£2

D1349118

# Gaelic-English
# English-Gaelic
# DICTIONARY

# Gaelic-English
# English-Gaelic
# DICTIONARY

**LOMOND BOOKS**

Gaelic-English dictionary compiled by Dougal Buchanan,
English-Gaelic dictionary compiled by RLS Ltd

© 1998 Geddes & Grosset,
an imprint of Children's Leisure Products Limited,
David Dale House, New Lanark, Scotland.

First published for Lomond Books 1998.
Reprinted 2000.

ISBN 0 947782 31 1

Printed and bound in Scotland

# Introduction

Within its convenient coat-pocket compass, this dictionary aims to provide a generous range of vocabulary. It is designed both for the student of Gaelic and for those with a more general interest in Scotland's languages and cultures — for all, in fact, who wish to have a sample, a handy *vade mecum*, an *aide-mémoire*, of the ancient tongue.

The emphasis remains on mainstream language while touching on a wide range of activity and experience, from the traditional and rural way of life still to be found in the Highlands and Islands to some of the innovations of the later twentieth century. The Gaelic-English section also includes a significant number of common phrases and expressions and so will reward the browser as well as the searcher for a particular word.

In a publication of this size, it is not possible to include all the different inflections of the items listed or to give much help with grammar. Anyone wishing to learn the language is recommended to use this dictionary in conjunction with one or more of the printed, audio and audiovisual courses readily available in bookshops. They should also find it very useful to get in touch with the Gaelic learners' organisation, CLI, 62 High Street, Invergordon, Ross-shire IV18 0DH, e-mail cli@sol.co.uk, which runs and co-ordinates courses and support for learners and publishes a quarterly magazine.

Gaelic is a language the structure of which is markedly different from that of English. In particular, in common with the other Celtic languages, Gaelic can show grammatical change at the beginning of many words, a process known as lenition or aspiration. This involves the softening of certain initial consonants and is represented in writing by the insertion of *h* immediately after the consonant concerned. By mentally removing this *h*, the newcomer to the language will be able to identify the radical or basic form of an aspirated word, and so on coming across *mhaighdeann*, *bhaile* or *chuir*, for example, will look up *maighdeann*, *baile* and *cuir* respectively.

# Format

Words are given in alphabetical order. It is not uncommon in Gaelic for words to express a variety of meanings, and in such cases the most common meaning or meanings are given. Often further meanings are given, with significant differences separated by a semicolon. In many cases, an explanatory note is inserted in brackets to help with clarification.

# Abbreviations

| | | | |
|---|---|---|---|
| *abbrev* | abbreviation | *m/f* | a noun the gender of which may change according to what it names, its case (often the genitive) or its dialect |
| *adj* | adjective | | |
| *adv* | adverb | | |
| *anat* | anatomy | | |
| *arith* | arithmetic | | |
| *art* | article | *milit* | military |
| *coll* | colloquial/collective | *mus* | music |
| *comput* | computing | *neg* | negative |
| *conj* | conjunction | *occas* | occasionally |
| *corres* | correspondence | *orthog* | orthography |
| *derog* | derogatory | *part* | particle |
| *esp* | especially | *pers* | personal |
| *excl* | exclamation | *phys* | physical |
| *f* | noun (feminine gender) | *pl* | plural |
| *fam* | familiar | *poss* | possessive |
| *fig* | figurative | *pp* | present or past participle |
| *fin* | financial | *prep* | preposition |
| *fml* | formal | *pron* | pronoun |
| *govt* | government | *refl* | reflexive |
| *gram* | grammar | *rel* | relative |
| *imper* | imperative | *relig* | religion |
| *interrog* | interrogative | *sing* | singular |
| *lit* | literature | *usu* | usually |
| *m* | noun (masculine gender) | *v* | verb |
| *med* | medical | *vulg* | vulgar |

# Gaelic-English Dictionary

# A

**a** *prep* to. •*el pron* that.

**a'**[1] *art* the; of the.

**a'**[2] *see* **ag**.

**a' cnàmh na cìre** chewing the cud; mulling things over.

**ab** *m* abbot.

**abachadh** *m* ripening.

**abaich** *adj* mature, ripe. •*□* mature, ripen.

**abaichead** *m* maturity, ripeness.

**abaid** *f* abbey.

**abair** *v* say.

**abair amadan!** *excl* what a fool!

**abairt** *f* phrase, expression.

**àbhacas** *m* mirth, ridicule.

**àbhachd** *f* humour.

**àbhachdach** *adj* amusing.

**abhag** *f* terrier.

**abhainn** *f* river.

**àbhaist** *f* custom, habit.

**àbhaisteach** *adj* usual.

**a-bhàn** *adv* down.

**a bhon-dè** *adv* day before yesterday.

**a bhon-raoir** *adv* night before last.

**a bhon uiridh** *adv* year before last.

**a bhos** *adv* over here, hither.

**ablach** *m* carcase.

**abstol** *m* apostle.

**aca** *prep pron* their.

**acadamh** *m* academy.

**acaid** *f* stabbing pain.

**acainn** *f* apparatus; tools.

**acainneach** *adj* equipped.

**acair** *f* anchor.

**acaire** *f* acre.

**acarsaid** *f* harbour, mooring.

**ach** *conj* but.

**achadh** *m* field.

**ach a-mhàin** *prep* except, apart from.

**a-chaoidh** *adv* always, for ever.

**achd** *f* (*politics*) act.

**a cheana** *adv* already.

**a chèile** *pron* each other.

**a chiall!** *excl* good heavens!

**a chionn** *prep* because of.

**a chionn is gu** *conj* because.

**achlais** *f* armpit.

**achlasan** *m* armful.

**achmhasan** *m* reprimand.

**a-chum** *prep* for.

**a-chum is gu** *conj* in order that.

**acraich** *v* anchor, moor.

**acras** *m* hunger.

**acrasach** *adj* hungry.

**actair** *m* actor.

**a' cur** part snowing.

**ad** *f* hat.

**adag** *f* haddock.

**adha** *m* liver.

**a dh'aindeòin** *prep* in spite of.

**a dh'aithghearr** *adv* soon.

**adhaltraiche** *m* adulterer.

**adhaltranas** *m* adultery.

**a dh' aon ghnothach** *adv* expressly, deliberately.

**a dh'aon rùn** *adv* expressly, deliberately.

**adhar** *m* air, sky.

**adharc** *f* horn.

**adharcach** *adj* horned.

**a dh' easbaidh** *adv* lacking, needed.

**a dh' ionnsaigh** *prep* to, towards; against.

**a dhìth** *adv* lacking, required; in short supply.

**adhartach** *adj* progressive.

**adhartas** *m* progress.

**adhbhar** *m* cause, reason.

**adhbhar-gàire** *m* laughing stock.

**adhbrann** *f* ankle.

**a dheòin no a dh'aindeòin** *adv* willy-nilly.

**a dh' fhad** *adv* long, in length.

**adhradh** *m* worship.

**a' dol bàs** *part* dying out.

**Afraga** *m* Africa.

**Afraganach** *m/adj* African.

**ag, a'** *part introducing pres part*.

**agad** *prep pron* your (*sing*).

**agaibh** *prep pron* your (*pl*).

**againn** *prep pron* our.

**agallamh** *m* interview; conversation.

**agam** *prep pron* my.

**ag eudach rithe** jealous about her.

**àgh** *m* joy; good fortune.

**agh** *f* heifer.

**aghaidh** *f* face; nerve, cheek.

**aghaidh-choimhich** *f* mask.

**aghann** *f* frying pan.

**a ghaoil!** *excl* love! dear!

**àghmhor** *adj* pleasant; joyful.

**a ghràidh!** *excl* dear! love!

**agus** *conj* and.

**a h-uile càil** everything.

**a h-uile duine** everyone, everybody.

**a h-uile sian** *f* everything.

**aibidil** *f* alphabet.

**aibidealach** *adj* alphabetical.

**aice** *prep pron* her.

**àicheadh** *m* denial.

**àicheidh** *v* deny.

**aideachadh** *m* confession.

**aidich** *v* confess, own up.

**aifrionn** *m* Mass.

**aig** *prep* at; in the possession of.

**aig a' cheann thall** *adv* in the end, eventually.

**aig àmannan** *adv* at times.

**aig an taigh** *adv* at home.

**aig baile** *adv* at home.

**aige** *prep pron* his.

**àigeach** *m* stallion.

**aighearach** *adj* cheerful, merry.

**aighearachd** *f* cheerfulness.

**aigne** *f* spirit; mind.

**aig Sealbh tha brath!** *excl* Heaven knows!

**ailbhinn** f flint.

**àile** m air, atmosphere.

**àileach** adj airy.

**aileag** f (with art) **an aileag** hiccups.

**àill** f desire, will.

**àilleag** f jewel.

**àillidh** adj shining; beautiful.

**aillse** f cancer.

**ailseag** f caterpillar.

**ailtire** m architect.

**ailtireachd** f architecture.

**aimbealains** m ambulance.

**aimhreit** f disorder, trouble.

**aimhreiteach** adj quarrelsome.

**aimsir** f weather.

**aimsireil** adj temporal; climatic.

**ain-** prefix un-.

**aindeòin** f reluctance.

**aindeònach** adj reluctant.

**aineach** adj (gram) imperative.

**aineolach air** adj unfamiliar with.

**aineolas** m ignorance.

**aingeal** m angel.

**ainm** m name.

**ainmeachadh** m naming; mentioning.

**ainmear** m noun.

**ainmeil** adj famous.

**ainmhidh** m animal.

**ainmich** v name; mention.

**ainmneach** adj (gram) nominative.

**ainneamh** adj scarce, rare.

**ainneart** m violence.

**aintighearn** m tyrant, oppressor.

**air** prep on; about. •⧄rep pron on him, on it (m).

**air adhart** adv forwards, onwards.

**air a dheagh dhòigh** on good form; chuffed.

**air aghaidh** adv forward(s).

**air ais** adv back; ago.

**air allaban** adv wandering.

**air alt is gu** conj so that.

**air an dùthaich** adv in the country.

**air an spot** adv on the spot.

**air a phronnadh** adv drunk.

**air ball** adv immediately.

**air banais** adv at a wedding.

**air beulaibh** prep in front of.

**air bhàinidh** adv mad with rage.

**air bhog** adv afloat.

**air bhoile** adv furious, raging.

**air bith** adv any at all.

**air bòrd** adv aboard, on board.

**air chall** adv lost.

**airchealladh** m sacrilege.

**air chois** adv up and about.

**air choreigin** adj some or other.

**air chor is gu** conj so that.

**air chrith** adv shaking, shivering.

**air chuthach** adv mad; furious.

**air chothrom a** conj able to, fit to.

**air corra-biod** adv on tiptoe.

**air cùl** prep behind.

**air cùlaibh** prep behind.

**air cumha is gu** conj on condition that.

**àird** *f* point, promontory.
**air dàir** *adv* on heat, rutting.
**àirde** *f* height; (*mus*) pitch.
**aire** *f* attention.
**air deireadh** *adv* last.
**air dheireadh** *adv* lagging behind.
**air dhòigh is gu** *conj* so that; in order that.
**air dòigh** *adv* in good order.
**air do shocair!** *excl* steady on! go easy!
**air dreach** *adv* looking like.
**air eagal gu** *conj* lest; for fear that.
**àireamh** *f* number.
**àireamhair** *m* calculator.
**àireamh fòn** *f* phone number.
**air èiginn** *adv* hardly, barely; with difficulty.
**air fad** *adv* entirely, completely; all.
**air falbh** *adv* away, gone.
**air feadh** *prep* throughout, all over.
**air fleòdradh** *adv* floating.
**air flod** *adv* floating, afloat.
**airgead** *m* money; silver.
**airgeadach** *adj* well-off, monied.
**airgead pòcaid** *m* pocket-money.
**airgead pronn** *m* small change.
**airgead ullamh** *m* ready money, cash.
**air iasad** *adv* on loan.
**airidh** *adj* worthy, deserving.
**àirigh** *f* shieling.

**air iomrall** *adv* wandering; astray, erring.
**air iteig** *adv* flying, on the wing.
**air leth** *adv* apart; exceptional.
**air leth-mhisg** *adv* tipsy.
**air leth-shùil** *adv* one-eyed.
**air m'aigne** *adv* on my mind.
**air m'aire** *adv* on my mind.
**air mhisg** *adv* drunk.
**air mhodh eile** *adv* otherwise, alternatively.
**air mo chùram** *adv* on my mind; under my responsibility.
**air mo sgàth** *adv* for my sake.
**àirneis** *f* furniture.
**air neo** *conj* or else, otherwise.
**air sgàth** *prep* on account of.
**air sgàth is gu** *conj* because.
**airson** *prep* for; in favour of. •□*onj* in order to.
**airson a reic** *adv* sale, for.
**air snàmh** *adj* inundated, flooded.
**air stailc** *adv* on strike.
**air thoiseach air** *prep* ahead of.
**airtnealach** *adj* sad, weary.
**air tuaiream** *adv* at random.
**air uairean** *adv* at times.
**air uaireann** *adv* occasionally.
**air urras** *adv* on bail.
**aiseag** *f* ferry.
**aiseal** *f* axle.
**aisean** *m* rib.
**aiseirigh** *f* resurrection; resurgence.
**Aisia** *f* (*with art*) **an Aisia** Asia.

**Aisianach** *m/adj* Asian.

**aisling** *f* dream; vision.

**aiste**[1] *f* essay.

**aiste**[2] *prep pron* from her, from it (*f*).

**àite** *m* place.

**àiteach** *m* cultivation.

**àiteachas** *m* agriculture.

**àite-coise** *m* pedestrian crossing.

**aiteal** *m* glimpse.

**aiteamh** *m* thaw.

**àite-còmhnaidh** *m* dwelling place.

**àite-fuirich** *m* dwelling place.

**àiteigin** *m* some place or other.

**àite-suidhe** *m* seat, sitting place.

**aithghearr** *adj* short; quick; abrupt.

**aithghearrachd** *f* short cut. •◻*dv* **an aithghearrachd** swiftly, sharpish.

**aithne** *f* acquaintance.

**aithnich** *v* know, recognise.

**aithreachail** *adj* repentant.

**aithreachas** *m* repentance.

**aithris** *v* recite. •◻*h* report.

**àitich** *v* cultivate.

**aitreabh** *m* building; dwelling.

**àl** *m* litter, young.

**àlainn** *adj* lovely; fine.

**a laoigh!** *excl* my love! my dear!

**Alba** *f* Scotland.

**Albais** *f* Scots language.

**Albannach** *m/adj* Scotsman, Scot; Scottish.

**alcol** *m* alcohol.

**allaban** *m* wandering.

**allaidh** *adj* wild.

**allt** *m* stream, burn.

**alt** *m* joint; method; (*gram*) article.

**altachadh** *m* (*prayer*) grace.

**altair** *f* altar.

**altraim** *v* foster; nurse.

**am**[1] *poss adj* their.

**am**[2] *art* the.

**àm** *m* time. •◻*dv* **aig àmannan** at times. •◻**an t-àm a dh'fhalbh** the past.

**a-mach** *adv* out.

**a-mach air a'bhus** *adv* overflowing.

**a-mach à seo!** *excl* get out!

**amadan** *m* fool, silly man.

**amaideach** *adj* foolish, silly.

**amaideas** *m* foolishness.

**a-màireach** *adv* tomorrow.

**amais** *v* aim; hit upon.

**amaiseach** *adj* accurate.

**amalach** *adj* complicated.

**amar** *m* basin; pool.

**amar-ionnlaid** *m* wash basin.

**amar-snàmh** *m* swimming pool.

**am bitheantas** *adv* usually, normally.

**am bliadhna** *adv* this year.

**am broinn** *prep* inside, within.

**am bròn** *adv* in mourning.

**Ameireagaidh** *f* America.

**Ameireaganach** *m/adj* American.

**am feasd** *adv* ever; for ever.

**amh** *adj* raw; unripe.

**amhaich** *f* neck; throat.

**a-mhàin** *adv* only.

**àmhainn** *f* oven.

**amharas** *m* suspicion.

**amharasach** *adj* suspicious, distrustful.

**amharc** *m* sight.

**amhran** *m* song.

**am measg** *prep* among.

**a-muigh** *adv* outside.

**an**[1] *art* the; of the.

**an**[2] *poss adj* their.

**an**[3] *prep* in.

**an-abaich** *adj* unripe; premature.

**anabarrach** *adj/adv* extreme(ly).

**an aghaidh** *prep* against.

**anail** *f* breath.

**an ainm an àigh!** *excl* in Heaven's name!

**anainn** *f* eaves.

**an àite** *prep* instead of.

**a-nall** *adv* over here, hither.

**anam** *m* soul.

**ana-mhiann** *m/f* lust.

**an àrd** *adv* up.

**anart** *m* linen.

**anart bàis** *m* shroud.

**an-asgaidh** *adv* free of charge.

**an ath-bhliadhna** *adv* next year.

**an ath dhoras** *m* next door.

**an ath-oidhche** *adv* tomorrow night.

**an ceann** *prep* (*of time*) in, after.

**an ceann a chèile** *adv* one after the other, in succession.

**an ceartuair** *adv* just now, presently.

**an clàr a aodainn** *adv* full in the face.

**an coimeas ri** *prep* compared to.

**an coinneimh** *prep* towards.

**an cois** *adv* near; accompanying.

**an comhair** *prep* in the direction of.

**an comhair a chinn** *adv* head first.

**an comhair a thoisich** *adv* frontwards.

**an-còmhnaidh** *adv* always, constantly.

**an crochadh** *adv* hanging.

**an crochadh air** *prep* depending on.

**an cumantas** *adv* commonly, normally.

**an dà chuid** *pron* both.

**an dà là** *m* changed days.

**an dàn** *adv* destined, ordained.

**an dara cuid a no b** either a or b.

**an-dè** *adv* yesterday.

**dèideadh** *m* (*with art*) **an dèideadh** toothache.

**an dèidh** *prep* after.

**an dèidh sin?** *adv* so?.

**an-diugh** *adv* today.

**an dòlas!** *excl* woe is me!

**an-dràsta** *adv* just now.

**an-dràsta fhèin** *adv* this instant.

**an droch-shùil** *f* the evil eye.

**an ear** eastern.

**an-earar** *adv* day after tomorrow.

**an eisimeil** *adv* dependent (on).

**anfhann** *adj* infirm.

**an-fhoiseil** *adj* restless, uneasy.

**an impis** *conj* about to.

**an-ìochdmhor** *adj* merciless, pitiless.

**an iomadh-chomhairle** in a quandary.

**an ìre mhath** *adv* quite, fairly; just about.

**an làthair** *adv* present.

**a-nìos** *adv* up.

**a-nise** *adv* now.

**an là roimhe** *adv* the other day.

**an lùib** *prep* involved in/with.

**anmoch** *adj* late.

**ann**[1] *adv* there.

**ann**[2] *prep pron* in him; in it (*m*).

**annad** *prep pron* in you (*sing*).

**annaibh** *prep pron* in you (*pl*).

**annainn** *prep pron* in us.

**annam** *prep pron* in me.

**ann an** *prep* in.

**ann an cabhag** *adv* in a hurry.

**ann an dà-rìreadh** *adv* serious, in earnest.

**ann an droch staid** *adv* in a bad way.

**ann an sheo** *adv* here.

**ann an shin** *adv* there.

**ann an shiud** *adv* there, yonder.

**annas** *m* rarity; novelty.

**annasach** *adj* novel; odd.

**anns a' bhad** *adv* immediately.

**anns a' chiad dol-a-mach** in the first instance.

**anns an** *prep* in the.

**anns an dealachadh** *adv* on parting.

**annta** *prep pron* in them.

**a-nochd** *adv* tonight.

**an-raoir** *adv* last night.

**an sàs** *adv* captured; involved.

**an seo** *adv* here.

**anshocrach** *adj* uneasy.

**an sin** *adv* there.

**an siud** *adv* there, yonder.

**an taca ri** *prep* compared to, alongside.

**an taic ri** *prep* leaning on/against; in comparison with.

**an taobh a-muigh** *m* outside.

**an taobh an ear** *m* the east.

**an taobh an iar** *m* the west.

**an taobh a-staigh** *m* inside.

**an taobh sear** *m* the east.

**an taobh siar** *m* the west.

**an t-Eilean Sgitheanach** *m* (the Isle of) Skye.

**an tòir air** *prep* in pursuit of; looking for.

**an toiseach** *adv* at first.

**an uair a** *conj* when.

**an uair sin** *adv* then, next.

**a-nuas** *adv* down.

**an-uiridh** *adv* last year.

**a-null** *adv* thither; over.

**a-null thairis** *adv* abroad, overseas.

**an urra ri** *prep* responsible for; in charge of.

**aocoltach** *adj* dissimilar.

**aodach** *m* cloth; clothes.
**aodach-leapa** *m* bedclothes.
**aodach oidhche** *m* nightclothes.
**aodann** *m* face; hillface.
**ao-dìonach** *adj* leaky.
**aoibhneach** *adj* glad.
**aoigh** *m* guest; resident.
**aoigheachd** *f* hospitality.
**aoigheil** *adj* generous; hospitable.
**aoir** *f* satire.
**aois** *f* age.
**aol** *m* lime.
**aon** *adj* one.
**aonach** *m* moor, moorland.
**aonad** *m* unit.
**aona deug** *adj* eleventh.
**aonadh** *m* union.
**aonadh-cèaird** *m* trade union.
**aonaich** *v* unite, combine.
**aonaran** *m* hermit; loner.
**aonaranach** *adj* lonely; desolate.
**aon chuid a no b** either a or b.
**aon deug** *n* eleven.
**aon-fhillte** *adj* uncomplicated.
**aon-inntinneach** *adj* unanimous.
**aonta** *m* agreement.
**aontaich** *v* agree.
**aosta** *adj* old, aged.
**aotrom** *adj* light; trivial.
**aotromaich** *v* lighten; alleviate.
**aotroman** *m* bladder.
**aparan** *m* apron.
**ar** *poss adj* our.
**àr** *m* slaughter.
**àra** *f* kidney.

**àrach** *m* rearing, upbringing.
**àrachas** *m* insurance.
**àradh** *m* ladder.
**àraich** *v* raise, bring up.
**àraid** *adj* particular; peculiar.
**àraidh** *adj* particular; exceptional.
**ar-a-mach** *m* rebellion, rising.
**aran** *m* bread.
**ar-aon** *adv* both.
**arbhar** *m* corn.
**àrc** *f* cork.
**Arcach** *adj/n* Orcadian.
**Arcaibh** *m* Orkney.
**àrdachadh** *m* promotion; rise.
**àrdaich** *v* raise; increase.
**àrdan** *m* pride, arrogance.
**àrdanach** *adj* proud, arrogant.
**àrd-doras** *m* lintel.
**àrd-easbaig** *m* archbishop.
**àrd-ìre** *adj* (*education, etc*) higher, high-level.
**àrd mo chlaiginn** *adv* at the top of my voice.
**àrd-ollamh** *m* professor.
**àrd-sgoil** *f* secondary school.
**àrd-ùrlar** *m* stage, platform.
**àrd-urram** *m* honour, distinction; reverence.
**a-rèir** *prep* according to.
**a-rèir choltais** *adv* seemingly, apparently.
**a-rèist** *adv* in that case.
**argamaid** *f* argument.
**a-riamh** *adv* ever.
**a-rithist** *adv* again.

**ar leam** *v* I consider.

**arm** *m* army.

**armachd** *f* armour.

**armaich** *v* arm.

**arm-lann** *f* armoury.

**arsa** *v* say, says, said.

**àrsaidh** *adj* ancient.

**àrsaidheachd** *f* archaeology.

**àrsair** *m* archaeologist.

**às** *prep* from, out of. •⬛*prep pron* from him, from it (*m*).

**às a' cheud** *adv* percent.

**às a' chumantas** *adv* out of the ordinary.

**asad** *prep pron* from you (*sing*).

**asaibh** *prep pron* from you (*pl*).

**asaid anabaich** *f* miscarriage.

**asainn** *prep pron* from us.

**asal** *f* ass; donkey.

**asam** *prep pron* from me.

**às an amharc** *adv* out of sight.

**às an làthair** *adv* out of sight.

**às aonais** *prep* without.

**as bith cò** *prep* whoever.

**as bith cuine** *adv* whenever.

**as bith dè** *prep* whatever.

**às d'aonais** without you.

**à sealladh** *adv* out of sight.

**às eugmhais** *prep* without.

**asgaidh** *f* present, gift.

**a shìorraidh!** *excl* for Heaven's sake!

**às leth** *prep* on behalf of.

**às mo chiall** *adv* out of my mind.

**às mo rian** *adv* out of my mind.

**asta** *prep pron* from them.

**a-staigh** *adv* in, inside.

**astar** *m* distance; speed.

**a-steach** *adv* in, inside.

**a-steach do** *prep* into.

**as t-fhodhar** *adv* in Autumn.

**Astràilia** *f* Australia.

**Astràilianach** *m/adj* Australian.

**as ùr** *adv* afresh; anew.

**at** *v* swell, puff up. •⬛*n* swelling.

**ataireachd** *f* (*of sea*) swell, surge.

**ath** *adj* next.

**àth**[1] *f* kiln.

**àth**[2] *m* ford.

**ath-** *prefix* re-.

**athair** *m* father; progenitor.

**athair-cèile** *m* father-in-law.

**athaireil** *adj* fatherly.

**athaiseach** *adj* dilatory.

**ath-aithris** *v* repeat.

**a thaobh** *prep* concerning.

**atharrachadh** *m* change, alteration.

**atharraich** *v* change, alter.

**atharrais** *v* imitate, mimic.

**ath-bheothachadh** *m* renaissance.

**ath-bheothaich** *v* revive.

**ath-chruthaich** *v* re-create.

**ath-dhìol** *v* repay.

**ath-leasachadh** *m* redevelopment; (*with art*) **an t-Ath-leasachadh** the Reformation.

**ath-leasaich** *v* redevelop.

**ath-nuadhachadh** *m* renewal.

**ath-nuadhaich** *v* renew.

**athraichean** *mpl* forefathers.

**ath-sgrìobh** *v* rewrite.
**ath-sgrùdadh** *m* revision.

**a thuilleadh air** *prep* in addition to.

# B

**bac** *v* prevent; obstruct.
**bacach** *adj* lame. •☐*n* lame person.
**bacadh** *m* prevention; obstacle.
**bacan** *m* hobble.
**bachall** *m* crozier.
**bachlach** *adj* curly.
**bachlag** *f* curl, ringlet.
**bachlaich** *v* curl.
**bad** *m* place; clump.
**badan** *m* thicket.
**baga** *m* bag; hand-bag.
**bagaid** *f* bunch; cluster.
**bagair** *v* threaten.
**bagairt** *f* threat.
**bàgh** *m* bay, cove.
**bagradh** *m* threat.
**bàidh** *f* affection; favour.
**bàidheil** *adj* kindly.
**baidhsagal** *m* bicycle.
**baile** *m* township, village. •☐*dv*
  **aig baile** at home.
**bailead** *m* ballad.
**baile beag** *m* village, small town.
**baile mòr** *m* town, city.
**baile-margaid** *m* market town.
**baile-puirt** *m* sea port.
**bàillidh** *m* bailiff; baillie.
**b'àill leam?** *adv* pardon?.
**bàine** *adj* whiter, whitest.

**bàinead** *f* whiteness.
**bainne** *m* milk.
**bainne lom** *m* skimmed milk.
**bàirdse** *f* barge.
**bàirlinn** *f* (*law*) summons.
**bàirneach** *f* barnacle, limpet.
**baist** *v* baptise, christen.
**Baisteach** *adj/m* Baptist.
**baisteadh** *m* baptism.
**bàl** *m* (*dance*) ball.
**balach** *m* boy, lad.
**balachan** *m* wee boy.
**balbh** *adj* dumb; speechless.
**balbhan** *m* dumb person.
**balg** *m* abdomen; blister.
**balgair** *m* fox; rogue.
**balgam** *m* sip; swig.
**balgan** *m* mushroom; toadstool.
**balgan-buachair** *m* edible mushroom.
**ball** *m* organ; member.
**balla** *m* wall.
**bàlla** *m* ball.
**ball-acainn** *m* tool.
**ballach** *adj* speckled, spotted.
**ball-airm** *m* weapon.
**ball-àirneis** *m* piece of furniture.
**ballan** *m* tub.
**ball-aodaich** *m* garment.
**ball-basgaid** *m* basketball.

**ball-bodhaig** m bodily organ.

**ball-coise** m football.

**ball-dòbhrain** m (on skin) mole.

**ball-maise** m ornament.

**ball pàrlamaid** m MP.

**ballrachd** f membership.

**ball-seirce** m beauty spot.

**ball-stèidhe** m baseball.

**bàn** adj blonde; white; blank; fallow.

**bana-bhuidseach** f witch.

**bana-charaid** f female friend or relative; (corres) **A Bhanacharaid** Dear Madam.

**bana-chliamhainn** f daughter-in-law.

**ban-adhaltraiche** f adulteress.

**bànag** f sea trout.

**bana-ghaisgeach** f heroine.

**banail** adj womanly, feminine.

**banais** f wedding.

**Ban Albannach** f Scotswoman.

**banaltram** f nurse.

**bana-mhaighistir-sgoile** f schoolmistress.

**bana-phrionnsa** f princess.

**banarach** f milkmaid, dairymaid.

**banca** m bank.

**bancair** m banker.

**bancaireachd** f banking.

**bàn-dhearg** adj light red.

**ban-dia** f goddess.

**ban-diùc** f duchess.

**bàn-ghorm** adj pale blue.

**ban-ìompaire** f empress.

**ban-leòmhann** f lioness.

**bann** m strip; bandage.

**banntach** m hinge.

**banntrach** m/f widow(er).

**ban-ogha** f grand-daughter.

**bànrigh** f queen.

**ban-rùnaire** f (female) secretary.

**baoghalta** adj stupid.

**baoghaltachd** f stupidity.

**baoit** f (fishing) fly, bait.

**baoiteag** f (fishing) fly, bait.

**baoth** adj foolish, simple.

**bàr** m (hotel, etc) bar.

**barail** f opinion.

**baraille** m barrel.

**bàrd** m poet, bard.

**bàrdachd** f poetry.

**bàrr** m top; cream; crop.

**Barrach** m/adj from Barra.

**barrachd** f surplus; more. •rep **barrachd air** more than. •dv **a bharrachd** extra, in addition, **a bharrachd air sin** moreover.

**barragach** adj creamy.

**Barraidh** m Barra.

**barrall** m shoelace.

**barrantas** m pledge, guarantee.

**bàrr na teangaidh** m tip of the tongue.

**bas** f palm.

**bàs** m death.

**bàsaich** v die.

**bas-bhualadh** m applause.

**basgaid** f basket.

**bàsmhor** adj mortal; deadly.

**bàsmhorachd** f mortality.

**bata** m stick.

**bàta** *m* boat.

**bata-coiseachd** *m* walking stick.

**bàt' aisig** *m* ferry.

**bàta-ràmh** *m* rowing boat.

**bàta-sàbhalaidh** *m* lifeboat.

**bàta-siùil** *m* sailing boat.

**bàta-smùide** *m* steamer.

**bàta-teasairginn** *m* lifeboat.

**bàth** *v* drown; muffle.

**bàthach** *f* byre, cow-shed.

**bathais** *f* forehead; impudence.

**bathar** *m* goods, merchandise.

**bàthte** *adj* drowned.

**bàt'-iasgaich** fishing boat.

**beach** *m* bee; wasp.

**beachd** *m* idea; opinion.

**beachdail** *adj* abstract.

**beachd-smaoinich, beachd-smaointich** *v* meditate.

**beachlann** *m* beehive.

**beag** *adj* little, •◫ a' bheag the least bit. •◫*dv* beag air bheag bit by bit; beag is beag little by little.

**beagan** *adv* a bit, slightly. •◫ a little; few.

**beag-nàrach** *adj* shameless.

**bealach** *m* pass, col; detour.

**bealaidh** *m* broom.

**Bealltainn** *f* May Day, Beltane.

**bean**[1] *f* wife.

**bean**[2] *v* touch, meddle with.

**bean-** *prefix* woman-, female.

**bean-an-taighe, bean-taighe** *f* housewife; landlady.

**bean-bainnnse** *f* bride.

**bean-eiridinn** *f* nurse.

**bean-ghlùine** *f* midwife.

**beannachadh** *m* beatification; greeting.

**beannachd** *f* blessing; regards.

**beannachd leibh!** *excl* goodbye!

**beannaich** *v* bless.

**beannaich do** *v* greet.

**beannaichte** *adj* blessed.

**bean phòsda** *f* married woman, Mrs.

**bean ri** *v* brush against.

**bean-shithe** *f* fairy woman.

**bean-an-taighe** *see* **bean-taighe**.

**bean-teagaisg** *f* (female) teacher.

**bean-uasal** *f* noblewoman; (*fml*) a Bhean-uasal! *excl* Madam! (*corres, fml*) Dear Madam.

**beàrn** *f* gap; notch.

**beàrnan-bròïde** *f* dandelion.

**Beàrnarach** *m* Berneray person.

**Beàrnaraigh** *f* Berneray.

**beàrr** *v* shave; shear.

**bearradair** *m* barber.

**beart** *f* machine.

**beartach** *adj* rich, wealthy.

**beartas** *m* riches, wealth.

**beart-fhighe** *f* loom.

**beatha** *f* life.

**beathach** *m* animal.

**beathach-mara** *m* sea-creature.

**beathaich** *v* feed; maintain.

**beath-eachdraidh** *f* biography.

**beic** *f* curtsey.

**Beilg** *f* (*with art*) a' Bheilg Belgium.

**Beilgeach** *m/adj* Belgian.

**being** *f* bench.

**beinn** *f* ben, mountain.

**Beinn Nibheis** *f* Ben Nevis.

**beinn-teine** *f* volcano.

**beir** *v* irreg bear; give birth to.

**beir air** *v* seize; overtake.

**beir air làimh air** *v* shake hands with.

**beirm** *f* yeast.

**beò** *adj* alive, living.

**beò-ghlacadh** *m* obsession.

**beòshlaint** *f* livelihood.

**beothaich** *v* revive; liven up.

**beothail** *adj* lively, active.

**beothalachd** *f* vivacity.

**beuc** *m* roar, bellow. •◻ roar, bellow.

**beud** *m* harm, loss.

**beul** *m* mouth.

**beul a bhi** *adv* about to be.

**beul-aithris** *f* oral tradition.

**beulchar** *adj* plausible, smooth-talking.

**beul-ìochdair** *m* lower lip.

**beul-oideachas** *f* lore.

**beul ri** *prep* nearly.

**beul-uachdair** *m* upper lip.

**beum** *m* stroke; blow.

**beum-grèine** *m* sunstroke.

**Beurla** *f* (*often with art*) **a' Bheurla** English.

**beusach** *adj* modest; well-behaved.

**beus-eòlas** *m* ethics.

**bha** *past tense of v* **bith**.

**bhàrr** *prep* off, down from.

**bha spòrs agam** *v* I enjoyed myself/had fun.

**Bhèineas** *f* Venus.

**bheir** *future tense of v* **thoir**.

**bho** *prep* from; since.

**bho àm gu àm** *adv* from time to time.

**bhòt** *v* vote.

**bho thùs** *adv* originally.

**bhuaibh** *prep pron* from you (*pl*).

**bhuainn** *prep pron* from us.

**bhuaipe** *prep pron* from her, from it (*f*).

**bhuaithe** *prep pron* from him, from it (*m*).

**bhuam** *prep pron* from me.

**bhuapa** *prep pron* from them.

**bhuat** *prep pron* from you (*sing*).

**bhur** *adj* your (*pl*).

**biadh** *m* food; meal.

**biadhlann** *m* refectory, canteen.

**bian** *m* fur, hide.

**biast** *f* beast.

**biastail** *adj* bestial.

**biath** *v* feed; fodder.

**bìd**[1] *v* bite.

**bìd**[2] *m* chirp.

**bideag** *f* fragment, crumb.

**bidse** *f* bitch. •◻*xcl* **a bhidse!** sod it!

**bile**[1] *f* lip, rim.

**bile**[2] *m* (*politics*) bill.

**bileag** *f* petal; (*commerce*) bill.

**binid** *f* rennet.

**binn**[1] *adj* sweet.

**binn²** *f* judgement; sentence.

**binnean** *m* peak.

**binneas** *m* sweetness.

**bìoball** *m* bible.

**bìoballach** *adj* biblical.

**biodach** *adj* tiny; trifling.

**biodag** *f* dirk, dagger.

**bìog** *f* chirp. •◻ cheep, chirp.

**biolar** *f* cress.

**biona** *f* bin.

**biona-stùir** *f* dustbin.

**bior** *m* point; prickle.

**biorach** *adj* sharp, pointed.

**bioran** *m* a pointed stick.

**biorra-crùidein** *m* kingfisher.

**bior-ròstaidh** *m* (*cooking*) spit.

**biotais** *m* beet.

**bìrlinn** *f* galley, birlinn.

**bith¹** *f* existence, being. •◻ be.

**bìth²** *f* tar, pitch.

**bith-** *prefix* ever-.

**bith-bheò** *adj* ever-living, immortal.

**bith-bhuan** *adj* eternal, everlasting.

**bitheanta** *adj* frequent, common.

**bitheantas** *m* frequency.

**bith-eòlas** *m* biology.

**bithis** *f* screw.

**bithiseach** *adj* spiral.

**blais** *v* taste.

**blàr** *m* plain; battle(field).

**blas** *m* flavour; accent.

**blasad** *m* taste.

**blasad bìdh** *m* bite to eat.

**blasaich** *v* flavour.

**blasmhor** *adj* full of flavour.

**blasta** *adj* tasty.

**blàth¹** *m* bloom, blossom.

**blàth²** *adj* warm; affectionate.

**blàthaich** *v* warm.

**blàth-chridheach** *adj* warm-hearted.

**blàths** *m* warmth.

**bleideag** *f* flake.

**bleith** *v* grind, pulverise.

**bleoghainn** *v* milk.

**bliadhna** *f* year.

**bliadhnach** *adj* yearling.

**bliadhnail** *adj* annual, yearly.

**bliadhna-leum** *f* leap year.

**bliadhna ùr** *f* new year.

**blian** *v* sunbathe.

**bloigh** *f* half.

**bloighd** *f* fragment, splinter.

**bloinigean-gàraidh** *m* spinach.

**blonag** *f* lard.

**bò** *f* cow.

**bò bhainne** *f* milk cow.

**bobhla** *m* bowl.

**boc** *m* billy goat; roebuck.

**bòc** *v* swell, bloat.

**bòcan** *m* apparition; bogy-man.

**boc-earba** *m* roe-buck.

**bochd** *adj* poor; unfortunate; poorly.

**bochdainn** *f* poverty; misfortune.

**bocsa** *m* box.

**bocsa-ciùil** *m* accordion.

**bocsa-fòn** *m* phonebox.

**bocsair** *m* boxer.

**bocsa-litrichean** *m* letterbox.

**bod** *m* penis.

**Bòd** *m* Bute.

**bodach** *m* old man, old guy.

**Bodach na Nollaig** *m* Santa Claus.

**bodach-ròcais** *m* scarecrow.

**bodach-sneachda** *m* snowman.

**bodhaig** *f* body.

**bodhair** *v* deafen.

**bodhar** *adj* deaf. •🔲 deaf person.

**bòdhran** *m* bodhran.

**bodraig** *v* bother, trouble.

**bog**[1] *adj* soft; tender. •🔲 soak, steep.

**bog**[2] *v* bob, dip.

**bogadaich** *f* bouncing, bobbing.

**bogaich** *v* soften.

**bog fliuch** *adj* soaking wet.

**bogha** *m* bow; curve.

**bogha-frois** *m* rainbow.

**boglach** *f* bog.

**bòid** *f* oath; swearing.

**Bòideach'** *m/adj* from Bute.

**bòidhchead** *f* beauty.

**bòidheach** *adj* pretty, beautiful.

**boile** *f* madness; frenzy.

**boillsg** *m* flash; gleam. •🔲 flash; glitter, shine.

**boillsgeach** *adj* gleaming; glittering.

**boinne** *f* drop.

**boinneag** *f* droplet.

**boireann** *adj* female, feminine.

**boireannach** *m* woman, female.

**boireannaich** *mpl* womenfolk.

**boireannta** *adj* effeminate.

**boiseag** *f* slap; palmful.

**boladh** *m* smell.

**bò laoigh** *f* in-calf cow.

**bolgan** *m* bulb.

**boltrach** *m* smell; perfume.

**boma** *m* bomb.

**bonaid** *m/f* bonnet, cap.

**bonaid bhiorach** *f* Glengarry.

**bonn** *m* base; coin.

**bonnach** *m* bannock; scone.

**bonnach-uighe** *m* omelette.

**bonn airgid** *m* coin; silver medal.

**bonn còmhraidh** *m* chat.

**bonn-cuimhne** *m* medal.

**bonn-dubh** *m* heel.

**borb** *adj* wild, barbarous.

**borbair** *m* barber.

**bòrd** *m* board; table.

**bòrd ceadachaidh** *m* licensing board.

**bòrd-dàmais** *m* draught board.

**bòrd-dubh** *m* blackboard.

**bòrd-geal** *m* whiteboard.

**bòrd-iarnaigidh** *m* ironing board.

**bòrd-sgrìobhaidh** *m* desk.

**bòrd slàinte** *m* health board.

**bòstail** *adj* boastful.

**botal** *m* bottle.

**botal teth** *m* hotwater bottle.

**bòtann** *m* boot, wellie.

**bothan** *m* cottage; shebeen.

**bothan àirigh** *m* sheiling bothy.

**bracaist** *f* breakfast.

**brach** *v* ferment; (*boil, etc*) gather.

**brachadh** *m* fermentation; pus.
**bradan** *m* salmon.
**brag** *m* bang.
**bragail** *adj* boastful.
**braich** *f* malt.
**braid** *f* theft, thieving.
**bràigh**[1] *m* upper part; upland.
**bràigh**[2] *m* captive; hostage.
**bràighdeanas** *m* captivity.
**braim** *m* fart.
**braisead** *f* impetuosity.
**bràiste** *f* brooch.
**bràmair** *m* girlfriend.
**branndaidh** *f* brandy.
**braoisg** *f* grin; grimace.
**braoisgeil** *adj* grinning.
**braon** *v* drizzle. •*n* drop;.
**bras** *adj* hasty; bold.
**brat** *m* cover; mat; cloak.
**bratach** *m* banner, flag.
**brath**[1] *v* betray; inform on.
**brath**[2] *m* knowledge; advantage.
**bràth** *m* judgement; **gu bràth tu-illeadh** *adv* (*with neg v*) never again.
**brathadair** *m* betrayer.
**brathadh** *m* betrayal.
**bràthair** *m* brother.
**bràthair athar** *m* uncle.
**bràthair-cèile** *m* brother-in-law.
**bràthair-màthar** *m* uncle.
**brat-leapach** *m* bedcover, coverlet.
**brat-ùrlair** *m* carpet.
**breab** *v* kick. •*n* kick.
**breabadair** *m* weaver; daddy-long-legs.

**breac**[1] *adj* speckled, variegated.
**breac**[2] *m* trout.
**breacadh-seunain** *m* freckles.
**breacag** *f* bannock.
**breacan** *m* plaid, tartan cloth.
**breacanach** *adj* tartan.
**breac-bhallach** *adj* freckled.
**breac-òtraich** *f* (*with art*) **a' bhreac-òtraich** chicken pox.
**buinneach** *f* (*with art*) **a' bhuinneach** diarrhoea.
**brèagha** *adj* fine, lovely.
**Breatannach** *m/adj* Briton; British.
**breice** *f* brick.
**breicire** *m* bricklayer.
**brèid** *m* kerchief; patch.
**brèid-shoithichean** *m* dishcloth.
**brèige** *adj* deceitful; artificial.
**breisleach** *m* confusion; delirium.
**breislich** *v* talk irrationally.
**breith**[1] *f* birth.
**breith**[2] *f* decision; sentence.
**breith anabaich** *f* abortion.
**breithnich** *v* judge; assess.
**breug** *f* lie.
**breugach** *adj* lying.
**breugaire** *m* liar.
**breug-riochd** *m* disguise.
**breun** *adj* putrid, corrupt.
**briathar** *m* term.
**briathran** *mpl* statements, words.
**briathran teicneolach** *mpl* technical terms.
**brìb** *v* bribe. •*n* bribe.

**brìgh** *f* meaning; essence; energy.
**brìghmhor** *adj* pithy; energetic.
**briogais** *f* trousers, breeches.
**briosgaid** *f* biscuit.
**bris** *v* break, smash.
**briseadh** *m* break, fracture.
**briseadh-cridhe** *m* heartbreak.
**briseadh-dùil** *m* disappointment.
**briseadh-là** *m* daybreak.
**brisg** *adj* crisp; brittle.
**briste** *adj* broken, smashed.
**britheamh** *m* judge.
**broc** *m* badger.
**brochan** *m* porridge.
**brod** *v* drive on; encourage. •*n* goad, prod.
**bròg** *f* shoe, boot.
**broilleach** *m* bosom, chest.
**broinn** *f* interior.
**bròn** *m* sadness, sorrow.
**brònach** *adj* sad, sorrowful.
**brosnachadh** *m* encouragement.
**brosnachail** *adj* encouraging.
**brosnaich** *v* encourage; arouse.
**brot** *m* soup, broth.
**broth** *m* rash.
**brù** *f* womb; belly; bulge.
**bruach** *f* (*river, etc*) bank.
**bruadair** *v* dream.
**bruadar** *m* dream.
**brùchd** *v* burst out; belch. •*n* belch.
**brù-dhearg** *m* robin.
**bruich** *v* cook; boil. •*adj* cooked; boiled.
**bruicheil** *adj* sultry.

**brùid** *m* brute; beast.
**brùidealachd** *f* brutality.
**brùideil** *adj* brutal.
**bruidhinn** *v* talk, speak. •*n* talk, talking.
**bruidhinn ri** *v* talk to.
**bruidhneach** *adj* talkative, chatty.
**bruis** *f* brush.
**bruis-aodaich** *f* clothes brush.
**bruis-fhiaclan** *f* toothbrush.
**bruisig** *v* brush.
**brùite** *adj* bruised; oppressed.
**brùth** *v* bruise; shove.
**bruthach** *m/f* bank, slope.
**bruthainneach** *adj* sultry.
**bu** *v* was, were; would be.
**buachaille** *m* cowherd.
**buachailleachd** *f* cattle herding.
**buachaillich** *v* herd cattle.
**buachar** *m* cowdung.
**buadh** *f* quality, virtue.
**buadhair** *m* adjective.
**buadhmhor** *adj* effective; successful.
**buaic** *f* wick.
**buaidh** *f* victory; success; influence.
**buail** *v* hit.
**buail a-steach** *v* call in, drop in.
**buail bas** *v* applaud.
**buaile** *f* sheepfold.
**buailteach** *adj* liable, apt to.
**buain** *f* reaping, harvest(ing).
**buair** *v* upset; tempt.
**buaireadh** *m* temptation.

**buaireas** *m* anxiety; confusion.

**buaireasach** *adj* troublesome.

**bualadh** *m* blow.

**buan** *adj* lasting, durable.

**buannachd** *f* profit, advantage.

**buannaich** *v* win.

**buar** *m* herd.

**bucaid** *f* bucket.

**bucas** *m* box.

**bu chiatach orm** *v* I should.

**bu chòir dhomh** *v* I ought, I should.

**bugair** *m* bugar.

**buideal** *m* bottle.

**buidhe** *adj* yellow; lucky.

**buidheach** *adj* thankful, grateful.

**buidheachas** *m* gratitude.

**buidheagan** *f* yolk.

**buidheann** *m/f* group; firm.

**buidheann-cluich** *m* playgroup.

**buidheann-obrach** *m* working party.

**buidheann òigridh** *m/f* youth club/group.

**buidheann-strì** *m* pressure group.

**buidhe-ruadh** *adj* auburn.

**buidhinn** *v* win.

**buidhre** *f* deafness.

**buidseach** *m/f* wizard.

**bùidsear** *m* butcher.

**buige** *f* softness; moistness.

**buil** *f* consequence; conclusion.

**buileach** *adv* completely, quite.

**buileann** *f* loaf.

**builgean** *f* bubble.

**builgeanach** *adj* bubbly.

**builich air** *v* bestow upon.

**buill a' chuirp** *mpl* parts of the body.

**buille** *f* blow; emphasis; (*mus*) beat.

**buille cridhe** *f* heartbeat.

**buill-ghineamhain** *mpl* genitals.

**buin do** *v* belong to; be related to.

**buinnig** *v* win.

**buin ri** *v* interfere with.

**buinteanas** *m* links, relationship.

**buirbe** *f* barbarity, wildness.

**bumailear** *m* oaf; no-user.

**bun** *m* base, bottom, foot.

**bunait** *f* foundation, fundamentals.

**bunaiteach** *adj* stable; fundamental(ist).

**bunasach** *adj* radical.

**bun-dealain** *m* power point.

**bun-os-cionn** *adv* upside down.

**bun-sgoil** *f* primary school.

**buntàta** *m* potato(es).

**buntàta pronn** *m* mashed potato(es).

**bùrach** *m* mess, guddle.

**bùrn** *m* water.

**burraidh** *m* fool, blockhead.

**bus**[1] *m* bus.

**bus**[2] *m* mouth; grimace, pout.

**bùth** *f* shop.

**bùth-chungaidh** *f* pharmacist's.

**bùth-eisg** *f* fish shop.

# C

**cab** *f* gob.
**cabach** *adj* talkative.
**cabadaich** *f* chatter.
**cabaireachd** *f* chatter.
**càball** *m* cable.
**cabar** *m* rafter, pole; caber.
**cabar-droma** *m* ridge pole.
**cabar-fèidh** *m* deer's antlers.
**cabhag** *f* haste.
**cabhagach** *adj* hurried, hasty.
**cabhlach** *m* fleet.
**cabhsair** *m* pavement, causeway.
**cabstair** *m* horse's bit.
**cac** *v* defecate. •◻*n* excrement.
**càch** *pron* other people, the others.
**càch-a-chèile** *pron* each other.
**cadal** *m* sleep.
**cadalach** *adj* sleepy.
**cafaidh** *m/f* café.
**cagailt** *f* hearth, fireside.
**cagainn** *v* chew.
**cagair** *v* whisper.
**cagar** *m* whisper; secret.
**caibe** *m* spade; mattock.
**caibeal** *m* chapel.
**caibideil** *m/f* chapter.
**caibideil a h-aon** chapter one.
**caidil** *v* sleep.
**caidil gu math!** *excl* sleep well!
**càil**[1] *f* desire; appetite.
**càil**[2] *m* thing.
**cailc** *f* chalk.

**caileag** *f* girl, lassie.
**cailin** *f* girl.
**caill** *v* lose; miss.
**caill do rian** *v* go out of your mind.
**cailleach** *f* old woman; wifie; hag.
**cailleach dhubh** *f* nun.
**cailleach-oidhche** *f* owl.
**caill mùn** *v* wet oneself.
**caillte** *adj* lost.
**caillteach** *adj* ruinous.
**càil sam bith** *m* anything at all.
**càin**[1] *v* scold.
**càin**[2] *f* tax.
**cainb** *f* hemp.
**caineal** *m* cinnamon.
**cainnt** *f* speech, language.
**caiptean** *m* captain, skipper.
**càir** *v* repair.
**càirdeach do** related to.
**càirdean** *mpl* friends; relations.
**càirdeas** *m* friendship; kinship.
**càirdeas fola** *m* blood relationship.
**càirdeil** *adj* friendly.
**càirdineal** *m* cardinal.
**càireas** *m* (*in mouth*) gum(s).
**cairgein** *m* carrageen.
**cairt**[1] *v* tan (leather); muck out.
**cairt**[2] *f* card; chart.
**cairt**[3] *f* cart.
**cairt-bhòrd** *m* cardboard.

**cairt-chluiche** *f* playing card.

**cairteal** *m* quarter.

**cairteal na h-uarach** *m* quarter hour.

**cairt-iùil** *f* navigation chart.

**cairt-Nollaig** *f* Xmas card.

**cairt-phuist** *f* postcard.

**càise** *m* cheese.

**caise** *f* abruptness; impetuosity.

**caisg** *v* abate; prevent.

**Càisg** *f* (*with art*) **a' Chàisg** Easter.

**caismeachd** *f* alarm; march.

**caisteal** *m* castle.

**càite?** *interrog adv* where?

**caith** *v* wear; spend; consume; waste.

**caitheamh** *m* (*with art*) **a' chaitheamh** tuberculosis.

**caithte** *adj* worn-out; consumed.

**caithteach** *adj* wasteful.

**Caitligeach** *m/adj* Catholic.

**càl** *m* cabbage, kale.

**cala** *m* harbour.

**càl-colaig** *m* cauliflower.

**calg** *m* prickle.

**calg-dhìreach** *adv* completely.

**calg-dhìreach an aghaidh** *adv* dead against.

**call** *m* loss; waste.

**calla** *adj* tame, domesticated.

**callaich** *v* tame, domesticate.

**callaid** *f* fence; hedge.

**calltainn** *m* hazel.

**calma** *adj* stout; sturdy.

**calman** *m* dove, pigeon.

**calpa**[1] *m* (*leg*) calf.

**calpa**[2] *m* (*fin*) capital.

**cam** *adj* bent, curved.

**camacasach** *adj* bow-legged.

**camag** *f* curl, ringlet; bracket.

**camagach** *adj* curled, curly.

**caman** *m* shinty stick.

**camanachd** *f* shinty.

**camara** *m* camera.

**camas** *m* bay.

**càmhal** *m* camel.

**camhanach** *f* dawn, twilight.

**campa** *m* camp.

**campaich** *v* camp.

**can** *v* say.

**cana** *m* tin, can.

**canabhas** *m* canvas.

**canach** *m/f* bog cotton.

**cànain** *f* language, tongue.

**can air** *v* say for.

**cànan** *m* language, tongue.

**cànanach** *adj* linguistic.

**canastair** *m* tin, can, canister.

**Canèidianach** *m/adj* Canadian.

**can ri** *v* call.

**caochail** *v* change, alter; die.

**caochladh** *m* change, alteration.

**caochlaideach** *adj* changeable, fickle.

**caog** *v* blink; wink.

**caogad** *m* fifty.

**caoidh** *v* lament, weep; mourn.

**caol** *adj* narrow; thin. •*m* strait, kyle.

**caolan** *m* gut, intestine.

**caol an droma** *m* small of the back.

**caol an dùirn** *m* wrist.

**caolas** *m* strait, kyle(s).

**Caolas Bòideach** *m* Kyles of Bute.

**caol na coise** *m* ankle.

**caol-shràid** *f* vennel, alley.

**caon** *adj* wily.

**caomh** *adj* dear, beloved.

**caomhain** *v* save, economise.

**caora** *f* sheep, ewe.

**caorann** *f* rowan.

**car**[1] *m* turn; stroll; trick. •▱*s adv* a bit, somewhat.

**car**[2] *prep* during, for.

**càr** *f* car.

**carabhaidh** *m* boyfriend.

**carach** *adj* wily; unreliable.

**carachd** *f* wrestling.

**caractar** *m* (*play, etc*) character.

**càradh** *m* repair; state, condition.

**caraich** *v* move.

**càraich** *v* repair.

**caraiche** *m* wrestler.

**caraid**[1] *m* friend, relative; (*corres*) **A Charaid** Dear Sir; **A Chàirdean** Dear Sirs.

**càraid**[2] *f* pair; twins.

**càraid phòsda** *f* married couple.

**car a' mhuiltein** *m* somersault.

**caran** *adv* a bit, slightly.

**carbad** *m* vehicle; carriage; craft.

**carbad-eiridinn** *m* ambulance.

**cargu** *m* cargo.

**càrn** *v* pile up; accumulate. •▱*h* heap; cairn; hill.

**càrnaid** *f* carnation.

**càrnan** *m* cockroach.

**càrn-cuimhne** *m* monument.

**càrr** *f* dandruff.

**carragh** *m* rock; stone pillar.

**carraig** *f* rock.

**carson?** *interrog adv* why?

**carson a chiall?** *excl* why on earth?

**cartadh** *m* mucking out.

**carthannas** *m* kindness; charity.

**cas**[1] *f* foot; leg; handle.

**cas**[2] *adj* steep; impetuous;.

**càs** *m* difficulty, predicament.

**casad** *m* cough.

**casadaich** *v* cough.

**casa-gobhlach air** *prep* astride.

**casaid** *f* complaint; accusation.

**cas-chrom** *f* foot-plough.

**casgadh** *m* prevention.

**casgair** *v* slay, massacre.

**casgairt** *f* slaughter, butchery.

**casgan** *m* brake.

**casg-gineamhainn** *m* contraception; contraceptive.

**cas-lom** *adj* barefoot, barelegged.

**cas-ruisgte** *adj* barefoot, barelegged.

**cas toisich** *f* foreleg.

**cat** *m* cat.

**cat fiadhaich** *m* wildcat.

**cath** *m* battle; warfare.

**càth** *f* chaff.

**cathadh** *m* snowdrift.

**cathag** *f* jackdaw.

**cathair** *f* chair; city.

**cathair-chuibhle** *f* wheelchair.

**cathair-eaglais** *f* cathedral.

**cath-bhuidheann** *f* batallion.

**cead** *m* permission; permit, licence.

**ceadach** *adj* tolerant.

**ceadachail** *adj* permissive.

**ceadaich** *v* permit, allow.

**ceadaichte** *adj* allowed.

**cead-dol-thairis** *m* passport.

**cead dràibhidh** *m* driving licence.

**cead telebhisein** *m* television licence.

**ceàird** *f* trade, craft.

**cealg** *f* deceit; hypocrisy.

**cealgach** *adj* deceitful; hypocritical.

**cealgair** *m* deceiver, cheat; hypocrite.

**cealla** *f* (*biol*) cell.

**ceanalta** *adj* pretty, comely.

**ceangail** *v* tie; join.

**ceangal** *m* connection; bond.

**ceann** *m* head; end.

**ceannach, ceannachd** *m* purchase, buying; trading.

**ceannaich** *v* buy.

**ceannaich air dhàil** *v* buy on credit.

**ceannaiche** *m* purchaser; merchant.

**ceannard** *m* leader; chief.

**ceann-bliadhna** *m* birthday.

**ceann-cinnidh** *m* clan chief.

**ceann daoraich** *m* hangover.

**ceann-feadhna** *m* clan chief.

**ceann goirt** *m* sore head, headache.

**ceann-làidir** *adj* headstrong.

**ceann-pholan** *m* tadpole.

**ceann-ruisgte** *adj* bareheaded.

**ceannsaich** *v* conquer; control; tame.

**ceannsal** *m* authority.

**ceannsalach** *adj* authoritative.

**ceann-simid** *m* tadpole.

**ceann-suidhe** *m* president.

**ceann-uidhe** *m* destination.

**ceap**[1] *m* block; lump.

**ceap**[2] *m* cap.

**ceapach** *m* (garden) plot, bed.

**ceapaire** *m* sandwich.

**cearb** *f* rag; defect.

**cearbach** *adj* clumsy; ragged.

**cearc** *f* hen.

**cearcall** *m* circle, ring.

**cèard** *m* tinker, smith.

**cèardach** *f* smithy.

**cèard-airgid** *m* silversmith.

**ceàrd-copair** *m* coppersmith.

**ceàrn** *m* corner; district.

**ceàrnach** *adj* square.

**ceàrnag** *f* square.

**ceàrr** *adj* wrong; left.

**ceàrraiche** *m* gambler.

**ceart** *adj* correct; just; same.

**ceartachadh** *m* correction; marking.

**ceartaich** *v* correct; put right.

**ceartas** *m* justice.

**ceart gu leòr** *adv* right enough; okay!

**ceart-mheadhan** *m* dead centre.

**ceart-uilinn** *f* right angle.

**ceasnachadh** *m* questioning; questionnaire.

**ceasnaich** *v* question; interrogate.

**ceathach** *m* mist.

**ceathrad** *m* forty.

**ceathramh** *adj* fourth. •◻*h* quarter.

**ceathrar** *m* foursome.

**cèic** *f* cake.

**cèidse** *f* cage.

**ceil (air)** *v* hide, conceal (from).

**cèile** *m/f* spouse; counterpart.

**cèilidh** *m/f* visit; ceilidh.

**ceilir** *v* sing sweetly, warble.

**ceilp** *f* kelp.

**Ceilteach** *m/adj* Celt; Celtic.

**ceimig** *f* chemical substance.

**ceimigeachd** *f* chemistry.

**ceimigear** *m* chemist.

**cèin** *adj* foreign; faraway.

**cèir** *f* wax.

**cèir-chluaise** *f* ear wax.

**cèis** *f* frame; envelope.

**cèiseag** *f* cassette.

**ceist** *f* question; problem; point.

**ceisteachan** *m* questionnaire.

**ceistear** *m* questioner; question master.

**Cèitean** *m* (*with art*) **an Cèitean** May.

**ceithir** *m/adj* four.

**ceò** *m* mist; haze; smoke.

**ceòl** *m* music.

**ceòl beag** *m* light music for the pipes.

**ceòlmhor** *adj* musical; melodious.

**ceòl mòr** *m* classical pipe music, pibroch.

**ceòthach** *adj* misty.

**ceud** *m* hundred.

**ceudameatair** *m* centimetre.

**ceudamh** *adj* hundredth.

**ceud mìle fàilte!** *excl* a hundred thousand welcomes!

**ceudna** *adj* same.

**ceud taing!** *excl* many thanks! thanks a lot!

**ceum** *m* step; pace; degree.

**ceum air cheum** *adv* step by step.

**ceumnachadh** *m* graduation.

**ceumnaich** *v* graduate.

**ceus**[1] *v* crucify.

**ceus**[2] *m* suitcase.

**ceusadh** *m* crucifixion.

**cha, chan** *part negating the clause or sentence.*

**cha bheir mi ho-ro-gheallaidh air**◻.◻.◻don't give a toss for◻.◻.◻.

**cha b'urrainn dhomh gun**◻.◻.◻. couldn't help.

**chaidh** *past tense of v* **rach**.

**chaidh agam air** *v* I managed it.

**cha mhòr** *adv* nearly.

**cha mhòr nach** *conj* almost.

**chan** *see* **cha**.

**chan fhad' thuige!** it won't be long!

**chan iongnadh e!** no wonder!

**cha ruig thu leas**□.□.□you don't need to.

**chì** *future tense of v* **faic**.

**chleachd mi** *v* I used to.

**cho** *adv* so, as.

**cho luath is**□.□.□*conj* as soon as□.□.□.

**cho math sin** *adv* that good, as good as that.

**chuala** *past tense of v* **cluinn**.

**chuca** *prep pron* to them.

**chugad** *prep pron* to you (*sing*).

**chugaibh** *prep pron* to you (*pl*).

**chugainn** *prep pron* to us.

**chugam** *prep pron* to me.

**chuice** *prep pron* to her, to it (*f*).

**chuige** *prep pron* to him, to it (*m*).

**chun** *prep* to, towards, up to.

**chun a seo** *adv* up to now, so far.

**chunnaic** *past tense of v* **faic**.

**ciad** *adj* (*with art*) **a' chiad**. the first.

**ciad-fhuasladh** *m* first aid.

**ciall** *f* sense(s); meaning.

**ciallach** *adj* sensible.

**ciallaich** *v* mean.

**ciamar?** *interrog adv* how?

**cia mheud?** *interrog adv* how many? how much?

**cian** *adj* distant; long. •□*h* distance; remoteness.

**cianail** *adj* sad.

**cianalach** *adj* homesick.

**cianalas** *m* sadness.

**ciar** *adj* dark; swarthy; dun.

**ciatach** *adj* pleasant; attractive.

**cidhe** *m* quay.

**cidsin** *m* kitchen.

**cileagram** *m* kilogram.

**cilemeatair** *m* kilometre.

**cill** *f* cell; church; kirkyard.

**cineal** *m* race; species.

**cinn** *v* grow; multiply.

**cinneadail** *adj* clannish.

**cinneadh** *m* clan; people; surname.

**cinneas** *m* growth.

**cinne-daona** *m* (*with art*) **an cinne-daona** mankind.

**cinnt** *f* certainty.

**cinnteach** *adj* certain; confident.

**ciobair** *m* shepherd.

**cìoch** *f* breast.

**cìochag** *f* valve.

**ciomach** *m* prisoner; detainee.

**cion** *m* lack; desire.

**cionta** *m* guilt; guilty action.

**ciontach** *adj* guilty. •□*h* guilty person; offender.

**ciontaich** *v* commit an offence.

**ciora** *f* (*fam*) sheep.

**ciorram** *m* disability, handicap.

**ciorramach** *adj* disabled, handicapped. •□*h* disabled person; (*pl with art*) **na ciorramaich** the disabled.

**ciotach** *adj* left-handed.

**cipean** *m* stake; tether post.

**cìr** *v* comb. •□comb; cud.

**cìrean** *m* (*of hen, etc*) comb, crest.

**cìr-mheala** *f* honeycomb.

**cìs** f tax; taxation.
**cìs-chusbainn** f customs duty.
**cìs-cinn** f poll tax.
**cìs oighreachd** f inheritance tax.
**ciste** f (*furniture*) chest.
**ciste-chàir** f car boot.
**ciste-laighe** f coffin.
**ciste-urrais** f trust fund.
**ciùb** m cube.
**ciùbach** adj cubic.
**ciùbhran** m drizzle, shower.
**ciudha** f queue.
**ciùin** adj gentle; quiet; calm.
**ciùineas** m calm, calmness.
**ciùinich** v quieten, calm down.
**ciùraig** v (*bacon, etc*) cure.
**ciùrr** v hurt; torture.
**ciùrrte** adj hurt, injured.
**clabar-snàimh** m flipper.
**clabhstair** m cloister.
**clach** v stone. •*f* stone; (*fam*) testicle.
**clachach** adj stony.
**clachair** m (stone-)mason.
**clachan** m village; kirktown; kirkyard.
**clach-bhalg** f (*toy, etc*) rattle.
**clach cuimhne** f memorial, monument.
**clach-ghràin** f granite.
**clach-mheallain** f hailstone.
**Clach na Cineamhainn** f the Stone of Destiny.
**clach sùla** f eyeball.
**clach uasal** f precious stone.
**cladach** m shore, beach.

**cladh** m kirkyard, cemetry.
**cladhaich** v dig.
**cladhaire** m coward.
**cladhaireach** adj cowardly.
**clag** m bell.
**clagarsaich** f clinking; rattling.
**clag-rabhaidh** m alarm bell.
**claidheamh** m sword.
**claidheamhair** m swordsman.
**claidheamh caol** m rapier.
**claigeann** m skull.
**clàimhean** m latch.
**clais** f ditch; furrow.
**claisdeachd** f hearing.
**claisneachd** f hearing.
**clamhan** m buzzard.
**clann** f children; clan.
**clann-nighean** f (*collective*) girls.
**claoidh** v exhaust; vex.
**claoidhte** adj exhausted.
**claon** v incline; go astray; pervert. •*adj* awry; oblique; perverse.
**claonadh** m slant, slope; squint; perversion.
**clàr** m board; table; record.
**clàraich** v record.
**clàr-amais** m index.
**clàr-aodainn** m brow, forehead.
**clàr-dùthcha** m map.
**clàr-fhiacail** f incisor.
**clàr-gnothaich** m agenda.
**clàr-innsidh** m table of contents.
**clàr-oideachais** m curriculum.
**clàrsach** f harp; Celtic harp, clarsach.

**clàrsair** *m* harper.

**clàr-tìde** *m* timetable.

**clas** *m* class.

**clasaigeach** *adj* classical.

**cleachd** *v* use; accustom.

**cleachdadh** *m* habit; practice.

**cleachdte ri** *adj* accustomed to, used to.

**cleas** *m* feat; trick.

**cleasachd** *f* conjuring; juggling.

**cleasaiche** *m* actor; comic; conjurer.

**cleas-chluich** *f* comic film/play.

**clèir** *f* clergy; Presbytery.

**clèireach** *m* clergyman; clerk. •◨*n*/*adj* Presbyterian.

**clèireachail** *adj* clerical.

**cleoc** *m* clock.

**cleòc** *m* cloak.

**clì** *adj* left.

**cliabh** *m* pannier; creel; (*anat*) chest.

**cliamhainn** *m* son-in-law.

**cliath** *v* (*agric*) harrow. •◨ grate, bars; harrow.

**cliathaich** *f* side, flank.

**cliath-theine** *f* fire grate.

**cliath-uinneig** *f* window bars.

**clìomaid** *f* climate.

**clis** *adj* nimble.

**cliseachd** *f* nimbleness, agility.

**clisg** *v* start, jump; startle.

**clisgeach** *adj* jumpy, on edge; timid.

**clisgeadh** *f* start, fright.

**clisgear** *m* exclamation.

**clisg-phuing** *f* exclamation mark.

**cliù** *m* fame; reputation.

**cliùiteach** *adj* famous, celebrated.

**cliùthaich** *v* praise.

**clò**[1] *m* cloth; tweed.

**clò**[2] *m* print; printing press.

**clòbha** *f* clove.

**clobha** *m* tongs.

**clòbhar** *m* clover.

**clobhsa** *m* (*in tenement, etc*) close.

**clò-bhuail** *v* print.

**clò-bhuailte** *adj* printed.

**clò-bhualadair** *m* printer(s).

**clò-bhualadh** *m* printing; publication.

**clò-chadal** *m* doze, dozing.

**clochar** *m* convent.

**clogaid** *f* helmet.

**clòimh** *f* wool.

**clòimhteachan** *m* eiderdown.

**Clò Mòr na Hearadh** *m* Harris Tweed.

**closach** *f* carcase.

**clòsaid** *f* closet.

**clò-sgrìobh** *v* type.

**clò-sgrìobhadair** *m* typewriter.

**clò-sgrìobhadh** *m* typing; typescript.

**clò-sgrìobhaiche** *m* typist.

**cluain** *f* meadow, pasture.

**cluaineas** *m* retirement.

**cluaran** *m* thistle.

**cluas** *f* ear; handle.

**cluasag** *f* pillow.

**cluas-fhail** *f* earring.

**club** *m* club.

**clùd** *m* rag; cloth.

**cluich** *m* play; game. •◻ play.

**cluich-bùird** *m* board game.

**cluicheadair** *m* player; actor.

**cluinn** *v* hear.

**cnag** *v* crunch; bang, knock. •◻ bang, knock.

**cnag-aodaich** *f* clothes peg.

**cnag-dealain** *f* electric plug.

**cnag na cùise** *f* the crux of the matter.

**cnàimh** *m* bone.

**cnàimh an droma** *m* the spine, the backbone.

**cnàimheach** *m* skeleton.

**cnàimhseag** *f* acne; blackhead.

**cnàimh-slinnein** *f* shoulder-blade.

**cnàimh uga** *m* collarbone.

**cnàmh** *v* chew; digest.

**cnàmh** *m* potato blight.

**cnàmhach** *adj* bony.

**cnàmh a' chìr** *v* chew the cud.

**cnap** *m* block; lump, knob.

**cnapach** *adj* lumpy, nobbly.

**cnap-starra** *m* stumbling block.

**cnatan** *m* (*often with art*) cold, **tha an cnatan orm** I have a cold; **an cnatan mòr** *m* influenza.

**cnead** *m* groan.

**cnèadaich** *v* caress; stroke.

**cneutag** *f* small ball, puck.

**cnò** *f* nut.

**cnoc** *m* hill.

**cnocach** *adj* hilly.

**cnocan** *m* hillock.

**cnò challtainne** *m* hazelnut.

**cnò Fhrangach** *m* walnut.

**cnò-thalmhainn** *m* peanut.

**cnuas** *v* chew; ponder.

**cnuimh-thalmhainn** *f* earthworm.

**co-** *prefix* co-.

**cò?** *interrog pron* who? which?

**co aca** *conj* whether.

**co-aimsireil** *adj* contemporary.

**cò air bith?** *interrog pron* who-ever?

**co-alta** *m/f* foster brother/sister.

**cò am fear?** which one?.

**co-aoiseach** *m/adj* contemporary.

**co-aontaich** *v* agree.

**cò às?** *adv* where from?

**cobhair** *f* help; relief.

**cobhair orm!** *excl* help! help me!

**cobhar** *m* foam.

**cobhartach** *m/f* plunder; prey.

**co-bhuail** *v* collide.

**còc** *m* (*fuel*) coke.

**còcaire** *m* cook, chef.

**còcaireachd** *f* cookery.

**cochall** *m* husk; hood.

**co-cheangail** *v* tie together; connect.

**co-cheangailte** *adj* linked together.

**co-chomann** *m* commune; co-operative.

**co-chòrd** v agree mutually.

**co-chothrom** m balance, equilibrium.

**co-chruinnich** v assemble.

**co-chruinneachadh** m assembly; collection.

**còco** m cocoa.

**co-dhèanta** adj put together.

**co dhiubh** conj whether.

**co-dhiubh, co-dhiù** adv anyway; at least.

**co-dhlùthaich** v condense.

**co-dhùin** v conclude; end.

**co-dhùnadh** m conclusion; end.

**co-èigneachadh** m compulsion.

**co-èignich** v compel.

**cofaidh** m coffee.

**co-fharpais** f competition.

**co-fharpaiseach** m competitor.

**co-fhlaitheachd** f republic; republicanism.

**co-fhlaitheas** m commonwealth.

**co-fhoghar** m consonant.

**co-fhreagair** v match; correspond.

**co-fhulangach** adj sympathetic.

**co-fhulangas** m sympathy.

**cofhurtachd** f consolation; comfort.

**cofhurtaich** v comfort, console.

**cofhurtail** adj comfortable.

**cò fon ghrèin'.**□.□. **?**who on earth□.□.□.□?

**cogadh** m war; warfare.

**cogais** f conscience.

**co-ghin** v mate, copulate.

**co-ghineadh** m mating, copulation.

**co-ghnìomhair** m adverb.

**coibhneas** m kindness, kindliness.

**coibhneil** adj kind, kindly.

**coidse** f coach.

**còig** m/adj five.

**còigeamh** adj fifth.

**còignear** m fivesome.

**coigreach** m foreigner; stranger.

**coileach** m (fowl) cock.

**coilleach-gaoithe** m weathercock.

**coilean** v accomplish; complete.

**coileanta** adj completed; perfect.

**coilear** m collar.

**coill** f guilt; sin.

**coille** f wood.

**coilleag** f cockle.

**coillear** m forestry worker; woodcutter.

**coille mhòr** f forest.

**coimeas** f comparison; like(s) of. •□ compare, liken.

**coimeasach** adj comparable.

**coimh-** prefix co-.

**coimheach** adj foreign; unfamiliar. • m foreigner; stranger.

**coimhead** v watch; look.

**coimhead air** v look at.

**coimhead ri** v expect.

**coimhearsnach** m neighbour.

**coimhearsnachd** f neighbourhood.

**coimheatailt** f alloy.

**coimhlion** *v* accomplish; complete.

**coimisean** *m* commission.

**coimpiutair, coimpiutar** *m* computer.

**coineanach** *m* rabbit.

**còinneach** *f* moss.

**coinneal** *f* candle.

**coinneamh** *f* meeting.

**coinnich** *v* congregate.

**coinnich ri** *v* meet.

**coinnleir** *m* candlestick.

**co-ionann** *adj* identical, the same.

**còir** *f* obligation; right; justice. •*adj* decent; worthy; kindly.

**coirbte** *adj* corrupt.

**coirce** *m* oats.

**coire**[1] *f* wrong; blame.

**coire**[2] *m* kettle; cauldron; corrie.

**coireach** *adj* guilty; responsible. •*n* guilty person; offender.

**coirich** *v* blame.

**còir-slighe** *f* right of way.

**coiseachd** *f* walking.

**coisich** *v* walk.

**coisiche** *m* walker, pedestrian.

**coisinn** *v* win; earn.

**còisir** *f* choir.

**còisir-chiùil** *f* choir.

**coisrig** *v* consecrate; devote.

**coitcheann** *adj* common, communal; general, universal.

**coithional** *adj* congregation.

**coitich** *v* urge.

**co-labhairt** *f* conference.

**co-là-breith** *m* birthday.

**cola-deug** *m* fortnight.

**colaiste** *f* college.

**colann** *f* body.

**colbh** *m* column.

**Colla** *m* Coll.

**Collach** *m/adj* from Coll.

**collaidh** *adj* sensual, carnal.

**coltach** *adj* likely.

**coltach ri** *prep* like.

**coltaich ri** *v* compare to.

**coltas** *m* appearance.

**com** *m* bosom, chest area.

**coma** *adj* indifferent; unconcerned.

**coma co-dhiubh** *adj* quite indifferent.

**comain** *f* obligation.

**coma leat!** *excl* never mind! don't worry!

**comanachadh** *m* Communion.

**comanaich** *v* take Communion.

**comanaiche** *m* communicant.

**comann** *m* association; club, society.

**comann eachdraidh** *m* history society.

**comar** *f* confluence.

**comas** *m* ability; faculty.

**comasach** *adj* able.

**comasach air** capable of.

**comas inntinn** *m* mental ability.

**comataidh** *f* committee.

**combaist** *f* compass.

**comh-** *prefix* co-.

**comhachag** *f* owl.

**comhair** *f* direction.

**comhairle** *f* advice; council.

**comhairleach** *m* adviser.

**comhairlich** *v* advise.

**comhairliche** *m* councillor.

**comharrachadh** *m* marking, correction.

**comharradh** *m* mark; sign; symbol.

**comharradh-ceiste** *m* question mark.

**comharradh-rathaid** *m* road sign.

**comharradh-stiùiridh** *m* landmark.

**comharraich** *v* mark, correct.

**comhart** *m* (*of dog*) bark.

**comhartaich** *v* (*of dog*) bark.

**còmhdach** *m* cover, covering.

**còmhdaich** *v* cover.

**còmhdaichte** *adj* covered.

**còmhdhail** *f* congress, conference.

**co-mheasgaich** *v* intermix, mix; amalgate; mingle.

**co mheud?** *interrog adv* how much? how many?

**còmhla**[1] *adv* together.

**còmhla**[2] *m/f* door.

**còmhlan** *m* band; company.

**còmhlan-ciùil** *m* (*mus*) band, group.

**còmhla ri** *prep* with, along with.

**còmhnaich** *v* live, dwell.

**còmhnaidh** *f* dwelling.

**còmhnard** *adj* level; smooth. •*n* plain; level ground.

**còmhradh** *m* conversation, talk.

**còmhradh beag** *m* chat.

**còmhrag** *f* combat; conflict.

**còmhrag-dithis** *f* duel.

**còmhraiteach** *adj* talkative, chatty.

**còmhstri** *f* strife; competition.

**com-pàirtich** *v* take part.

**companach** *m* companion; pal.

**companaidh** *m/f* firm, company.

**companas** *m* companionship.

**comraich** *f* sanctuary.

**còn** *m* cone.

**conaire** *f* rosary.

**conaltrach** *adj* social; sociable.

**conaltradh** *m* conversation; company.

**conasg** *m* gorse, whins.

**conastabal** *m* constable.

**connadh** *m* fuel.

**connadh-làmhaich** *m* munitions.

**connlach** *f* straw.

**connrag** *f* consonant.

**connsachail** *adj* quarrelsome; argumentative.

**connsaich** *v* argue, quarrel.

**connspaid** *f* dispute; controversy; wrangling.

**connspaideach** *adj* disputatious; controversial.

**conntraigh** *f* neap tide.

**consal** *m* consul.

**consan** *m* consonant.

**co-obrachadh** *m* co-operation; co-operative.

**co-obraich** *v* co-operate.

**co-ogha** *m* cousin.

**co-oibrich** *v* work together.

**co-oibriche** *m* fellow worker.

**cop** *m* foam, froth.

**copach** *adj* frothy, foaming.

**copag** *f* dock, docken.

**copan** *m* cup.

**copar** *m* copper.

**co-phòitear** *m* drinking companion.

**cor** *m* state, condition.

**còraichean daonna** *fpl* human rights.

**còrcair** *adj* purple.

**corcais** *f* cork.

**còrd**[1] *v* agree.

**còrd**[2] *m* cord.

**còrdadh** *m* agreement, understanding.

**còrd ri** *v* please.

**còrn** *m* drinking horn; corn.

**Còrn** *f* (*with art*) **a' Chòrn** Cornwall.

**Còrnach** *m/adj* Cornishman; Cornish.

**còrnair** *m* corner.

**corp** *m* body; corpse.

**corpailear** *m* corporal.

**corp-làidir** *adj* able-bodied.

**corporra** *adj* bodily, corporal.

**còrr** *adj* (*number*) odd. •⬛*h* (*with art*) **an còrr** the rest, everything else; anything else.

**corra** *adj* odd, occasional.

**corrag** *f* finger.

**corra-ghritheach** *f* heron.

**corran** *m* sickle.

**còrr is** *prep* more than.

**còs** *m* hollow.

**còsach** *adj* hollow.

**cosamhlachd** *f* parable.

**cosg** *v* cost; spend; waste. •⬛*h* cost; waste.

**cosgail** *adj* costly.

**cosgais** *f* cost.

**cosgaisean siubhail** *fpl* travel costs.

**co-sheirm** *f* harmony.

**co-shìnte** *adj* parallel.

**cosnadh** *m* earning; employment; work.

**costa** *m* coast.

**còta** *m* coat.

**còta-bàn** *m* petticoat.

**còta-leapa** *m* dressing gown, housecoat.

**còta mòr** *m* overcoat.

**cotan** *m* cotton.

**cothrom** *adj* (*number*) even. •⬛*h* chance, opportunity; balance.

**cothromach** *adj* fair; decent.

**cothromaich** *v* weigh; balance.

**cothrom na Feinne** *m* fair chance.

**co-thuit** *v* coincide.

**co-thuiteamas** *m* coincidence.

**cràbhach** *adj* devout, pious.

**cràdh** *m* pain; anguish.

**craiceann** *m* skin.

**cràidh** *v* pain; torment.

**cràidhteach** *adj* grievous, painful.

**cràin** f sow.

**crann** m mast; plough; crane; bolt; tree; (with art) **an Crann** the Saltire, St Andrew's Cross; **an Crann-Ceusaidh** Christ's Cross.

**crannag** f pulpit; milk churn; crannog.

**crannchur** m drawing lots; fate.

**crann-fìona** m vine.

**crann-sgaoilidh** m transmitter; TV mast.

**crann-sneachda** m snowplough.

**crann-tarsainn** m crossbar.

**craobh** f tree.

**craobh-sgaoil** v diffuse; broadcast.

**craos** m maw; gluttony.

**craosach** adj gluttonous.

**craosaire** m glutton.

**crasg** f crutch (for walking).

**crasgag** f starfish.

**crath** v shake, tremble; brandish.

**creach** v plunder; ruin. •🔲 ruination; plunder.

**creachan** m scallop.

**crèadh** f clay.

**crèadhadair** m potter.

**crèadhadaireachd** f pottery.

**creag** f crag; hill.

**creagach** adj craggy.

**creamh** m garlic.

**creamh-gàrraidh** m leek.

**creapan** m stool.

**creathail** f cradle.

**creid** v believe; think, consider.

**creideamh** m belief; trust; religion.

**creideas** m trust.

**creim** v nibble.

**crèis** f grease, fat.

**crèiseach** adj greasy, fatty.

**creithleag** f cleg, horsefly.

**creud** f creed.

**creutair** m creature.

**creutair bochd** m poor soul.

**criadh** f clay.

**criathar** m sieve, riddle.

**criathraich** v sieve, riddle.

**cridhe** m heart; courage.

**cridhealas** m heartiness; conviviality.

**cridheil** adj hearty; jovial.

**crìoch** f end; boundary.

**Crìochan Shasainn** the Borders.

**crìochnach** adj finite.

**crìochnaich** v finish.

**crìochnaichte** adj finished.

**criomag** f bit; crumb; (pl) **criomagan** bits and pieces, odds and ends.

**crìon** v wither; dry up. •🔲 adj tiny; petty; withered.

**crioplach** m cripple.

**crios** m belt.

**Crìosdachd** f Christendom.

**Crìosdaidh** m Christian.

**Crìosdaidheachd** f Christianity.

**Crìosdail** adj Christian.

**Crìosdalachd** f Christian-ness.

**criostal** m crystal.

**cripleach** m cripple.

**crith** *v* tremble, shiver. •🔲 trembling, shivering.

**critheanach** *adj* shaky; scary.

**crith-thalmhainn** *f* earthquake.

**crò** *m* cattle pen, fold.

**croch** *v* hang.

**crochadair** *m* hangman; hanger.

**crochadh** *m* hanging.

**crochte** *adj* hung; hanged.

**crodh** *m* cattle, livestock.

**crodh-bhainne** *m* dairy cows.

**crodh-dàra** *m* breeding cattle.

**crodh-eadraidh** *m* milk cows.

**crò-dhearg** *adj* crimson.

**cròg** *f* paw; fist.

**cròic** *f* antler.

**croich** *f* gallows. •🔲*xcl* **X na croiche!** damned X! bloody X!

**crois** *f* cross; crucifix.

**crois rathaid** *f* crossroads.

**croit**[1] *f* croft.

**croit**[2] *f* (*on back*) hump.

**croitear** *m* crofter.

**croitse** *f* (*for walking*) crutch.

**crom** *v* bend, incline; descend, climb down. •🔲*dj* bent, crooked; curved.

**cromag** *f* hook; comma; cromag, crook.

**cromagan turrach** *fpl* inverted commas.

**crom air** *v* set to.

**crom-chasach** *adj* bandy-legged.

**cron** *m* harm; fault.

**cronaich** *v* chide, scold.

**cronail** *adj* harmful, hurtful.

**crònan** *m* humming; murmuring; buzzing; (*stags*) belling.

**crò snàthaid** *m* eye of needle.

**crosta** *adj* cross; naughty.

**crotach** *adj* hump-backed.

**crotal** *m* lichen.

**cruach** *v* heap, stack. •🔲 heap; rick.

**cruachann** *f* hip.

**cruadal** *m* hardship; hardihood.

**cruadalach** *adj* difficult; hardy.

**cruadhaich** *v* harden; solidify.

**cruaidh** *f* steel. •🔲*dj* hard; harsh; hardy.

**cruaidh-chàs** *m* emergency; tight corner.

**cruaidh-chridheach** *adj* hard-hearted.

**cruan** *m* enamel.

**cruas** *m* hardness; harshness; toughness.

**crùb** *v* crouch; cringe; crawl.

**crùbach** *adj* lame. •🔲*h* lame person.

**crùbag** *f* crab.

**crùban** *m* crouch, squat.

**crùdh** *v* (*horse*) shoe.

**crudha** *m* horseshoe.

**cruinn** *adj* round; accurate; assembled.

**cruinne** *m/f* sphere, globe; (*with art*) **an cruinne** the earth, the globe.

**cruinneachadh** *m* gathering, assembly; collection.

**cruinne-cè** *m/f* (*with art*) **an cruinne-cè** the world.

**cruinn-eòlas** *m* geography.

**cruinnich** *v* gather, assemble; (*fruit, etc*) pick.

**cruinn-leum** *m* standing jump.

**crùisgean** *m* oil lamp, cruisie.

**cruit**[1] *f* croft.

**cruit**[2] *f* harp.

**cruit-chòrda** *f* harpsichord.

**cruitear** *m* harper.

**cruitheachd** *f* creation; (*with art*) **a' Chruitheachd** the world; the universe, Creation.

**cruithear** *m* creator; (*with art*) **an Cruithear** God, the Creator.

**Cruithneach** *m/adj* Pict; Pictish.

**cruithneachd** *f* wheat.

**crùn** *v* crown. •*n* crown.

**crùnadh** *m* crowning, coronation.

**cruth** *m* shape; figure; appearance.

**cruthaich** *v* create.

**cù** *m* dog.

**cuach** *f* bowl, quaich.

**cuagach** *adj* bent; limping.

**cuaille** *m* club, cudgel.

**cuairt** *f* circuit; stroll; trip.

**cuan** *m* sea, ocean; **an Cuan Sgìth** the Little Minch; **an Cuan Siar** the Atlantic Ocean.

**cuaraidh** *m* quarry.

**cuaran** *m* sandal.

**cuartaich** *v* surround; enclose.

**cùbaid** *f* pulpit.

**cubhaidh** *adj* fitting.

**cùbhraidh** *adj* sweet, fragrant.

**cucair** *f* cooker.

**cù-chaorach** *m* sheepdog.

**cùdainn** *f* large tub.

**cudthrom** *m* weight; importance; stress.

**cudthromach** *adj* weighty, important.

**cugullach** *adj* unsteady; dodgy; unreliable.

**cuibhle** *f* wheel.

**cuibhle-stiùiridh** *f* steering wheel.

**cuibhreach** *m* chain.

**cuibhreann** *m* portion; allowance.

**cuibhreann-ciorraim** *m* disability allowance.

**cuibhrich** *v* chain.

**cuibhrig** *f* quilt, coverlet.

**cuid** *f* share; part. •*pron* some.

**cuid-aodaich** *f* clothes, clothing.

**cuideachadh** *m* help.

**cuideachail** *adj* helpful.

**cuideachd**[1] *f* company; companions.

**cuideachd**[2] *adv* too, also.

**cuideachdail** *adj* sociable, fond of company.

**cuideigin** *m/f* someone, somebody.

**cuide ri** *prep* with, along with.

**cuidhteag** *f* whiting.

**cuidhteas** *m* receipt; riddance.

**cuidich** *v* help, assist.

**cuid oidhche** *f* night's lodging.

**cùil** f corner, nook.

**cuilbheart** f trick; stratagem.

**cuilc** f reed; cane.

**cùil-chumhang** f tight corner, fix.

**cuilc Innseanach** f bamboo.

**cuileag** f fly, house-fly.

**cuilean** m puppy; cub.

**cuimhne** f memory; remembrance.

**cuimhneachan** m memorial; memorandum.

**cuimhneachan-cogaidh** m war memorial.

**cuimhnich** v remember.

**cuimir** adj succinct; neat; shapely.

**Cuimreach** m/adj Welshman; Welsh.

**Cuimrigh** f (with art) **a' Chuimrigh** Wales.

**cuimsich** v aim.

**cuine?** interrog adv when?

**cuing** f yoke; (with art) **a' chuing** f asthma.

**cuinneag** f bucket; milking pail.

**cuinnean** m nostril.

**cuip** v whip. •⊞whip.

**cuir** v put; send; (seed, etc) sow, plant.

**cuir a dh'iarraidh** v send for.

**cuir air** v light, turn/switch on; put on, don.

**cuir air an spàrr** v save; stow away.

**cuir air an teine** v light the fire.

**cuir air ath là** v defer, put off.

**cuir air bhonn** v found, set up.

**cuir air chois** v found, set up.

**cuir air dòigh** v organise; put right.

**cuir air earalas** v forewarn, alert.

**cuir air flod** v float; launch.

**cuir air leth** v put aside; save.

**cuir air meidh** v balance.

**cuir air mheomhair** v commit to memory.

**cuir air snàmh** v inundate, flood.

**cuir aithne air** v get to know.

**cuir a-mach** v bring up, vomit.

**cuir am bogadh** v steep.

**cuir am fad** v lengthen, make longer.

**cuir an cèill** v express, put into words.

**cuir an clò** v print; publish.

**cuir an cràdh** v torture.

**cuir an eanchainn à** v brain.

**cuir an geall gu** v bet that.

**cuir an òrdugh** v put in order.

**cuir an sàs** v capture; arrest.

**cuir an suarachas** v belittle, disparage.

**cuir an tairgse** v make available.

**cuir an teagamh** v cast doubt upon.

**cuir às an teine** v put the fire out.

**cuir às do** v abolish; kill.

**cuir às mo leth.** v accuse me of.

**cuir bacadh air** v obstruct; prevent.

**cuir bun-os-cionn** v upend, overturn.

**cuir bus air** *v* grimace, pout.

**cuir cabhag air** *v* rush, hurry.

**cuir car de** *v* move.

**cuir ceart** *v* correct, put right.

**cuir cèilidh air** *v* go to see, visit.

**cuir cleas air** *v* play a trick/joke on.

**cuir clisgeadh air** *v* startle.

**cuir coire air** *v* blame, lay blame on.

**cuir crainn** *v* toss coin.

**cuir crìoch air** *v* complete, finish.

**cuir dàil air** *v* delay.

**cuir dath air** *v* colour.

**cuir dheth** *v* turn/switch off; doff, take off; talk away, jabber on.

**cuir do taic orm/rium** *v* lean on me; depend on me.

**cuir dragh air** *v* worry; bother, trouble.

**cuireadh** *m* invitation.

**cuir eagal air** *v* frighten.

**cuir earbsa ann** *v* put trust in, rely on.

**cuir eòlas air** *v* get to know.

**cuir fàilte air** *v* welcome.

**cuir fios do** *v* let know, inform.

**cuir fodha** *v* sink, scuttle.

**cuir fon choill** *v* outlaw.

**cuir geall** *v* place a bet.

**cuir gruaim air** *v* frown, scowl.

**cuir gu feum** *v* use, utilise.

**cuir impidh air** *v* persuade, urge.

**cuir iongantas air** *v* amaze, astound.

**cuir luach air** *v* value; evaluate.

**cuirm** *f* feast, banquet.

**cuir ma sgaoil** *v* set free.

**cuirm-bainnse** *f* wedding reception.

**cuirm-chnuic** *f* picnic.

**cuirmeach** *adj* festive.

**cuir meal an naidheachd air** *v* congratulate.

**cuir mo chùl ri** *v* turn my back on.

**cuir mùig air** *v* frown, scowl.

**cuir oillt air** *v* terrify; horrify.

**cuir rian air** *v* put in order, organise.

**cuir romham** *v* make up my mind, resolve (to).

**cuir smùid** *v* smoke, emit smoke.

**cuir seachad** *v* pass, spend.

**cuir sneachd** *v* snow.

**cuir stad air** *v* put a stop/end to.

**cuir suim ann** *v* take an interest in.

**cùirt** *f* court.

**cùirtean** *m* curtain.

**cùirteil** *adj* courteous; courtly.

**cuir thairis** *v* overflow.

**cuir thar a chèile** *v* set at loggerheads.

**cuir timcheall** *v* send/pass round.

**cùirt-lagha** *f* law court.

**cuir urram air** *v* honour.

**cùis** *f* matter, business; (*pl*) **cùisean** things, matters.

**cùis-bheachd** *f* abstraction, abstract idea.

**cùisear** *m* (*gram*) subject.

**cùis-ghràin** *f* abomination.

**cùis lagha** *f* lawsuit.

**cuisle** *f* vein; pipe.

**cuislean** *m* flute.

**cuisle-chinn** *f* aorta.

**cuisle-chiùil** *f* flute.

**cuisle-mhòr** *f* artery.

**cùl** *m* nape; hair of head; back.

**cùlaibh** *m* back part. •*adv* **cùlaibh air beulaibh** back to front; vice versa.

**culaidh** *f* garment; suit of clothes; butt, object.

**culaidh-choimheach** *f* fancy dress.

**culaidh-fharmaid** *f* object of envy.

**cularan** *m* cucumber.

**cùl-chàin** *v* slander.

**cùl-chàineadh** *m* slander, backbiting.

**cullach** *m* boar.

**cùl-mhùtaire** *m* smuggler.

**cùl-mhùtaireachd** *f* smuggling.

**cùl na h-amhaich** *f* the back of the neck.

**cùl na làimh** *m* the back of the hand.

**cultar, cultur** *m* culture.

**cum** *v* shape, form.

**cùm** *v* keep.

**cumadh** *m* shape, form.

**cùm air** *v* continue, go on. •*excl* **cùm ort!** keep at it! on you go!

**cùm air ais** *v* hold back, delay.

**cùm a-mach** *v* assert, claim.

**cuman** *m* bucket; milking pail.

**cumanta** *adj* common, ordinary.

**cumantas** *m* usualness, normality.

**cùm às an làthair** *v* keep away; keep out of sight.

**cùm caismeachd ri** *v* keep time to.

**cùm faire** *v* keep watch/guard.

**cumha**[1] *f* lament, elegy.

**cumha**[2] *m* stipulation, condition.

**cumhach** *adj* conditional.

**cumhachd** *m/f* power; might; (electric) power.

**cumhachdach** *adj* powerful; mighty.

**cumhachd tuinne** *m* wave power.

**cumhang** *adj* narrow.

**cùmhnant** *m* covenant; contract.

**cùm ris!** *excl* stick at it! keep it up!

**cùm smachd air** *v* keep control of.

**cùm suas** *v* maintain, support.

**cùm sùil air** *v* keep an eye on.

**cùm taic ri** *v* support.

**cùm taobh ri** *v* side with, favour.

**cunbhalach** *adj* even, regular; steady.

**cungaidh** *f* materials; ingredients.

**cungaidh-leighis** *f* medicine, drug.

**cunnart** *m* danger, risk.

**cunnartach** *adj* dangerous, risky.

**cùnnradh** *m* contract; deal.
**cùnnt** *v* count.
**cùnntas** *m* counting; (*finance*) account; narration; score.
**cùnntasachd** *f* accountancy.
**cùnntasair** *m* accountant.
**cuntair** *m* (*shop, etc*) counter.
**cùp** *m* cup.
**cupa** *m* cup.
**cuplachadh** *m* copulation, mating.
**cuplaich** *v* couple, copulate.
**cùpon** *m* coupon, voucher.
**cur** *m* placing; sending.
**curach** *f* coracle.
**curach Innseanach** *f* canoe.
**curaidh** *m* hero.
**cùram** *m* care; responsibility.

**cùramach** *adj* careful; prone to worry.
**cur na mara** *m* seasickness.
**curran** *m* carrot.
**currcag** *f* lapwing.
**cùrsa** *m* course.
**cur-seachad** *m* hobby, pastime.
**cùrtair** *m* curtain.
**cus** *m* excess, too much.
**cusbainn** *f* (*tax*) customs.
**cusp** *f* chilblain.
**cuspair** *m* subject, topic; (*gram*) object.
**cut** *v* gut.
**cutair** *m* fish-gutter.
**cuthach** *m* madness; rage.
**cuthag** *f* cuckoo.

# D

**dà** *n/adj* two.
**dachaigh** *f* home.
**dà-chànanach** *adj* bilingual.
**dad** *f* thing, anything.
**dadaidh** *m* dad, daddy.
**dadam** *m* atom; tiny piece.
**dà-dheug** *n/adj* twelve.
**dad ort!** *excl* never mind! don't worry!
**dag** *m* pistol.
**dail** *f* meadow; dale.
**dàil** *f* delay.
**dàimh** *m/f* relationship, ties.
**dàimheach** *adj* relative.

**daingeann** *adj* firm, solid.
**daingneach** *f* fort; stronghold.
**daingnich** *v* fortify; consolidate; confirm.
**dàir** *m* rutting, heat.
**dall** *v* blind. •*adj* blind. •*n* blind man.
**dàmais** *f* draughts.
**damh** *m* stag.
**dàmhair** *f* rutting; (*with art*) **an Dàmhair** October.
**damhan-aillidh** *m* spider.
**dàn**¹ *m* fate, destiny.
**dàn**² *m* poem; song.

**dàna** *adj* daring; impudent; arrogant.

**dànachd** *f* poetry, verse.

**danns** *v* dance.

**dannsa** *m* dance.

**dannsadh** *m* dancing.

**dannsair** *m* dancer.

**dàn spioradail** *m* hymn.

**daoimean** *m* diamond.

**daoine** *mpl* people; kinsfolk.

**daoine mòra** *mpl* big shots, bigwigs.

**daoine-sìth** *mpl* fairyfolk.

**daolag** *f* beetle.

**daolag-bhreac-dhearg** *f* ladybird.

**daonna** *adj* human.

**daonnan** *adv* always, constantly.

**daor** *adj* dear, expensive.

**daorach** *f* drunkenness; spree.

**daorachail** *adj* intoxicating.

**daorsa** *f* captivity.

**dara** *adj* second; one.

**darach** *m* oak.

**dara-deug** *adj* twelfth.

**dàrna** *adj* second.

**dà-sheaghach** *adj* ambiguous.

**dàta** *m* data.

**dath** *v* colour; dye. •*n* colour; dye.

**dath-bhacadh** *m* colour bar.

**dath-dhall** *adj* colour-blind.

**dathte** *adj* coloured; dyed.

**dà uair** *adv* twice.

**de** *prep* of; from; made of.

**dè** *pron* what, what?

**deacair** *adj* hard, difficult.

**deachd** *v* dictate.

**deachdadh** *m* dictation.

**deachdaire** *m* dictator.

**deagh** *adj* good. •*adv* well.

**deagh-bheusan** *f* morals.

**deagh-chritheach** *adj* good-hearted.

**deagh-thoil** *f* good will.

**dealachadh** *m* parting.

**dealachadh-pòsaidh** *m* divorce, separation.

**dealaich** *v* part; separate; (*elec*) insulate.

**dealan** *m* electricity.

**dealanach** *m* lightning.

**dealanaich** *v* electrify.

**dealanair** *m* electrician.

**dealan-dè** *m* butterfly.

**dealasach** *adj* eager, zealous.

**dealbh** *m/f* picture; painting; shape. •*n* picture; design; construct.

**dealbh-chluich** *m/f* play.

**dealbh-chumadh** *m/f* plan, diagram.

**dealbh-èibhinn** *m/f* cartoon.

**dealg** *f* prickle, thorn; pin.

**deàlrach** *adj* shining, shiny.

**deàlraich** *v* shine, flash, glitter.

**dealt** *m/f* dew.

**dè am fonn?** (*fam*) how are you?

**deamhais** *m* shears.

**deamhan** *m* demon.

**dèan** *v* do; make.

**dèan a' chùis** *v* suffice, do the job/trick.

**dèan a' chùis air** v manage; defeat.

**dèanadach** adj industrious, active.

**dèan adhradh** v worship.

**dèan altachadh** v say grace.

**dèan an gnothach** v be just the job, do the trick.

**dèan bàidh do** v do a favour for.

**dèan beic** v curtsey.

**dèan braoisg** v grin; grimace.

**dèan breug** v lie, tell a lie.

**dèan bruadar** v dream.

**dèan cabhag** v hurry, make haste.

**dèan cadal** v sleep.

**dèan casad** v cough.

**dèan casaid air** v accuse; make a complaint against.

**dèan cnead** v groan.

**dèan coimeas eadar** v compare.

**dèan còmhradh** v talk, converse.

**dèan cron air** v harm, injure.

**dèan crùban** v crouch, squat.

**dè an dòigh?** (fam) how're you doing?.

**dèan dragh** v worry oneself.

**dèan dragh do** v cause worry to.

**dèan dùrdail** v coo.

**dèan faire** v be on guard.

**dèan faite-gàire** v smile.

**dèan fanaid air** v mock, ridicule.

**dèan faoighe** v beg.

**dèan fead** v whistle.

**dèan feum** v come in handy.

**dèan feum do** v do good to; be useful to.

**dèan foill air** v cheat.

**dèan gàirdeachas** v rejoice.

**dèan gàire** v laugh.

**dèan gràgail** v caw, croak.

**dèan imrich** v move house.

**dèan iolach** v shout.

**dèan iomradh air** v mention.

**dèan malairt** v trade, do business.

**dèan mèirle** v steal.

**dèan miodal (do)** v flatter, fawn (on).

**dèan mo dhìcheall** v do my utmost.

**dèan mùn** v urinate.

**deanntag** f nettle.

**dèan oilbheum (do)** v give offence (to).

**dè an rud?** what?

**dèan sèisd air** v besiege.

**dèan sgairt** v yell.

**dèan sodal do** v fawn on, butter up.

**dèan sreothart** v sneeze.

**dèan stad** v stop, call a halt.

**dèan sùgradh** v make merry, sport.

**dèan suidhe!** excl sit down! take a seat!

**dèan sùil bheag ri** v wink at.

**dèan suiridhe ri** v court.

**dèan tàir air** v despise, disparage.

**dèan tarcais air** v despise.

**dèan ulfhart** v howl.

**dèan ùrnaigh ri** v pray to.

**dearbh** adj same. •◻ prove; test.

**dearbhadh** m proof; test, trial.

**dearc** f berry.

**dearcag** f berry.

**dearg** *adj* red; (*fam*) utter.

**deargad** *f* flea.

**deargann** *f* flea.

**deargnaich** *v* redden.

**dearmad** *m* neglect, negligence; omission.

**dearmadach** *adj* negligent; neglectful.

**dearmaid** *v* omit, neglect (to do something).

**deàrrs** *v* shine.

**deas** *f* south. •*dj* south; right(-hand); ready; finished; active.

**deasachadh** *m* preparation; editing.

**deasaich** *v* prepare; edit.

**deasaich biadh** *v* cook.

**deasbad** *m* discussion, debate.

**deasg** *m* desk.

**deas-ghnàth** *m* ceremony.

**dè a tha dhìth air?** what does he require?

**dè a tha a' dol?, dè tha dol?** *excl* (*fam*) what's doing?

**dè a tha thu ris?** *excl* what are you up to?

**de chlòimh** *adj* woollen.

**de chois** *adv* on foot.

**de dh' fhad** *adv* long, in length.

**dè do bheachd?** what do you think?

**dè do chor?** *excl* (*fam*) how're you doing?

**dè fon ghrèin'?** *excl* what on earth?

**deich** *n*/*adj* ten.

**deichead** *m* decade.

**deicheamh** *adj* tenth.

**deichnear** *m*/*f* ten (people).

**dèideadh** *m* (*with art*) **an dèideadh** toothache.

**dèideag** *f* pebble; toy.

**dèidheil air** *adj* fond of, keen on.

**deigh** *f* ice.

**dèile** *f* board, plank.

**dèilig ri** *v* deal with, handle.

**deimhinne** *adj* sure, certain.

**dèine** *f* eagerness; fervour.

**dèirc** *f* charity, alms.

**dèirceach** *m* beggar. •*dj* charitable.

**deireadh** *m* end.

**deireannach** *adj* last, final.

**deisciobal** *m* disciple.

**deise** *f* suit (of clothes).

**deiseil** *adj* ready; finished; clockwise; sunwise; handy.

**dè na tha e?** how much is it?

**deò** *f* (*with art*) **an deò** the breath of life.

**deoch** *f* drink; booze.

**deoch-làidir** *f* alcohol; alcoholic drink.

**deoch-an dorais** *f* parting drink.

**deoch-slàinte** *f* (*drink*) toast.

**deoghail** *v* suck; absorb.

**deòin** *f* consent; willingness.

**deònach** *adj* willing.

**deònach air** prepared to.

**dè tha dol?** *see* **dè a tha a' dol?**

**deuchainn** *f* examination, test; trying time.

**deuchainn-lann** *m* laboratory.

**deudach** *adj* dental.

**deug** *suffix* -teen.

**deugaire** *m* teenager.

**deur** *m* tear, teardrop.

**dh', dha** (*for* **do**) *prep* to.

**dhà** *prep pron* to him; for him; to it; for it (*m*).

**dhachaigh** *adv* home(wards).

**dhaibh** *prep pron* to them; for them.

**dheth**[1] *adv* off.

**dheth**[2] *prep pron* of him; off him; of it; off it (*m*).

**dhì** *prep pron* of her; off her; of it; off it (*f*).

**dhibh** *prep pron* of you; off you (*pl*).

**dhinn** *prep pron* of us; off us.

**dhìom** *prep pron* of me; off me.

**dhìot** *prep pron* of you; off you (*sing*).

**dhith** *prep pron* to her; for her; to it; for it (*f*).

**dhiubh** *prep pron* of them; off them.

**dhomh** *prep pron* to me; for me.

**dhuibh** *prep pron* to you; for you (*pl*).

**dhuine! dhuine!** *excl* oh dear! oh dear!

**dhuinn** *prep pron* to us; for us.

**dhut** *prep pron* to you; for you (*sing*).

**dia** *m* god.

**diabhal** *m* devil.

**diabhlaidh** *adj* devilish, fiendish.

**diadhachd** *f* godhead; godliness; theology.

**diadhaidh** *adj* pious, godly.

**dìallaid** *f* saddle.

**dian** *adj* eager; fierce; intense.

**dian-ruith** *f* headlong rush.

**Diardaoin** *m* Thursday.

**dias** *f* ear of corn.

**dibhearsan** *m* fun; entertainment.

**dìblidh** *adj* abject.

**dìcheall** *m* diligence, application.

**dìcheallach** *adj* diligent; hard-working.

**dì-cheannaich** *v* behead.

**Diciadain** *m* Wednesday.

**Didòmhnaich** *m* Sunday.

**dìg** *f* ditch.

**Dihaoine** *m* Friday.

**dìle** *f* heavy rain; flood.

**dìleab** *f* legacy.

**dìleas** *adj* faithful, trusty.

**dìle bhàthte** *f* downpour.

**Diluain** *m* Monday.

**Dimàirt** *m* Tuesday.

**dìmeas** *m* disrespect; contempt.

**dìnichean** *npl* jeans.

**dinn** *v* stuff, cram.

**dìnnear** *f* dinner.

**dìobair** *v* desert, abandon.

**dìobhair** *v* vomit, sick up.

**dìochuimhne** *f* forgetfulness; oblivion.

**dìochuimhneach** *adj* forgetful.

**dìochuimhnich** *v* forget.

**diofar** f difference; importance.
**diofarach** adj different.
**diogail** v tickle.
**diogalach** adj ticklish.
**dìoghail** v repay; take revenge.
**dìoghaltas** m revenge.
**dìoghras** m zeal; enthusiasm.
**dìolain** adj bastard, illegitimate.
**diomb** m indignation; displeasure.
**diombach** adj out of sorts; indignant.
**dìombuan** adj transient, fleeting.
**dìomhain** adj vain; idle.
**dìomhair** adj secret.
**dìomhanas** m vanity, futility.
**dìon** v protect, shelter. •☐n protection, shelter.
**dìonach** adj sheltering; safe; wind and watertight.
**dìorrasach** adj keen; tenacious.
**dìosail** m diesel.
**dìosgail** m/f creaking; crunching.
**dìosgan** m/f grating; squeaking.
**diosgo** m disco.
**dìreach** adj straight; upright; just.
**dìreach!** excl quite!, just so!, exactly!
**dìreadh** m ascent; climbing.
**dìrich**[1] v straighten.
**dìrich**[2] v climb.
**Disathairne** m Saturday.
**dìsne** m/f dice.
**dìt** v condemn, sentence.
**dìteadh** m condemnation; sentence.

**dìth** m lack, want.
**dìthean** m flower.
**dithis** f two, twosome, pair.
**dithreabh** f desert, wilderness.
**diùc** m duke.
**diùid** adj shy, timid.
**diùlt** v refuse; disown.
**diù nan.** the worst of..
**Diùra** f Jura.
**Diùrach** m/adj from Jura.
**dleasdanas** m duty.
**dlighe** f right, due.
**dligheach** adj rightful, legitimate.
**dlùth** adj near; dense.
**dlùthaich** v draw near, approach.
**dlùths** m density.
**do**[1] poss adj your (sing).
**do**[2] prep to; into; for.
**do-** prefix un-, in-, im-.
**dòbhran** m otter.
**do bhrìgh** prep because of.
**dòchas** m hope.
**do-dhèanta** adj impossible.
**dòigh** m way, manner; condition.
**dòigh-beatha** m lifestyle, way of life.
**dòighean** mpl customs; manners.
**dòigheil** adj proper; in good order.
**dòil** m dole.
**doille** f blindness.
**doilleir** adj dark; gloomy.
**doilleirich** v darken; obscure.
**doimhne** f (with art) **an doimhne** the deep.

**doimhneachd** *f* depth.

**doimhnich** *v* deepen.

**doinnean** *f* storm, tempest.

**doirbh** *adj* hard, difficult.

**doire** *m/f* grove, thicket, copse.

**dòirt** *v* pour; shed; flow.

**do-labhairt** *adj* unspeakable.

**dolair** *m* dollar.

**dol-a-mach** *m* behaviour, conduct.

**dòlas** *m* grief.

**dol-às** *m* way out, escape.

**dol fodha na grèine** *m* sunset.

**dòmhail** *adj* crowded; dense.

**domhainn** *adj* deep; profound.

**domhan** *m* (*with art*) **an Domhan** the Universe.

**dona** *adj* bad; naughty.

**donas** *m* badness, evil; (*with art*) **an Donas** the Devil.

**donn** *adj* brown; brown-haired.

**donnal** *m* howl.

**donnalaich** *f* howling.

**doras** *m* door.

**dorcha** *adj* dark.

**dorchadas** *m* darkness.

**dòrlach** *m* fistful, handful.

**dòrn** *m* fist.

**dòrtadh-fala** *m* bloodshed.

**dos**[1] *m* bush.

**dos**[2] *m* bagpipe drone.

**dotair** *m* doctor.

**doth** *v* singe, scorch.

**drabasda** *adj* obscene.

**dràbhail** *adj* grotty.

**drabhair** *m* drawer.

**dràc** *m* drake.

**dragh** *m* trouble, bother; worry.

**draghail** *adj* worrying; annoying.

**dràibh** *v* (*car, etc*) drive.

**dràibhear** *m* driver.

**drama** *m* dram.

**dràma** *m* drama.

**dranndan** *m* snarl(ing), growl(ing).

**draoidh** *m* druid; magician.

**draoidheachd** *f* wizardry, magic.

**draoidheil** *adj* magic, magical.

**draosda** *adj* smutty, lewd.

**draosdachd** *f* smut, lewdness.

**drathais** *fpl* underpants; pants, knickers.

**dreach** *m* appearance, aspect; complexion.

**dreag** *f* meteor.

**dreallag** *f* (child's) swing.

**drèana** *f* drain, drainage ditch.

**dreasa** *f* dress.

**dreasair** *m* dresser.

**dreathan-donn** *m* wren.

**dreuchd** *f* occupation, profession.

**dreuchdail** *adj* professional.

**driamlach** *m/f* fishing line.

**drile** *f* drill, auger.

**drip** *f* bustle, state of being busy.

**dripeil** *adj* busy.

**dris** *f* bramble; brier.

**drithleann** *m* sparkle, flash.

**driùchd** *f* dew.

**dròbh** *m* cattle drove.

**dròbhair** *m* cattle-drover.

**droch** *adj* bad.

**drochaid** *f* bridge.

**droch-bheart** *f* vice; evil deed.

**droch bheus** *f* bad manners.

**droch chainnt** *f* bad language, swearing.

**droch chòrdadh** *m* disagreement, bad terms.

**droch-ionnsaigh** *f* physical assault.

**droch isean** *m* brat, naughty child.

**droch nàdarrach** *adj* ill-natured, ill-tempered.

**droga** *f* drug; *pl* **drogaichean** (*illegal, etc*) drugs.

**drùdhag** *f* drop; sip.

**druid** *f* starling.

**drùidh** *v* soak, penetrate (to skin).

**drùidh air** *v* affect, make an impression on.

**druim** *m* back; ridge.

**drùis** *f* lust, lechery.

**drùiseach** *adj* lustful, lecherous.

**druma** *f* drum.

**duais** *f* wages; reward; award.

**dual**[1] *m* character; birthright.

**dual**[2] *m* curl, lock; plait.

**dualaich** *v* curl; twist, plait.

**dual-chainnt** *f* dialect.

**dualchas** *m* hereditary character.

**dualtach** *adj* inherent, natural; **dualtach a bhith** inclined to be.

**duan** *m* poem, song.

**duanag** *f* song, ditty.

**dùbailte** *adj* double; dual.

**dubh** *v* blacken. •◨*n* black; ink. •◨*adj* black; dark-haired.

**dubhach** *adj* gloomy; in a bad mood.

**dubhadh** *m* eclipse.

**dubhag** *f* kidney.

**dubhaigeann** *m* abyss, the deep.

**dubhan** *m* hook.

**dubhar** *m* shade.

**dubh às** *v* erase; blot out.

**dubh-dhonn** *adj* dark brown.

**dubh-ghorm** *adj* dark blue.

**Dùbhlachd** *f* (*with art*) **an Dùbhlachd** December.

**dùbhlan** *m* challenge.

**dubh-nota** *m* (*mus*) crochet.

**dùblaich** *v* double.

**dùdag** *f* bugle.

**duibhre** *f* dusk.

**dùil**[1] *f* hope; expectation.

**dùil**[2] *f* created being; element.

**duileasg** *m* dulse.

**duilgheadas** *m* difficulty; problem.

**duilgheadasan sòisealta** *mpl* social problems.

**duilich** *adj* hard, difficult; unfortunate. •◨*xcl* **tha mi duilich!** I'm sorry!

**duilleach** *m* foliage.

**duilleachan** *m* leaflet.

**duilleag** *f* leaf; page, sheet.

**dùin** *v* shut, close.

**duine** *m* man; person; human being; husband. •◨*ron* someone; **duine sam bith** anyone at all.

**duinealas** *m* manliness; decisiveness.

**duine cloinne** *m* child.

**duineil** *adj* manly; decisive; mannish.

**duine lag-chùiseach** *m* stick-in-the-mud.

**duine-uasal** *m* gentleman; nobleman.

**dùinte** *adj* closed, shut; introvert.

**dùisg** *v* wake, awaken.

**Duitseach** *m/adj* Dutch person; Dutch.

**dùn** *m* heap; castle; hill fort; conical hill.

**dùnan** *m* small hill; dung heap.

**dùr** *adj* stubborn; dour.

**dùrachd** *f* seriousness; sincerity; greeting.

**dùrachdach** *adj* serious, earnest.

**dùraig** *v* dare.

**durcan** *m* pine cone, fir cone.

**dùrdail** *f* cooing.

**dùsal** *m* slumber, snooze.

**dusan** *m* dozen.

**dùsgadh** *m* awakening.

**duslach** *m* dust.

**dust** *m* dust.

**dustach** *adj* dusty.

**dustair** *m* duster.

**dùthaich** *f* country; homeland; countryside.

**dùthchas** *m* cultural inheritance.

**dùthchasach** *adj* native, indigenous.

# E

**e** *pron* he; him; it (*m*).

**eabar** *m* mud, mire.

**Eabhra** *f* Hebrew (language).

**Eabhrach** *m/adj* Hebrew.

**eacarsaich** *f* exercise.

**each** *m* horse.

**each-aibhne** *m* hippopotamus.

**eachdraiche** *m* historian.

**eachdraidh** *f* history.

**eachdraidheil** *adj* historical.

**each-oibre** *m* workhorse.

**each-uisge** *m* water-horse, kelpie.

**eaconamachd** *f* economics.

**eaconomaidh** *m* economy.

**eaconomair** *m* economist.

**Eadailt** *f* (*with art*) **an Eadailt** Italy.

**Eadailteach** *m/adj* Italian.

**eadar** *prep* between; among; both.

**eadaraibh** *prep pron* between you; among you.

**eadarainn** *prep pron* between us; among us.

**eadar-dhà-lionn** *adv* undecided; between two stools.

**eadar-dhealachadh** *m* difference; distinction.

**eadar-dhealaich** *v* differentiate; distinguish.

**eadar-dhealaichte** *adj* different; distinct, separate.

**eadar-nàiseanta** *adj* international.

**eadar-sholas** *m* twilight.

**eadar-theangachadh** *m* translation.

**eadar-theangaich** *v* translate.

**eadhon** *adv* even.

**eadradh** *m* milking.

**eag** *f* nick, notch.

**eagal** *m* fear, fright; **eagal mo bheatha** the fright of my life.

**eagalach** *adj* prone to fear; terrible, dreadful. •*adv* terribly, dreadfully.

**eaglais** *f* church; (*with art*) **an Eaglais Shaor** the Free Church; **Eaglais na h-Alba** the Church of Scotland.

**eala** *f* swan.

**èalaidh** *v* creep; sneak away.

**ealain** *f* art; **Comhairle nan Ealain an Albainn** the Scottish Arts Council.

**ealanta** *adj* artistic.

**eallach** *m* load, burden.

**ealta** *f* (*birds*) flock.

**ealtainn** *f* razor.

**eanchainn** *f* brain.

**eanraich** *f* soup, broth.

**ear** *f* east.

**ear air** *prep* east of.

**earalachadh** *m* exhortation.

**earalaich** *v* exhort; caution.

**Earranta** *adj* (*company*) Limited, Ltd.

**earb**¹ *v* trust.

**earb**² *f* roe-deer.

**earb à** *v* trust in.

**earball** *m* tail.

**earbsa** *f* trust; confidence; reliance.

**earbsach** *adj* trusting; trustworthy.

**eàrlas** *m* (*financial*) advance.

**earrach** *m* spring; **as t-earrach** in spring.

**earrann** *f* part, section; piece.

**eas** *m* waterfall.

**eas-** prefix in-, dis-, un-.

**easag** *f* pheasant.

**easaonta** *f* disagreement; dissent.

**easbaig** *m* bishop.

**Easbaigeach** *m/adj* Episcopalian. •*adj* episcopal.

**easbhaidh** *f* lack, want, need.

**easbhaidheach** *adj* needy; needful, lacking.

**eascaraid** *m* foe.

**èasgaidh** *adj* active; willing; **èasgaidh a dhèanamh** willing/keen to do it.

**easgann** *f* eel.

**eas-ùmhail** *adj* disobedient, insubordinate.

**eas-urramach** *adj* dishonourable.

**eathar** *m/f* rowing boat.

**eatorra** *prep pron* between them; among them.

**èibhinn** *adj* funny, amusing.

**èibhleag** *f* ember.

**èideadh** *m* dress, garb; uniform.

**eidheann** *f* ivy.

**èifeachdach** *adj* effective; efficient.

**eigh** *f* ice.

**èigh** *v* shout, call. •◻shout, cry.

**eighe** *f* (*tool*) file.

**-eigin** *suffix* some-.

**èiginn** *f* difficulty; trouble; need; violence.

**Eilbheis** *f* (*with art*) **an Eilbheis** Switzerland.

**Eilbheiseach** *n/adj* Swiss.

**èildear** *m* church elder.

**eile** *adj* other; another.

**eilean** *m* island.

**eileanach** *m* islander.

**Eilean a' Cheò** *m* (*nickname*) Skye.

**Eilean I** *m* Iona.

**Eilean Luing** *m* Luing.

**Eilean Ruma** *m* (the Isle of) Rum.

**eilid** *f* hind.

**eilthireach** *m* foreigner; exile.

**einnsean** *m* engine.

**einnsean-smàlaidh** *m* fire engine.

**Eipheit** *f* (*with art*) **an Eipheit** Egypt.

**Eipheiteach** *m/adj* Egyptian.

**eireachdail** *adj* elegant; handsome.

**eireag** *f* pullet.

**Eireannach** *m/adj* Irishman; Irish.

**Eirinn** *f* Ireland.

**èirich** *v* rise, get up; rebel.

**èirich do** *v* happen to, befall, become of.

**eiridinn** *m* nursing.

**eiridnich** *v* nurse, tend.

**èirig** *f* ransom.

**èirigh na grèine** *f* sunrise.

**eirmseach** *adj* witty.

**èisd (ri)** *v* listen (to).

**eisimealachd** *f* dependence.

**eisimeileach** *adj* dependent.

**eisimpleir** *m* example.

**eist!** *excl* hush! be quiet!

**eitean** *m* kernel; core.

**eòlach** *adj* knowledgeable; acquainted.

**eòlach air** *adv* familiar with.

**eòlaiche** *m* expert.

**eòlas** *m* knowledge; acquaintance.

**eòlas-leighis** *m* (*science of*) medicine.

**eòrna** *m* barley.

**Eòrpa** *f* Europe; (*with art*) **an Roinn Eòrpa** *m* Europe.

**Eòrpach** *m/adj* European.

**esan** *pron* (*emphatic form of* **e**) he; him.

**eu-** prefix un-, dis-, -less.

**euchd** *m* feat; achievement.

**eucoir** *f* crime.

**eucoireach** *m* criminal.

**eu-coltach** *adj* dissimilar; unlikely.

**eud** *m* jealousy; zeal.

**eudach** *adj* jealous; zealous.

**eudail** *f* treasure; **m'eudail!** my dear!

**eu-dòchas** *m* hopelessness.

**eun** *m* bird, fowl.

**eun-àir** *m* bird of prey.

**eun-eòlas** *m* ornithology.

**eun-mara** *m* seabird.

**eun-uisge** *m* waterfowl.

**euslaint** *f* illness, ill-health.

**euslainteach** *adj* ill, unhealthy. •*n* invalid; patient.

# F

**fàbhar** *m* favour.

**fabhra** *m* eyelash; eyelid.

**facal** *m* word; saying.

**fa chomhair** *prep* opposite; in front of.

**faclach** *adj* wordy, verbose.

**faclair** *m* dictionary.

**faclaireachd** *f* lexicology; lexicography.

**fad** *m* length; the whole, all the.

**fada** *adj* long; tall. •*adv* far, much.

**fada air falbh** *adv* faraway, distant.

**fadachd** *f* longing; nostalgia; impatience; boredom.

**fadalach** *adj* late; tedious; long drawn out.

**fada nas fheàrr** much/far better.

**fad an là** *adv* all day, the whole day.

**fada 'nur comain** much obliged to you.

**fad às** *adj* remote, distant; (*person*) withdrawn.

**fàd mònach** *m* a single peat.

**fad na h-oidhche** *adv* all night.

**fad na h-ùine** *adv* all the time, constantly.

**fad-shaoghalach** *adv* long-lived.

**fad-shaoghalachd** *f* longevity.

**fàg** *v* leave; abandon.

**faic** *v* see.

**faiceall** *f* care, caution.

**faiceallach** *adj* careful, cautious.

**faiche** *f* meadow, grass park.

**faicsinneach** *adj* visible; conspicuous.

**faide** *f* length.

**fàidh** *m* prophet, seer.

**fàidheadaireachd** *f* prophecy.

**faigh** *v* get, obtain; find.

**faigh air.** *v* get to., manage to..

**faigh air adhart** *v* get on, progress.

**faigh a-mach** *v* find out, discover.

**faigh bàs** *v* die, get killed.

**faigh cron do** *v* blame.

**faigh cuidhteas de** *v* get rid/shot of.

**faigh do sheise** *v* meet your match.

**faighean** *m* vagina.

**faigh fàire air** *v* spot, catch sight of.

**faigh lorg air** *v* track down, locate.

**faigh muin** *v* have sex, copulate.

**faighneach** *adj* inquisitive, enquiring.

**faighnich** *v* ask, enquire.

**faigh seachad air** *v* get over.

**faigh seòl air** *v* contrive to, manege to.

**failc** *v* bathe.

**faileas** *m* shadow; reflection.

**faileasach** *adj* shadowy.

**faillean** *m* eardrum.

**fàillig** *v* fail.

**fàillinn** *f* failing, fault; blemish; failure.

**failmean** *m* kneecap.

**fail-mhuc** *f* pigsty.

**fàilte** *f* welcome.•*excl* **fàilte oirbh!** welcome to you! you're welcome!

**fàilteach** *adj* welcoming; hospitable.

**fàilteachail** *adj* welcoming; hospitable.

**fàiltich** *v* welcome.

**faing** *f* sheepfold, fank.

**fàinne** *m/f* (*finger*) ring.

**fàinne-pòsaidh** *f* wedding ring.

**fàinne-solais** *f* halo.

**faire** *f* guard; watch.

**fàire** *f* horizon, skyline.

**faireachdainn** *f* sensation; emotion, feeling.

**fàireag** *f* gland.

**fairge** *f* (*in songs, etc*) sea, ocean.

**fairich** *v* feel; smell.

**fairtlich air** *v* get the better of, defeat; baffle.

**faisg** *adj* near, close.

**fàisg** *v* squeeze; wring.

**faisge** *f* nearness, closeness.

**fàisneachd** *f* prophecy.

**faite-gàire** *f* smile.

**faitheam** *m* hem.

**faitich** *v* smile.

**fàl** *m* hedge; verge.

**falach** *m* hiding, concealment.

**falachd** *f* feud.

**falach-fead** *m* hide-and-seek.

**falaich** *v* hide.

**falaichte** *adj* hidden, concealed.

**falamh** *adj* empty.

**falamhachd, falmhachd** *f* emptiness; void.

**falbh** *v* leave, go away.

**falbh a dh'iarraidh** *v* go to fetch/get.

**fa leth** *adv* separate; apart.

**fallain** *adj* sound, healthy; wholesome; able-bodied.

**fallas** *m* sweat; **tha fallas orm** I'm sweating.

**fallasach** *adj* sweaty.

**fallsa** *adj* false, deceitful.

**falmadair** *m* helm.

**falmhachd** *see* **falamhachd**.

**falmhaich** *v* empty.

**falt** *m* (*of head*) hair.

**famh** *m/f* (*animal*) mole.

**famhair** *m* giant.

**fan** *v* wait; stay.

**fanaid** *f* mockery, ridicule.

**fan aig** *v* lodge with.

**fan air** *v* wait for.

**fànas** *m* space; void.

**fànas-long** *f* spaceship.

**fa-near dhomh** *adv* on my mind, in my thoughts.

**fann** *adj* weak, faint.

**fannaich** *v* weaken.

**fanntaig** *v* faint, swoon.

**faobhar** *m* (*of blade*) edge.

**faobharaich** *v* sharpen.

**faochadh** *m* relief, respite.

**faochag** *f* whelk, winkle.

**faod** *v* can, may, might.

**faoighe** *f* begging, cadging.

**faoileag** *f* seagull.

**faoilidh** *adj* hospitable; generous; frank.

**Faoilteach** *m* (*with art*) **am Faoilteach** January.

**faoin** *adj* silly, foolish; empty-headed; futile.

**faoineas** *m* silliness, vacuity; futility.

**faoinsgeul** *m* myth, legend.

**faoisid** *f* confession.

**faoisidich** *v* confess.

**faol** *m* wolf.

**faothachadh** *m* *same as* **faochadh**.

**faothaich** *v* relieve, alleviate.

**far** *prep* from, down from.

**far a** *conj* where.

**faradh** *m* (*rail, etc*) fare.

**fàradh** *m* ladder.

**far-ainm** *m* nickname.

**faram** *m* loud noise.

**faramach** *adj* loud, noisy.

**farchluais** *f* eavesdropping.

**fàrdach** *f* house; dwelling, lodging.

**farmad** *m* envy.

**farpais** *m* competition.

**farpaiseach** *m* competitor.

**farranaich** *v* tease.

**farsaing** *adj* wide, broad.

**farsaingeachd** *f* width, breadth; area.

**farspag** *f* black-backed gull.

**fàs**[1] *v* grow; become.

**fàs**[2] *adj* waste, uncultivated; barren.

**fàsach** *m/f* desert, wilderness; deserted place.

**fàsaich** *v* empty; depopulate.

**fàsail** *adj* desolate.

**fasan** *m* fashion.

**fasanta** *adj* fashionable.

**fasgach** *adj* sheltered; sheltering.

**fasgadh** *m* shelter, protection.

**fasgain** *v* winnow.

**fa sgaoil** *adv* free, at liberty.

**fastaich** *v* hire, employ.

**fastaidhear** *m* employer.

**fàth** *m* cause; reason; opportunity.
**fathann** *m* rumour.
**feabhas** *m* improvement; excellence.
**feachd** *f* army.
**fead** *v* whistle. •⬚ (*noise*) whistle.
**feadag** *f* (*instrument*) whistle; plover.
**feadaireachd** *f* whistling; playing a whistle.
**feadan** *m* chanter; pipe, tube, spout.
**feadhainn** *f* some; (*with art*) **an fheadhainn** those, the ones.
**feagal** *m* fear, fright.
**feàirrde** *adj* better.
**fealladh** *m* foul; foul play.
**fealla-dhà** *f* joke, jest.
**feall-falach** *m* ambush.
**feallsanach** *m* philosopher.
**feallsanachd** *f* philosophy.
**feamainn** *f* seaweed. •⬚ manure (*usu with seaweed*).
**feannag** *f* crow; ridge; lazybed.
**feannag ghlas** *f* hooded crow.
**feanntag** *f* nettle.
**feansa** *f* fence.
**fear** *m* man; one.
**fearail** *adj* manly.
**fearalachd** *f* manliness.
**fear-allabain** *m* wanderer.
**fearann** *m* ground, land.
**fear-bainnse** *m* bridegroom.
**fear-brèige** *m* puppet.
**fear-ceàirde** *m* craftsman.
**fear-ceuma** *m* graduate.

**fear-cinnidh** *m* clansman, fellow clansman.
**fear-ciùil** *m* musician.
**fear-deasachaidh** *m* editor.
**fear-ealain** *m* artist.
**fear-faire** *m* guard.
**fear-fianais** *m* witness.
**fear-foille** *m* cheat.
**fear-fòirneart** *m* oppressor.
**fear-fuadain** *m* wanderer; exile.
**fearg** *f* anger.
**feargach** *adj* angry.
**fear-giùlain** *m* carrier, bearer.
**fear-ionnsaigh** *m* assailant, attacker.
**fear-labhairt** *m* speaker; spokesman.
**fear lagha** *m* lawyer, solicitor.
**feàrna** *f* alder.
**fear-naidheachd** *m* journalist.
**feàrr** *adj* better; best.
**fear-reic** *m* salesman.
**fear-riaghlaidh** *m* manager; administrator.
**fear seach fear** in turn; one by one.
**fear-siubhail** *m* traveller.
**fear-stiùiridh** *m* director.
**feart** *f* attention, heed; quality, characteristic.
**fear-taice** *m* supporter; patron, backer.
**fear-tomhais** *m* surveyor.
**feasgar** *m* afternoon; evening. •⬚ *dv* in the afternoon/evening, p.m.

**fèath** m/f (weather) calm.

**fèichear** m debtor.

**fèile, fèileadh, fèile beag** m kilt.

**fèill** f feast, festival, fair; sale, market.

**Fèill Brìde** f (with art) **an Fhèill Brìde** Candlemas.

**fèin**[1], **fhèin** refl pron self; own.

**fèin**[2] m (with art) **am fèin** the ego, the self.

**fèin-eachdraidh** f autobiography.

**fèinealachd** f selfishness.

**fèineil** adj selfish.

**fèin-moladh** m conceit.

**fèin-riaghladh** m self-government.

**fèin-spèis** f conceit, self-regard.

**fèis, fèisd, fèist** f festival; feast, banquet.

**feith** v wait; stay.

**fèith**[1] f muscle; sinew; vein.

**fèith**[2] f bog, marsh.

**feòil** f meat; flesh.

**feòladair** m butcher.

**feòil-muice** f pork.

**feòrag** f squirrel.

**feòraich** v ask, enquire.

**feuch, fiach** v try, attempt; try out, test.

**feuch deuchainn** v sit an exam.

**feudail** f treasure.

**feum** v must, have to; need. •▯n need; use, usefulness, good.

**feumach** adj needy, in need.

**feumail** adj useful, handy; necessary.

**feur** m grass; hay.

**feurach** adj grassy.

**feuraich** v graze.

**feusag** f beard.

**feusgan** m mussel.

**fhad is a** conj while, as long as.

**fhathast** adv yet; still.

**fhèin**[1] refl pron same as **fèin**[1].

**fhèin**[2] adv even.

**fhuair** past tense of v **faigh**.

**fiabhras** m fever.

**fiacail** f tooth; pl **fiaclan-fuadain** false teeth, dentures.

**fiach**[1] adj worth, worthwhile; of value.

**fiach**[2] m value, worth; debt.

**fiach**[3] see **feuch**.

**fiach!** excl lo! behold!

**fiachail** adj worthy, respectable; valuable.

**fiaclach** adj toothed, toothy; dental.

**fiaclaire** m dentist.

**fiaclan-fuadain** see **fiacail**.

**fiadh** m deer.

**fiadhaich** adj wild; angry, furious.

**fial** adj generous; hospitable; tolerant.

**fiamh** adj hue, tint; complexion; expression; fear.

**fiamh-ghàire** m smile.

**fianais** f evidence, testimony.

**fiar** adj bent; slanting; squinting; cunning.

**fiar** v bend, curve; slant; squint.

**fiaradh** *m* slant; squint.

**fiar-shùileach** *adj* squint-eyed.

**fichead** *m* twenty, a score.

**ficheadamh** *adj* twentieth.

**fideag** *f* (*instrument*) whistle.

**fidheall** *f* fiddle, violin.

**fìdhlear** *m* fiddler, violinist.

**fidir** *v* appreciate, comprehend.

**fìge** *f* fig.

**figear** *m* (*numerical*) figure.

**figh** *v* weave; knit.

**fighe** *f* weaving; knitting.

**figheachan** *m* pigtail, pony-tail.

**figheadair** *m* weaver; knitter.

**fighte** *adj* woven; knitted.

**fileanta** *adj* eloquent, articulate; fluent.

**fileantach** *m* native speaker; fluent speaker.

**filidh** *m* poet.

**fill** *v* fold; pleat; plait.

**filleadh** *m* fold; pleat; plait.

**fillte** *adj* folded; pleated; plaited.

**film** *m* film.

**fine** *f* clan; tribe.

**fiodh** *m* wood, timber.

**fìogais** *f* fig.

**fiolan-gòbhlach** *m* earwig.

**fìon** *m* wine.

**fìonan** *m* vine.

**fìon-dearc** *f* grape.

**fìon-geur** *m* vinegar.

**fionn**[1] *v* flay.

**fionn**[2] *adj* white.

**fionnach** *adj* hairy; rough, shaggy.

**fionnadh** *m* (*animal*) hair.

**fionnaireachd** *f* coolness.

**fionnan-feòir** *m* grass-hopper.

**fionnar** *adj* cool, fresh; cold, off-hand.

**fionnaraich** *v* cool; refrigerate.

**fionnsgeul** *m* legend.

**fìor**[1] *adj* real; genuine.

**fìor**[2] *adv* very.

**fìor-uisge** *m* pure water.

**fios** *m* knowledge; information; word, message, news.

**fiosaiche** *m* prophet, seer; fortune teller.

**fiosrach** *adj* well-informed.

**fiosrachadh** *m* information.

**Fir Chlis** *mpl* (*with art*) **na Fir Chlis** the Northern Lights, Aurora Borealis.

**fireann** *adj* masculine, male.

**fireannach** *m* man; male.

**fìreannach** *adj* truthful.

**fireanta** *adj same as* **fireann**.

**fìrinn** *f* truth.

**fìtheach** *m* raven.

**fiù** *m* worth, value. •*adj* worth.

**fiù agus/is** *adv* even.

**fiùdalach** *adj* feudal.

**flanainn** *f* flannel.

**flath** *m* king, prince; ruler.

**fleadh** *m* feast, banquet.

**fleasgach** *m* youth, stripling; bachelor.

**fleisg** *f* (*elec*) flex.

**fleòdradh** *m* floating; buoyancy.

**fliuch** *v* wet. •*adj* wet.

**flùr¹** *m* flower.

**flùr²** *m* flour.

**flùranach** *adj* flowery.

**fo** *prep* under, beneath, below; affected by.

**fo-aodach** *m* underwear.

**fo bhlàth** *adv* in bloom.

**fo bhròn** *adv* sad, sorrowful.

**fo chasaid** *adv* accused.

**fo chomain** *adv* obliged.

**fo chùram** *adv* anxious; preoccupied.

**fòd, fòid** *f* (single) peat; sod; clod of earth.

**fodar** *m* fodder.

**fodha** *prep pron* under him, under it (*m*).

**fodhad** *prep pron* under you (*sing*).

**fodhaibh** *prep pron* under you (*pl*).

**fodhainn** *prep pron* under us.

**fodham** *prep pron* under me.

**fo-dhearg** *adj* infra-red.

**fo dhìmeas** *adv* despised.

**fòdhpa** *prep pron* under them.

**fo eagal** *adv* afraid.

**fo fhiachaibh** *adv* obliged, under an obligation.

**fògair** *v* banish, exile; drive out.

**foghain** *v* suffice, do, be enough.
•*xcl* **fòghnaidh!** that will do!

**foghar** *m* autumn; harvest.

**fo gheasaibh** *adv* spellbound, enchanted.

**foghlaim** *v* educate.

**foghlaimte** *adj* educated, learned.

**foghlam** *m* education; scholarship.

**fòghnadh** *m* sufficiency.

**fòghnan** *m* thistle.

**fo ghruaim** *adv* gloomy; grumpy, in ill-humour.

**fògrach** *m* exile; fugitive; refugee.

**fògradh** *m* exile, banishment.

**fòid** *see* **fòd**.

**foidhpe** *prep pron* under her, under it (*f*).

**foighidinn** *f* patience.

**foighidneach** *adj* patient.

**foileag** *f* pancake.

**foill** *f* deceit; fraud, deception; cheating.

**foilleil** *adj* deceitful; fraudulent.

**foillsich** *v* publish.

**foillsichear** *m* publisher.

**fo imcheist** *adv* anxious; perplexed.

**fo iomagain** *adv* anxious, troubled.

**fo iongnadh** *adv* amazed; abashed.

**foinne** *m* wart.

**foirfe** *adj* perfect; full-grown.

**foirfeach** *m* (church) elder.

**foirmeil** *adj* formal.

**fòirneart** *m* violence, force; oppression.

**fois** *f* rest, ease, leisure; peace.

**fo-lèine** *f* vest.

**follais** *f* evidentness, obviousness; clarity; openness.

**follaiseach** *adj* evident, clear; public.

**fo-mhothachail** *adj* subconscious.

**fo mhulad** *adv* sad.

**fòn** *v* telephone. •⊠telephone.

**fònaig** *v* telephone.

**fo nàire** *adv* ashamed.

**fonn** *m* tune; mood, state of mind.

**fonnmhor** *adj* tuneful, melodious.

**for** *m* attention; notice; concern.

**fo-rathad** *m* underpass.

**forc** *f* fork.

**forladh** *m* (*army, etc*) leave.

**forsair** *m* forester, forestry worker.

**fortan** *m* fortune; luck. •⊠*xcl* **fortan leat!** good luck!

**for-thalla** *m* foyer.

**fosgail** *v* open.

**fosgailte** *adj* open, opened; frank.

**fosgladh** *m* opening, gap; opportunity.

**fo smachd** *adj* under subjection.

**fo smalan** *adv* gloomy, melancholy.

**fo-thiotalan** *mpl* subtitles.

**fo uallach** *adv* under stress.

**fradharc** *m* eyesight; sight, view.

**Fraingis** *m* (*with art*) **an Fhraingis** French (language).

**Frangach** *m*/*adj* Frenchman; French.

**fraoch** *m* heather, heath, ling.

**fraoidhneas** *m* fringe.

**fras** *v* rain lightly, shower. •⊠ shower; seed.

**frasair** *m* (*bathroom*) shower.

**freagair** *v* answer, reply; suit.

**freagairt** *f* answer, reply.

**freagarrach** *adj* suitable.

**frèam** *m* frame, framework.

**freasdail** *v* serve, wait on.

**freiceadan** *m* watch; guard; (*with art*) **am Freiceadan Dubh** the Black Watch.

**freiceadan-oirthire** *m* coastguard.

**freumh** *m* root.

**frìde** *f* corpuscle; insect.

**frids** *m* refrigerator, fridge.

**frioghan** *m* bristle.

**frionasach** *adj* worried; upset; vexing, niggling.

**frìth** *f* moorland; deer forest.

**frith-ainm** *m* nickname.

**frithealadh** *m* attendance, service.

**frithearra** *adj* touchy; peevish.

**fritheil** *v* serve, wait on.

**frith-rathad** *m* footpath; track.

**froca** *m* frock.

**fuachd** *f* cold, coldness; (*with art*) **am fuachd** a/the cold.

**fuadach** *m* banishment; driving away; *pl* (*with art*) **na Fuadaichean** (*hist*) the Highland Clearances.

**fuadachadh** *m same as* **fuadach**.

**fuadaich** *v* banish; drive away.

**fuadain** *adj* artificial, false.

**fuadan** *m* wandering; exile.

**fuaigh** *v* sew; stitch; seam.

**fuaigheal** *m* sewing; stitching; seaming.

**fuaigheil** *v* sew; stitch.

**fuaighte** *adj* sewn; stitched.

**fuaim** *m/f* noise; sound.

**fuaimneach** *adj* noisy.

**fuaimneachadh** *m* pronunciation.

**fuaimnich** *v* pronounce.

**fuaimreag** *f* vowel.

**fuaim-thonn** *m* sound wave.

**fual** *m* urine.

**fuar** *adj* cold.

**fuaradair** *m* refrigerator.

**fuaraich** *v* cool, chill.

**fuaraidh** *adj* (*lit and fig*) cool, chilly.

**fuaran** *m* spring, well.

**fuasgail** *v* release; untie; disentangle; solve.

**fuasgladh** *m* solution; absolution.

**fuath** *f* hatred, loathing.

**fuathach** *adj* hateful, detestable.

**fuathaich** *v* hate, loathe, detest.

**fùdar** *m* powder.

**fùdaraich** *v* powder.

**fuidheall** *m* relic; remainder.

**fuighleach** *m* rubbish, refuse.

**fuil** *f* blood.

**fuiling** *v* suffer; bear, put up with.

**fuil-mìos** *f* menstruation, period.

**fuilteach** *adj* bloody, gory.

**fuiltean** *m* (*single*) hair.

**fuin** *v* bake; knead.

**fuineadair** *m* baker.

**fuirich** *v* stay; live, dwell; wait; **fuirich aig X** lodge with X. •*xcl* **fuirich ort!** hang on! wait a minute! **fuirich orm□.□.□**et me see now□.□.□.

**fùirneis** *f* furnace.

**fulang** *m* suffering; endurance, hardiness.

**fulangach** *adj* hardy; long-suffering; passive.

**fulmair** *m* fulmar.

**furachail** *adj* watchful; observant; **furachail air** on the watch for.

**furan** *m* welcome, hospitality.

**furasda** *adj* easy.

**furm** *m* form, bench.

**furtachd** *f* relief; consolation, solace.

**furtaich** *v* console, comfort.

# G

**gabh** *v* take; capture; perform.

**gàbhadh** *m* danger, peril.

**gabh a' ghrian** *v* sunbathe.

**gàbhaidh** *adj* dangerous, perilous.

**gabhail** *m/f* lease; course; reception, welcome.

**gabh air** *v* make for.

**gabh air do shocair** *v* take things easily.

**gabh air màl** *v* rent.

**gabhaltach** *adj* infectious.

**gabhaltas** *m* tenancy; rented holding.

**gabh an cùram** be converted, become devout.

**gabh beachd** *v* form an opinion.

**gabh brath air** *v* take advantage of.

**gabh cead (de)** *v* take one's leave (of).

**gabh cuairt** *v* take a stroll; take a trip.

**gabh d'anail!** take a rest/breather!

**gabh eagal** *v* become afraid, take fright.

**gabh fois** *v* take a rest/break.

**gabh gnothach ri** *v* interfere with/in; get involved in.

**gabh grèim air** *v* take hold of, seize.

**gabh iongantas** *v* be amazed.

**gabh mo leisgeul!** *excl* excuse me!

**gabh mo thaobh** *v* take my side.

**gabh nàire** *v* be/feel ashamed.

**gabh os làimh** *v* undertake, take on.

**gabh pàirt** *v* participate.

**gabh ri** *v* accept.

**gabh seilbh air** *v* take possession of.

**gabh smùid** *v* (*fam*) get drunk.

**gabh socair** *v* take one's ease.

**gabh suim** *v* care.

**gabh truas de** *v* take pity on.

**gabh ùidh ann** *v* take an interest in.

**gach** *adj* each, every.

**gach aon** *adj* every single.

**gach uile** *adj* each and every.

**gad** *m* supple stick, switch.

**gadaiche** *m* thief.

**gagach** *adj* stammering, stuttering.

**Gaidheal** *m* Gael; Highlander; Gaelic speaker.

**Gaidhealach** *adj* Highland.

**Gaidhealtachd** *f* (*with art*) **a' Ghaidhealtachd** the Highlands.

**Gàidhlig** *f* (*also with art*) **Gàidhlig/a' Ghàidhlig** Gaelic (language).

**gail** *v* weep, cry.

**gailbheach** *adj* stormy.

**gaileiridh** *m* art gallery.

**gailleann** *f* storm, tempest.

**gainmheach** *f* sand.

**gainne** *f* scarcity.

**gainnead** *m* scarcity.

**gàir** *v* laugh.

**gàir** *m* cry; outcry.

**gairbhe** *f* roughness; wildness.

**gairbhead** *m* roughness; wildness.

**gàirdeachas** *m* joy; rejoicing.

**gàirdean** *m* arm.

**gàireachdainn** *f* laughing, laughter.

**gairm** *v* cry; call; crow. •*n* cry; call; cock-crow.

**gairm-chogaidh** *f* war-cry.

**gairmeach** *adj* (*gram*) vocative.

**gàirnealair** *m* gardener.

**gàirnealaireachd** *f* gardening.

**gaisge** *f* bravery, heroism.

**gaisgeach** *m* hero; champion.

**gaisgeil** *adj* brave, heroic.

**gal** *m* crying, weeping.

**galan** *m* gallon.

**galar** *m* disease.

**Gall** *m* Lowlander; non-Gael.

**galla** *f* bitch.

**gallan** *m* standing stone.

**Gallda** *adj* Lowland.

**Galldachd** *f* (*with art*) **a' Ghalldachd** the Lowlands.

**gàmag** *f* octave.

**gamhainn** *m* stirk.

**gamhlas** *m* malice, ill-will.

**gamhlasach** *adj* malevolent, spiteful.

**gann** *adj* scarce, scant, rare.

**gaoid** *f* blemish, defect.

**gaoir** *f* (*of anguish*) cry.

**gaoisid** *f* animal hair; horsehair.

**gaol** *m* love. •*excl* **a ghaoil!** darling! (my) love!

**gaolach** *adj* loving; beloved.

**gaoth** *f* wind; (*with art*) **a' ghaoth** wind, flatulence.

**gaothach** *adj* windy; flatulent.

**gàradh** see **gàrradh**.

**garbh** *adj* rough; harsh; coarse. •*adv* (*fam*) very, terribly.

**garg** *adj* fierce; unruly.

**gàrradh, gàradh** *m* wall, stone wall; garden.

**gartan** *m* garter.

**gas** *f* stalk; shoot.

**gasda** *adj* handsome; splendid; (*fam*) great.

**gath** *m* barb; sting; spear; beam.

**gath-grèine** *f* sunbeam.

**ge** *conj* though.

**gèadh** *m/f* goose.

**geal** *adj* white. •*n* white part of anything.

**gealach** *f* moon.

**gealach-an-abachaidh** *f* harvest moon.

**gealagan** *m* egg white.

**gealaich** *v* whiten.

**gealbhonn** *m* sparrow.

**geall** *v* promise, pledge. •*n* bet, wager; promise.

**gealladh** *m* promise.

**gealladh-pòsaidh** *m* engagement, betrothal.

**gealltanach** *adj* promising.

**gealtach** *adj* cowardly; fearful.

**gealtaire** *m* coward.

**geama** *m* game, match.

**geamair** *m* gamekeeper.

**geamhradh** *m* winter.

**gean** *m* mood, frame of mind.

**geanmnachd** *f* chastity.

**geanmnaidh** *adj* chaste.

**geansaidh** *m* jersey, jumper.

**gèar** *f* (*engine*) gear.

**gearain** *v* complain, grumble.

**gearan** *m* complaining; complaint.

**gearanach** *adj* complaining, querulous.

**gearastan** *m* garrison; (*with art*) **An Gearastan** Fort William.

**Gearmailt** *f* (*with art*) **a' Ghearmailt** Germany.

**Gearmailteach** *m/adj* German.

**Gearmailteis** *f* (*with art*) **a' Ghearmailtis** German (language).

**geàrr**[1] *v* cut; castrate. •*adj* short.

**geàrr**[2] *f* hare.

**gearradh** *m* cut; *pl* **gearraidhean** (*financial*) cuts.

**Gearran** *m* (*with art*) **an Gearran** February.

**gearran** *m* gelding; pony, garron.

**geàrr-shealladh** *m* short-sightedness.

**geas** *f* enchantment, spell.

**geata** *m* gate.

**ge b'e cò** *pron* whoever.

**ged a** *conj* though, although.

**ged-thà** *adv* though.

**gèile** *m* gale.

**gèill** *v* yield, surrender.

**geimheal** *m* fetter, shackle.

**geimhlich** *v* fetter, shackle.

**geinn** *m* chunk; wedge.

**geir** *f* suet; fat.

**gèire** *f* sharpness; bitterness.

**geòcach** *adj* greedy, gluttonous.

**geòcaire** *m* glutton.

**geòcaireachd** *f* greed, gluttony.

**geodha** *m/f* cove, narrow bay.

**geòla** *f* yawl, small boat.

**geòlas** *m* geology.

**ge-tà** *adv* though.

**geug** *f* branch.

**geum** *m* bellow; bellowing; lowing. •□ bellow; low.

**geur** *adj* sharp; bitter; sarcastic.

**geuraich** *v* sharpen.

**geur-chùiseach** *adj* smart, shrewd.

**gheibh** *future tense of v* **faigh**.

**giall** *f* jaw.

**gibht** *f* gift.

**Giblean** *m* (*with art*) **an Giblean** April.

**Giblinn** *f* (*with art*) **a' Ghiblinn** April.

**gidheadh** *adv* nevertheless.

**gilb** *f* chisel.

**gile** *f* whiteness.

**gilead** *m* whiteness.

**gille** *m* boy, lad; young man.

**gille-brìghde** *m* oyster-catcher.

**gin**[1] *v* beget; conceive; breed.

**gin**[2] *□ron* any; (*with neg v*) none.

**gineal** progeny; race.

**ginealach** *m* generation.

**gineamhainn** *m* conception; breeding.

**ginideach** *adj* (*gram*) genitive.

**giodar** *m* sewage.

**giodhar** *m* (*engine*) gear.

**giomach** *m* lobster.

**gioma-goc** *m* piggy-back.

**gionach** *adj* keen, ambitious; greedy.

**gionaiche** *f* greed: ambition.

**giorrachadh** *m* shortening; curtailment; abbreviation.

**giorrad** *m* shortness.

**giorraich** *v* shorten; abbreviate; curtail.

**gìosg** *v* gnash.

**giùlain** *v* carry.

**giùlan** *m* carrying; carriage; behaviour.

**giùran** *m* (*of fish*) gill.

**giuthas** *m* (*wood and tree*) pine, fir tree.

**glac**[1] *f* small valley; hollow; palm of hand.

**glac**[2] *v* catch, trap; grasp; apprehend.

**glacte** *adj* captured, trapped.

**glagadaich** *f* clattering; rattling.

**glaine** *f* cleanliness.

**glainne** *f* glass.

**glainneachan** *fpl* glasses, spectacles.

**glais** *v* lock.

**glaiste** *adj* locked.

**glam, glamh** *v* gobble, devour.

**glan** *v* clean, cleanse. •*□adj* clean; (*fam*) fine, grand.

**glaodh**[1] *v* call, shout, yell. •*□n* call, shout, yell.

**glaodh**[2] *v* glue. •*□n* glue.

**glaodhan** *m* paste; pulp.

**glas**[1] *f* lock.

**glas**[2] *adj* grey; green.

**glas-làmh** *f* handcuff.

**glasraich** *f* vegetable(s), greens.

**glè** *adv* very.

**gleac** *v* struggle; wrestle. •*□n* struggle; wrestling.

**gleacadair** *m* wrestler.

**gleadhar** *m* uproar.

**gleadhraich** *f* clamour, din.

**gleann** *m* glen, valley.

**glèidh** *v* keep; save; conserve.

**glèidhteachas** *m* conservation.

**Glèidhteachas Nàdair** *m* Nature Conservancy.

**glè mhath** *adv/adj* very good; very well.

**gleoc** *m* clock.

**gleus** *v* get ready; put in trim; adjust; (*mus*) tune. •*□n/f* condition, trim; mood; (*mus*) tuning.

**gleusda** *adj* ready; handy; in good trim; in good humour; (*mus*) tuned.

**glic** *adj* wise; clever; sensible.

**gliog** *m* (*sound*) drip, dripping.

**gliongartaich** *m* clinking, jingling.

**gloc** *v* cackle.

**glocail** *f* cackle, cackling.

**gloinne** *f* glass.

**gloinneachan** *fpl* glasses, spectacles.

**glòir** *m* glory; fame.

**glòirich** *v* glorify.

**glòir-mhiann** *m/f* ambition.

**glòrmhor** *adj* glorious.

**gluais** *v* move; touch, affect.

**gluasad** *m* movement; gait; emotional arousal.

**gluasadach** *adj* capable of moving.

**glug** *m* gurgling; gulping.

**glugan** *m* gurgling.

**glug caoinidh** *m* sob.

**glumag** *f* pool (*in burn, etc*); puddle.

**glùn** *m/f* knee.

**gnàth, gnàths** *m* custom; habit.

**gnàthach** *adj* customary, normal.

**gnàthaich** *v* use; accustom; behave towards, treat.

**gnè** *f* kind; species; gender.

**gnìomh** *m* act, action.

**gnìomhach** *adj* active; enterprising; hardworking.

**gnìomhachas** *m* industry; business; industriousness.

**gnìomhaiche** *m* executive.

**gnìomhair** *m* verb.

**gnog** *v* knock; nod.

**gnothach** *m* business; matter, affair; errand.

**gnù** *adj* surly, sullen.

**gnùis** *f* face; complexion; expression.

**gob** *m* beak, bill; (*fam*) gob; point.

**gobach** *adj* prattling, chattering.

**gobaireachd** *f* prattle, prattling.

**gobha** *m* blacksmith.

**gobhal** *m* fork; (*anat*) crotch.

**gobhal-gleusaidh** *m* tuning fork.

**gobhar** *m/f* goat.

**gobhlach** *adj* forked.

**gobhlag**[1] *f* pitch-fork, hay-fork.

**gobhlag**[2] *f* earwig.

**gobhlan-gaoithe** *m* swallow.

**goc** *m* tap; stopcock.

**gogail** *f* cackling; clucking.

**goid** *v* steal, thieve. •⚑ stealing, thieving.

**goil** *v* boil; seethe.

**goile** *f* stomach.

**goileach** *adj* boiling.

**goileam** *m* prattle, tittle-tattle.

**goireas** *m* resource, facility; (*pl*) **goireasan** public conveniences.

**goireasach** *adj* handy, convenient.

**goireasan** see **goireas**.

**goirid** *adj* short; brief.

**goirt** *adj* painful, sore; sour; bitter; severe.

**goirtich** *v* hurt.

**goistidh** *m* godfather; sponsor; gossip.

**gòrach** *adj* stupid; foolish, daft.

**gòraiche** *f* stupidity; foolishness.

**gorm** *adj* blue; green.

**gort** *f* famine; starvation.

**gràbhail** *v* engrave.

**grad** *adj* sudden; alert; agile.

**gràdh** *m* love. •*excl* **a ghràidh!** love! dear!

**gràdhach** *adj* loving, affectionate.

**graf** *m* graph.

**gràg** *m* croak, caw.

**gràgail** *f* croaking, cawing.

**gràin** *f* hatred; loathing, disgust; **tha gràin agam air** I hate him/it.

**gràineag** *f* hedgehog.

**gràineil** *adj* hateful, abominable, loathsome.

**gràinne** *f* (*single*) grain (*of corn*).

**gràinnean** *m* grain (*of sugar, etc*).

**gràisg** *f* (*derog*) crowd; mob.

**gràisgeil** *adj* uncouth, yobbish.

**gram** *m* gram(me).

**gramail** *adj* persistent.

**gràmar** *m* grammar.

**gràmarach** *adj* grammatical.

**gràn** *m* cereal; (*coll*) grain.

**granaidh** *f* granny.

**grànda, grànnda** *adj* ugly.

**gràpa** *m* (*agricultural*) fork.

**gràs** *m* grace; graciousness.

**gràsmhor** *adj* gracious.

**greadhnach** *adj* gorgeous; magnificent.

**greallach** *f* entrails, innards.

**greannach** *adj* ill-tempered.

**greannmhor** *adj* cheerful, joyful.

**greas** *v* hurry, urge on. •*excl* **greas ort!** hurry up!

**grèata** *m* grate; grating.

**greideal** *f* griddle.

**Grèig** *f* (*with art*) **a' Ghrèig** Greece.

**greigh** *f* herd; flock; (*of horses*) stud.

**greigheach** *adj* gregarious.

**grèim** *m* grip, grasp, hold; (*med*) stitch.

**grèim bìdh** *m* bite to eat.

**greim-cluaise** *m* earache.

**greimeil** *adj* resolute.

**greimich ri/air** *v* seize, grasp.

**greimire** *m* (*table*) fork.

**greis** *f* while, time.

**grèis** *f* needlework, embroidery (*i.e. the activity, see* **obair-ghrèise**).

**greiseag** *f* short while.

**Greugach** *m/adj* Greek person; Greek.

**Greugais** *f* (*with art*) **a' Ghreugais** Greek (language).

**greusaiche** *m* shoemaker, cobbler.

**grian** *f* sun.

**grinn** *adj* elegant, fine; neat; accurate.

**grinneal** *m* gravel; (*of sea, etc*) bottom.

**grinneas** *m* elegance; fineness; neatness.

**grìogag** *f* bead.

**Grioglachan** *m* (*with art*) **an Grioglachan** the Pleiades.

**Griomasach** *m/adj* from Grimsay.

**Griomasaigh** *m* Grimsay.

**grìos** *m* (*cookery*) grill.

**grìosaich** *v* (*food*) grill.

**griùlach** *f* (*with art*) **a' ghriùlach** measles.

**grod** *v* rot, putrefy. •*adj* rotten, rotted, putrid.

**grodach** *adj* grotty.

**grodach-coimhead** *adj* (*fam*) grotty-looking.

**grodadh** *m* rot, putrefaction.

**gròiseid** *f* gooseberry.

**grosair** *m* grocer.

**gruag** *f* (head of) hair.

**gruagach** *f* maid, girl, young woman.

**gruagaire** *m* hairdresser.

**gruag-bhrèige** *f* wig.

**gruaidh** *f* cheek.

**gruaim** *f* gloom, melancholy; scowl; sulkiness; grumpiness.

**gruamach** *adj* gloomy; morose; sulking; grumpy.

**grùdair** *m* brewer.

**grùdaireachd** *f* brewing.

**grùid** *f* lees, dregs, grounds; sediment.

**grunn** *m* crowd; many, lots of.

**grunnd** *m* base; sea-bed.

**grùnsgal** *m* growl, growling.

**gruth** *m* curd(s); crowdie.

**grùthan** *m* (*usu animal*) liver.

**gu**[1] *prefix introducing an adverb.*

**gu**[2] see **gus.**

**gual** *m* coal.

**gualan** *m* carbon.

**gualann, gualainn** *f* shoulder. *f* shoulder.

**gual-fiodha** *m* charcoal.

**guanach** *adj* giddy, scatter-brained; coquettish.

**guanag** *f* scatter-brained girl; coquettish girl.

**gu bochd** *adv* poorly.

**gu bràth** *adv* ever; for ever.

**gu bràth tuilleadh** *adv* (*with neg v*) nevermore.

**gu buileach** *adv* entirely.

**gucag** *f* (*botany*) bud; bubble.

**gucag-uighe** *f* egg-cup.

**gu chùl** *adv* through and through.

**gu dè?** *pron* what?, whatever?.

**gu dearbh** *adv* indeed; definitely.

**gu dearbh fhèin** *adv* extremely.

**gu diofair** *adv* of importance.

**gu dubh dona** *adv* absolutely terribly.

**guga** *m* young gannet, young solan goose.

**gu grad** *adv* suddenly; shortly.

**gu h-aon sgeulach** *adv* unanimously.

**gu h-àraid, gu h-àraidh** *adv* especially, particularly.

**gu h-iomlan** *adv* fully, absolutely.

**guidh** *v* beg, beseech; pray.

**guidhe** *m/f* plea, entreaty; prayer.

**guil** *v* weep, cry.

**guilbneach** *m* curlew.

**guin** v sting. •☐n sting.
**guineach** adj sharp; acerbic; wounding.
**guir** v hatch.
**guirean** m pimple, spot.
**gul** m crying, weeping.
**gu lèir** adv entire, entirely.
**gu leòr** adv enough, plenty.
**. . . gu leth** adv . . . and a half.
**gum, gun** conj that.
**gu mì-fhortanach** adv unfortunately.
**gu minig** adv often.
**gun**[1] see **gum**.
**gun**[2] prep without.
**gùn** m gown.
**gun bhuannachd** adv fruitless.
**gun chadal** adv sleepless.
**gun chaomhnadh** adv unsparingly.
**gun chiall** adv senseless; meaningless.
**gun chùnntas** adv countless, innumerable.
**gun dòchas** adv hopeless.
**gun fheum** adv useless.
**gun fhios do X** without X's knowledge.
**gun fhios nach** conj lest, in case.
**gun fhiù** adv worthless.
**gun ghluasad** adv still, motionless.
**gun luach** adj worthless.
**gun mheang** adj flawless.
**gunna** m gun.
**gunnair** m gunner.

**gun nàire** adv shameless.
**gun obair** adv unemployed.
**gùn-oidhche** m nightgown.
**gun sgillinn ruadh** adv (stony) broke.
**gun smior** adj spineless, wet.
**gun teagamh** adv doubtless, without a doubt.
**gun tomhas** adj incalculable, immeasurable.
**gun uiread is** adv without so much as.
**gurraban** m crouch, crouching position.
**gu ruige** prep up to, as far as; until.
**gu ruige an seo** adv this far; so far, up to now.
**gus, gu** conj to, in order to. •☐prep to, towards, up to; until.
**gus bhith . . .** about to (be) . . .;
**gus bhith 'falbh** about to leave.
**gu sealladh orm!** excl my goodness!
**gu sealladh sealbh oirnn!** excl Heaven preserve us!
**gu sìorraidh** adv for ever.
**gu sìorraidh bràth** adv for ever and ever.
**gu sònraichte** adv especially, particularly.
**guth** m voice; news, word; mention; **gun guth air X** not to mention X.
**gu tur** adv completely, totally, entirely.

# H

**hàidraidean** *m* hydrogen.
**halò** *excl* hello/hullo.
**heactair** *m* hectare.
**Hearach** *m/adj* from Harris.
**Hearadh** *f* (*with art*) **na Hearadh** Harris.

**heileacoptair, heileacoptar** *m* helicopter.
**Hiort** *f* St Kilda.
**Hiortach** *m/adj* St Kildan.
**ho-ro-gheallaidh** *m* party, knees-up, hoolie.

# I

**i** *pron* she, her, it (*f*).
**iad** *pron* they, them.
**iadh-shlat** *f* honeysuckle.
**iadsan** *pron* (*emphatic*) they, them.
**iall** *f* thong; dog's leash; strap; strop.
**iall bròige** *f* shoe-lace.
**ialtag** *f* (*creature*) bat.
**iar** *f* west.
**iar-**[1] *prefix* under-, deputy-; **iar-stiùiriche** *m* deputy director.
**iar-**[2] *prefix* post-; **iar-cheumaiche** *m* postgraduate.
**iar air** *prep* west of.
**iarann** *m* iron.
**iargalt, iargalta** *adj* churlish, surly.
**iarla** *m* earl.
**iarmad** *m* remnant.
**iarmailt** *f* (*with art*) **an iarmailt** the firmament, the heavens.
**iarnaich** *v* iron.

**iar-ogha** *m* great-grandchild.
**iarr** *v* want; ask for; invite.
**iarrtas** *m* request; demand; (*job, etc*) application.
**iasad** *m* borrowing; loan.
**iasg** *m* fish.
**iasgach** *m* (*deep-sea, etc*) fishing; angling.
**iasgaich** *v* fish.
**iasgair** *m* fisherman; angler.
**iath** *v* surround; enclose.
**idir** *adv usu with neg* (not) at all.
**ifrinn** *f* hell.
**ifrinneach** *adj* hellish, infernal.
**Ìle** *f* Islay.
**Ìleach** *m/adj* from Islay.
**ìm** *m* butter.
**imcheist** *f* anxiety, perplexity, dilemma. •*adv* **an imcheist** in a dilemma, perplexed.
**imcheisteach** *adj* worried; worrying.
**imich** *v* depart, go.

**imleag** *f* navel.

**imlich** *v* lick, lap. •⊡lick; licking.

**impidh** *m* persuasion, urging.

**impidheach** *adj* persuasive.

**ìmpireil** *adj* imperial.

**ìmpireileas** *f* imperialism.

**imrich** *v* move house. •⊡ moving house, flitting.

**inbhe** *f* rank; level; adulthood.

**inbheach** *adj* adult. •⊡ adult, grown-up.

**inbheil** *adj* high-ranking.

**inbhir** *m* confluence; (*of watercourse*) mouth.

**inc** *m* ink.

**ìne** *f* toenail, fingernail; claw, talon.

**inneal** *m* machine; implement.

**innealach** *adj* mechanical.

**inneal-ciùil** *m* musical instrument.

**inneal-clàir** *m* record-player.

**inneal-nighe** *m* washing machine.

**inneal-smàlaidh** *m* fire extinguisher.

**innean** *m* anvil.

**innear** *f* dung, manure.

**innidh** *f* bowels; intestines.

**innis**[1] *v* tell, inform; (*story, etc*) recount.

**innis**[2] *f* island; haugh, inch.

**innis breug** *v* lie, tell a lie.

**Innis Tìle** *m* Iceland.

**innleachd** *f* device; inventiveness; intelligence; artfulness; stratagem.

**innleachdach** *adj* inventive; resourceful; intelligent; cunning.

**innleadair** *m* engineer, mechanic.

**innleadair-dealain** *m* electrical engineer.

**innleadaireachd** *f* engineering.

**innleadair-thogalach** *m* civil engineer.

**innlich** *v* invent, devise; plot.

**Innseachan** *mpl* (*with art*) **na h-Innseachan** India; the Indies.

**Innseanach** *m/adj* Indian.

**innte** *prep pron* in her, in it (*f*).

**inntinn** *f* mind, intellect.

**inntinneach** *adj* interesting; mental, intellectual.

**inntrig** *v* (*building, etc*) enter.

**iobair** *v* (*relig*) sacrifice, offer up.

**iobairt** *f* (*relig*) sacrifice, offering.

**ìoc** *v* pay. •⊡ payment.

**ìochd** *f* compassion, mercy.

**ìochdar** *m* bottom, base.

**ìochdarach** *adj* lower; inferior, subordinate.

**ìochdaran** *m* inferior, subordinate; subject.

**ìochdaranachd** *f* inferiority.

**ìochdmhor** *adj* compassionate, merciful.

**ìocshlàint** *f* medicine, remedy.

**iodhal** *m* idol.

**iodhlann** *f* stack-yard.

**iolach** *f* shout.

**iolaire** *f* eagle.

**iolaire bhuidhe** *f* golden eagle.

**iolra** *m/adj* (*gram*) plural.

**ioma-** *prefix* multi-.

**iomadach** *adj* many (a).

**iomadach uair** *adv* often, many a time.

**iomadh** *adj adv* many (a).

**iomadh-fhillte** *adj* complex, complicated; manifold.

**iomagain** *f* anxiety, worry.

**iomagaineach** *adj* anxious; worrying.

**iomain** *v* drive on (*esp livestock*); propel; play shinty. •⏢shinty.

**iomair** *v* (*boat*) row.

**iomair an aon ràmh** co-operate, pull together.

**iomall** *m* edge, periphery; limit; verge; rim.

**iomall a' bhaile** *m* suburbs.

**iomallach** *adj* remote, isolated; marginal.

**iomchaidh** *adj* suitable; decent, proper.

**iomchair** *v* carry, transport.

**ìomhaigh** *f* image; likeness; idol.

**iomlaid** *f* exchange, barter; (*money*) change.

**iomlan** *adj* complete, full, absolute.

**iomnaidh** *f* solicitude.

**iompachadh** *m* conversion.

**iompachan** *m* convert, neophyte.

**iompaich** *v* persuade; (*relig*) convert.

**ìompaire** *m* emperor.

**ìompaireachd** *f* empire.

**iomradh** *m* mention; report.

**iomraiteach** *adj* celebrated; notorious.

**iomrall** *m* mistake; going astray.

**iomrallach** *adj* mistaken, erroneous.

**iomramh** *m* rowing.

**ion-** *prefix indicating* able to, worthy of.

**ionad** *m* place, spot; centre.

**ionadail** *adj* local.

**ionad-cosnaidh** *m* job centre.

**ionad-latha** *m* day centre.

**ionad-margaid, ionad-margaidh** *m* marketplace.

**ionad-obrach** *m* job centre.

**ionad-slàinte** *m* health centre.

**ionad-stiùiridh** *m* management centre.

**ionaltair** *v* graze.

**ionaltradh** *m* grazing, pasture.

**ionann, ionnan** *adj* alike, identical.

**ion-dhèanta** *adj* feasible, possible.

**iongantach** *adj* strange; surprising; marvellous.

**iongantas** *m* surprise, amazement; phenomenon, amazing thing.

**iongna** *f* toenail, fingernail; claw, talon.

**iongnadh** *m* amazement.

**ion-ithe** *adj* eatable, edible.

**ionmhainn** *adj* dear, beloved.

**ionmhas** *m* treasure; finance.

**ionmhasair** *m* treasurer.

**ionmholta** *adj* praiseworthy.

**ionnan** *see* **ionann**.

**ionndrainn** *v* miss, long for.

**ionnlad** *m* washing, ablutions.

**ionnlaid** *v* wash, bathe.

**ionnsachadh** *m* learning.

**ionnsaich** *v* learn, study.

**ionnsaichte** *adj* educated; trained.

**ionnsaigh** *m/f* attack, assault; attempt.

**ionnsramaid, ionnstramaid** *f* instrument.

**ionracas** *m* honesty; justice; righteousness.

**ionraic** *adj* honest; just; righteous.

**iorghail** *f* tumult.

**iorghaileach** *adj* tumultuous.

**ioronas** *m* irony.

**ioronta** *adj* ironic.

**Iosa** *m* Jesus.

**ìosal, ìseal** *adj* low; lowly; humble; (*voice, etc*) quiet.

**Ioslamach** *adj* Islamic.

**ìotmhor** *adj* (*land, etc*) parched; very thirsty.

**ìre** *f* degree, level; stage.

**iriosal** *adj* low, lowly; humble.

**irioslachd** *f* humility; lowliness.

**irioslaich** *v* humble; humiliate.

**iris** *f* magazine, periodical.

**is**[1] *v* am, is, are.

**is**[2] (*for* **agus**) *conj* and.

**is beag orm X** *v* I don't like X.

**isbean** *m* sausage.

**is caomh leam X** *v* I like X.

**is ciar leam X** *v* I take a dim view of X.

**is cubhaidh dhomh** *v* it befits me.

**is dòcha!** maybe!

**is dòcha gun** *conj* perhaps.

**is duilich leam** *v* I find it hard to.

**is duilich sin!** *excl* that's a shame!

**ise** *pron* (*emphatic*) she, her.

**ìseal** *adj* same as **ìosal**.

**isean** *m* chick; baby animal.

**is e do bheatha!** *excl* you're welcome!

**is e sin a'cheist!** that's the question/point!

**is e sin a' chùis!** that's the point!

**is fheàirrde mi X** *v* I'm better for X, X is good for me.

**is fheàrr leam X** *v* I prefer X.

**is fheudar dhomh** *v* I must, I have to.

**is leisg dhomh.** *v* I hesitate to.

**ìslich** *v* become lower; demote.

**is math leam X** *v* I find X good.

**is math sin!** *excl* smashing!

**is miann leam** *v* I wish.

**is mòr am beud e!** *excl* it's a great pity!

**isneach** *f* rifle.

**Israel** *f* Israel.

**Israelach** *m/adj* Israeli, Israelite.

**ist!** *excl* hush! be quiet!

**is toigh leam** X *v* I like X.

**is truagh e/sin!** *excl* it's/that's a pity.

**is urrainn dhomh** v I can.
**ite** f feather; plumage; fin.
**iteach** adj feathered.
**iteachan** m bobbin, spool.
**iteag** f small feather; flying, flight.
**iteagach** adj feathered.
**itealaich** v fly.
**itealan** m aeroplane, aircraft.
**iteileag** f kite.

**ith** v eat.
**iubhar** m yew.
**iuchair** f key; **iuchair-gnìomha** f (IT) function key.
**luchar** m (with art) **an t-luchar** July.
**lùdhach** m/adj Jew; Jewish.
**iùil-tharraing** f magnetism.
**iùil-tharraingeach** adj magnetic.
**iutharn, iutharna** f hell.

# L

**là** m day.
**là a' bhràtha** m judgement day.
**labhair** v speak, talk.
**labhairt** f speech, speaking.
**là-breith** m birthday.
**lach** f (bird) duck.
**lachdann** adj dun, tawny; khaki; swarthy.
**ladar** m ladle, scoop.
**ladarna** adj bold; shameless.
**ladhar** m hoof.
**lag**[1] adj weak, feeble.
**lag**[2] m/f hollow; pit.
**lagaich** v weaken.
**lag-chùiseach** adj unenterprising.
**lagh** m law.
**laghach** adj nice; kind.
**laghail** adj lawful, legal.
**laghairt** m/f lizard.
**Laideann** f Latin (language).

**Laidinneach** adj Latin.
**làidir** adj strong; potent.
**laigh** v lie (down); (plane, etc) land; subside.
**laighe** m/f recumbent position.
**laighe na grèine** m/f sunset.
**laigse** f weakness; infirmity; faint.
**làimhsich** v touch, handle; wield.
**lainnir** f glint, sparkle; radiance.
**lainnireach** adj sparkling; radiant.
**làir** f mare.
**làithean-saora** mpl holidays.
**làitheil** adj daily; everyday.
**là-luain** m doomsday.
**làmh** f hand; handle.
**làmhainn** f glove.
**làmh an uachdair** m the upper hand.
**làmh-lèigh** m surgeon.

**làmh-sgrìobhadh** *m* handwriting; manuscript.

**làmhthuagh** *f* hatchet, chopper.

**lampa** *m/f* lamp.

**làn** *adj* full. •◻*dv* fully. •◻*t* one's fill.

**Là na Sàbaid** *m* Sunday, the Sabbath.

**làn beòil** *m* mouthful.

**làn-chinnteach** *adj* completely certain, convinced.

**làn-chumhachd** *m* absolute power.

**làn-chumhachdach** *adj* all-powerful.

**làn dùirn** *m* handful, fistful.

**làn-fhada** *adj/adv* full-length.

**langa** *f* (*fish*) ling.

**langanaich** *v* (*animals*) bellow; low.

**langasaid** *f* sofa, couch.

**làn-mara** *m* high tide.

**làn mo bhroinn de**. *m* (*fam*) my bellyful of.

**lann** *f* blade; (*fish*) scale; enclosure; repository.

**lanntair** *m* lantern.

**là no latheigin** *adv* some day or other, one fine day.

**làn spàine** *m* spoonful.

**laoch** *m* hero; warrior.

**laochan** *m* wee boy, wee hero.

**laogh** *m* calf.

**laoidh** *m/f* poem; hymn.

**laoigh-fheòil** *f* veal.

**làr** *m* ground, floor.

**làrach** *f* trace, mark; ruin; site.

**làrna-mhàireach** *m* the morrow, the next day.

**las** *v* set alight; blaze; (*fig*) light up.

**lasadair** *m* match (*for striking*).

**lasaich** *v* loosen; soothe.

**lasair** *f* flame(s); flash.

**lasgan** *m* outburst; (*of anger, etc*) fit.

**lasrach** *adj* flaming; blazing.

**lastaig** *f/adj* elastic.

**latha** *m* day.

**latha-fèille** *m* holiday, feastday.

**làthair** *f* presence; sight, view.

**latheigin** *m* some day.

**là-trasg** *m* fast day.

**le** (*before art* **leis**) *prep* with; by; belonging to.

**leabaidh** *f* bed.

**leabhar** *m* book.

**leabharlann** *f* library.

**leabhar-latha** *m* diary, journal.

**leabhra, leabhrachan** *m* booklet; brochure.

**leac** *f* (*rock*) slab, ledge.

**leacag** *f* tile.

**leac teallaich** *f* hearthstone.

**leac uaighe** *f* gravestone.

**leac-ùrlair** *f* paving stone.

**leag** *v* fell; demolish; (*carpet, etc*) lay; (*window, etc*) lower.

**leag càin air** *v* tax, subject to taxation.

**leag gu làr** *v* raze (*to ground*).

**leagh** *v* melt, thaw; dissolve.

**leam** *prep pron* with/by me.

**leamhaich** *v* exasperate; plague.

**leamhach** *adj* insipid.

**leamhan** *m* elm.

**lean** *v* follow; continue; understand. •*excl* **lean ort!** keep going! □.□.□.□a leanas following□.□.□.

**leanabail** *adj* childish, silly; infantile.

**leanaban** *m* baby; small child.

**leanabh** *m* baby; infant; child.

**leanailteach** *adj* continuous, incessant.

**leann** *m* beer, ale.

**leannan** *m* lover; sweetheart, boyfriend, girlfriend.

**leannanachd** *f* courting, courtship.

**leannra** *m* sauce.

**leantainneach** *adj* continuous; persevering; lasting.

**leas** *m* benefit, advantage; improvement; **cha leig thu leas**□.□.□.you don't need to□.□.□.

**leasachadh** *m* improvement; development.

**leasaich** *v* improve; develop.

**leasan** *m* lesson.

**leat** *prep pron* with/by you (*sing*).

**leatha** *prep pron* with/by her, with/by it (*f*).

**leathad** *m* slope, hillside.

**leathann** *adj* broad, wide.

**leathar** *m* leather.

**le chèile** *adv* together; both.

**le deagh dhùrachd** (*corres*) with compliments.

**le dùrachd** (*corres*) yours sincerely.

**le foill** *adv* fraudulently.

**leibh** *prep pron* with/by you (*pl*).

**leig** *v* let, allow; leave to; let out, utter; (*weapon*) fire.

**leig air** *v* pretend; give away.

**leig air dhearmad** *v* neglect.

**leig anail** *v* take a breather.

**leig às** *v* let off/out.

**leig braim** *v* fart.

**leig brùchd** *v* belch.

**leig cnead** *v* groan.

**leig de** *v* give up, cease.

**leig fead** *v* whistle.

**leigheas** *m* cure, remedy.

**leighis** *v* cure, heal.

**leig le** *v* leave alone, let be.

**leig leas** *see* **leas**.

**leig ma sgaoil** *v* free.

**leig 'na theine** *v* set on fire.

**leig osna, leig osnadh** *v* heave/breathe a sigh.

**leig seachad** *v* give up, relinquish.

**lèine** *f* shirt.

**leinn** *prep pron* with/by us.

**lèir** *adj* visible; evident; **is lèir dhomh (gu)** (*fml*) it's clear to me (that).

**lèirmheas** *m* (*book, etc*) review.

**lèirsinn** *f* sight; perceptiveness.

**lèirsinneach** *adj* visible; perceptive.

**leis¹** *f* thigh.

**leis²** *prep pron* with/by him, with/by it (*m*).

**leis a' bhruthaich** *adv* with the slope.

**leis an t-sruth** *adv* downstream.

**leis a sin, leis sin** *adv* whereupon, at that.

**leisg** *adj* lazy; reluctant. •◻ laziness.

**leis gach deagh dhùrachd** (*corres*) with best wishes.

**leisge** *f* laziness.

**leisgeadair** *m* lazy person, lazybones.

**leisgeul** *m* excuse; pretext.

**leis sin** *see* **leis a sin**.

**leiteis** *f* lettuce.

**leitheach** *adv* half, semi-.

**leitheach-slighe** *adv* halfway.

**leithid (de)** *f* the like(s) (of); **a leithid de◻.◻.◻**ch a◻.◻.◻.

**leitir** *f* slope, hillside.

**Leòdhasach** *m*/*adj* Lewisman; from Lewis.

**leòghann** *m* lion.

**leòinteach** *m* casualty, victim; *pl* (*with art*) **na leòintich** the injured; the wounded.

**leòman** *m* moth.

**leòn** *v* wound; hurt; injure. •◻ wound; hurt; injury.

**leònte** *adj* wounded; hurt; injured.

**leòr** *f* enough, sufficiency; **mo leòr de◻.◻.◻**y fill of◻.◻.◻.

**leotha** *prep pron* with/by them.

**le sùrd** *adv* with a will.

**leth** *m* half; side; **sia gu leth** six and a half; **leth-** one of a pair.

**leth-asal** *f* mule.

**lethbhreac** *m* (*book, etc*) copy, reproduction; match.

**lethcheann** *m* cheek; side of head.

**leth-cheud** *m* fifty.

**leth-chuid** *f* half.

**leth-fhuar** *adj* lukewarm.

**leth shean** *adj* middle-aged.

**le tuiteamas** *adv* by accident, by chance.

**leud** *m* breadth, width.

**leudaich** *v* widen; extend.

**leudaichte** *adj* widened; flattened.

**leug** *f* jewel.

**leugh** *v* read.

**leum** *v* jump, leap; (*nose*) bleed. •◻ jump, leap.

**leum-sròine** *m* nosebleed.

**leum-uisge** *m* waterfall.

**le ur cead** by your leave.

**leus** *m* light; ray of light; torch; blister.

**liagh** *f* ladle, scoop.

**liath** *v* make or become grey. •◻ *dj* grey.

**liath-reothadh** *m* frost, hoar frost.

**libhrig** *v* (*goods, etc*) deliver.

**lide** *m* syllable.

**lighiche** *m* doctor, physician.

**lili, lilidh** *f* lily.

**lìnig** *v* line.

**linn** *m* age, period; generation; century; *(pl with art)* **na Linntean Dorcha** the Dark Ages.

**linne** *f* pool; waterfall.

**liomaid** *f* lemon.

**lìomh** *v* polish, shine. •🎵 polish, gloss.

**lìomharra** *adj* polished, glossy.

**lìon**[1] *v* fill; *(tide)* come in.

**lìon**[2] *m* net; web.•🎵 flax, lint.

**lìon damhain-allaidh** *m* cobweb.

**lìonmhor** *adj* numerous; abundant.

**lionn** *m* liquid.

**lionsa** *f* lens.

**liopard** *m* leopard.

**lios** *m/f* garden; enclosure.

**Liosach** *m/adj* from Lismore.

**liosda** *adj* boring.

**Lios Mòr** *m* Lismore.

**liosta** *f* list.

**liotair** *m* litre.

**lip** *f* lip.

**lite** *f* porridge.

**litir** *f* letter.

**litreachadh** *m* spelling.

**litreachas** *m* literature.

**litrich** *v* spell.

**liùdhag** *f* doll.

**liut** *f* knack.

**lobh** *v* rot, decay.

**lobhadh** *m* rot, putrefaction.

**lobhar** *m* leper.

**lobht, lobhta** *m* flat; storey; loft.

**locair** *m/f* *(tool)* plane.

**lòcast** *m* locust.

**loch** *m* loch, lake.

**lochan** *m* small loch, pond.

**lochd** *m* fault; harm.

**lochdach** *adj* harmful.

**Lochlann** *f* Norway; Scandinavia.

**Lochlannach** *m/adj* Norseman; Norse; Norwegian; Scandinavian; Viking.

**lòchran** *m* lamp, lantern.

**lof** *m/f* loaf.

**loidhne** *f* line.

**loingeas** *m* shipping; fleet; navy.

**lòinidh** *m/f* *(with art)* **an lòinidh** rheumatism.

**loisg** *v* burn; *(gun)* fire.

**loisgte** *adj* burnt.

**lòistear** *m* lodger.

**lòistinn** *m* lodging(s); digs; accommodation.

**lom** *v* strip; shave; shear; mow. •🎵*adj* bare; bleak; thin.

**lomadair** *m* shearer.

**loma-làn** *adj* full to the brim.

**lomnochd** *adj* naked.

**lòn**[1] *m* food, provisions.

**lòn**[2] *m* pool; puddle; meadow.

**lònaid** *f* lane.

**lon-dubh** *m* blackbird.

**long** *f* ship.

**long-bhriseadh** *m* shipwreck.

**long-chogaidh** *f* warship, battleship.

**lorg** *v* find; track down, trace. •🎵 vestige; footprint; track.

**los** *m* purpose, intention. •*conj* **los gu, los gun** in order that.

**lòsan** *m* pane.

**losgadh-bràghad** *m* heartburn.

**losgann** *m* frog.

**lot**[1] *f* croft; piece of land.

**lot**[2] *v* wound. •*n* wound.

**loth** *f* filly.

**luach** *m* worth, value.

**luachachadh** *m* valuation.

**luachaich** *v* evaluate, value.

**luachair** *f* rushes.

**luachmhor** *adj* valuable, precious.

**luadhadh** *m* (*cloth*) waulking, fulling.

**luaidh**[1] *v* praise. •*n* praise; beloved person. •*excl* **a luaidh!** my love! (my) darling!

**luaidh**[2] *v* (*cloth*) waulk, full.

**luaisg** *v* rock, sway, toss.

**luaithre, luath** *f* ash(es).

**luas, luaths** *m* speed; agility.

**luath**[1] *adj* fast, quick.

**luath**[2] *f* same as **luaithre**.

**luathaich** *v* accelerate; hurry on.

**luaths** *m* same as **luas**.

**luath-thrèana** *f* express (train).

**lùb** *v* bend; bow. •*n* bend; loop.

**lùbach** *adj* bending; winding; flexible.

**lùb a' ghlùin** *v* kneel, pray.

**luch** *f* mouse.

**lùchairt** *f* palace.

**luchd**[1] *m* cargo.

**luchd**[2] *m* people.

**luchdaich** *v* load.

**luchd-càraidh** *m* repairers.

**luchd-ciùil** *m* musicians.

**luchd-eòlais** *m* acquaintances.

**luchd-frithealaidh** *m* attendants.

**luchdmhor** *adj* capacious.

**luchd-obrach** *m* workers; workforce.

**luchd-poileataics** *m* politicians.

**luchd-siubhail** *m* (*coll*) travellers.

**luchd-stiùiridh** *m* managers, management.

**luchd-turais** *m* (*coll*) tourists.

**luchraban** *m* dwarf, midget.

**Lucsamburg** *m* Luxembourg.

**Lucsamburgach** *m/adj* from Luxembourg.

**lùdag** *f* little finger; hinge.

**lugha** *comp adj* smaller, smallest.

**lùghdachadh** *m* reduction; abatement.

**lùghdaich** *v* lessen; shrink; abate.

**luibh** *m/f* herb; plant; weed.

**luibh-eòlas** *m* botany.

**luibhre** *f* leprosy.

**luideach** *adj* shabby, scruffy.

**luideag** *f* rag.

**luidhear** *m* funnel, chimney.

**Luinn** *f* Luing.

**Luinneach** *m/adj* from Luing.

**luinneag** *f* song, ditty.

**Lùnasdal** *m* (*with art*) **an Lùnasdal** August; **Là Lùnasdail** Lammas Day.

**lurach** *adj* pretty; nice; beloved.

**lurgann** _f_ shin.

**lus** _m_ herb; plant; weed.

**lùth, lùths** _m_ power of movement; energy.

**lùthmhor** _adj_ strong; agile; energetic.

**lùths** _m_ _same as_ **lùth**.

# M

**ma** _conj_ if.

**màb** _v_ revile, vilify.

**mac** _m_ son; **mac bràthair, mac piuthar** _m_ nephew.

**mac-an-aba** _m_ ring finger.

**mac an donais!** _excl_ damn it!

**mac an duine** _m_ humanity, humankind.

**macanta** _adj_ meek, submissive.

**machair** _m/f_ machair; plain; (_with art_) **a' Mhachair Ghallda** the Lowlands.

**machlag** _f_ womb, uterus.

**mac-meanmna** _m_ imagination.

**mac-meanmnach** _adj_ imaginary; imaginative.

**mac-na-bracha** _m_ (_nickname_) whisky.

**mac-samhail** _m_ equal, match; likeness.

**mac-talla** _m_ echo.

**madadh** _m_ dog.

**madadh-allaidh** _m_ wolf.

**madadh ruadh** _m_ fox.

**madainn** _f_ morning. •⊠_dv_ **sa' mhadainn** a.m.

**ma dh'fhaoidte** _adv/conj_ maybe, perhaps.

**mag (air)** _v_ mock, make fun (of).

**màg** _f_ paw.

**magadh** _m_ mockery.

**magail** _adj_ mocking, jeering.

**magairle** _m/f_ testicle.

**maghar** _m_ fly, bait.

**maide** _m_ wood, timber; stick; **maide-droma** _m_ ridge pole, roof-tree.

**maide poite** _m_ spirtle.

**maids, maidse** _m_ match (_for striking_).

**màidsear** _m_ (_rank_) major.

**Màigh** _f_ (_with art_) **a' Mhàigh** May.

**maighdeann** _f_ maiden; virgin; spinster. (_address_) **a Mhaighdeann X!** Miss X!

**maighdeannas** _m_ maidenhood, virginity.

**maighdeann-mhara** _f_ mermaid.

**maigheach** _m_ hare.

**maighistir, maighstir** _m_ master; (_address_) **a Mhaighstir X!** Mister X!

**maighistir-sgoile, maighstir-sgoile** _m_ schoolmaster.

**màileid** _f_ suitcase; briefcase; bag.

**màileid-droma** *f* rucksack.

**màileid-làimh** *f* handbag.

**maille** *f* slowness; delay.

**maille ri** *prep* with, along with.

**maillich** *v* delay; procrastinate.

**mair** *v* last, continue; **mair beò** live, survive.

**maireann** *adj* living; enduring; **X nach maireann** the late X.

**maireannach** *adj* eternal; durable; long-lived.

**màirnealach** *adj* dilatory; boring.

**mairtfheoil** *f* beef.

**maise** *f* beauty.

**maiseach** *adj* beautiful.

**maisich** *v* beautify; decorate; (*face*) make up.

**màithreil** *adj same as* **màthaireil**.

**màl** *m* rent.

**mala** *f* brow; eyebrow.

**malairt** *f* trade, business; barter.

**malairtich** *v* trade; barter.

**màlda** *adj* coy, bashful.

**mall** *adj* slow, tardy.

**mallachd** *f* curse.

**mallaich** *v* curse.

**mallaichte** *adj* cursed, damned.

**mamaidh** *f* Mummy.

**manach** *m* monk.

**manachainn** *f* monastery.

**manadh** *m* omen.

**manaidsear** *m* manager.

**Manainneach** *m/adj* Manxman; Manx.

**mang** *f* fawn.

**maodal** *f* paunch.

**maoidh** *v* threaten.

**maoil** *f* forehead, brow.

**Maoil** *f* (*with art*) **a' Mhaoil** the Minch.

**maoile** *f* baldness.

**maoin** *f* wealth; goods, chattels.

**maol** *m* cape, promontory; rounded hill. •*adj* blunt; bald.

**maorach** *m* shellfish.

**maor-eaglais** *m* church officer.

**maor-obrach** *m* foreman, gaffer.

**maoth** *adj* soft; tender-hearted.

**maothaich** *v* soften.

**mapa** *m* map.

**mar** *prep* as; like. •*conj* **mar a** as, how; **mar gun** as if, as though.

**mar a bheatha** *adv* for dear life.

**marag** *f* pudding.

**maraiche** *m* sailor, seafarer.

**mar an ceudna** *adv* likewise, too.

**marbh** *v* kill. •*adj* dead.

**marbhaiche** *m* killer; murderer.

**marbhan** *m* corpse.

**marbhrann** *m* elegy.

**marbhtach** *adj* deadly, fatal.

**mar bu chòir** *adv* fittingly.

**marcachadh** *m* riding; horsemanship.

**marcaich** *v* ride.

**marcaiche** *m* rider, horseman.

**marcaid** *m/f* market.

**mar eisimpleir** (*abbrev* **m e**) *adv* for example.

**margadh** *m/f* market; **am Mar-**

gadh Coitcheann the Common Market.

**margarain** *m* margarine.

**màrmor** *m* marble.

**mar ri** *prep* with, along with.

**màrsail** *f* march; marching.

**mar sin** *adv* so.

**mar sin leat/leibh!** *excl* good-bye!

**Màrt** *m* Mars; (*with art*) **am Màrt** March.

**mart** *m* beef animal.

**màs** *m* buttock; (*fam*) arse, bum.

**ma's e do thoil e** *adv* please.

**ma's fhìor** *adv* kidding, pretending.

**masg** *m* mask.

**maslach** *adj* disgraceful, shameful.

**masladh** *m* disgrace, shame.

**maslaich** *v* disgrace, put to shame.

**ma-tà** *adv* then, in that case.

**matamataig, matamataigs** *m* mathematics.

**math** *m* good. •*dj* good.

**ma-tha** *adv* then, in that case.

**mathachadh** *m* manure; fertilizer.

**mathaich** *v* manure; enrich.

**màthair** *f* mother.

**màthair-chèile** *f* mother-in-law.

**màthaireil, màithreil** *adj* motherly, maternal.

**màthair-uisge** *m* fountainhead.

**mathan** *m* (brown) bear.

**mathanas** *m* forgiveness, pardon.

**mathan bàn** *m* polar bear.

**mathas** *m* goodness.

**math dhà-rìreadh!** *excl* excellent!

**math do** *v* forgive.

**ma thogras tu** if you like.

**math thu-fhèin!** *excl* well done! good for you!

**meadhan** *m* middle, centre; medium, mechanism; waist; average; *pl* **na meadhanan** (*press, etc*) the media.

**meadhanach** *adj* middling, so-so; average.

**meadhan-aois** *f* middle age.

**meadhan-aoiseil** *adj* medieval.

**meadhan-chearcail** *m* equator.

**meadhan-là** *m* midday, noon.

**meadhan-oidhche** *m* midnight.

**Meadhan-thìreach** *adj* Mediterranean.

**meal** *v* enjoy. •*excl* **meal do/ur naidheachd!** congratulations!

**meal-bhucan** *m* melon.

**meall**[1] *v* deceive; cheat; entice.

**meall**[2] *m* lump; lumpy hill.

**meallach** *adj* beguiling, bewitching.

**mealladh** *m* deceit, deception; enticement.

**meall an sgòrnain** *m* Adam's apple.

**meallta** *adj* deceived; cheated.

**mealltach** *adj* deceitful; cheating; deceptive.

**mealltair** *m* deceiver; cheat.

**meall-uisge** *m* heavy shower.

**mean** *adj* little, tiny; **mean air mhean** little by little.

**mèanan** *m* yawn.

**mèananaich** *f* yawning.

**meanbh** *adj* tiny, minute.

**meanbh-chuileag** *f* midge.

**meang** *f* fault, flaw; abnormality.

**meangach** *adj* abnormal.

**meangan, meanglan** *m* branch, bough.

**meann** *m* (*goat*) kid.

**mearachadh** *m* aberration.

**mearachd** *f* mistake, error.

**mearachdach** *adj* wrong, erroneous.

**mèaran** *m* yawn.

**mèaranaich** *f* yawning.

**mèarrsaidh** *m* march, marching.

**meas**[1] *m* valuation; respect, esteem; **is mise le meas** (*corres*) yours sincerely. •⊡ estimate; evaluate; esteem; think.

**meas**[2] *m* fruit.

**measach** *adj* fruity.

**measail** *adj* respected; respectable; valued.

**measail (air)** *adj* fond (of).

**measarra** *adj* moderate; temperate.

**measarrachd** *f* moderation; abstinence.

**meas-chraobh** *f* fruit tree.

**measgaich** *v* mix, mingle.

**measgaichear** *m* mixer.

**measgaich suas** *v* confuse, mix up.

**meata** *adj* faint-hearted; feeble.

**meatailt** *f* metal.

**meatair** *m* metre.

**meatrach** *adj* metric.

**meidh** *f* scales; equilibrium.

**meil** *v* mill, grind.

**meileabhaid** *f* velvet.

**meilich** *v* chill; numb.

**mèilich** *f* bleat, bleating; baa, baa-ing.

**mèinn**[1] *f* temperament; appearance.

**mèinn**[2]**, mèinne** *f* mine; ore.

**mèinneach** *adj* mineral.

**mèinneadair** *m* miner.

**mèinnear, mèinnearach** *m* mineral.

**mèinnearachd** *f* mining; mineralogy.

**mèinne-ghuail** *see* **mèinn-ghuail**.

**mèinneil** *adj* mineral.

**mèinn-eòlas** *m* mineralogy.

**mèinn-ghuail, mèinne-ghuail** *f* coalmine.

**meirg** *v* rust. •⊡ rust.

**meirg-dhìonach** *adj* rustproof.

**meirgeach** *adj* rusty.

**meirgich** *v* rust.

**mèirle** *f* theft.

**mèirleach** *m* thief.

**meomhair** *f* (*faculty*) memory.

**meòmhraich** *v* recollect; muse.

**meud** *m* size; amount; extent.

**meudachd** *f* magnitude.

**meudaich** *v* increase; enlarge.

**m' eudail!** *excl* love! darling!

**meur** *f* finger; branch; (*piano, etc*) key.

**meuran** *m* thimble.

**meur-chlàr** *m* keyboard.

**meur-lorg** *f* fingerprint.

**mi** *pron* I, me.

**mì-** *prefix* un-, dis-, in-, mis-, un-, -less.

**mial** *f* (*parasite*) tick.

**mialaich** *f* mewing, miauling.

**mial-chaorach** *f* sheep-tick.

**miann** *m/f* wish; longing; (*sexual*) desire.

**miannaich** *v* wish for; lust after.

**mias** *f* platter; basin.

**mias-ionnlaid** *f* wash-basin.

**mì-bhlasta** *adj* tasteless;.

**mì-cheartas** *m* injustice.

**mì-dhileas** *adj* disloyal.

**mì-earbsa** *m* mistrust.

**mì-fhoighidinn** *f* impatience.

**mì-fhoighidneach** *adj* impatient.

**mì-ghnàthach** *adj* abnormal; unusual.

**mil** *f* honey.

**mìle** *m* thousand; mile.

**milis** *adj* sweet.

**mill** *v* damage; spoil; destroy.

**millean** *m* million.

**millte** *adj* damaged; spoilt; destroyed.

**millteach** *adj* destructive.

**mìlseachd** *f* sweetness.

**mìlsean** *m* dessert, pudding.

**mì-mhodhail** *adj* rude, ill-mannered.

**mìn**[1] *adj* smooth; soft.

**min**[2] *f* (*ground*) meal; **min-choirce** *f* oatmeal.

**mì-nàdarra** *adj* unnatural.

**mineachadh** *m* explanation; interpretation.

**mineachail** *adj* explanatory.

**min-flùir** *f* flour.

**min-iarainn** *f* iron filings.

**minich** *v* explain, illustrate; interpret; mean.

**mìnich** *v* smoothe.

**minig** *adj* frequent.

**ministear** *m* (*church, govt*) minister.

**ministrealachd** *f* (*church, govt*) ministry.

**min-sàibh** *f* sawdust.

**miodal** *m* flattery, fawning.

**mìog** *f* smirk.

**miogadaich** *f* bleat, bleating.

**mìolchu** *m* greyhound.

**mion** *adj* small; minute; detailed; punctilious.

**mionach** *m* entrails, guts; (*fam*) belly.

**mionaid** *f* minute.

**mionaideach** *adj* thorough; detailed.

**mion-aoiseach** *adj* minor.

**mion-bhraide** *f* pilfering.

**mion-chànan** *m* minority language.

**mion-cheasnaich** *v* question minutely, grill.

**mion-chuid** *f* (*proportion*) minority.

**mion-chùiseach** *adj* meticulous.

**mion-eòlas** *m* detailed knowledge.

**mion-fhacal** *m* (*gram*) particle.

**mion-gheàrr** *v* cut up finely.

**mionnaich** *v* curse, swear.

**mionnan** *m* curse, swearword.

**mion-phuing** *f* detail.

**mìorbhail** *f* marvel; miracle.

**mìorbhaileach** *adj* marvellous; miraculous.

**mìos** *m/f* month; **mìos nam pòg** honeymoon.

**mìosach** *adj* monthly.

**mìosachan** *m* calendar.

**miotag** *f* glove; mitten.

**mìr** *m* bit, particle; scrap.

**mire** *f* mirth; light-heartedness.

**mì-rùn** *m* malice, ill-will.

**misde** *adj* same as **miste**.

**mise** *pron emphatic form of* **mi**.

**misg** *f* drunkenness, intoxication.

**misgear** *m* drunkard, boozer.

**mì-shealbhach** *adv* unlucky, unfortunate.

**misneachadh** *m* encouragement.

**misneachail** *adj* courageous; spirited; in good heart; encouraging.

**misneach, misneachd** *f* courage.

**misnich** *v* encourage; inspire courage in.

**miste, misde** *adj* the worse for; **cha bu mhisde mi X** I'd be none the worse for X.

**mithich** *adj* timely.

**mo** poss *adj* my.

**moch** *adj* early; **bho mhoch gu dubh** from morning til night.

**mòd** *m* (*with art*) **am Mòd (Nàiseanta)** the (National) Mod.

**modh** *f* manner, mode; manners; (*gram*) mood.

**modhail** *adj* polite, well-bred.

**Mohamadanach** *m/adj* Mohammedan, Muslim.

**mòine** *f* (*collective*) peat; **dèan/buain mòine** *v* cut peat.

**mòinteach** *f* moor, moorland.

**moit** *f* pride.

**moiteil** *adj* proud.

**mol**[1] *v* praise; recommend.

**mol**[2] *m* shingle; shingly beach.

**molach** *adj* hairy; rough.

**moladh** *m* praise; recommendation.

**moll** *m* chaff.

**molldair** *m* (*jelly, etc*) mould.

**molt, mult** *m* wether.

**mòmaid** *f* moment, second.

**monadail** *adj* hilly, mountainous.

**monadh** *m* moor, moorland; common hill grazing.

**mòr** *adj* big; great; **mòr aig a chèile** great friends/pals.

**mòrachd** *f* greatness, grandeur.

**morair** *m* lord.

**mòran** *m* many, a lot of; much.

**mòrchuis** *f* pride, conceit.

**mòr-chuid** *f* (*with art*) **a' mhòr-chuid** the majority; most people.

**morghan** *m* gravel, shingle.

**mòr-inbhe** *f* eminence; high rank.

**mòr iongnadh** *m* astonishment, stupefaction.

**mòr-roinn** *f* continent.

**mòr-sluagh** *m* multitude.

**mort, murt** *v* murder, assassinate. •*n* murder, assassination, manslaughter.

**mortair, murtair** *m* murderer, assassin.

**mòr-uasal** *m* nobleman, aristocrat.

**mosach** *adj* nasty; scruffy; niggardly.

**mosg** *m* mosque.

**mosgail** *v* (*from sleep*) wake, waken, rouse.

**mo sgrios!** *excl* woe is me!

**motair** *m* motor.

**motair-rothar** *m* motorbike.

**motha** *adj* bigger, greater.

**mothachail** *adj* aware; observant; sensitive; conscious.

**mothaich** *v* notice; feel; experience.

**mo thruaighe!** *excl* woe is me!

**mo thruaighe ort!** *excl* woe unto you!

**mu** *prep* around, about; concerning.

**muc** *f* pig; sow.

**mu choinneimh** *prep* opposite.

**mucfheoil** *f* pork.

**mùch** *v* extinguish, quench; smother; strangle; repress.

**muc-mhara** *f* whale.

**mu dheas** *adv* to/in the South.

**mu dheidhinn** *prep* about, concerning.

**mu dheireadh** *adj* last. •*adv* at last; **mu dheireadh thall** at long last.

**muga** *f* (*drinking*) mug.

**mùgach** *adj* morose, surly.

**muidhe** *m* churn.

**mùig** *f* frown, scowl.

**muilcheann, muinichill** *m* sleeve.

**Muileach** *m/adj* from Mull.

**muileann, muilinn** *m/f* mill.

**muileann-gaoithe** *m/f* windmill.

**muile-mhàg** *f* toad.

**muilinn** *m/f* same as **muileann**.

**muillean** *m* million.

**muillear** *m* miller.

**muilt-fheoil** *f* mutton.

**muime** *f* stepmother.

**muin** *f* (*esp of animal*) back; top.

**muineal** *m* neck.

**muing** *f* mane.

**muinichill** *m* same as **muilcheann**.

**muinntir** *f* people; followers.

**muir** *m/f* sea.

**muir-làn** *m* high tide.

**mulad** *f* grief, sadness.

**muladach** *adj* sad.

**m' ulaidh** my darling, my love.
**mullach** *m* top; summit; roof.
**mult** *m same as* **molt**.
**mun, mus** *conj* before.
**mùn** *m* urine, piss.
**muncaidh** *m* monkey.
**mun cuairt** *adv* around, about.
**mun cuairt air** *prep* around, about.
**mùr** *m* bulwark, rampart.
**mura** *conj* if not.
**murt** *v/m same as* **mort**.

**murtair** *m same as* **mortair**.
**mus** *conj same as* **mun**.
**mu seach** *adv* in turn, one by one.
**mùth** *v* change, alter; mutate; deteriorate.
**mùthadh** *m* change, alteration; mutation; deterioration.
**mu thimcheall** *adv* around.
**mu thràth** *adv* already.
**mu thuath** *adv* to/in the North.

# N

**'n** *art/poss pron/prep* **an** *after words ending with a vowel*.
**na**[1] *imper part* do not, don't.
**na**[2] *conj* than.
**na**[3] *rel pron* what, that which, those which.
**na**[4] *art* (*f sing*) of the; (*pl*) the.
**nàbachas** *m* neighbourliness.
**nàbaidh** *m* neighbour.
**nàbaidheachd** *f* neighbourhood.
**nàbaidheil** *adj* neighbourly.
**nach** *neg rel pron* that not.
**nach math a rinn thu!** *excl* well done!
**'na chrùbagan** *adv* crouched down.
**'na chrùban** *adv* crouching, squatting.
**nàdar, nàdur** *m* nature; temperament.

**nàdarrach** *adj* natural.
**'na dhùisg** *adv* awake.
**'na dhùsgadh** *adv* awake.
**nàdur** *m same as* **nàdar**.
**na h-uile** *pron* everybody, everyone.
**naidheachd** *f* piece of news; anecdote; (*pl TV, etc*) **na naidheachdan** the news.
**naidheachdair** *m* journalist.
**nàidhlean** *m* nylon.
**nàire** *f* shame, ignominy; bashfulness. •*excls* **mo nàire!** for shame! **mo nàire ort!** shame on you!
**nàisean** *m* nation.
**nàiseanta** *adj* national.
**nàiseantach** *m* nationalist.
**nàiseantachd** *f* nationalism; nationhood.

**naisgear** *m* (*gram*) conjunction.

**nàimhdeas** *m* enmity, hostility.

**nàimhdeil** *adj* inimical, hostile.

**nàireach, nàrach** *adj* shame-faced; bashful; diffident.

**naisgear** *m* (*gram*) conjunction.

**nam** *see* **nan**.

**'nam aonar** *adv* on my own.

**'nam bheachd-sa** in my opinion.

**'nam chomain** *adj* obliged to me.

**nàmhaid** *m* enemy.

**nan**[1] (**nam** *before b, f, p*) *conj* if.

**nan**[2] (**nam** *before b, f, p*) *pl art* of the.

**naodh, naoi** *m/adj* nine.

**naoidhean** *m* baby; infant.

**naoinear** *m/f* nine (people).

**naomh** *m* saint. •*adj* holy, sacred; saintly.

**naomhachd** *f* holiness; saintliness.

**nàr** *adj* shameful; disgraceful.

**nàrach** *adj same as* **nàireach**.

**nàraich** *v* put to shame; disgrace.

**nas motha** *adv* either, (*with neg v*) neither.

**'na stad** *adj* stationary; in abeyance.

**'na shuidhe** *adv* seated, sitting.

**nathair** *f* adder; serpent, snake.

**'na thràill do** addicted to.

**'na trasg** *adv* fasting.

**neach** *m* person; one, someone.

**neach chungaidhean** *m* chemist, pharmacist.

**neach-teagaisg** *m* teacher.

**neach-treòrachaidh** *m* guide.

**neactair** *m* nectar.

**nead** *m* nest.

**nèamh** *m* heaven(s).

**nèamhaidh** *adj* heavenly, celestial.

**neapaigear** *m* handkerchief.

**neapaigin** *f* napkin.

**nearbhach** *adj* nervous; nervy.

**neart** *m* strength, might; vigour; **an trèine a neirt** in his prime.

**neartaich** *v* strengthen; invigorate.

**neartmhor** *adj* strong; mighty.

**neas** *m/f* weasel; ferret; **neas mhòr** stoat.

**neasgaid** *f* boil; ulcer, abscess.

**nèibhi, nèibhidh** *m/f* navy.

**neimh, nimh** *m* poison; malice.

**Neiptiùn** *m* Neptune.

**neo** *conj same as* **no**.

**neo-** *prefix* un-, in-, non-.

**neo-chrìochnach** *adj* infinite.

**neo-eisimeileach** *adj* independent.

**neo-eisimeileachd** *f* independence.

**neòinean** *m* daisy.

**neòinean-grèine** *m* sunflower.

**neò-làthaireachd** *f* absence.

**neònach** *adj* strange, curious.

**neo-sheachanta** *adj* unavoidable, inevitable.

**neul** *m* cloud; complexion; faint.

**neulach** *adj* cloudy.

**neulaich** *v* cloud over; obscure.

**nì¹** *m* thing; matter; circumstance;
**an Nì Math** God.

**nì²** *future tense of v* **dèan**.

**Nic** (*in surnames*) daughter of.

**nigh** *v* wash.

**nigheadair** *m* washer, washing machine.

**nigheadaireachd** *f* washing.

**nigheadair-shoithichean** *m* dishwasher.

**nighean** *f* girl; young woman; daughter; **nighean bràthar/peathar** niece.

**nimh** *m same as* **neimh**.

**nimheil** *adj* poisonous; malicious.

**Nirribhidh** *f* Norway.

**nitheigin** *pron* something.

**nitheil** *adj* concrete, actual.

**no, neo** *conj* or.

**nobhail** *f* novel.

**nochd** *v* show; appear; **nochd an clò** be printed/published.

**Nollaig** *f* Christmas.

**norrag** *f* nap, snooze; **norrag cadail** a wink of sleep.

**nòs** *m* way; custom; style.

**nota** *f* note; (*money*) pound.

**nuadh** *adj* new.

**nuadhaich** *v* renovate.

**nuallaich** *v* howl; roar; bellow.

**nurs** *f* nurse.

# O

**o** *prep* from; since.

**òb** *m* bay.

**obair** *f* work; job, employment.

**obair-ghrèise** *f* (*the product of*) embroidery, needlework.

**obair-làimhe** *f* handiwork.

**obair-taighe** *f* housework.

**obann** *adj* sudden.

**obh! obh!** *excl* dear oh dear! good heavens!

**obraich, oibrich** *v* work, function; operate.

**och (nan och)!** *excl* alas! woe is me!

**ochd** *m/adj* eight.

**ochdad** *m* eighty.

**ochdamh** *adj* eighth.

**ochd-deug** *m/adj* eighteen.

**ochdnar** *m/f* eight (people).

**o chionn** *prep* ago; since; **o chionn ghoirid** recently; **o chionn fhada** long ago.

**ocsaidean** *m* oxygen.

**odhar** *adj* dun(-coloured); sallow.

**òg** *adj* young.

**ògan** *m* shoot, tendril.

**òganach** *m* young man; adolescent.

**ogha** *m* grandchild.

**Og-mhìos** *m* (*with art*) **an t-Og-mhìos** June.

**oibrich** *v same as* **obraich**.

**oibriche** *m* worker, workman.

**oide** *m* stepfather.

**oideachas** *m* education; learning.

**oidhche** *f* night; **oidhche mhath leat/leibh!** goodnight! **Oidhche Challainn** Hogmanay, New Year's Eve; **Oidhche Shamhna** Halloween.

**oidhirp** *f* attempt, try; effort.

**oifig** *f* same as **oifis**.

**oifigeach, oifigear** *m* officer; official.

**oifigeil** *adj* official.

**oifis, oifig** *f* office; position; **oifis a' phuist** post office; **Oifis na h-Alba** the Scottish Office.

**òige** *f* youth.

**òigear** *m* youngster, adolescent.

**òigh** *f* virgin; young woman.

**òigheil** *adj* virginal.

**oighre** *m* heir, inheritor.

**oighreachd** *f* (*land*) estate; inheritance.

**òigridh** *f* (*collective*) young people.

**oilbheum** *m* offence.

**oilbheumach** *adj* offensive.

**oileanach** *m* student.

**oileanaich** *v* train; instruct.

**oillt** *f* terror; horror.

**oillteil** *adj* frightful, dreadful; horrible.

**oilltich** *v* terrify.

**oilthigh** *m* university.

**òinseach** *f* fool, idiot.

**oir** *f* edge, margin; rim; **oir an rathaid** verge; **oir a' chabhsair** kerb.

**oir** *conj* for.

**oirbh** *prep pron* on you (*pl*).

**òirdheirc** *adj* magnificent; illustrious.

**òirleach** *m/f* inch.

**oirnn** *prep pron* on us.

**oirre** *prep pron* on her, on it (*f*).

**oirthir** *f* coast, seaboard.

**oisean, oisinn** *m* corner.

**oiteag** *f* breeze; breath of wind.

**òl** *v* drink.

**ola** *f* oil.

**olann** *f* wool.

**olc** *m* evil, wickedness. •▢*dj* evil, wicked.

**ollamh** *m* learned man; (*academic*) doctor.

**òmar** *m* amber.

**on a** *conj* since, as.

**onair** *f* honour; honesty; esteem. •▢*xcl* **air m'onair!** honestly!

**onorach** *adj* honourable; honest; honorary.

**onoraich** *v* honour.

**on taigh** *adv* out; away from home.

**opairèisean** *m* (*med*) operation.

**òr** *m* gold.

**òraid** *f* speech, address; lecture.

**òraidiche** *m* speaker.

**orainds, orains** *adj* orange.

**oraindsear, orainsear** *m* orange.

**òran** *m* song; **òrain luadhaidh** waulking songs; **na h-òrain**

**mhòra** the classic(al) songs.
**òr-chèard** *m* goldsmith.
**òrd** *m* hammer.
**òrdag** *f* thumb.
**òrdag-coise** *f* toe.
**òrdaich** *v* order, command; organise, tidy.
**òrdaighean** *mpl* (*with art*) **na h-òrdaighean** (*relig*) communion.
**òrdail** *adj* orderly; ordinal.
**òrdugh** *m* order, sequence; command.
**òrgan** *m* organ.
**orm** *prep pron* on me.
**orra** *prep pron* on them.
**òrraiseach** *adj* squeamish.
**ort** *prep pron* on you (*sing*).
**ortha** *f* spell, charm.
**osan** *m* stocking, hose.

**osann** *m* same as **osna**.
**os cionn** *prep* above, over.
**òsdair, òstair** *m* hotelier, landlord, licensee.
**o shean** *adv* of old, long ago.
**os ìosal** *adv* quietly; secretly.
**osna, osnadh** *m/f*, **osann** *m* sigh; breeze.
**osnaich** *v* sigh.
**ospadal** *m* hospital.
**ospag** *f* sigh; breath of wind.
**òstair** *m* same as **òsdair**.
**Ostair** *f* (*with art*) **an Ostair** Austria.
**Ostaireach** *m/adj* Austrian.
**othail** *f* hubbub, uproar.
**othaisg** *f* hogg, ewe-lamb.
**o thùs** *adv* originally.
**òtrach** *m* dunghill, midden.

# P

**paca** *m* pack.
**pacaid** *f* packet.
**pàganach** *m/adj* pagan, heathen.
**paidh** *m* pie.
**paidhir** *m/f* pair.
**paidir** *f* Lord's Prayer.
**paidirean** *m* rosary.
**pàigh** *v* pay (for); atone (for).
**pàigh, paigheadh** *m* pay, remuneration.
**pàileis** *f* palace.

**pàillean** *m* pavilion; large tent.
**pailt** *adj* plentiful.
**pailteas** *m* plenty.
**pàipear** *m* paper.
**pàipear-balla** *m* wallpaper.
**pàipear-gainmhich** *m* sandpaper.
**pàipear-naidheachd** *m* newspaper.
**pàirc** *f* field; park.
**paireafain** *m* paraffin.

**pàirt** *m* part.

**pàirt-càraidh** *m* spare, spare part.

**pàirtich** *v* share out; divide up.

**pàisde, pàiste** *m* baby; infant; small child.

**paisg** *v* wrap (up); fold (up).

**pàiste** *m same as* **pàisde**.

**pàiteach** *adj* thirsty.

**pana** *m* pan.

**pannal** *m* panel.

**Pàpa** *m* Pope.

**pàpanach** *m/adj* (*derog*) papist, popish.

**pàrant** *m* parent.

**pàrlamaid** *f* parliament.

**pàrlamaideach** *adj* parliamentary.

**parsail** *m* parcel, package.

**pàrtaidh** *m* party.

**partan** *m* (*edible*) crab.

**pasgadh** *m* packing.

**pasgan** *m* bundle; package.

**pastra** *f* pastry.

**pathadh** *m* thirst.

**pàtran** *m* pattern.

**peacach** *m* sinner. •*adj* sinful.

**peacadh** *m* sin.

**peacadh-bàis** *m* mortal sin.

**peacadh-gine** *m* original sin.

**peacaich** *v* sin.

**peanas** *m* punishment; penalty.

**peanasaich** *v* punish.

**peann** *m* pen.

**peansail** *m* pencil.

**peant** *v* paint.

**peanta** *m* paint.

**peantair** *m* painter.

**pearraid** *f* parrot.

**pearsa** *m* person; (*play, etc*) character.

**pearsanta** *adj* personal.

**pearsantachd** *f* personality.

**pears-eaglais** *m* clergyman.

**peasair** *f* pea.

**peata** *m* pet.

**peatroil, peatrol** *m* petrol.

**peighinn** *f* penny.

**peile** *m* pail.

**pèileag** *f* porpoise.

**peilear** *m* bullet; pellet.

**peile-frasaidh** *m* watering can.

**peinnsean** *m* pension.

**peirceall** *m* jaw, jawbone.

**pèist** *f* reptile.

**peitean** *m* vest; waistcoat.

**pèitseag** *f* peach.

**peur** *f* pear.

**pian** *v* pain, distress; torture. •*m* pain.

**piàna** *m* piano.

**pianail** *adj* painful.

**pic** *m* (*tool*) pick.

**picil** *f* pickle.

**pile** *f* pill.

**pìleat, piodhlead** *m* pilot.

**pillean** *m* cushion; pillion.

**pinc** *adj* pink.

**pinnt** *m* pint.

**pìob** *f* pipe; tube.

**pìobaire** *m* piper.

**pìobaireachd** *f* (bag-)piping; pibroch.

**piobar** *m* pepper.

**pìob mhòr** *f* Highland bagpipes.

**piobraich** *v* add pepper to; pep up.

**pìob-thombaca** *f* (tobacco) pipe.

**pìob-uilne** *f* uileann pipes.

**pioc** *v* peck; nibble.

**piodhlead** *m same as* **pìleat**.

**pìos** *m* piece, bit; packed lunch.

**piseach** *m* progress, improvement.

**piseag** *f* kitten.

**pit** *f* vulva.

**piuthar** *f* sister.

**piuthar-chèile** *f* sister-in-law.

**plaide** *f* blanket.

**plàigh** *f* plague; infestation; nuisance.

**plàigheil** *adj* pestilential.

**plana** *m* plan.

**planaid** *f* planet.

**planaig** *v* plan.

**plangaid** *f* blanket.

**plap** *v* flutter. •*☐t* fluttering.

**plaoisg** *v* shell; peel; skin.

**plaosg** *m* shell; peel; skin; husk.

**plàsd** *m* sticking plaster.

**plastaig** *f*/*adj* plastic.

**plathadh** *m* glance; glimpse; instant.

**pleadhag** *f* (*canoe, etc*) paddle.

**pleadhagaich** *v* paddle.

**plèana** *f* (aero)plane.

**ploc** *m* clod; turf; block; lump.

**ploc-prìne** *m* pinhead.

**plosg** *v* gasp, pant; palpitate,

throb. •*☐t* gasp; palpitation; throb.

**plub, plubraich** *m* splash, plop. •*☐* splash, plop, slosh.

**plucan** *m* pimple; (*sink, etc*) plug.

**pluic** *f* (plump) cheek.

**plumair** *m* plumber.

**Pluta** *m* Pluto.

**poball** *m* people.

**poballach, poblach** *adj* public.

**poballachd, poblachd** *f* republic.

**poca** *m* bag; sack.

**pòca** *m*, **pòcaid** *f* pocket.

**poca-cadail** *m* sleeping-bag.

**pòcaid** *see* **pòca**.

**pòg** *v* kiss. •*☐* kiss.

**poidsear** *m* poacher.

**poileas** *m same as* **polas**.

**poileasman** *m same as* **polasman**.

**poileataiceach** *adj* political.

**poileataics** *f* politics.

**poit** *f* pot.

**poit-dhubh** *f* (whisky) still.

**pòitear** *m* drinker, boozer.

**pòitearachd** *f* boozing, tippling.

**poit-fhlùran** *f* flowerpot.

**poit-mhùin** *f* chamberpot.

**poit-teatha** *f* teapot.

**pòla** *m* pole; **am Pòla a Tuath/a Deas** the North/South Pole.

**Pòlach** *m*/*adj* Pole; Polish.

**Pòlainn** *f* (*with art*) **a' Phòlainn** Poland.

**polas, poileas** *m* police; policeman.

**polasman, poileasman** m policeman.

**poll** m mud; bog.

**poll-mòna, poll-mònach** m peat bog.

**pònaidh** m pony.

**pònair** f bean(s); **pònair leath-ann** broad bean(s); **pònair Fhrangach** French bean(s).

**pong** m (mus) note.

**pongail** adj concise; punctual; punctilious.

**pòr** m seed; crops; growth.

**port**[1] m port, harbour; **port-ad-hair** airport.

**port**[2] m tune; **port a-beul** mouth music.

**Portagail** f (with art) **a' Phorta-gail** Portugal.

**Portagaileach** m/adj Portuguese.

**portair** m porter; doorman.

**pòs** v marry.

**pòsadh** m marriage.

**pòsda, pòsta** adj married; **pòs-da aig** married to; **nuadh-phòsda** newly married.

**post** m post, stake; post, mail; postman; **post-adhair** air mail.

**posta** m postman.

**pòsta** adj same as **pòsda**.

**post dealain** m electronic mail.

**prabar** m rabble, mob.

**prab-shùileach** adj bleary-eyed.

**prais** f cooking pot.

**pràis** f brass.

**pràiseach** adj brass.

**preantas** m apprentice.

**preas**[1] v crease; corrugate; crush.

**preas**[2] m bush, shrub.

**preas**[3], **preasa** m cupboard.

**preasach** adj wrinkly, wrinkled.

**preasadh** m wrinkle.

**preasag** f wrinkle, crease.

**preas-aodaich** m wardrobe.

**preas-leabhraichean** m book-case.

**prìne** m pin.

**prìne-banaltraim** m safety pin.

**priob** v wink; blink.

**priobadh** m wink; blink; instant.

**prìobhaideach** adj private.

**prìomh** adj main, head.

**prìomhaire** m prime minister.

**prionnsa** m prince.

**prionnsabal** m principle.

**prìosan** m prison.

**prìosanach** m prisoner.

**prìs** f price, cost.

**prìseil** adj precious; valuable.

**prògram** m programme; (comput) program.

**proifeasair** m professor.

**proifeiseanta** adj professional.

**pròis** f pride.

**pròiseict** f project.

**pròiseil** adj proud.

**pronn** v mash, pulverise; (fam) bash, beat up. •adj mashed, pulverised.

**pronnasg** m sulphur; brimstone.

**prosbaig** f binoculars; telescope.

**Pròstanach** m/adj Protestant.

**prothaid** *f (fin)* profit; gain, benefit.

**puball** *m* marquee.

**pùdar** *m* powder.

**pùdaraich** *v* powder.

**puing** *f* point (in scale, etc); *(orthog)* stop, mark; **stad-phuing** full stop; **clisg-phuing** exclamation mark; **dà-phuing** colon.

**puinnsean** *m* poison.

**puinnseanach** *adj* poisonous.

**puinnseanaich** *v* poison.

**pumpa** *m* pump.

**punnd** *m (weight and money)* pound; **punnd Eireannach** punt; **punnd Sasannach** pound sterling.

**purpaidh** *adj* purple.

**purpar, purpur** *m* purple.

**put**[1] *v* push, jostle.

**put**[2] *m* buoy.

**putan** *m* button.

# R

**rabaid** *f* rabbit.

**rabhadh** *m* warning; alarm.

**rabhd, ràbhart** *m* idle talk; obscene talk.

**ràc**[1] *v* rake.

**ràc**[2] *m* drake.

**racaid** *f (sports)* racket.

**ràcan** *m* rake.

**rach** *v* go.

**rach à bith** *v* cease to be.

**rach a cadal** *v* go to bed.

**rach à cuimhne** *v* be forgotten.

**rach a dhìth** *v* go short.

**rach air dìochuimhne** *v* be forgotten.

**rach air iomrall** *v* wander; go astray, err.

**rach air iteig** *v* fly.

**rach air muin** *v* have sex with; *(animals)* serve.

**rach air seachran** *v* wander; go astray.

**rach am fad** *v* get/grow longer.

**rach am feabhas** *v* improve, get better.

**rach am meud** *v* get bigger.

**rach an geall gu** *v* bet that.

**rach an laigse** *v* faint.

**rach an neul** *v* faint, pass out.

**rach an sàs an** *v* get involved in.

**rach an urras (air)** *v* guarantee, vouch (for).

**rach an urras gu** *v* guarantee that.

**rach à sealladh** *v* disappear, go out of sight.

**rach às mo chuimhne** *v* be forgetten.

**rach às mo leth** *v* side with me.

**rach bhuaithe** *v* deteriorate.

**rach car mu char** *v* roll over and over.

**rach fodha** *v* sink; (*firm, etc*) fail.

**rach 'na laighe** *v* lie down; go to bed.

**rach 'na lasair** *v* go up in flames.

**rach 'na shaighdear** *v* become a soldier.

**rach ri taobh X** *v* take after X.

**rach seachad (air)** *v* pass by, go past.

**rach thar a chèile** *v* fall out, quarrel.

**radan** *m* rat.

**ràdh** *m* saying, proverb.

**radharc** *m* eyesight; sight; view.

**rag** *adj* stiff; stubborn.

**ragaich** *v* stiffen.

**rag-mhuinealach** *adj* pig-headed.

**raidhfil** *f* rifle.

**raineach** *f* bracken, fern(s).

**ràinig** *past tense of v* **ruig**.

**ràith** *f* season; quarter (of year); while.

**ràitheachan** *m* (*magazine*) quarterly, periodical.

**ràmh** *m* oar.

**ràn** *v* roar, yell; weep. • *m* roar, yell; weeping.

**rann** *f* poetry; a verse.

**rannsaich** *v* search; rummage; research; ransack.

**raon** *m* field.

**raon-adhair** *m* airfield.

**raon-cluiche** *m* playing field.

**rapach** *adj* slovenly, scruffy.

**rathad** *m* road; way, route.

**rathad mòr** *m* main road.

**Ratharsach** *m/adj* from Raasay.

**Ratharsair** Raasay.

**rè** *f* time, period.

**rè** *prep* during, throughout.

**reachd** *m* rule; command; law.

**reamhar** *adj* fat.

**reamhraich** *v* fatten.

**reic** *v* sell. • *m* sale; selling.

**reiceadair** *m* vendor; salesman; auctioneer.

**rèidh** *adj* level; smooth; cleared; **rèidh ri** on good terms with.

**rèidhlean** *m* green.

**rèidio** *m* radio.

**rèile** *f* rail, railing.

**rèilig** *f* kirkyard.

**rèis** *f* (*sport, etc*) race.

**rèiseamaid** *f* regiment.

**rèite** *f* agreement; reconciliation; betrothal; atonement.

**rèiteach, rèiteachadh** *m* betrothal.

**rèitear** *m* referee.

**reithe** *m* tup, ram.

**rèitich** *v* reconcile; appease; arbitrate; settle; adjust.

**reòdh** *v* freeze.

**reòiteag** *f* ice cream.

**reòta** *adj* frozen.

**reòth** *v* same as **reòdh**.

**reothadair** *m* freezer, deep freeze.

**reothadh** *m* frost.

**reothairt** f spring-tide.

**reub** v tear; lacerate; mangle.

**reubadh** m rip, rent.

**reubalach** m rebel.

**reudan** m wood-louse.

**reul** f star.

**reuladair** m astronomer.

**reul-bhad** m constellation.

**reul-eòlas** m astronomy.

**reul-iùil** f pole star.

**reusan** m reason; sanity.

**reusanta** adj reasonable; sensible; fair.

**ri** prep to; against; during.

**riabhach** adj brindled; grizzled; drab; dun.

**riadh** (fin) interest.

**riaghail** v rule (over), govern; regulate; manage.

**riaghailt** f rule, regulation; system, order.

**riaghailteach** adj regular; systematical.

**riaghailteachd** f orderliness; regularity.

**riaghailtich** v regularise; regulate.

**riaghaltas** m government.

**riaghladair** m ruler, governor.

**riaghladh** m governing; administration; management.

**rian** m orderliness; system; reason; (mus) arrangement.

**rianadair** m (mus) arranger; computer.

**rianail** adj methodical.

**riaraich** v please; satisfy; distribute; (cards) deal.

**riatanach** adj essential.

**rib** v trap, ensnare.

**ribe** f trap, snare.

**ribean-tomhais** m tape measure.

**ribh** prep pron to you (pl).

**ribheid** f (mus) reed.

**rìbhinn** f (songs) maiden, girl.

**ridhil** m (dance) reel; **ridhil-och-dnar** eightsome reel.

**ridire** m knight.

**rìgh** m king.

**Rìgh nan Dùl** m Lord of the Universe, God.

**righinn** adj (material, etc) tough.

**rim bheò** adv all my life; in my lifetime.

**rinn**[1] past tense of v **dèan**.

**rinn**[2] m point, promontory.

**rinn**[3] prep pron to us.

**rioban** m ribbon.

**riochd** m likeness, form; appearance.

**riochdaich** v represent; portray; impersonate.

**riochdair** m (gram) pronoun.

**riochdaire** m representative.

**rìoghachadh** m reign; reigning.

**rìoghachd** f kingdom.

**rìoghaich** v reign.

**rìoghail** adj royal; kingly, regal.

**rìomhach** adj beautiful; splendid.

**rionnach** m mackerel.

**rionnag** f star.

**ris**[1] prep pron to him, to it (m).

**ris²** *adv* showing, exposed.

**ris a' bhruthaich** *adv* against the slope.

**ris a' ghaoith** *adv* against the wind.

**ris an t-sruth** *adv* against the current.

**ri taobh** *prep* beside, alongside.

**ri taobh a chèile** *adv* abreast.

**ri teachd** *adv* future, to come.

**rithe** *prep pron* to her, to it (*f*).

**ri tìde** *adv* in time, eventually.

**ri uchd bàis** *adv* at the point of death.

**rium** *prep pron* to me.

**riut** *prep pron* to you (*sing*).

**riutha** *prep pron* to them.

**ro** *prep* (*time and space*) before; in front of.

**ro** *adv* too; very, extremely.

**ro-** *prefix* fore-, pre-.

**robach** *adj* hairy, shaggy; slovenly.

**robh** *past tense, neg and interrog, of v* **bith**.

**roc** *f* wrinkle.

**rocaid** *f* rocket.

**ròcail** *f* croak(ing), caw(ing).

**ròcais** *f* rook.

**ro-chraiceann** *m* foreskin.

**roghainn** *m* choice; preference.

**roghnaich** *v* choose.

**roilig** *v* roll.

**roimhe** *prep pron* before him, before it (*m*).

**roimhe** *adv* before.

**roimhear** *m* preposition.

**roimh-innleachd** *f* strategy.

**roimhpe** *prep pron* before her, before it (*f*).

**ròineag** *f* (*single*) hair.

**roinn** *v* divide (up); distribute; (*cards*) deal; (*arith*) divide.

**roinn** *f* division; share; department; (*govt*) region; continent.

**ròisd** *v* roast; fry.

**ro làimh** *adv* beforehand.

**ròlaist** *m* romance, romantic novel.

**ro-leasachan** *m* (*gram*) prefix.

**ròmach** *adj* woolly, hairy, shaggy; bearded.

**Romàinia** *f* Romania.

**Romàinianach** *m/adj* Romanian.

**romhad** *prep pron* before you (*sing*).

**romhaibh** *prep pron* before you (*pl*).

**romhainn** *prep pron* before us.

**romham** *prep pron* before me.

**romhpa** *prep pron* before them.

**ròn** *m* (*animal*) seal.

**rong¹** *f* rung; spar; hoop.

**rong²** *m* vital spark.

**ron mhithich** *adv* premature(ly).

**ronn** *m* mucus, phlegm.

**ro-nochd** *v* overexpose.

**ro-òrdachadh** *m* predestination.

**ro-òrdaich** *v* predestine, predetermine.

**ròpa** *m* rope.

**ròp-aodaich** *m* clothes-line.

**ro-ràdh** *m* foreword, preamble.

**ròs** *m* rose.

**ròsda** *adj* roast(ed); fried.

**rosg**[1] *m* eyelash.

**rosg**[2] *m* prose.

**rosg-rann** *f* sentence.

**ròst** *v same as* **ròisd**.

**ròsta** *adj same as* **ròsda**.

**roth** *m/f* wheel.

**rothach** *adj* wheeled.

**rothar** *m* bicycle.

**ro-throm** *adj* overweight.

**ruadh** *adj* red; red-haired, ginger.

**ruaig** *v* chase; put to flight, (*milit*) rout. • *f* chase, pursuit; flight; rout; hunt.

**ruamhair** *v* dig; rummage.

**rubair** *m* rubber.

**rubha** *m* point, promontory.

**rùchd** *v* grunt; belch; retch. • *m* grunt; belch; retching.

**rud** *m* thing; fact.

**rùda** *m* ram, tup.

**rudail** *adj* concrete, actual, real.

**rùdan** *m* knuckle, finger-joint.

**rudbeag** *adv* a bit, somewhat.

**rudeigin** *pron* something, anything. • *adv* somewhat.

**rudhadh** *m* blush(ing), flush(ing).

**rud sam bith** *m* anything at all.

**rug** *past tense of v* **beir**.

**rugadh mi** *v* I was born.

**ruidhle** *m same as* **ridhil**.

**ruig** *v* arrive (at), reach.

**ruig air** *v* reach for; take, seize;.

**ruighe** *m/f* forearm; hillslope.

**rùilear** *m* (*measuring*) rule, ruler.

**Ruis** *f* (*with art*) **an Ruis** Russia.

**ruisean** *m* (*with art*) **an ruisean** the midday meal.

**Ruiseanach** *m/adj* Russian.

**rùisg** *v* bare, strip; shear, fleece; peel; chafe.

**rùisgte** *adj* stripped; shorn; peeled.

**Ruisia** *f* Russia'.

**ruiteach** *adj* ruddy; blushing, flushed.

**ruith** *v* run; flow; chase. • *f* run, running; pursuit; rout; rate, pace.

**rùm** *m* room; space.

**Rumach** *m/adj* from Rum.

**rùm-bidhe** *m* dining-room.

**rùm ionnlaid** *m* bathroom.

**rùn** *m* secret; love, affection; wish, purpose; ambition.

**rùnaich** *v* wish, desire; resolve.

**rùnaire** *m* secretary; **Rùnaire na Stàite** the Secretary of State.

**rùraich** *v* rummage, grope; explore.

**rus** *m* rice.

**rùsg** *m* fleece; peel, skin, husk; (*tree*) bark.

# S

**'s** (*for* **agus, is**) *conj* and.

**-sa** *suffix* this.

**sabaid** *v* fight, scrap, brawl. • *f* fight(ing), scrap(ping), brawl-(ing).

**sàbaid** *f* sabbath.

**sàbh** *v* saw. • *m* saw.

**sàbhail** *v* save, rescue; economise.

**sàbhailte** *adj* safe.

**sabhal** *m* barn.

**sàbhaladh** *m* rescuing; (*relig*) salvation; savings.

**sabhs** *m* sauce.

**sac** *m* sack.

**sad** *v* throw, toss, chuck.

**sagart** *m* priest.

**saibhear** *m* culvert; sewer.

**saideal** *m* satellite.

**saidhbhir** *adj* wealthy, affluent.

**saidhbhreas** *m* wealth, affluence.

**saighdear** *m* soldier.

**saighead** *f* arrow.

**saidheans** *m* science.

**sail** *f* beam, joist.

**sàil** *f* heel.

**sailead** *m* salad.

**saill**[1] *v* salt; season (*with salt*).

**saill**[2] *f* fat, grease.

**saillear** *f* salt-cellar.

**saillte** *adj* salt, salted; salty.

**saimeant** *m* concrete, cement.

**sal** *m* filth; dross; stain.

**sàl** *m* salt water, brine; (*with art*) **an sàl** (*songs, etc*) the sea, the briny.

**salach** *adj* dirty, filthy; foul.

**salaich** *v* dirty, soil; defile, sully.

**salann** *m* salt.

**salchar** *m* dirt, filth.

**salm** *m/f* psalm.

**saltair** *v* tread, trample.

**sàmhach** *adj* quiet, peaceful, tranquil; silent.

**samhail** *m* likeness; match; the like(s) of.

**Samhain** *f* Hallowtide; All Saints'/Souls' Day; **Oidhche Shamhna** *f* Halloween; (*with art*) **an t-Samhainn** November.

**sàmhchair** *f* quiet(ness), tranquility; silence.

**samhla, samhladh** *m* resemblance; sign; (*lit*) symbol, simile, comparison, allegory; parable.

**samhlaich (ri)** *v* resemble; compare, liken (to).

**samhradh** *m* summer.

**sanas** *m* announcement; notice; hint.

**sanas-reic** *m* advertisement.

**san fharsaingeachd** *adv* generally, broadly speaking.

**san fhradharc** *adv* in sight.

**sannt** *m* avarice, covetousness.

**sanntach** *adj* greedy, avaricious.

**sanntaich** *v* covet.

**saobh** *adj* foolish, wrong-headed.

**saobhaidh** *f* den, lair.

**saobh-chràbhadh** *m* superstition.

**saobh-shruth** *m* eddy, counter-current.

**saobh-smuain** *m* whim.

**saoghal** *m* world; life; lifetime.

**saoghalta** *adj* wordly; materialistic.

**saoil** *v* think, believe; suppose.

**saor**[1] *v* free; (*relig*) save, redeem.
• *adj* free (of charge); cheap; free, at liberty.

**saor**[2] *m* joiner, carpenter.

**saoradh** *m* liberation; absolution; salvation.

**saor-àirneis** *m* cabinet maker.

**saor-làithean** *mpl* holiday(s).

**saor o** *adv* free from, untroubled by.

**saorsa** *f* freedom; (*relig*) redemption.

**saor 's an asgaidh** *adv* free of charge.

**saor-thoileach** *adj* voluntary.

**saothair** *f* labour, toil.

**saothraich** *v* labour, toil.

**sàr** *adv* very, extremely; through and through.

**sàraich** *v* oppress; distress; vex; weary.

**sàr-mhath** *adj* excellent.

**sàr obair** *f* masterpiece.

**sàsaich** *v* content, satisfy; satiate.

**sàsaichte** *adj* contented, satisfied; sated.

**Sasainn** *f* England.

**Sasannach** *m/adj* Englishman; English.

**sàsar** *m* saucer.

**sàth** *v* stab; push, shove.

**seabhag** *f* hawk, falcon.

**seacaid** *f* jacket.

**seac àraidh** *adv* especially, particularly.

**seach**[1] *prep* instead of; rather than; in comparison to.

**seach**[2] *adv/prep* past, by.

**seachad**[1] *adj* over, finished; (*space and time*) past.

**seachad**[2] *adv* past, by.

**seachad air** *prep* past, by.

**seachain, seachainn** *v* avoid; shun, abstain from.

**seachanta** *adj* avoidable.

**seachd** *n/adj* seven.

**seachdad** *m* seventy.

**seachdain** *f* week.

**seachdamh** *adj* seventh.

**seachdnar** *m/f* (*people*) seven.

**seachran** *m* wandering; going astray.

**seac searbh sgìth (de)** sick and tired (of).

**seada** *m/f* shed.

**seadag** *f* grapefruit.

**seadh** *adv* (*non-affirmative*) yes, uh-uh.

**seagal** *m* rye.

**seagh** *m* sense, meaning.

**seàla** *f* shawl.

**sealbh** *m* luck; fortune, providence; heaven. • *excl* **sealbh ort!** good luck! **aig Sealbh tha brath** Heaven knows.

**sealbh** *f* property; possession.

**sealbhach** *adj* lucky; possessive.

**sealbhadair** *m* owner, proprietor.

**sealbhaich** *v* own, possess.

**sealg** *v* hunt.

**sealg** *f* hunt, hunting.

**sealgair** *m* hunter, huntsman; **an Sealgair Mòr** Orion.

**seall** *v* see; look; show; watch over.

**seall air** *v* look at.

**sealladh** *m* sight; view, prospect; eyesight; look; **an dà shealladh** second sight.

**sealladh-taoibh** *m* sideways look/glance.

**Sealtainn** *m* Shetland.

**Sealtainneach** *m/adj* Shetlander; from Shetland.

**seamrag** *f* shamrock; clover.

**sean** *adj* old; former.

**seana-ghille** *m* old batchelor.

**seanair** *m* grandfather; ancestor, forebear.

**seanalair** *m* general.

**seana-mhaighdeann** *f* old maid.

**seanchaidh** *m* shenachie, tradition-bearer; story-teller.

**seanchas** *m* traditional lore; chat, gossip; news.

**seanfhacal** *m* proverb, saying, adage.

**sean-fhasanta** *adj* old-fashioned.

**sean-fhleasgach** *m* old bachelor.

**seang** *adj* thin; slim; lank, skinny.

**seangan** *m* ant.

**seanmhair** *m* grandmother.

**seann** *adj* same as **sean**.

**seann-phàrant** *m* grandparent.

**sean-seanair** *m* great grandfather.

**sean-sheanmhair** *f* great grandmother.

**seantans** *m* (*gram*) sentence.

**Seapan** *f* (*with art*) **an t-Seapan** Japan.

**Seapanach** *m/adj* Japanese.

**sear** *adj/adv* east, eastern.

**sear air** *adv* east of.

**searbh** *adj* bitter; sour, acrid; pungent; harsh; disagreeable; sharp, sarcastic.

**searbhadair** *m* towel.

**searbhanta** *m/f* servant, maid.

**searg** *v* wither, shrivel, dry up; fade away; pine away; blight.

**seargach** *adj* (*tree*) deciduous.

**searmon** *f* sermon.

**searmonaich** *v* preach.

**searrach** *m* colt, foal.

**searrag** *f* flask; bottle.

**seas** *v* stand (up); stand by; support; last.

**seasamh** *m* standing position; **'na sheasamh** standing (up).

**seasamh-chas** *m* footing.

**seasg** *adj* barren, sterile; (*cattle, etc*) dry.

**seasgad** *m* sixty.

**seasgair** *adj* cosy, snug; comfortably off.

**seasmhach** *adj* firm, stable; reliable; enduring; durable.

**seathar** *m* chair.

**seathar-tulgaidh** *m* rocking-chair.

**seatlair** *m* settler.

**seic** *f* cheque.

**Seic** *f* (*with art*) **an t-Seic** the Czech Republic.

**Seiceach** *m/adj* Czech.

**seiche** *f* skin, pelt, hide.

**seic-leabhar** *m* chequebook.

**sèid** *v* blow; swell, puff up.

**seilbh, seilbheach, seilbheadair, seilbhich** *same as* **sealbh, sealbhach, sealbhadair, sealbhaich**.

**seilcheag** *f* snail; slug.

**seile** *m* saliva, spittle.

**seileach** *m* willow.

**seillean** *m* bee.

**seillean mòr** *m* bumble-bee.

**sèimh** *adj* calm, mild, gentle.

**sèimhe** *f* calm(ness), mildness, gentleness.

**seinn** *v* sing; (*instrument, etc*) play, sound.

**seinn** *m* singing; sounding.

**seinneadair** *m* singer.

**seirbheis** *f* service; favour.

**seirbheiseach** *m* servant.

**seirc** *f* love, affection; (Christian) charity.

**seirm** *v* ring (out), sound.

**sèisd** *m/f* siege.

**seis, seise** *m* like(s) of; equal, match.

**seisean** *m* (*meeting, etc*) session; kirk session.

**sèist** *m/f* refrain, chorus.

**seo** *adj/pron* this.

**seòbhrach** *f* primrose.

**seòclaid** *f* chocolate.

**seòd** *m* hero.

**seòl** *v* sail; steer; navigate; guide, direct; manage; govern. • *m* sail; course; method; means.

**seòladair** *m* sailor, seaman.

**seòladh** *m* sailing; (*house, etc*) address.

**seòl-beatha** *m* way of life.

**seòl-mara** *m* (high) tide.

**seòlta** *adj* cunning; resourceful; shrewd.

**seòmar** *m* room.

**seòmar-cadail** *m* bedroom.

**seòmar-ionnlaid** *m* bathroom.

**seòmar-leapa** *m* bedroom.

**seòmar-mullaich** *m* attic.

**seòrsa** *m* sort, kind; genus, species; class.

**seòrsaich** *v* classify; sort.

**seud** *m* jewel, gem.

**seumarlan** *m* factor, land-agent; chamberlain.

**seun** *m* spell; charm, amulet.

**seunta** *adj* enchanted, spellbound.

**'s e ur beatha!** *excl* you're welcome!

**sgadan** *m* herring.

**sgàil** *v* shade, darken, eclipse; veil, mask. • *f* shade, shadow; covering; (*occas*) ghost, spectre.

**sgailc** *v* slap, smack. • *f* slap, sharp blow; sharp sound; (*liquid*) swig; baldness.

**sgàilc** *n* same as **sgàil**.

**sgàilean-grèine** *m* parasol.

**sgàilean-uisge** *m* umbrella.

**sgàil-lampa** *f* lampshade.

**sgàil-sùla** *f* eyelid.

**sgàin** *v* burst, crack, split.

**sgàineadh** *m* split, crack.

**sgàird** *f* (*with art*) **an sgàird** diarrhoea.

**sgairt**[1] *f* diaphragm.

**sgairt**[2] *f* yell; gusto; vigour, activity.

**sgairteil** *adj* brisk; active, bustling; enthusiastic; (*weather*) blustery.

**sgait** *f* (*fish*) skate.

**sgal** *v* yell, squeal. • *m* yell; outburst; squall.

**sgàl** *m* tray.

**sgàla** *f* (*mus*) scale.

**sgalag** *f* farm servant; skivvy.

**sgalanta** *adj* shrill.

**sgall** *m* baldness; bald patch.

**sgallach** *adj* bald-headed.

**Sgalpach** *m/adj* from Scalpay.

**Sgalpaigh** *n* Scalpay.

**sgamhan** *m* lung.

**sgaoil** *v* spread (out); stretch out; disperse; release.

**sgaoth** *m* mass, multitude, swarm.

**sgaothaich** *v* (*crowds, etc*) flock, mass, swarm.

**sgap** *v* scatter.

**sgar** *v* separate; sever.

**sgaradh** *m* separation.

**sgaradh-pòsaidh** *m* divorce, separation.

**sgarbh** *m* cormorant.

**sgarbh an sgumain** *m* (*bird*) shag.

**sgarfa** *m* scarf.

**sgàrlaid** *f/adj* scarlet.

**sgath** *v* cut off; prune.

**sgàth** *m* shadow; protection; fear.

**sgàthan** *m* mirror.

**sgeadaich** *v* adorn, embellish; dress up; (*lamp, fire, etc*) attend to, trim.

**sgealb** *v* split; shatter; chip; carve. • *f* chip; splinter, fragment.

**sgealbag** *f* index finger.

**sgealp** *f* slap, smack; sharp sound.

**sgeap** *f* beehive.

**sgeilb** *f* chisel.

**sgeileid** *f* skillet.

**sgeilp** *f* shelf.

**sgeir** *f* rock, skerry.

**sgeith** *v* vomit, throw up.

**sgeul** *m* story; (*of person*) news, sign.

**sgeulach** *adj* like a story; fond of stories.

**sgeulachd** *f* story.

**sgeulachd ghoirid** *f* short story.

**sgeulaiche** *m* storyteller.

**sgeumhach** *adj* beautiful.

**sgeumhaich** *v* beautify; adorn, ornament.

**sgeunach** *adj* timid, shy; skittish, mettlesome.

**sgi, sgith** *f* ski.

**sgiamh** *v* squeal, shriek. • *m* squeal, shriek.

**sgian** *f* knife.

**sgiath** *f* wing; shield; shelter.

**sgiathaich** *v* fly.

**Sgiathanach, Sgitheanach** *m/adj* from Skye. • *m* **an t-Eilean Sgitheanach** (the Isle of) Skye.

**sgil** *m* skill.

**sgileil** *adj* skilled; skilful.

**sgillin** *f* penny.

**sgillinn ruadh** *f* brass farthing.

**sgioba** *m/f* crew; team.

**sgiobair** *m* skipper, captain.

**sgiobalta** *adj* neat, tidy; quick, active; handy.

**sgioblaich** *v* tidy; put right/ straight.

**sgiorradh** *m* accident; stumble, slip.

**sgiort** *f* skirt.

**sgìos** *f* tiredness; weariness.

**sgìre** *f* (*local govt*) district; area, locality; parish.

**sgìreachd** *f* parish.

**sgith** *f same as* **sgi**.

**sgìth** *adj* tired; weary.

**sgitheach** *m* whitethorn, hawthorn.

**Sgitheanach** *m/adj same as* **Sgiathanach**.

**sgìtheil** *adj* tiring; wearisome.

**sgìthich** *v* tire; weary.

**sgithich** *v* ski.

**sgìths** *adj same as* **sgìos**.

**sgiùrs** *v* whip, scourge.

**sgiùrsair** *m* whip, scourge.

**sglàib** *f* (*building, etc*) plaster.

**sglàibeadair** *m* plasterer.

**sglèat** *m* slate.

**sglèatair** *m* slater.

**sgleog** *f* slap.

**sgob** *v* snatch; sting; peck; sprain.

**sgoil** *f* school; schooling.

**sgoil-àraich** *f* nursery school.

**sgoilear** *m* pupil; scholar.

**sgoilearachd** *f* scholarship; bursary.

**sgoilt, sgolt** *v* split, cleave; slit.

**sgoinneil** *adj* (*fam*) great, smashing.

**sgol** *v* rinse.

**sgolt** *see* **sgoilt**.

**sgoltadh** *m* split, cleft; chink; slit.

**sgona** *f* scone.

**sgonn** *m* lump, hunk.

**sgòr** *m* (*games, etc*) score.

**sgòrnan** *m* throat; gullet, windpipe.

**sgoth** *f* skiff, sailing boat.

**sgòth** *f* cloud.

**sgòthach** *adj* cloudy.

**sgoth long** *f* yacht.

**sgraing** *f* frown, scowl.

**sgreab** *f* scab.

**sgread** *v* scream, shriek. • *m* scream, shriek.

**sgreadhail** *f* trowel.

**sgreamh** *m* loathing, disgust.

**sgreamhail** *adj* loathsome, disgusting.

**sgreataidh** *adj* loathsome, nauseating.

**sgreuch** *v* scream, screech. • *m* scream, screech.

**sgrìob** *v* scratch, scrape; furrow. •⚏ scratch, scrape; furrow; trip, jaunt.

**sgrìobach** *adj* abrasive.

**sgrìoban** *m* hoe.

**sgrìobh** *v* write.

**sgrìobhadair** *m* writer.

**sgrìobhadh** *m* writing; handwriting.

**sgrìobhaiche** *m* writer.

**sgriobtar** *m* scripture.

**sgrios** *v* destroy; ruin. • *m* destruction; ruin.

**sgriosail** *adj* destructive; pernicious; (*fam*) terrible, dreadful.

**sgriubha** *f* screw.

**sgriubhaire** *m* screwdriver.

**sgròb** *v* scratch; cross out.

**sgrùd** *v* scrutinize; investigate; research; audit.

**sgrùdadh** *m* scrutiny; investigation; research; audit.

**sguab**[1] *v* sweep, brush. • *f* brush, broom.

**sguab**[2] *f* sheaf of corn.

**sguabadair** *m* hoover, vacuum-cleaner.

**sguab fhliuch** *f* mop.

**sgud** *v* chop.

**sgudal** *m* rubbish, refuse; nonsense.

**sguir** *v* stop, cease; desist.

**sguir de** *v* give up, stop.

**sgur** *m* stopping, ceasing.

**sgùrr** *m* peak, pinnacle.

**shìos** *adv* down; below.

**shìos bhuam** *adv* below me, down from me.

**shuas** *adv* up; above.

**shuas bhuam** *adv* above me, up from me.

**sia** *n/adj* six.

**siab** *v* wipe, rub; (*snow*) drift.

**siabann** *m* soap.

**siach** *v* sprain, strain.

**sia-deug** *m/adj* sixteen.

**sian**[1] *f* storm; (*wind*) blast; *pl* (*with art*) **na siantan** the elements.

**sian**[2] *m* thing; anything, (*with neg v*) nothing.

**sianar** *m/f* (*people*) six.

**siar** *adj/adv* west, western. • **na h-Eileanan Siar** *mpl* the Western Isles; **an Cuan Siar** *m* the Atlantic Ocean; **an taobh siar** *m* the west.

**siar air** *prep* west of.

**sibh** *pers pron pl* you.

**sìde** *f* weather; **sìde nan seachd sian** appalling weather.

**sil** *v* (*liquids*) drip, drop, flow, rain.

**silidh** *m* jam; jelly.

**silteach** *adj* (*liquids*) dripping, dropping, flowing.

**similear** *m* chimney.

**simplidh** *adj* simple, uncomplicated; simple-minded.

**sin** *adj* that; those. • *pron* that.

**sìn** *v* stretch, extend; pass, hand.

**sinc** *m* zinc.

**since** *f* (*kitchen*) sink.

**sine** *f* nipple, teat.

**sineach** *adj* mammal.

**sìneadh** *m* stretching; recumbent position. • **'na shìneadh** *adv* stretched out, lying down.

**singilte** *adj* single; (*gram*) singular.

**sinn** *pron* we.

**sinn-seanair** *m* great-grandfather.

**sinn-seanmhair** *f* great-grandmother.

**sinnsear** *m* ancestor, forefather.

**sinn-sinn-seanair** *m* great-great-grandfather.

**sinn-sinn-seanmhair** *f* great-great-grandmother.

**sìnteag** *f* hop; stride.

**sin thu!, sin thu-fhèin!** *excl* well done! good for you!

**siobhag** *f* wick.

**sìobhalta** *adj* civil, polite.

**sìobhaltair** *m* civilian.

**sìochail** *adj* peaceful.

**sìoda** *m* silk.

**sìol** *m* seed; race; progeny.

**sìolachan** *m* strainer, filter.

**sìolaidh** *v* subside, settle; filter, strain.

**sìol-cuir** *m* seed corn.

**sìol-ghinidh** *m* semen.

**sìoman** *m* straw rope.

**sìon** *m* same as **sian**².

**Sìona** *f* China.

**Sìonach** *m/adj* Chinaman; Chinese.

**sionnach** *m* fox.

**sionnsar** *m* (*bagpipe*) chanter.

**sìor-** *prefix* ever-.

**sìor-mhaireannach** *adj* everlasting; immortal.

**siorrachd** *f* sheriffdom; county, shire.

**siorraidh** *m* sheriff.

**sìorraidh** *adj* everlasting, eternal.

**sìorraidheachd** *f* eternity.

**siorram** *m* same as **siorraidh**.

**siorramachd** *f* same as **siorrachd**.

**sìor-uaine** *adj* evergreen.

**sìos** *adv* down.

**siosar** *f* scissors.

**siosarnaich** *f* hissing; whispering; rustling.

**sìos 'na inntinn** *adv* depressed.

**sir** *v* seek, search for; require.

**siris, sirist** *f* cherry.

**siteag** f dunghill, midden.

**sìth**[1] f peace; tranquility.

**sìth**[2] adj fairy.

**sithean** m fairy hill.

**sitheann** f venison; game.

**sìtheil** adj peaceable; tranquil.

**sìthich** v pacify.

**sìthiche** m fairy.

**sitir** f braying, neighing, whinny-ing.

**siubhail** v travel; seek; die.

**siubhal** f travel.

**siùbhlach** adj speedy; fluent; flu-id.

**siùcar** m sugar; pl **siùcairean** sweets.

**siud** pron that, yonder.

**siuga** f jug.

**siuthad** (sing), **siuthadaibh** (pl) imper on you go! get on with it!

**slabhraidh** f chain.

**slac** v thrash, beat, thump; bruise, maul.

**slàinte** f health. • excls **slàinte!** cheers! good health! **slàinte mhath/mhòr!** good health! **air do dheagh shlàinte!** your very good health!

**slaman** m curds, crowdie.

**slàn** adj well, healthy; complete. •excl **slàn leat!** goodbye! fare-well!

**slànaich** v heal, cure; get better.

**slànaighear** m (with art) **an Slànaighear** the Saviour.

**slàn is fallain** safe and sound.

**slaod** v drag, haul. • m sledge.

**slaodach** adj slow; long-drawn-out, boring.

**slaodair** m trailer.

**slaod-uisge** m raft.

**slaoightear** m rascal, rogue.

**slapag** f slipper.

**slat** f (length) yard; twig; rod; (vulg) penis, cock; spear, javelin.

**slat-iasgaich** m fishing rod.

**slat-rìoghail** f sceptre.

**slat-thomhais** f yardstick.

**sleamhainn** adj slippy, slippery.

**sleamhnag** f (children's) slide.

**sleamhnaich** v slip, slide.

**sleuchd** v bow down; prostate oneself.

**sliabh** m moor, moorland; hill.

**sliasaid** f thigh.

**slige** f (mollusc, military) shell.

**slighe** f path, road, track; way, route.

**slinnean** m shoulder.

**slìob** v stroke.

**sliochd** m descendants, lineage.

**slios** m side, flank.

**slis** f slice.

**sliseag-èisg** f fish slice.

**slisnich** v slice.

**sloc, slochd** m hollow; pit.

**sloinneadh** m surname, family name.

**sluagh** m people, populace; crowd; army.

**sluagh-ghairm** m war-cry; slo-gan.

**sluaghmhor** *adj* populous.

**sluasaid** *f* shovel.

**slugadh** *m* swallow, gulp; swallowing.

**sluig** *v* swallow; devour.

**smachd** *m* authority, discipline; control; rule.

**smachdail** *adj* commanding, authoritative.

**smàil, smàl** *v* (*fire*) put out; quench.

**smal** *m* spot, stain.

**smàl** *v same as* **smàil**.

**smàladair** *m* candle snuffers.

**smàladh** *m* extinguishing.

**smalan** *m* gloom, melancholy.

**smalanach** *adj* gloomy, melancholy.

**smaoin** *f* thought, notion, idea.

**smaoinich, smaointich** *v* think, reflect; consider.

**smàrag** *f* emerald.

**'s mar sin air adhart** and so on.

**smèid (air)** *v* beckon (to); wave (to).

**smeòrach** *f* thrush.

**smeur**[1] *v* smear, daub; grease.

**smeur**[2] *f* blackberry, bramble.

**smid** *f* (*with neg v*) word, syllable.

**smig, smiogaid** *m* chin.

**smior** *m* marrow; courage, spirit, guts; manliness, strength, vigour; best/pick of.

**smiorail** *adj* strong; spirited; plucky; manly, vigorous.

**smiùr** *v same as* **smeur**[1].

**smoc** *v* (*tobacco*) smoke.

**smocadh** *m* smoking; **chan fhaodar smocadh** no smoking.

**smuain** *f same as* **smaoin**.

**smuainich, smuaintich** *v same as* **smaoinich**.

**smuais** *v* smash, splinter.

**smugaid** *f* spit.

**smùid** *v* smoke; smash. • *f* smoke, steam, vapour, fumes; drunkenness.

**smùr** *m* dust; dross.

**snagan-daraich** *m* woodpecker.

**snaidhm** *m* knot.

**snàig** *v* crawl, creep; grovel.

**snaigh** *v* hew; carve.

**snàmh** *v* swim; float. • *m* swimming, floating.

**snasail, snasmhor** *adj* neat, trim; elegant.

**snàth** *m* (*coll*) thread.

**snàthad** *m* needle.

**snàthainn** *m* (*single*) thread.

**sneachd** *m* snow.

**snèap** *f* turnip, swede.

**snigh** *v* drip, seep.

**snìomh** *v* spin; twist; wring.

**snìomhaire** *m* (*tool*) drill.

**snodha-gàire** *m* smile.

**snog** *adj* pretty; nice.

**snuadh** *m* appearance; complexion.

**so-** *prefix* -able, -ible.

**sòbair** *adj* sober.

**sòbhrach** *f same as* **seòbhrach**.

**socair** *adj* mild; tranquil, relaxed;

at peace. • *f* comfort; ease, leisure. •*excl* **socair!** take it easy!

**socais** *f* sock.

**sochar** *f* bashfulness; weakness, compliance; indulgence.

**socharach** *adj* bashful; weak; soft, over-indulgent.

**socrach** *adj* at ease; sedate, leisurely.

**socraich** *v* abate; assuage; settle; set, fix.

**sodal** *m* adulation; fawning, flattery.

**so-dhèanta** *adj* possible, feasible.

**sòfa** *f* sofa.

**soilire** *m* celery.

**soilleir** *adj* bright, clear; obvious.

**soilleirich** *v* brighten (up); clarify, explain.

**soillse** *m* light.

**soillsich** *v* shine; gleam.

**soirbh** *adj* easy.

**soirbheachail** *adj* successful; prosperous.

**soirbhich le** *v* turn out well for.

**sòisealach** *adj* socialist.

**sòisealta** *adj* social. • *fpl* **seirbhisean shòisealta** social services.

**soisgeul** *m* gospel.

**soisgeulach** *adj* evangelical.

**soisgeulaiche** *m* evangelist.

**soitheach** *m* (*sailing*) vessel; dish, container.

**soitheamh** *adj* gentle, good-natured.

**sòlaimte** *adj* solemn; ceremonious.

**solair** *v* supply, purvey.

**solas** *m* light.

**sòlas** *m* solace, consolation; joy.

**sòlasach** *adj* comforting, consoling; joyful.

**solta** *adj* meek, gentle.

**so-lùbadh** *adj* flexible, pliable.

**sona** *adj* happy, content.

**sònraich** *v* distinguish; specify, single out.

**sònraichte** *adj* special, particular; specific.

**sop** *m* wisp.

**soraidh** *f* farewell; greeting. •*excl* **soraidh leat!** farewell!

**so-ruighinn** *adj* attainable; accessible.

**so-thuigsinn** *adj* intelligible, comprehensible.

**spàid** *f* spade.

**spaideil** *adj* (*esp dress*) smart.

**spaidirich** *v* strut.

**spàin** *f* spoon.

**spàin-mìlsein** *f* dessert spoon.

**Spainn** *f* (*with art*) **an Spàinn** Spain.

**Spàinneach, Spàinnteach** *m/adj* Spaniard; Spanish.

**Spàinnis** *f* (*language*) Spanish.

**spàirn** *f* exertion, effort; struggle.

**spanair** *m* spanner.

**spàrr**[1] *v* drive, thrust.

**spàrr**[2] *m* joist, beam; roost.

**speach** *f* wasp.

**speal** *f* scythe.

**spealg** *v* smash, splinter. • *f* splinter, fragment.

**spèil** *v* skate. • *f* ice-skate.

**spèis** *f* love; affection; regard.

**speuclairean** *mpl* spectacles, glasses.

**speuclairean-grèine** *mpl* sunglasses.

**speur** *m* sky; space; *pl* **na speuran** the heavens.

**speur-sheòladh** *m* space travel.

**speuradair** *m* astrologer.

**speuradaireachd** *f* astrology.

**speurair** *m* spaceman, astronaut.

**spìc** *f* spike.

**spideag** *f* nightingale.

**spìocach** *adj* miserly, mean.

**spìocaire** *m* miser.

**spìon** *v* snatch, grab; pluck.

**spionnadh** *m* strength; energy.

**spiorad** *m* spirit, ghost; **an Spiorad Naomh** the Holy Spirit/ Ghost.

**spioradail** *adj* spiritual.

**spiosradh** *m* spice.

**spiosraich** *v* spice; embalm.

**spiris** *f* perch, roost.

**spleuchd** *v* stare, gape; squint. • *m* stare; squint.

**spliuchan** *m* pouch.

**spòg** *f* paw; *(of clock or watch)* hand; spoke.

**spong** *m* sponge.

**sporan** *m* purse; sporran.

**spòrs** *f* sport; fun.

**spot** *m* spot, stain.

**spoth** *v* castrate.

**spreadh** *v* burst; explode.

**spreadhadh** *m* explosion.

**sprèidh** *f* livestock.

**sprèig** *v* incite, urge.

**sprùilleach** *m* crumbs.

**sprùilleag** *f* crumb.

**spùill** *v* plunder, despoil.

**spùinneadair** *m* plunderer, brigand.

**spùinneadair-mara** *m* pirate, buccaneer.

**spuir, spur** *m* claw, talon.

**spùt** *v* spurt; squirt. • *m* spout; spurt, gush; waterfall.

**sràbh** *m* drinking straw.

**srac** *v* rip, tear.

**sradag** *f* spark.

**sràid** *f* street.

**sràidearaich** *v* stroll, saunter.

**srainnsear** *m* stranger.

**srann** *v* snore.

**srann** *f* snore; snoring.

**srannartaich** *f* snoring.

**sreang** *f* string.

**sreath** *m* row, line, rank; layer; series.

**sreothart** *m* sneeze.

**sreothartaich** *f* sneezing.

**srian** *f* bridle, rein(s); streak, stripe.

**sròn** *f* nose; ridge; point, promontory.

**sròn-adharcach** *m* rhinoceros.

**srùb** *v* spout; spurt; slurp. • *m* *(pot, etc)* spout.

**srùbag** f sip; snack, stroupach.

**srùban** m cockle.

**sruth** v flow, stream, run. • m stream, burn; flow; current.

**stàball** m stable.

**stad** v stop, cease; halt, pause. • m stop, end; halt, pause.

**stad-phuing** f (orthog) full stop.

**staid** f state, condition.

**staidhre** f stair, staircase.

**stailc** f (industry, etc) strike.

**stàillinn** f steel.

**staing** f difficulty, tight corner, fix.

**stàirn** f crashing, clattering, rumbling.

**stairseach, stairsneach** f threshold.

**stàit** f (nation) state; (pl) **na Stàitean Aonaichte** the United States. • m **Rùnaire na Stàite** the Secretary of State.

**stàiteil** adj stately.

**stalc** m starch.

**stalcaire** m fool, blockhead.

**stalcaireachd** f stupidity; stupid action.

**stamag** f stomach.

**stamh** m (seaweed) tangle.

**stamp** v stamp. • f (postage) stamp.

**staoig** f steak.

**staoin** f (the metal) tin.

**steall** v spout, squirt, spurt, gush. • f outpouring. spout, spurt; (fam) swig, slug.

**steallair, steallaire** m syringe.

**stèidh** f base, foundation, basis.

**stèidhich** v found, establish.

**stèidhichte** adj founded, established. • f **an Eaglais Stèidhichte** the Established Church.

**stèisean** m station.

**stiall** v stripe, streak.

**stiall** f stripe; tape; (of clothing) stitch, scrap.

**stìopall** m steeple.

**stiùbhard** m steward.

**stiùir** v steer, direct; run, manage. • f rudder, helm.

**stiùireadair** m steersman, helmsman.

**stiùireadh** m steering, directing; managing.

**stob** m fence post; stake; (tree) stump.

**stòbha** f stove.

**stoc** m (tree) trunk, stump; livestock; scarf, cravat.

**stocainn** f stocking.

**stoidhle** f style.

**stòir, stòr** v store.

**stòiridh** m story; humorous anecdote.

**stoirm** f storm.

**stòl** m stool.

**stòlda** adj sedate, staid, serious; sober.

**stòr**[1] m store; riches, wealth.

**stòr**[2] v same as **stòir**.

**stòras** m riches, wealth.

**stòr-dàta** m database.

**stràc** *m* stroke, blow; (*orthog*) accent.

**stràic** *m* (*school, formerly*) belt, tawse.

**streap** *v* climb.

**streap-monaidhean** *f* hillwalking, mountain climbing.

**strì** *v* struggle; compete. • *f* struggle, strife; contest.

**strìoch** *f* hyphen.

**strìochag** *f* (*marking, etc*) tick.

**strìochd** *v* surrender, yield; cringe.

**strìopach** *f* prostitute.

**structair** *m* structure.

**struidheil** *adj* extravagant, prodigal. • *m* **am mac struidheil** the prodigal son.

**struth** *m/f* ostrich.

**stuadh** *f* (*sea*) wave; (*house*) gable.

**stuaim** *f* abstemiousness, moderation, temperance; sobriety.

**stuama** *adj* abstemious, moderate, temperate; sober.

**stuamachd** *f* abstinence, sobriety.

**stùiceach** *adj* surly, morose.

**stuig** *v* incite, urge.

**stùr** *m* dust.

**stuth** *m* material, stuff.

**suaicheantas** *m* badge, emblem.

**suaimhneach** *adj* calm, quiet.

**suain**[1] *v* wrap, entwine.

**suain**[2] *f* sleep, slumber.

**Suain** *f* (*with art*) **an t-Suain** Sweden.

**Suaineach** *m/adj* Swede; Swedish.

**suairc, suairce** *adj* kind; courteous; affable.

**suarach** *adj* insignificant; petty; despicable.

**suarachas** *m* insignificance; pettiness.

**suas** *adv* up.

**suath** *v* rub, wipe.

**suath ri** *v* brush against.

**sùbailte** *adj* supple, flexible.

**subh** *m* berry.

**subh-làir** *m* strawberry.

**sugan** *m* straw rope.

**sùgh** *v* absorb; suck (up).

**sùgh** *m* juice; sap.

**sùghach** *adj* absorbent.

**sùgh-measa** *m* fruit juice.

**sùghmhor** *adj* juicy; sappy.

**sùgradh** *m* mirth, merrymaking; lovemaking.

**suidh** *v* sit (down); **suidh sìos** sit down.

**suidhe** *m* seat; sitting position. •*adv* **'na shuidhe** *adv* sitting.

**suidheachadh** *m* setting, site; situation.

**suidheachan** *m* seat; stool; pew.

**suidhich** *v* seat; place; decide/ agree upon;.

**suidhichte** *adj* settled, arranged; resolute; sedate, grave.

**suidse** *f* switch.

**suigeart** *m* cheerfulness.

**sùil** *f* eye; look, glance.

suilbhir *adj* cheerful.

sùil-chritheach *f* quagmire.

sùileach *adj* forward-looking, far-sighted.

sùilich *v* expect.

suim¹ *f* regard; attention.

suim² *f* (*money*) amount, sum; (*arith*) sum.

suipear *f* supper.

suirghe, suiridhe *f* courting, courtship.

suiteas *m* sweet.

sùith *m* soot.

sùlaire *m* solan goose.

sult *m* fat, fatness;.

Sultain, Sultuine *f* (*with art*) an

t-Sultain, an t-Sultuine September.

sultmhor *adj* fat, plump; lusty, in rude health.

sumainn *f* (*sea*) surge, swell.

sùnnd *m* cheerfulness; mood.

sùnndach *adj* cheerful, in good spirits.

Suòmach *m/adj* Finn; Finnish.

Suòmaidh *f* Finland.

sùrd *m* cheerfulness; alacrity.

sùrdag *f* jump, skip; bounce; caper.

sùrdagaich *v* jump, skip; bounce; caper.

suth *m* embryo.

sutha *f* zoo.

# T

tàbhachdach *adj* sound, substantial.

tabhairteach, tabhairtaiche *m* donor, benefactor.

tabhannaich *v* bark. • *f* barking.

tabhartach *adj* generous, liberal; (*gram*) dative.

tabhartas *m* donation; presentation; grant.

taca *f* proximity.

tacaid *f* tack, tacket.

tacan *m* little while.

tachair *v* happen.

tachair ri *v* meet.

tachais *v* scratch; itch, tickle.

tachartas *m* happening; incident.

tachas *m* scratching; itching, tickling.

tachd *v* smother, choke, throttle.

tacsaidh *m* taxi.

tadhail (air) *v* visit, call (on).

tadhal *m* visit; (*sport*) goal.

tagair *v* claim; (*legal*) plead, argue.

tagh *v* choose; elect, vote in.

taghadh *m* choosing, choice; election.

taghta *adj* chosen; elected; (*fam*) great! perfect!

tagradh *m* claim; (*legal*) plea.

**taibhse** m/f ghost.

**taibhsearachd** f second sight.

**taic, taice** f contact; proximity; prop; (*moral and phys*) support; patronage

**taic airgid** f (*fin*) support, backing.

**taiceil** adj supporting, supportive.

**taidhir** f tyre.

**taifeid** m bowstring.

**taigeis** f haggis.

**taigh** m house. • adv **aig an taigh** at home. • m/f **fear/bean an taighe** the landlord/lady.

**taigh beag** m toilet.

**taigh-bìdh** m café, restaurant.

**taigh-cluiche** m theatre.

**taigh comhairle** m council house.

**taigh-dhealbh** m cinema.

**taigh-eiridinn** m hospital.

**taigh-grùide** m brewery.

**taigh na galla do X!** excl damn X! sod X!

**taigh-nighe** m wash-house, laundry.

**taigh-òsda** m hotel; inn, pub.

**taigh-tasgaidh** m museum.

**tailceas** m contempt, disdain.

**tailceasach** adj reproachful; contemptuous.

**tàileasg** m chess; backgammon.

**tàillear** m tailor.

**taing** f thanks, gratitude. • excl **taing dhut/dhuibh** thank you.

**taingeil** adj thankful, grateful.

**tàir**[1] v escape, make off.

**tàir**[2] f contempt, disparagement.

**tairbhe** f advantage, benefit; profit.

**tairbheach** adj advantageous, beneficial; profitable.

**tairbhich** v benefit, profit, gain.

**tàireil** adj contemptible.

**tairg** v propose, offer; bid.

**tairgse** f offer, bid.

**tàirneanach** m thunder.

**tairsgeir** f peat iron.

**tais** adj damp, moist, humid.

**taisbean** v show, reveal; display, exhibit; demonstrate.

**taisbeanach** adj clear, distinct; (*gram*) indicative.

**taisbeanadh** m display, exhibition; demonstration.

**taisbean-lann** f art gallery; exhibition hall.

**taise, taiseachd** f moisture, damp, dampness, humidity.

**taisg** v store; hoard.

**taisich** v dampen, moisten.

**taitinn (ri)** v please.

**taitneach** adj agreeable, pleasant.

**taitneas** m pleasantness; pleasure.

**tàladh** m attraction; allurement; soothing, calming; lullaby.

**talaich** v complain, grumble.

**tàlaidh** v attract; allure; tempt; calm; sing/rock to sleep.

**tàlaidheach** adj attractive.

**talamh** m earth, soil; land; (*with art*) **an Talamh** the Earth.

**tàlann** *m* talent, gift.

**tàlantach** *adj* talented, gifted.

**talla** *m* hall; **talla a' bhaile** the village/town hall.

**talmhaidh** *adj* earthly.

**tàmailt** *f* disgrace, shame; insult.

**tàmailteach** *adj* scandalous, shameful; insulting.

**tàmailtich** *v* insult.

**tamall** *m* while, time.

**tàmh**[1] *v* dwell, live.

**tàmh**[2] *m* rest, peace; inactivity, idleness; leisure.

**tana** *adj* thin, runny; shallow; sparse.

**tanaich** *v* thin.

**tancair** *m* tanker.

**tannasg** *m* ghost.

**taobh** *m* side; way, direction.

**taobh an teine** *m* fireside.

**taobh-duilleige** *m* page; **taobh-duilleige a dhà** page two.

**taobh ri taobh** *adv* side by side.

**taois** *f* dough.

**taom** *v* pour (out), flow (out); empty; bale.

**tap** *f* (*water*) tap.

**tapadh** *m* handiness, smartness; willingness.

**tapadh leat/leibh!** *excl* thank you!

**tapag** *f* slip of the tongue.

**tapaidh** *adj* clever, quick; sturdy, manly; active.

**tarbh** *m* bull.

**tarbh-nathrach** *m* dragonfly.

**tarcais** *m* contempt, disdain.

**tarcaiseach** *adj* reproachful; contemptuous.

**targaid** *f* target; shield.

**tàrmaich** *v* beget; breed; propagate; produce.

**tàrr** *v* escape, make off.

**tarrag** *f* (*joinery*) nail.

**tarraing** *v* draw; drag, pull; attract.

**tarraing à** *v* tease, kid.

**tarraingeach** *adj* attractive.

**tarraing gu** *v* approach.

**tarrang** *f* same as **tarrag**.

**tarsainn** *adv* across, over.

**tarsainn air** *prep* across, over.

**tart** *m* thirst.

**tartmhor** *adj* thirsty, dry.

**tasgadh** *m* storehouse; museum; investment.

**tasgaidh** *m* store, hoard.

**tastan** *m* shilling.

**tàth** *v* join together; glue; cement; weld; solder.

**tathaich** *v* frequent, haunt; visit.

**tathaich air** *v* call on.

**tàthan** *m* hyphen.

**tè** *f* one (*f*); woman.

**teachd** *defective v* come; fit, be contained. • *m* arrival, coming.

**teachdaire** *m* messenger; missionary.

**teachdaireachd** *f* message; mission, commission.

**teachd-an-tìr** *m* living, livelihood.

**teachd-a-steach** *m* entry, entrance; income.

**teadhair** *f* tether.

**teagaisg** *v* teach, instruct.

**teagamh** *m* doubt, uncertainty.

**teagamhach** *adj* doubtful, doubting; sceptical.

**teagasg** *m* teaching.

**teaghlach** *m* family.

**teallach** *m* hearth, fireside; fireplace.

**teallach ceàrdaich** *m* forge.

**teampall** *m* temple.

**teanchair** *m* clamp, vice; pincers; tongs.

**teanga** *f* tongue; (*occas*) language.

**teann**[1] *v* move, go, proceed.

**teann**[2] *adj* tight, tense; firm, secure; strict, severe.

**teannachair** *m same as* **teanchair**.

**teannaich** *v* tighten, tense; constrict, squeeze.

**teann air**[1] *v* approach; begin.

**teann air**[2] *prep* close to.

**teann ri** *v* begin (to), set about.

**teanta** *f* tent.

**tèarainte** *adj* safe, secure.

**tèarainteachd** *f* safety, security.

**tearc** *adj* scant, scarce, few.

**tèarmann** *m* protection; refuge, sanctuary.

**teàrr** *f* tar, pitch.

**teas** *m* heat.

**teasach** *f* fever.

**teasaich** *v* heat (up).

**teasairg** *v* save, rescue.

**teas-meadhan** *m* dead centre.

**teas-mheidh** *f* thermometer.

**teasraig** *v same as* **teasairg**.

**teatha** *f* (*drink*) tea.

**tè bheag** *f* nip, dram.

**teich** *v* flee, abscond; desert.

**teicheadh** *m* running away; desertion.

**teicneolach** *adj* technical, technological.

**teicneolaiche** *m* technician; technologist.

**teicneolas** *m* technology.

**teicneolas fiosrachaidh** *m* information technolology, IT.

**teignigeach** *adj* technical.

**teine** *m* fire.

**teinntean** *m* hearth, fireplace.

**teip** *f* tape; cassette.

**teip clàraidh** *f* recording tape.

**teip-tomhais** *f* measuring tape.

**teirinn** *v* come down; go down; climb down; dismount; alight, descend.

**teisteanas** *m* testimony, evidence; certificate, diploma; testimonial.

**teisteanas breith** *m* birth certificate.

**telebhisean** *m* television.

**teòclaid** *f*/*adj* chocolate.

**teodhachd** *f* temperature.

**teòthaich** *v* warm (up); warm to, take to.

**teòma** *adj* expert, skilful; ingenious.

**teòth ri** *v* take to.

**teth** *adj* hot.

**teud** *m* (*harp, etc*) string.

**tha** *present tense of v* **bith**.

**tha amharas agam** *v* I suspect.

**tha an t-eagal orm** I'm frightened.

**tha dùil agam air X** *v* I expect X.

**tha eagal orm** I'm afraid, I'm sorry to say.

**tha fallas orm** *v* I'm sweating.

**tha feum agam air X** *v* I need X.

**tha fios** *adv* of course, naturally.

**tha fios agam** *v* I know.

**tha gràin agam air** *v* I hate him/it.

**thàinig** *past tense of v* **thig**.

**thairis** *prep pron* over him, over it (*m*). • *adv* across, over; beyond.

**thairis air** *prep* across, over; beyond.

**thairte** *prep pron* over her, over it (*f*).

**thall** *adv* over there, over yonder.

**thalla** (*sing*), **thallaibh** (*pl*) *imper* go, off you go.

**thall 's a bhos** *adv* here and there; hither and thither.

**tha mi an dòchas** *v* I hope.

**tha mi an dùil** *v* I hope, I expect.

**tha mi duilich!** I'm sorry!

**tha mi gu dòigheil!** I'm fine!

**thar** *prep* across, over; beyond; more than.

**thar a chèile** *adv* in confusion; at loggerheads.

**tharad** *prep pron* over you (*sing*).

**tharaibh** *prep pron* over you (*pl*).

**tharainn** *prep pron* over us.

**tharam** *prep pron* over me.

**thar mo chomais** *adv* beyond my ability.

**tharta** *prep pron* over them.

**tha smùid orm** I'm drunk.

**tha ùidh agam ann** *v* I'm interested in it.

**theab** *defective v* nearly; **theab mi tuiteam** I nearly fell.

**theagamh** *conj* perhaps, maybe.

**thèid** *future tense of v* **rach**.

**thig** *v* come; approach; arrive.

**thig air adhart** *v* make progress.

**thig am bàrr** *v* surface.

**thig am follais** *v* come to light.

**thig an uachdar** *v* surface; manifest itself.

**thig a-steach air** *v* occur to.

**thig còmhla** *v* congregate, unite.

**thig do** *v* (*clothes, etc*) suit; please, suit.

**thig gu inbhe** *v* grow up.

**thig ri** *v* suit.

**thoir** *v* give; bring; take.

**thoir adhradh** *v* worship.

**thoir air** *v* make, force.

**thoir air èiginn** *v* rape.

**thoir air falbh** *v* abduct.

**thoir air gabhail** *v* lease.

**thoir am bith** *v* bring into being/existence.

**thoir am follais** *v* bring to light.

**thoir an aire** *v* pay attention; take care.

**thoir an car à** *v* cheat.

**thoir an t-siteag ort!** *v* get out! outside!

**thoir bàrr airr** *v* beat, cap, top.

**thoir breith** *v* pass judgement.

**thoir buaidh air** *v* defeat; influence, affect.

**thoir creideas do** *v* trust; believe.

**thoir cuireadh do** *v* invite.

**thoir do chasan leat!** get the hell out of here!

**thoir dùbhlan do** *v* challenge; defy.

**thoir facal air** *v* swear to.

**thoir fianais** *v* give evidence, testify.

**thoir fios air** *v* send for.

**thoir gealladh** *v* promise; vow.

**thoir gu buil** *v* achieve; see through.

**thoir gu stad** *v* bring to an end/a stop.

**thoir guth air** *v* mention.

**thoir ionnsaigh air** *v* attack, assault; have a shot/an attempt at.

**thoir na buinn asam** *v* take to my heels.

**thoir oidhirp (air)** *v* make an attempt (at).

**thoir rabhadh do** *v* warn; alert.

**thoir seachad** *v* give, give away.

**thoir seachad òraid** *v* give/deliver a speech.

**thoir sùil air** *v* have a look at.

**thoir tairgse (air)** *v* make an offer/a bid (for).

**thoir tarraing air** *v* mention, refer to.

**thoir tuaiream air** *v* guess at.

**thoir urram do** *v* respect.

**thoir uspag** *v* (*horse, etc*) start, shy.

**thoir X orm** *v* take myself off to X.

**thu** *pers pron sing* you.

**thuca** *prep pron* to them.

**thug** *past tense of v* **thoir**.

**thugad** *prep pron* to you (*sing*).

**thugaibh** *prep pron* to you (*pl*).

**thugainn** *prep pron* to us.

**thugam** *prep pron* to me.

**thuice** *prep pron* to her, to it (*f*).

**thuige** *prep pron* to him, to it (*m*).

**thun** *prep* to, towards, up to.

**thuirt** *past tense of v* **abair**.

**tì** *f* (*drink*) tea.

**tiamhaidh** *adj* melancholy; plaintive.

**tibhre** *m* dimple.

**ticead** *f* ticket.

**tìde** *m/f* time; weather; (*with art*) **an tìde, an tìde-mhara** the tide. • *excl* **bha a thìde aige!** he took his time!

**tidsear** *m* teacher.

**tigh** *m* house.

**tighearna** *m* lord; laird, landowner; (*with art*) **an Tighearna** the Lord, God. • *excl* **a Thighearna!** (Oh) Lord!

**Tìleach** *m/adj* Icelander; Icelandic.

**tilg** *v* throw; throw up; (*weapon*) fire.

**tilg air** *v* accuse of, reproach with.

**tilg smugaid** *v* spit.

**till** *v* return, come/go back.

**tilleadh** *m* return; returning.

**tìm** *f* time.

**timcheall**[1] *adv* round.

**timcheall**[2] *adv/prep* round, around, about.

**timcheall air** *prep* round, around, about.

**timcheallan** *m* roundabout.

**tinn** *adj* ill, sick.

**tinneas** *m* illness, disease.

**tinneas cridhe** *m* heart disease.

**tinneas mara** *m* seasickness.

**tinneas na dighe** *m* alcoholism.

**tiodhlac** *m* gift, present.

**tiodhlacadh** *m* burial, funeral.

**tiodhlaic** *v* give, donate; bury.

**tiomnadh** *m* will, testament; bequest; **an Seann Tiomnadh** the Old Testament; **an Tiomnadh Nuadh** the New Testament.

**tiomnaich** *v* bequeathe, leave.

**tiompan** *m* cymbal.

**tionail** *v* assemble, congregate; (*stock*) gather.

**tionndaidh** *v* turn.

**tionnsgail** *v* devise, invent.

**tionnsgal** *m* inventiveness; invention.

**tionnsgalach** *adj* inventive.

**tionnsgalair** *m* inventor.

**tioraidh!** *excl* cheerio!

**tioram** *adj* dry; thirsty.

**tiormachd** *f* dryness; drought.

**tiormadair** *m* dryer.

**tiormaich** *v* dry; dry up.

**tiota** *m* second, instant.

**tiotag** *f* instant, tick.

**tiotal** *m* title.

**tiotan** *m* second, instant.

**tìr** *m/f* land; country; area, region; ground, landscape.

**tìr-eòlas** *m* geography.

**tìr mòr** *m* mainland; continent.

**tiugainn!** *imper* come along! let us go!

**tiugh** *adj* thick, dense; slow-witted.

**tighead** *m* thickness; density.

**tlachd** *f* pleasure, enjoyment; affection, liking.

**tlachdmhor** *adj* pleasant; likeable.

**tnù** *m* envy; malice.

**tobar** *m/f* spring, well.

**tobhta** *m/f* ruin(s).

**tocasaid** *f* barrel, hogshead.

**tòchd** *m* stink.

**tochradh** *m* dowry.

**todha** *m* hoe.

**todhaig** *v* hoe.

**todhair** *v* manure; bleach.

**todhar** *m* manure, dung.

**tog** *v* raise, lift; pick up; build; (*family, etc*) bring up.

**togair** *v* wish for; covet; **ma thogras tu** if you like.

**togalach** *m* building.

**tog dealbhan** *v* take photos.

**tog ort** *excl* stir your stumps! get a move on!

**togradh** *m* wish, desire.

**toibheum** *m* blasphemy.

**toigh** *adj* pleasing; **is toigh leam X** I like X.

**toil** *f* will.

**toileach** *adj* willing; content; glad.

**toileachas** *m* contentment; gladness.

**toilich** *v* please, content.

**toilichte** *adj* happy; pleased, satisfied.

**toil-inntinn** *f* (*mental*) pleasure; peace of mind.

**toill** *v* deserve.

**toillteanach (air)** *adj* worthy (of).

**tòimhseachan** *m* puzzle; riddle.

**tòimhseachan-tarsainn** *m* crossword puzzle.

**toinisg** *f* common sense.

**toinisgeil** *adj* sensible; intelligent.

**toinn** *v* twist, wind, twine.

**tòir** *f* pursuit.

**toirm** *f* noise, din.

**toirmeasg** *m* forbidding; prohibition.

**toirmeasgach** *adj* prohibitive.

**toirmisg** *v* forbid, prohibit.

**toiseach** *m* start, beginning; vanguard; (*vehicle, etc*) front.

**tòiseachadh** *m* beginning.

**tòiseachadh ùr** *m* fresh start.

**tòisich (air/ri)** *v* start (to).

**tòisich as ùr** *v* start afresh.

**toit** *f* steam; smoke.

**toitean** *m* cigarette.

**toll** *v* bore, pierce, perforate; dig a hole. • *m* hole, pit, hollow; (*vulg*) arsehole.

**tolladh-chluasan** *m* ear-piercing.

**tolltach** *adj* full of holes.

**toll-tòine** *m* anus.

**tolman** *m* knowe, knoll.

**tom** *m* hillock; thicket.

**tomaltach** *adj* sizeable, bulky; burly.

**tombaca** *m* tobacco.

**tomhais** *v* measure; calculate; guess; survey.

**tomhas** *m* measuring; dimension; calculation; guess, guessing; surveying.

**tomhas-teas** *m* thermometer.

**tòn** *f* anus, rectum; (*fam*) arse, bum, backside; (*building, etc*) back.

**tonn** *m/f* wave.

**tonna** *m* ton, tonne.

**tonn teasa** *m* heat wave.

**torach** *adj* fruitful, productive; fertile, fecund; pregnant; (*egg, etc*) fertilised.

**torachadh** *m* fertilisation.

**torachas** *m* fertility.

**toradh** *m* produce, fruit(s); result, effect.

**toraich** *v* fertilise.

**torc** *m* boar.

**torman** *m* murmur, drone, hum; rumble.

**tòrr** *m* heap, mound; hill; (*fam*) lots, loads.

**tòrradh** *m* burial, funeral.

**tosd** *m* silence.

**tosdach** *adj* silent, quiet.

**tosgaire** *m* ambassador; envoy.

**tosgaireachd** *f* embassy.

**tractar** *m* tractor.

**trafaig** *f* traffic.

**tràghadh** *m* draining; subsiding; (*car*) exhaust.

**tràigh**[1] *v* drain, empty; subside, settle; ebb.

**tràigh**[2] *f* shore, beach; tide.

**tràill** *m/f* slave; drudge; addict.

**tràilleachd** *f* slavery; addiction.

**tràillich** *v* enslave.

**traisg** *v* fast.

**tràlair** *m* trawler.

**trang** *adj* busy.

**trannsa** *f* corridor, passage.

**trasg** *f* fast, fasting.

**tràth**[1] *adv* early.

**tràth**[2] *m* time, season; while, period; (*gram*) tense.

**tràth bìdh** *m* mealtime.

**tràthach** *m* hay.

**treabh** *v* plough.

**trealaich** *f* jumble; odds and ends, stuff, paraphernalia; trash, rubbish; (*pl*) **trealaichean** luggage, baggage.

**trèan** *v* train.

**trèana** *f* train.

**treas** *adj* third.

**treas deug** *adj* thirteenth.

**trèig** *v* leave; abandon; relinquish.

**trèigte** *adj* abandoned, deserted.

**treis** *f* while, time.

**treiseag** *f* short while.

**treòrachadh** *m* guiding, leading; guidance.

**treòraich** *v* guide, lead.

**treubh** *f* tribe.

**treud** *m* flock, herd; group; (*derog*) crowd, gang.

**treun** *adj* strong, stout. • *f* **treun a neirt** his prime.

**trì** *n/adj* three.

**triall (do)** *v* travel, journey (to).

**trian** *m* third.

**triath** *m* lord.

**tric** *adj/adv* frequent(ly).

**trì-cheàrnag** *f* triangle.

**trìd-shoilleir** *adj* transparent.

**trioblaid** *f* trouble.

**trìthead** *m* thirty.

**triubhas** *m* trews, trousers.

**triùir** *m/f* (*people*) three, threesome.

**triuthach** *f* (*with art*) **an triuthach** whooping cough.

**tro** *prep* through.

**trobhad** (*sing*), **trobhadaibh** (*pl*) *imper* come here, come to me; come along.

**tròcair** *f* mercy.

**tròcaireach** *adj* merciful.

**trod** *m* quarrel, row; quarreling.

**troich** *m/f* dwarf.

**troid** *v* quarrel, squabble, fight.

**troigh** *f* (*measure*) foot.

**troighean** *m* pedal.

**troimh** *prep same as* **tro**.

**troimh chèile** *adv* at logger-heads; in confusion; untidy.

**troimhe** *prep pron* through him, through it (*m*).

**troimhpe** *prep pron* through her, through it (*f*).

**trom** *adj* heavy; serious; important; depressed; pregnant.

**tromalach** *f* preponderance, majority.

**trombaid** *f* trumpet.

**tromhad** *prep pron* through you (*sing*).

**tromhaibh** *prep pron* through you (*pl*).

**tromhainn** *prep pron* through us.

**tromham** *prep pron* through me.

**tromhpa** *prep pron* through them.

**trom-laighe** *m/f* nightmare.

**trosg** *m* cod.

**trotan** *m* trot; trotting.

**truacanta** *adj* compassionate, humane.

**truacantas** *m* compassion, pity.

**truagh** *adj* sad; poor, pitiable, abject.

**truaghan** *m* wretch. • *excl* **a thruaghain!** poor man/creature!

**truaill** *v* pollute; corrupt, pervert; defile, profane.

**truas** *m* pity, compassion.

**truileis** *f* rubbish, junk.

**truimead** *m* heaviness.

**truinnsear** *m* plate.

**truis, trus** *v* bundle, roll up; (*skirt, etc*) tuck up; (*stock*) gather.

**trusgan** *m* clothes, clothing.

**tuagh** *f* axe.

**tuagh-chatha** *f* battleaxe, Lochaber axe.

**tuainealach** *adj* dizzy, giddy.

**tuainealaich** *f* dizziness, vertigo.

**tuaiream** *f* guess, conjecture.

**tuaireamach** *adj* random, arbitrary.

**tuairisgeul** *m* description.

**tuar** *m* complexion, hue; appearance.

**tuarasdal** *f* salary, wage(s); stipend; fee.

**tuasaid** *f* quarrel; scrap, tussle.

**tuath**[1] *adj/f* northern, north.

**tuath**[2] *f* peasantry; tenantry.

**tuath air** *prep* north of.

**tuathal** *adj* widdershins; anti-clockwise; awry, wrong.

**tuathanach** *m* farmer.

**tuathanachas** *m* farming.

**tuathanas** *m* farm.

**tubaist** *f* accident; mishap.

**tubhailte** *f* towel.

**tubhailte-shoithichean** *f* tea-towel.

**tùch** *v* make hoarse; smother; extinguish.

**tùchadh** *m* hoarseness.

**tùchanach** *adj* hoarse.

**tudan** *m* stack; turd.

**tugh** *v* thatch.

**tughadh** *m* thatch.

**tuig** *v* understand.

**tuigse** *f* comprehension; intelligence; sense, judgement.

**tuigseach** *adj* understanding; intelligent; sensible.

**tuil** *f* flood, deluge.

**tuilleadh** *m* more, additional; **tuilleadh 's a chòir** more than enough.

**tuinich** *v* settle; dwell.

**Tuirc** *m* (*with art*) **an Tuirc** Turkey.

**tuireadh** *m* mourning; lament.

**tùirse** *f* sorrow.

**tuiseal** *m* (*gram*) case.

**tuislich** *v* stumble, slip, trip.

**tuit** *v* fall.

**tuit do** *v* happen to, befall.

**tuiteamach** *adj* accidental, chance.

**tuiteamas** *m* occurence, event; incident; accident.

**tulach** *m* hillock.

**tulg** *v* rock, lurch, swing, toss.

**tulgach** *adj* rocking, lurching, swinging, tossing; rocky, unsteady.

**tulgadh** *m* rocking, lurching, swinging, tossing.

**tum** *v* dip, immerse; steep.

**tunnag** *f* duck.

**tur** *adj* whole, complete. • *adv* **gu tur** completely, altogether.

**tùr**[1] *m* understanding; sense.

**tùr**[2] *m* tower.

**turadh** *m* dry weather/spell.

**turaid** *f* tower; turret.

**tùrail** *adj* sensible.

**turas** *m* journey; trip; tour, touring; time.

**turasachd** *f* tourism.

**turas-mara** *m* voyage.

**turas-tillidh** *m* return journey.

**Turcach** *m/adj* Turk; Turkish.

**tursa** *m* standing stone.

**tùrsach** *adj* sorrowful.

**tùs** *m* beginning, origin.

**tùsanach** *adj* aborigene.

**tùthag** *f* patch.

# U

**uabhar** *m* pride, haughtiness, arrogance.

**uachdar** *m* surface; top; cream; upland.

**uachdarach** *adj* upper; superior; superficial.

**uachdaran** *m* superior; landowner, laird.

**uachdar-fhiaclan** *m* toothpaste.

**uaibh** *prep pron* from you (*pl*).

**uaibhreach** *adj* proud; haughty, arrogant.

**uaibhreas** *m* pride; haughtiness, arrogance.

**uaigh** *f* grave.

**uaigneach** *adj* lonely, solitary; secluded; private, secret.

**uaimh** *f* cave.

**uaine** *adj* green.

**uainn** *prep pron* from us.

**uaipe** *prep pron* from her, from it (*f*).

**uaipear** *m* botcher, bungler.

**uair** *f* hour; (*clock*) time; time, occasion. • *adv* once.

**uaireadair** *m* timepiece, clock; watch.

**uaireadair-gloinne** *m* hourglass.

**uaireadair-grèine** *m* sundial.

**uaireannan** *adv* sometimes.

**uaireigin** *adv* some time.

**uair is uair** *adv* time and time again.

**uair no uaireigin** *adv* some time or other.

**uair sam bith** *adv* any time.

**uaisle** *f* nobility, gentility.

**uaithe** *prep pron* from him, from it (*m*).

**uallach** *m* load, burden; onus, responsibility; stress, worry.

**uam** *prep pron* from me.

**uamhann** *m* dread, horror.

**uamhas** *m* dread, horror, terror; atrocity.

**uamhasach** *adj/adv* dreadful(ly), awful(ly), terrible, terribly.

**uamhasach fhèin math** *adv* (*fam*) wonderful, brilliant.

**uan** *m* lamb.

**uapa** *prep pron* from them.

**uasal** *adj* noble, aristocratic; genteel. • *m* gentleman; (*pl with art*) **na h-uaislean** the nobility, the aristocracy.

**uat** *prep pron* from you (*sing*).

**ubhal** *m* apple.

**ubhalghort** *m* orchard.

**uchd** *m* breast, bosom; lap.

**uchd-leanabh** *m* adopted child.

**uchd-mhacaich** *v* adopt.

**ud** *adj* that, yonder.

**ud ud!** *excl* tut tut! now now!

**uèir** *f* wire.

**ugan** *m* chest area.

**ugh** *m* egg.

**ughach** *m* oval. • *adj* oval.

**ughagan** *m* custard.

**ùghdar** *m* author.

**ùghdarras** *m* authority; (*govt*) **ùghdarras ionadail** local authority.

**ughlann** *f* ovary.

**uibhir** *f* number; amount, quantity; **na h-uibhir de** a certain amount of; such a lot of; **uibhir eile** as much again.

**uibhir ri** *prep* as much as.

**Uibhist** *m* Uist.

**Uibhisteach** *m/adj* from Uist.

**ùidh** *f* hope; fondness; interest.

**uidh** *f* step; gradation; journey; **uidh air n-uidh** step by step, gradually.

**uidheam** *f* equipment, tackle, gear; furnishings, trappings; harness; rigging.

**uidheamaich** *v* equip, fit out; get ready.

**uile** *adj/adv* all, every; fully, completely; **a h-uile** every. • *npl* **na h-uile** everybody.

**uileann** *f* angle; corner; elbow.

**uilebheist** *m* monster.

**uile-chumhachdach** *adj* all-powerful, omnipotent.

**uile fhiosrach** *adj* all-knowing.

**uile gu lèir** *adv* altogether, completely.

**ùilleach** *adj* oily.

**uilleagan** *m* spoilt brat.

**uillnich** *v* jostle, elbow.

**uime** *prep pron* about him, about it (*m*).

**uimpe** *prep pron* about her, about it (*f*).

**ùine** *f* time; while; (*pl fam*) **ùine-achan (is ùineachan)** ages (and ages).

**uinneag** *f* window.

**uinnean** *m* onion.

**uinnsean** *m* (*tree*) ash.

**ùir** *f* soil, earth.

**uircean** *m* piglet.

**uiread** *f* a certain amount/quanti-ty; **na h-uiread** such a lot; **uire-ad eile** as much again; **uiread ri** as much as. • *adv* (*sums*) times, multiplied by.

**uireasbhach** *adj* needy; lacking. • *m* needy person.

**uireasbhaidh** *f* indigence; lack, need; shortage.

**uirsgeul** *m* fable, legend, myth; fiction.

**uirsgeulach** *adj* legendary; fictional.

**uiseag** *f* skylark.

**uisge** *m* water; rain; **tha an t-uisge ann** it's raining.

**uisge-beatha** *m* whisky.

**uisge-dìonach** *adj* waterproof, watertight.

**uisge na stiùireach** *m* (*of boat, etc*) wake.

**uisgich** *v* water.

**ulaidh** *f* treasure; precious object.

**ulbhag** *f* large stone, boulder.

**ulfhart** *m* howl, howling.

**ullaich** *v* prepare; provide.

**ullamh** *adj* ready; handy; finished.

**ultach** *m* load; armful; bundle.

**umad** *prep pron* about you (*sing*).

**umaibh** *prep pron* about you (*pl*).

**ùmaidh** *m* blockhead, dolt, fool.

**umainn** *prep pron* about us.

**umam** *prep pron* about me.

**umha** *m* bronze.

**umhail, umhal** *adj* humble; lowly; obedient; obsequious.

**ùmhlachd** *f* humbleness; lowliness; obedience; obsequiousness; bow.

**ùmhlaich** *v* humble; humiliate.

**umpa** *prep pron* about them.

**Ungair** *f* (*with art*) **an Ungair** Hungary.

**Ungaireach** *m/adj* Hungarian.

**ùnnlagh** *m* fine.

**ùnnsa** *m* ounce.

**ùpag** *f* jostle, jab.

**ùpraid** *f* uproar; confusion; dispute.

**ùpraideach** *adj* rowdy, unruly.

**ùr** *adj* new; recent; fresh.

**ur** *poss adj* your.

**ùrachadh** *m* renewal; renovation; change.

**ùraich** *v* renew; renovate; refresh.

**urchair** *f* shot.

**urchair gunna** *f* gun-shot.

**urchasg** *m* antidote.

**ùrlar** *m* floor.

**ùrnaigh** *f* prayer; praying; **Urnaigh an Tighearna** the Lord's Prayer.

**ùr-nodha** *adj* brand new; up-to-date.

**urra** *f* person; authority; responsibility.

**urrainn** *f* power, ability.

**urram** *m* respect; honour.

**urramach** *adj* honourable; honorary; (*with art*) (*minister*) **an t-Urramach X** the Reverend X.

**urras** *m* guarantee, surety; bond; bail; insurance; (*fund, etc*) trust.

**ursainn** *f* prop, support; jamb.

**ursainn chatha** *f* (*warrior*) champion.

**usgar** *m* jewel.

**uspag** *f* (*horse, etc*) start, shy.

**ùth** *m* udder.

# English-Gaelic Dictionary

# A

**abandon** v tréig.

**abate** v lùghdaich.

**abbey** n abaid f.

**abbot** n aba m.

**abbreviate** v giorraich.

**abdicate** v leig dhe.

**abdication** n leigeil dhe m.

**abdomen** n balg m.

**abduct** v thoir air falbh.

**abet** v cuidich.

**abhor** v is lugha air.

**abhorrence** n gràin.

**abide** v fuirich.

**abject** adj truagh; dìblidh.

**ability** n comas m.

**able** adj comasach.

**able-bodied** adj fallain; corp-làidir.

**abnormal** adj mì-ghnàthach.

**abnormality** n mì-ghnàthas m.

**aboard** adv air bòrd.

**abode** n àite còmnaidh m.

**abolish** v cuir às do.

**abolition** n cur às m

**abominable** adj gràineil.

**aborigine** n prìomh neach-àiteach-aidh m.

**abortion** n breith an-abaich f.

**abound** v bi lìonmhor.

**about** adv timcheall; mun cuairt.
• prep mu; mu dheidhinn; mu thimcheall; mun cuairt air; tim-cheall air. • pron **about her** uimpe; **about him, it** uime; **about me** umam; **about them** umpa; **about us** umainn; **about you** (sing) umad; **about you** (pl) umaibh;

**above** adv shuas; gu h-àrd. • prep os cionn.

**abrade** v sgrìobaich.

**abridge** v giorraich.

**abridged** adj giorraichte.

**abroad** adv thall thairis.

**abrupt** adj cas; aithghearr.

**abruptness** n caise f.

**abscess** n niosgaid f.

**abscond** v teich, teich air falbh.

**absence** n neo-làthaireachd f.

**absent** adj nach eil an làthair.

**absent-minded** adj cian-aireach-al.

**absent oneself** v dìochuimh-neach cùm air falbh.

**absolve** v saor; sgaoil.

**absolute** adj iomlan; làn.

**absolutely** adv gu h-iomlan.

**absolution** n saoradh, fuasgladh m.

**absorb** v sùgh, deoghail.

**absorbent** adj sùghach.

**abstain** v na buin (ri).

**abstemious** adj stuama.

**abstinence** n stuamachd f.

**abstracted** *adj* beachdail.

**abstract** *n* às-tharraing *f*.

**abstract** *v* às-tharraing, tarraing à.

**absurd** *adj* gòrach.

**absurdity** *n* gòraiche *f*.

**abundance** *n* pailteas *m*.

**abundant** *adj* pailt.

**abuse**[1] *n* mì-ghnàthachadh *m*; (*verbal*) càin-eadh *f*.

**abuse**[2] *v* mì-ghnàthaich; (*verbally*) càin.

**abysmal** *adj* uabhasach.

**abyss** *n* àibheis *m*.

**academic** *adj* sgoileireach. • *n* oilthigheach *m*.

**academy** *n* àrd-sgoil *f*.

**accelerate** *v* luathaich, greas.

**acceleration** *n* luathachadh, greasad *m*.

**accelerator** *n* inneal-luathachaidh *m*.

**accent** *n* blas *m*.

**accept** *v* gabh.

**acceptable** *adj* furasda ghabhail.

**access** *n* inntrigeadh *m*.

**accessible** *adj* fosgailte.

**accident** *n* tubaist *f*.

**accidental** *adj* tubaisteach.

**accommodate** *v* gabh.

**accommodation** *n* rùm *m*.

**accompaniment** *n* compàirt *f*.

**accompanist** *n* compàirtiche *m*.

**accomplice** *n* fear-cuideachaidh *m*.

**accomplish** *v* coimhlion, thoir gu buil.

**accomplished** *adj* coimhlionta, deas.

**accord** *n* aonta, co-chòrdadh *m*.

**accordion** *n* bocsa-ciùil *m*.

**according to** *adv* a-rèir.

**accordingly** *adv* mar sin.

**account** *n* cùnntas, tuairisgeul *m*.
• *v* thoir cùnntas air.

**accountancy** *n* cùnntasachd *f*.

**accountant** *n* cùnntasair *m*.

**accounts book** *n* leabhar-cùnntais *m*.

**accumulate** *v* cruinnich.

**accumulation** *n* co-chruinneachadh *m*.

**accuracy** *n* cruinneas *m*.

**accurate** *adj* cruinn, grinn.

**accusation** *n* casaid *f*.

**accuse** *v* dèan casaid.

**accustom** *v* gnàthaich.

**accustomed** *adj* gnàthach; àbhaist.

**ace** *n* an t-aon *m*.

**acerbic** *adj* geur.

**acerbity** *n* goirte *f*.

**ache** *n* goirteas, cràdh *m*.

**achieve** *v* coimhlion.

**achievement** *n* euchd *m*.

**acid** *adj* searbh; geur.

**acidity** *n* searbhachd *f*.

**acknowledge** *v* aidich.

**acknowledgement** *n* aideachadh *m*.

**acoustic** *adj* fuaimneach.

**acoustics** *n* fuaimearrachd *f*.

**acquaintance** *n* fear-eòlais *m*.

**acquainted** *adj* eòlach.

**acquiesce** *v* aontaich.

**acquire** *v* faigh, buannaich.

**acquit** *v* fuasgail.

**acre** *n* acaire *m*.

**across** *adv* tarsainn, thairis.
• *prep* tarsainn air, thairis air,
thar.

**act** *n* gnìomh *m*; (*play*) earran *f*;
achd. • *v* obraich, dèan gnìomh;
cluich.

**action** *n* gnìomh *m*.

**active** *adj* deas, èasgaidh;
spreigeach.

**activity** *n* gnìomhachd *f*.

**actor** *n* cleasaiche, actair *m*.

**actress** *n* bana-chleasaiche, bana-
actair *f*.

**actual** *adj* dearbh, fìor.

**acute** *adj* dian, geur.

**adapt** *v* fàs suas ri, dèan freagarrach.

**adaptable** *adj* freagarrach.

**add** *v* cuir ri, meudaich, leasaich.

**adder** *n* nathair *f*.

**addict** *n* tràill *m/f*.

**addicted** *adj* fo bhuaidh.

**addiction** *n* tràilleachd *f*.

**addition** *n* meudachadh, leasachadh *m*.

**additional** *adj* a bharrachd, a thuilleadh.

**address** *n* seòladh *m*; (*oration*)
òraid *f*. • *v* cuir seòladh air; dèan
òraid ri.

**adequate** *adj* iomchaidh.

**adhere** *v* lean.

**adherent** *n* fear leanmhainn *m*.

**adhesive** *n* stuth leanmhainn *m*.

**adjacent** *adj* dlùth.

**adjective** *n* buadhair *m*.

**adjudication** *n* breitheamhnas *m*.

**adjust** *v* ceartaich, rèitich.

**adjustable** *adj* so-rèitichte.

**administer** *v* riaghlaich.

**administration** *n* riaghladh *m*.

**administrative** *adj* riaghlach.

**administrator** *n* fear-riaghlaidh
*m*.

**admirable** *adj* ionmholta.

**admiration** *n* meas *m*.

**admire** *v* tha meas air.

**admissible** *adj* ceadaichte.

**admission** *n* cead *m*; (*confession*) aideachadh *m*.

**admit** *v* leig a steach; (*confess*)
aidich.

**ado** *n* othail *f*.

**adolescence** *n* òigeachd *f*.

**adolescent** *n* òigear *m*.

**adopt** *v* uchd-mhacaich.

**adoption** *n* uchd-mhacachd *f*.

**adore** *v* trom-ghràdhaich.

**adorn** *v* sgeadaich.

**adrift** *adj* leis an t-sruth.

**adult** *adj* inbheach. • *n* inbheach
*m*.

**adulterate** *v* truaill.

**adulteration** *n* truailleadh *m*.

**adulterer** *n* adhaltraiche *m*.

**adultery** *n* adhaltranas *m*.

**advance** *n* dol air adhart *m*; (*fi-

*nancial*) eàrlas *m.* • *v* rach air thoiseach; (*financial*) thoir eàrlas.

**advanced** *adj* adhartach.

**advancement** *n* àrdachadh *m.*

**advantage** *n* tairbhe, buannachd *f.*

**advantageous** *adj* tairbheach.

**adventure** *n* tachartas *m.*

**adventurous** *adj* dàna.

**adverb** *n* co-ghnìomhair *m.*

**adverse** *adj* an aghaidh.

**adversity** *n* cruaidh-chas *f.*

**advertise** *v* thoir sanas.

**advertisement** *n* sanas, sanas-reic *m.*

**advice** *n* comhairle *f.*

**advise** *v* comhairlich.

**adviser** *n* comhairleach *m.*

**advocacy** *n* tagradh *m.*

**advocate** *n* fear-tagraidh *m.*

**advocate** *v* tagair.

**aerial** *n* aer-ghath *m.*

**aeronaut** *n* speur-sheòladair *m.*

**aeroplane** *n* pleuna *f*, itealan *m.*

**affable** *adj* suairce.

**affair** *n* gnothach *m.*

**affect** *v* drùidh air; (*let on*) leig air.

**affection** *n* gaol *m.*

**affectionate** *adj* gaolach.

**affinity** *n* dàimh *m/f.*

**affirm** *v* dearbh, daingnich.

**affirmative** *adj* aontach.

**aflict** *v* goirtich, sàraich.

**affliction** *n* doilgheas *m.*

**affluence** *n* beairteas *m.*

**affluent** *adj* beairteach.

**afford** *v* ruig air.

**affront** *v* maslaich.

**afloat** *adj* air fleòdradh.

**afoot** *adj* air chois; air bhonn.

**aforementioned** *adj* roimh-ainmichte.

**afraid** *adj* fo eagal, eagalach.

**afresh** *adv* às ùr, a-rithist.

**Africa** *n* Afraga *f.*

**African** *adj* Afraganach.

**after** *adv* an dèidh làimhe. • *prep* an dèidh.

**afternoon** *n* feasgar, tràth-nòin *m.*

**afterthought** *n* ath-smuain *f..*

**again** *adv* a-rithist.

**against** *prep* an aghaidh.

**age** *n* aois *f.* • *v* fàs aosda.

**aged** *adj* sean, aosda.

**agency** *n* ionadachd *f.*

**agent** *n* fear-ionaid *m*; dòigh *m.*

**aggravate** *v* antromaich.

**aggression** *n* (*phys*) ionnsaigh *m*; (*mental*) miann *m.*

**aggressive** *adj* ionnsaigheach.

**agile** *adj* lùthmhor.

**agitate** *v* gluais.

**agitation** *n* gluasad *m.*

**ago** *adv* air ais.

**agog** *adv* air bhiod.

**agonise** *v* bi an ioma-chomhairle.

**agony** *n* dòrainn *f.*

**agree** *v* aontaich; còrd.

**agreeable** *adj* taitneach.

**agreement** *n* còrdadh *m*, rèite *f.*

**agricultural** *adj* àiteachail.

**agriculture** *n* àiteachd *f*, tuathanachas *m*.

**aground** *adv* an sàs.

**ahead** *adv* air thoiseach.

**aid** *n* cuideachadh *m*. • *v* cuidich.

**ailment** *n* tinneas, galar *m*.

**ailing** *adj* tinn.

**aim** *n* (*missile*) cuimse *f*; (*intent*) amas *f*. • *v* cuimsich; amais.

**air** *n* àile; (*mus*) fonn; (*look*) aogas. • *v* leig an àile gu.

**airborne** *adj* air sgèith.

**airmail** *n* post-adhair *m*.

**airport** *n* port-adhair *m*.

**airwave** *n* tonn-adhair *m*.

**aisle** *n* trannsa *f*.

**ajar** *adv* leth-fhosgailte.

**akin** *adj* (*related*) càirdeach.

**alacrity** *n* sùrd *m*.

**alarm** *v* cuir eagal air.

**alarming** *adj* eagalach.

**album** *n* leabhar-chuimhneachan *m*.

**alcohol** *n* alcol *m*.

**alcoholic** *n* alcolach *m*.

**alcoholism** *n* alcolachd *f*.

**alder** *n* feàrna *f*.

**ale** *n* leann *m*.

**alert** *adj* furachail.

**algebra** *n* ailgeabra *f*.

**alias** *adv* fo ainm eile.

**alien** *adj* coigreach. • *n* coigreach *m*; Gall *m*.

**alienate** *v* fuadaich.

**alight** *v* teirinn.

**alike** *adj* co-ionnan.

**alimony** *n* airgead sgaraidh *m*.

**alive** *adj* beò.

**all** *adj* uile, na h-uile, iomlan.

**allay** *v* caisg.

**allegation** *n* cur às leth *m*.

**allegiance** *n* ùmhlachd *f*.

**allegory** *n* samhla *m*.

**alleviate** *v* aotromaich, lùghdaich.

**alleviation** *n* aotromachadh *m*.

**alliance** *n* càirdeas *m*.

**alliteration** *n* uaim *f*.

**allow** *v* leig le, ceadaich.

**allowance** *n* cuibhreann *f*.

**allusion** *n* iomradh *m*.

**ally** *n* caraid *m*; co-chòmraghaiche *m*.

**almighty** *adj* uile-chumhachdach.

**Almighty** *n* An t-Uile-chumhachdach *m*.

**almost** *adv* gu ìre bhig.

**alms** *npl* dèircean.

**aloft** *adv* gu h-àrd, shuas.

**alone** *adj* aonarach.

**along** *adv* air fad; **along with** còmhla ri.

**alongside** *adv* ri taobh.

**aloud** *adv* gu h-àrd ghuthach.

**alphabet** *n* aibidil *f*.

**alphabetical** *adj* aibidileach.

**already** *adv* mar thà.

**also** *adv* cuideachd.

**altar** *n* altair *f*.

**alter** *v* atharraich.

**alteration** *n* atharrachadh *m*.

**alternative** *adj* eile. • *n* roghainn eile *m*.

**although** *conj* ged a.

**altitude** *n* àirde *f*.

**altogether** *adv* gu lèir, uile gu lèir.

**aluminium** *n* almain *m*.

**always** *adv* an còmhnaidh, daonnan.

**amalgamate** *v* cuir le chèile.

**amateur** *adj* neo-dhreuchdail.

**amaze** *v* cuir iongnadh air.

**amazement** *n* iongantas *m*.

**amazing** *adj* iongantach.

**ambassador** *n* tosgaire *m*.

**ambidextrous** *adj* co-dheaslamhach.

**ambiguity** *n* dà-sheaghachas *m*.

**ambiguous** *adj* dà-sheaghach.

**ambit** *n* cuairt *f*.

**ambition** *n* glòir-mhiann *m*.

**ambitious** *adj* glòir-mhiannach.

**ambulance** *n* carbad-eiridinn *m*.

**ambush** *n* feallfhalach *m*.

**ameliorate** *v* dèan nas fheàrr.

**amen** *int* amen.

**amenable** *adj* fosgailte.

**amend** *v* leasaich.

**amendment** *n* leasachadh *m*.

**amenity** *n* goireas *m*.

**America** *n* Ameireagaidh *f*.

**American** *adj* Ameireaganach.

**amiable** *adj* càirdeil.

**amid, amidst** *prep* a-measg.

**amiss** *adv* gu h-olc.

**ammunition** *n* connadh làmhaich *m*.

**amnesty** *n* mathanas na coitcheann *m*.

**among, amongst** *prep* a-measg, air feadh.

**amorous** *adj* gaolach.

**amount** *n* suim, uimhir *f*; meud *m*.

**amphibian** *n* muir-thìreach *m*.

**amphibious** *adj* dà-bhitheach.

**ample** *adj* mòr, tomadach.

**amplification** *n* meudachadh *m*.

**amplify** *v* meudaich.

**amputate** *v* geàrr air falbh.

**amputation** *n* gearradh air falbh *m*.

**amuse** *v* toilich.

**amusement** *n* greannmhorachd *f*.

**amusing** *adj* greanmhor.

**anachronism** *n* às-aimsireachd *f*.

**anaemic** *adj* cìon-falach.

**anaesthetic** *n* an-fhaireachdair *m*.

**analogy** *n* co-fhreagarrachd *f*.

**analyse** *v* mion-sgrùdaich.

**analysis** *n* mion-sgrùdadh *m*.

**analyst** *n* mion-sgrùdaire *m*.

**anarchist** *n* ceannairceach *m*.

**anatomical** *adj* bodhaigeach.

**anatomy** *n* eòlas bodhaig *m*.

**ancestor** *n* sinnsear *m*.

**ancestry** *n* sinnsearachd *f*.

**anchor** *n* acair *f*.

**ancient** *adj* àrsaidh.

**and** *conj* agus, is, 's.

**anecdote** *n* naidheachd *f*.

**anew** *adv* às-ùr.

**angel** *n* aingeal *m*.

**angelic** *adj* mar aingeal.

**anger** *n* fearg *f.*

**angina** *n* grèim chridhe *m.*

**angle** *n* uilinn *f.*

**angler** *n* iasgair *f.*

**angling** *n* iasgachd *m.*

**angry** *adj* feargach.

**anguish** *n* dòrainn *f.*

**animal** *n* ainmhidh *m.*

**animate** *v* beothaich.

**animated** *adj* beothail.

**animation** *n* beothachadh *m.*

**ankle** *n* adhbrann *f.*

**annex** *n* ath-thaigh *m.*

**annihilate** *v* dìthich.

**annihilation** *n* lèirsgrios *m.*

**anniversary** *n* cuimhneachan, bliadhnail *m.*

**annotate** *v* notaich.

**annotation** *n* notachadh *m.*

**announce** *v* cuir an cèill.

**annoy** *v* cuir dragh air.

**annoyance** *n* dragh; buaireas *m.*

**annoyed** *adj* diombach.

**annoying** *adj* buaireil.

**annual** *adj* bliadhnail.

**annually** *adv* gach bhliadhna.

**annul** *v* cuir às.

**anoint** *v* ung.

**anon** *adv* a dh'aithghearr.

**anonymous** *adj* neo-ainmichte.

**another** *pron* fear eile. • *adj* eile.

**answer** *n* freagairt *f.*

**answer** *v* freagair.

**ant** *n* seangan *m.*

**antagonist** *n* nàmhaid *m.*

**antediluvian** *adj* roimh 'n Tuil.

**anthem** *n* laoidh *m.*

**anthology** *n* duanaire, cruinneachadh *m.*

**anthropology** *n* daonn-eòlas *m.*

**anticipate** *v* sùilich.

**anticipation** *n* sùileachadh *m.*

**antidote** *n* urchasg *m.*

**antipathy** *n* fuath *m.*

**antiquary** *n* àrsair *m.*

**antique** *adj* seann-saoghlach. • *n* seann-rud *m.*

**antiseptic** *n* loit-leigheas *m.*

**antler** *n* cabar fèidh *m.*

**anvil** *n* innean *m.*

**anxiety** *n* iomagain *m.*

**anxious** *adj* iomagaineach.

**any** *adj* sam bith, air bith, idir. • *pron* aon sam bith; aon; gin.

**anyone** *pron* neach sam bith.

**anything** *n* càil, dad *m.*

**apartheid** *n* sgaradh cinnidh *m.*

**apartment** *n* seòmar *m*; taigh *m.*

**apathy** *n* cion ùidhe *m.*

**ape** *n* apa *f.*

**aperture** *n* toll, fosgladh *m.*

**apex** *n* binnean *m*; bàrr *m.*

**apiece** *adv* an-t-aon.

**apologise** *v* dèan leisgeul.

**apology** *n* leisgeul *m.*

**apostle** *n* abstol *m.*

**apostrophe** *n* ascair *m.*

**appal** *v* cuir uabhas air.

**apparatus** *n* uidheam *m.*

**apparent** *adj* soilleir, faicsinneach.

**apparition** n taibhse f.

**appeal** n tarraing f; (*legal*) ath-agairt m. • v tarraing; ath-agair.

**appear** v nochd.

**appearance** n taisbeanadh m; teachd an làthair m.

**appease** v rèitich.

**append** v cuir ri.

**appendage** n sgòdan m.

**appendix** n (*anat*) aipeandaig f; (*book*) ath-sgrìobadh m.

**appetite** n càil f.

**applaud** v bas-bhuail.

**apple** n ubhal m.

**apple-tree** n craobh-ubhal f.

**appliance** n goireas m.

**applicable** adj freagarrach.

**applicant** n tagraiche m.

**application** n cur an sàs m; (*for a job*) tagradh m.

**applications** npl (*comput*) cleach-daidhean mpl.

**apply** v cuir a-steach.

**appoint** v suidhich.

**appointment** n suidheachadh m.

**apportion** v dèan rionn air.

**appraise** v meas.

**appreciate** v cuir luach air, lu-achaich; (*grow*) àrdaich.

**appreciation** n luachachadh m.

**apprehend** v (*infer*) thoir fa-near; (*arrest*) glac.

**approach** n modh-gabhail f. • v dlùthaich.

**appropriate** adj cubhaidh. • v gabh seilbh air.

**approval** n deagh bharail f.

**approve** v gabh beachd math air.

**approximate** adj dlùthach.

**apricot** n apracot m.

**April** n An Giblean m.

**apron** n aparan m.

**apropos** adv a thaobh.

**apt** adj deas; freagarrach.

**aptitude** n sgil m; buailteachd f.

**Arab** n Arabach m.

**Arabic** adj Arabach.

**arable** adj àitich.

**arbitrate** v rèitich.

**arbitrator** n neach-rèiteachaidh.

**arch** n stuagh m.

**archaeologist** n àrsair m.

**archbishop** n àrd-easbaig m.

**archetype** n prìomh-shamhla m.

**architect** n ailtire m.

**architecture** n ailtireachd f.

**archive** n tasg-lann f.

**ardent** adj dian, bras.

**arduous** adj deacair.

**area** n farsaingeachd, lann f.

**argue** v connsaich; dearbh.

**argument** n connsachadh m; arga-maid f.

**argumentative** adj connsachail.

**arid** adj loisgte.

**arise** v èirich suas.

**arithmetic** n cùnntas m.

**ark** n àirc f.

**arm** n gàirdean m. • v armaich.

**armchair** n cathair-ghàirdeanach f.

**armistice** n fosadh m.

**armour** n armachd f.

**armpit** n achlais f.

**army** n arm, armailt m.

**around** adv mun cuairt. • prep timcheall, mu chuairt.

**arouse** v dùisg.

**arrange** v rèitich, còirich.

**arrangement** n rèiteachadh m; (mus) rian m.

**array** v cuir an ordugh.

**arrears** n fiachan gun dìoladh m.

**arrest** v cuir an làimh.

**arrival** n teachd m.

**arrive** v ruig, thig.

**arrogance** n dànadas m.

**arrogant** adj dàna.

**arrow** n saighead f.

**arsenal** n arm-lann f.

**art** n ealdhain, ealain f; dòigh f; alt m; (artifice) seoltachd f.

**artery** n cuisle f.

**artful** adj innleachdach; seòlta.

**arthritis** n tinneas nan alt m.

**article** n alt m; (clause) bonn m.

**articulate** adj pongail.

**artifice** n seòltachd f.

**artificial** adj brèige.

**artist** n fear-ealain m.

**as** adv cho . . . ri, cho . . . is. • conj mar, ceart mar.

**ascend** v dìrich, streap.

**ascent** n dìreadh m.

**ascertain** v lorg; faigh fios.

**ascribe** v cuir às leth.

**ash** n uinnseann m.

**ashamed** adj nàraichte.

**ashes** n luaithre f.

**ashore** adv air tìr.

**ashtray** n soitheach-luaithre f.

**Asia** n An Aisia f.

**Asiatic, Asian** adj Aisianach.

**aside** adv a thaobh.

**ask** v (request) iarr; (inquire after) faighnich, feòraich.

**askew** adv cam; claon.

**asleep** adj an cadal.

**asparagus** n creamh na muice fiadhaich m.

**aspect** n snuadh m.

**aspen** n critheann m.

**asperity** n gairbhe f.

**aspiration** n dèidh m.

**aspire** v iarr, bi an dèidh air.

**ass** n asal f.

**assail** v thoir ionnsaigh air.

**assailant** n fear-ionnsaigh m.

**assassin** n mortair m.

**assassinate** v moirt, dèan mort.

**assault** n ionnsaigh f.

**assemble** v cruinnich.

**assembly** n mòrdhail m.

**assent** n aonta m.

**assert** v tagair.

**assertion** n tagradh m.

**assertive** adj tagrach.

**assess** v meas; (for taxation) meas a thaobh cis.

**assessment** n meas m; meas a thaobh cis m.

**assessor** n measadair m.

**asset** n taic f.

**assiduity** n dùrachd f.

**assiduous** *adj* leanmhainneach.
**assign** *v* cuir air leth.
**assignation** *n* cur air leth *m*; (*tryst*) coinneamh-leannan *f*.
**assignment** *n* obair shònraichte *f*.
**assimilate** *v* gabh a-steach.
**assist** *v* cuidich.
**assistance** *n* cuideachadh *m*.
**assistant** *n* fear-cuideachaidh.
**associate** *v* theirig am pàirt; cuir as leth.
**association** *n* comann *m*; ceangal *m*.
**assonance** *n* fuaimreagadh *m*.
**assortment** *n* measgachadh *m*.
**assuage** *v* caisg.
**assume** *v* gabh air.
**assumption** *n* gabhail *m*; (*supposition*) barail *f*.
**assurance** *n* dearbhachd *f*.
**assure** *v* dearbh.
**assuredly** *adv* gun teagamh.
**asterisk** *n* reul *f*.
**astern** *adv* an deireadh na luinge.
**asthma** *n* a' chuing *f*.
**astonish** *v* cuir iongnadh air.
**astonishment** *n* iongnadh *m*.
**astray** *adv* air seachran.
**astride** *adv* casa-gobhlach.
**astringent** *adj* ceangailteach; geur is tioram.
**astronaut** *n* speur-sheòladair *m*.
**astrologer** *n* speuradair *m*.
**astrology** *n* speuradaireachd *f*.
**astronomer** *n* reuladair *m*.

**astronomical** *adj* reul-eòlasach.
**astronomy** *n* reul-eòlas *m*.
**asunder** *adv* air leth.
**asylum** *n* àite-dìon *m*.
**at** *prep* aig.
**atheism** *n* neo-dhiadhachd *f*.
**atheist** *n* neo-dhiadhaire *m*.
**athletic** *adj* lùthmhor.
**athletics** *n* lùth-chleasachd *f*.
**athwart** *adv* trasd.
**Atlantic Ocean** *n* An Cuan Siar *m*.
**atlas** *n* atlas *m*.
**atmosphere** *n* àile *m*.
**atom** *n* dadam *m*.
**atomic** *adj* dadamach.
**atone** *v* dèan èiric.
**atonement** *n* rèite *f*.
**atrocious** *adj* uabhasach.
**atrocity** *n* buirbe *f*.
**attach** *v* ceangail.
**attached** *adj* ceangailte.
**attachment** *n* dàimh, gràdh *m*.
**attack** *n* ionnsaigh *m*. • *v* thoir ionnsaigh.
**attain** *v* ruig.
**attainable** *adj* so-ruigsinn.
**attainment** *n* ruigsinn *m*; (*ability*) sgil *m*.
**attempt** *n* oidhirp *f*. • *v* dèan oidhirp.
**attend** *v* fritheil; **attend to** thoir aire.
**attendance** *n* frithealadh *m*.
**attendant** *n* fear-frithealaidh *m*.
**attentive** *adj* furachail.

**attenuate** *v* tanaich.

**attest** *v* thoir fianais.

**attestation** *n* teisteas *m*.

**attire** *n* aodach, trusgan *m*. • *v* sgeadaich.

**attitude** *n* seasamh *m*.

**attract** *v* tarraing.

**attraction** *n* sùgadh *m*.

**attractive** *adj* tarraingeach.

**attribute** *v* cuir às leth.

**attrition** *n* bleith *f*.

**attune** *v* gleus.

**attuned** *adj* air ghleus.

**auburn** *adj* buidhe-ruadh.

**auction** *n* reic-tairgse *f*.

**audible** *adj* àrd-ghuthach.

**audience** *n* luchd-èisdeachd *m*.

**audiovisual** *adj* claistinn-léirsin-neach.

**audit** *n* sgrùdadh *m*. • *v* sgrùd.

**auditor** *n* sgrùdaire *m*.

**augment** *v* meudaich.

**augur** *n* fiosaiche *m*.

**augury** *n* tuar *m*.

**August** *n* Lùnasdal *m*.

**aunt** *n* antaidh *f*.

**aurora borealis** *n* Na Fir Chlis.

**auspicious** *adj* fàbharach.

**austere** *adj* teann.

**austerity** *n* teanntachd *f*.

**Australasia** *n* Astrailàisia *f*.

**Australia** *n* Astràilia *f*.

**Austria** *n* An Ostair *f*.

**authentic** *adj* cinnteach.

**author** *n* ùghdar *m*.

**authorise** *v* thoir ùghdarras.

**authority** *n* ùghdarras, smachd *m*.

**autobiography** *n* fèin-eachdra-ich *f*.

**automatic** *adj* fèin-ghluasadach.

**autumn** *n* Am Foghar *m*.

**auxiliary** *adj* taiceil.

**avail** *v* foghainn.

**available** *adj* ri fhaotainn.

**avarice** *n* sannt *m*.

**avaricious** *adj* sanntach.

**avenge** *v* dìol.

**average** *adj* gnàthach. • *n* mead-han *m*.

**aversion** *n* fuath *m*.

**avid** *adj* gionach.

**avoid** *v* seachainn.

**await** *v* fuirich ri.

**awake** *v* dùisg.

**award** *n* duais *f*. • *v* thoir duais.

**aware** *adj* fiosrach.

**away** *adv* air falbh.

**awesome** *adj* fuathasach.

**awful** *adj* eagalach, uabhasach.

**awhile** *adv* tacan.

**awkward** *adj* cearbach.

**awry** *adj* cam.

**ax, axe** *n* tuagh *f*.

**axle** *n* aiseil *f*.

# B

**babble** n glagais f.

**baby** n leanabh m.

**bachelor** n fleasgach m.

**back** adv air ais. • n cùl m; (person) druim m. • v theirig air ais; (support) seas.

**backbone** n cnàmh-droma m.

**backgammon** n tàileasg m.

**backside** n tòn f.

**backsliding** n cùl-sleamhnachadh m.

**backwards** adv an coinneamh a chùil.

**bacon** n muicfheòil f.

**bacterial** adj bacteridheach.

**bad** adj dona, olc.

**bad-tempered** adj greannach.

**badge** n suaicheantas m.

**badger** n broc m.

**badness** n donas m.

**baffle** v dèan a chuis air.

**bag** n poca m.

**baggage** n treallaichean f.

**bagpipe** n pìob, a' phìob mhor f.

**bail** n fuasgladh air urras m. • v thoir urras air.

**bailiff** n bàillidh m.

**bait** n maghar m. • v biadh.

**bake** v fuin; bruich ann an àmhainn.

**baker** n fuineadair, bèicear m.

**bakery** n taigh-fuine m.

**balance** n meidh f; (mental) co-throm m; (fin) còrr m. • v cuir air meidh; cothromaich.

**balcony** n for-uinneag f.

**bald** adj maol.

**baldness** n maoile f.

**baleful** adj millteach.

**ball** n ball m; (dance) bàl.

**ballad** n bailead m.

**ballast** n balaiste f.

**balloon** n bailiùn m.

**ballot** n bhòtadh m.

**balm** n ìocshlaint f.

**bamboo** n cuilc Innseanach f.

**bamboozle** v cuir an imcheist.

**ban** n toirmeasg f. • v toirmisg.

**banana** n banàna m.

**band** n bann m; còmhlan m; (mus) còmhlan ciùil m.

**bandage** n stìom-cheangail f.

**bandy-legged** adj camachasach.

**baneful** adj nimheil.

**bang** n cnag f; bualadh m. • v cnag; buail.

**banish** v fògair.

**banishment** n fògradh m.

**basking shark** n cearban m.

**battery** n bataraidh m.

**bawdy** adj drabasda.

**bead** n grìogag m.

**beak** n gob m.

**beans** npl pònair m.

**beard** n feusag m.

**beast** n beathach m, biast m.

**beat** v thoir buille.
**beautiful** adj bòidheach.
**beauty** maise, bòidhchead m.
**beckon** v smèid air.
**bed** n leabaidh m.
**bedroom** n seòmar leapa m.
**bee** n seillean, beach m.
**beef** n mairtheoil.
**beer** n leann m.
**beetle** n daolag m.
**beg** v iarr; dèan faoighe.
**beggar** n dèirceach m.
**behave** v giùlain.
**behaviour** n giùlan m; modh m.
**bell** n clag m.
**bellow** v beucaich.
**bellows** n balg-sèididh m.
**belly** n brù, broinn f.
**belong** v buin.
**beloved** adj gràdhach.
**below** adv shìos.
**belt** n crios m.
**bench** n being f.
**bend** n lùb m. • v lùb.
**beneath** prep fo.
**benediction** n beannachadh m.
**benefaction** n tabhartas m.
**benefactor** n taibheartach m.
**beneficent** adj deagh-ghnìomh-ach.
**beneficial** adj tairbheach.
**benefit** n sochair m.
**benevolence** n deagh-ghean m.
**benevolent** adj coibhneil.
**benign** adj suairc.
**bent** adj lùbte.

**benumb** v meilich.
**bequeath** v tiomnaich.
**bequest** n dìleab m.
**bereaved** adj rùisgte.
**berry** n dearc f, subh m.
**beseech** v dèan guidhe.
**beside** prep ri taobh.
**besides** adv a bhàrr air.
**besiege** v dèan sèisd air.
**best** adj as fheàrr. • n rogha m. • v fairtlich air.
**bestial** adj brùideil.
**bestow** v builich.
**bet** v cuir geall.
**betray** v brath.
**betrayer** n brathadair m.
**betrayal** n brathadh m.
**betroth** v rèitich.
**better** adj nas fheàrr.
**between** adv eadar. • prep eadar.
**bewail** v caoidh.
**beware** v thoir an aire.
**bewitch** v cuir fo gheasaibh.
**beyond** prep air taobh thall; seachad air.
**bias** n claonadh m.
**bible** n bìoball m.
**biblical** adj sgriobturail.
**bicycle** n bàidhseagal m.
**bid** n tairgse f. • v thoir tairgse.
**bidding** n (invitation) cuireadh m.
**bide** v fuirich.
**biennial** adj dà-bhliannach.
**bier** n carbad-adhlacaidh, giùlan m.
**big** adj mòr.

**bigamy** *n* dà-chèileachas *m*.

**bigot** *n* dalm-bheachdaiche *m*.

**bigotry** *n* dalm-bheachd *m*.

**bilateral** *adj* dà-thaobhach.

**bile** *n* domblas *m*.

**bilingual** *adj* dà-chànanach.

**bill** *n* gob *m*; (*account*) bileag.

**billion** *n* billean *m*.

**bin** *n* biona *f*.

**binary** *adj* càraideach.

**bind** *v* ceangail.

**binding** *n* ceangal *m*.

**biochemist** *n* bith-cheimicear *m*.

**biochemistry** *n* bith-cheimiceachd *f*.

**biography** *n* beath-eachdraidh *f*.

**biological** *adj* bith-eòlasach.

**biology** *n* bith-eòlas *m*.

**biped** *n* dà-chasach *m*.

**birch** *n* beithe *f*.

**bird** *n* eun *m*.

**bird-song** *n* ceilear *m/f*.

**birth** *n* breith *f*.

**birth certificate** *n* teisteanas-breith *m*.

**birthday** *n* ceann-bliadhna *m*.

**birthright** *n* còir-bhreith *f*.

**biscuit** *n* briosgaid *f*.

**bisect** *v* geàrr sa' mheadhan.

**bishop** *n* easbaig *m*.

**bit** *n* mìr, bìdeag *m*; (*horse*) cabstair *m*.

**bitch** *n* galla *f*.

**bite** *v* bìd, thoir grèim à.

**biting** *adj* bìdeach.

**bitter** *adj* geur.

**black** *adj* dubh, dorch.

**blackbird** *n* lon-dubh *m*.

**blackboard** *n* bòrd-dubh *m*.

**blacken** *v* dubh, dèan dubh.

**black-humoured** *adj* gruamach.

**blackness** *n* duibhead *m*.

**blacksmith** *n* gobha *m*.

**bladder** *n* aotroman *m*.

**blade** *n* (*of grass*) bilean; (*of weapon*) lann.

**blame** *n* coire *f*. • *v* coirich.

**blameless** *adj* neo-choireach.

**blanch** *v* gealaich.

**bland** *adj* mìn.

**blank** *adj* bàn.

**blanket** *n* plaide, plangaid *f*.

**blasphemy** *n* toibheum *m*.

**blast** *n* sgal *m*. • *v* sgrios.

**blaze** *n* teine lasrach *m*. • *v* las.

**bleach** *v* todhair.

**bleak** *adj* lom, fuar.

**bleat** *v* dèan mèilich.

**bleed** *v* leig fuil.

**blemish** *n* gaoid *f*.

**blend** *n* coimeasgadh *m*. • *v* coimeasgaich.

**bless** *v* beannaich.

**blessed** *adj* beannaichte.

**blessing** *n* beannachd *f*.

**blight** *n* fuar-dhealt.

**blind** *adj* dall. • *n* sgàil *m*.

**blind man** *n* dallaran *m*.

**blindness** *n* doille *f*.

**blink** *v* caog.

**bliss** *n* aoibhneas *m*.

**blissful** *adj* aoibhneach.

**blister** n leus m. • v thoir leus air; thig leus air.

**blithe** adj aoibhinn.

**block** n ploc m. • v caisg.

**blockhead** n bumailear m.

**blonde** n te bhàn f.

**blood** n fuil f.

**blood feud** n folachd f.

**blood group** n seòrsa fala m.

**blood pressure** n bruthadh fala m.

**bloodshed** n dòrtadh-fala m.

**blood transfusion** n leasachadh-fala m.

**bloody** adj fuileach.

**bloom** n blàth m.

**blot** n dubhadh m.

**blotting paper** n pàipear-sùghaidh m.

**blouse** n blobhsa f.

**blow** v sèid.

**blubber** n saill (muice-mara) f.

**blue** adj gorm.

**blueness** n guirme f.

**bluff** v meall.

**blunder** n iomrall m.

**blunt** adj maol. • v maolaich.

**blur** v dèan doilleir.

**blush** n rudhadh m.

**bluster** v bagair.

**boar** n torc m.

**board** n bòrd m, dèile f. • v rach air bòrd.

**boarding house** n taigh-aoigheachd m.

**boarding pass** n cead dol air bòrd m.

**boast** n bòsd. • v dèan bòsd.

**boaster** n bòsdair m.

**boastful** adj bòsdail.

**boat** n bàta m.

**body** n corp m; (person) neach, creutair m; (band) buidheann m.

**bog** n boglach, fèithe f.

**bog-cotton** n canach m.

**boggle** v bi an teagamh.

**boil** v goil; bruich.

**boiled** adj bruich.

**boiler** n goileadair m.

**boisterous** adj stoirmeil; iorgh-aileach.

**bold** adj dàna.

**boldness** n dànadas m.

**bolster** v misnich.

**bolt** n crann m. • v cuir crann air.

**bomb** n bom, boma m. • v leag bom air.

**bond** n ceangal m.

**bondage** n daorsa m.

**bone** n cnàmh m.

**boneless** adj gun chnàimh.

**bonfire** n tein-aighear m.

**bonnet** n bonaid f.

**bonny** adj maiseach.

**bonus** n còrr m.

**bony** adj cnàmhach.

**book** n leabhar m.

**bookcase** n lann leabhraichean f.

**bookish** adj dèidheil air leughadh.

**book-keeper** n fear chumail leabhraichean m.

**book-keeping** n leabhar-chùntas m.

**bookseller** n leabhar-reiceadair m.

**bookshop** n bùth-leabhraichean m.

**boor** n amhasg m.

**boorish** n amhasgail m.

**boot** n bròg m.

**booty** n cobhartach m/f.

**booze** n stuth òil m. • v òl.

**border** n crìoch f.

**borderer** n fear àiteach nan crìoch m.

**bore** n duine ràsanach m.

**bore** v cladaich.

**boring** adj fadalach.

**borrow** v faigh, gabh iasad.

**borrower** n fear gabhail iasaid m.

**bosom** n uchd m.

**boss** n ceann m.

**botanise** v cruinnich luibhean.

**botanist** n luibh-eòlaiche m.

**botany** n luibh-eòlas m.

**both** adj araon, le chèile, an dà; (people) an dithis.

**bother** n sàrachadh m. • v sàraich.

**bottle** n botal m.

**bottom** n lochdar m; grùnnd m; màs m.

**bottomless** adj gun ghrùnnd.

**bough** n geug f.

**bound** n sìnteag f. • v thoir leum.

**bountiful** adj fialaidh.

**bourgeois** adj bùirdeasach.

**bow** n bogha m; (ship) toiseach m; (head) ùmhlachd m.

**bowels** n innidh f.

**bowl** n cuach f, bòbhla m.

**bowsprit** n crann-spreòid m.

**bowstring** n taifeid m.

**box** n bocsa, bocas m. • v (sport) dèan sabaid.

**boxer** n fear-sabaid, bocsair m.

**boxer shorts** npl pantaichean bocsair.

**boy** n balach, gille m.

**brace** n (pair) dithis m.

**braces** npl galars.

**bracken** n raineach f.

**bracket** n camag f.

**brae** n bruthach f.

**brag** v dèan bòsd.

**bragging** n bòsd, spaglainn m.

**brain** n eanchainn f.

**bramble** n smeur f.

**bramble-bush** n dris f.

**branch** n meangan m, geug f. • v sgaoil.

**brandish** v beartaich.

**brandy** n branndaidh f.

**brass** n pràis f.

**brat** n isean m.

**brave** adj gaisgeil.

**bravery** n misneachd f.

**brawl** n stairirich m. • v dèan stairirich.

**bray** v dèan sitir.

**breach** n briseadh m. • v dèan briseadh.

**bread** n aran m.

**breadcrumb** n criomag arain f.

**breadth** n leud m.

**break** v bris; sgar.

**breakfast** n biadh-maidne m.

**breast** n cìoch f.

**breath** n anail f.

**breathe** v (out) leig anail; (in) tarraing anail.

**breathless** adj plosgartach.

**breed** n seòrsa m. • v tarmaich.

**breeding** n oilean m.

**breeze** n tlàth-ghaoth f.

**brevity** n giorrad m.

**brew** v dèan grùdaireachd; tarraing.

**brewer** n grùdaire m.

**bribe** n brìb f. • v brìb.

**bribery** n brìbeireachd f.

**brick** n breice f.

**bricklayer** n breicire m.

**bridal** adj pòsda.

**bride** n bean-bainnse f.

**bridegroom** n fear-bainnse m.

**bridesmaid** n maighdean-phòsaidh f.

**bridge** n drochaid f.

**brief** adj geàrr.

**brigand** n spùinneadair m.

**bright** adj soilleir; (mind) tuigseach.

**brighten** v soillsich.

**brightness** n soilleireachd f.

**brilliant** adj boillsgeach; (mind) air leth geur.

**brim** n oir m.

**brine** n sàl m.

**bring** v thoir.

**brink** n oir m.

**brisk** adj beothail.

**briskness** n beothalachd f.

**bristle** n calg m. • v cuir calg air.

**Britain** n Breatainn f.

**British** adj Breatannach.

**brittle** adj brisg.

**broach** v (open) toll; (introduce) tog.

**broad** adj leathann.

**broadcast** v craobh-sgaoil.

**broadcaster** n craobh-sgaoile-adair m.

**brochure** n leabhran m.

**brogue** n bròg èille f; (language) dual-chainnt f.

**broken** adj briste.

**broker** n fear-gnothaich m.

**brokerage** n duais fir-gnothaich f.

**bronchial** adj sgòrnanach.

**bronchitis** n at sgòrnain m.

**bronze** n umha m.

**bronzed** adj (tanned) donn, grian-loisgte.

**brooch** n bràiste f.

**brood** n àl m. • v àlaich.

**brook** n alltan m.

**broom** n bealaidh m; sguab m.

**broth** n eanraich f, brot m.

**brothel** n taigh-siùrsachd m.

**brother** n bràthair m.

**brotherhood** n bràithreachas m.

**brotherly** adj bràithreil.

**brow** n mala f; (of hill) maoilean m.

**brown** adj donn.

**brownness** n duinne f.

**browse** v criom; (book) thoir ruith air.

**bruise** n pronnadh m. • v pronn.

**brunette** n tè dhonn f.

**brush** n sguab f. • v sguab.

**Brussels** n A' Bhruiseal f.

**brutal** adj brùideil.

**brutality** n brùidealachd f.

**brute** n brùid m.

**bubble** n builgean m.

**buck** n boc m.

**bucket** n cuinneag f.

**buckle** n bucall m.

**bud** n gucag f.

**budge** v caraich.

**budget** n càin-aisneis f.

**buffet** n beum m; (food table) clàr bìdh m.

**bug** n (infection) galar m.

**bugle** n dùdach f.

**build** v tog.

**builder** n fear-togail m.

**building** n togalach m.

**building society** n comann thog-alach m.

**bulb** n bolgan m.

**bulk** n meudachd f.

**bulky** adj tomadach.

**bull** n tarbh m.

**bulldog** n tarbh-chù m.

**bulldozer** n tarbh-chrann m.

**bullet** n peilear m.

**bulletin** n cùirt-iomradh m.

**bullock** n tarbh òg m.

**bully** n pulaidh m.

**bum** n màs m.

**bump** n meall; bualadh m.

**bumper** n bumpair m.

**bun** n buna m.

**bunch** n bagaid f.

**bundle** n pasgan m.

**bung** n tùc m.

**bungle** v dèan gu cearbach.

**bungler** n cearbaire m.

**buoy** n put m.

**buoyancy** n fleodradh m.

**buoyant** adj aotrom.

**burden** n eallach m. • v uallaich.

**bureau** n biùro m.

**burgh** n borgh m.

**burglar** n gadaiche-taighe m.

**burglary** n gadachd-taighe f.

**burial** n adhlacadh m.

**burlesque** n sgeigeireachd f.

**burly** adj tapaidh.

**burn**[1] n losgadh m. • v loisg.

**burn**[2] n (stream) alltan m.

**burning** n losgadh m.

**burnish** v lìomh.

**burst** v spreadh.

**bury** v adhlaic.

**bus** n bus, baos m.

**bush** n preas m.

**bushy** adj preasach.

**business** n gnothach m, malairt f.

**businessman** n fear-gnothaich m.

**bust** n ceann is guaillean m.

**bustle** n othail f.

**busy** adj trang.

**busybody** n gobaire m.

**but** *conj*, *adv*, *prep* ach.

**butcher** *n* feòladair *m*. • *v* casgair.

**Bute** *n* Bòid.

**butler** *n* buidealair *m*.

**butt**[1] *n* cùis-bhùirt *m*; (*cask*) baraill *m*; (*target*) targaid *f*.

**butt**[2] *v* sàth.

**butter** *n* ìm *m*.

**buttercup** *n* buidheag-an-t-sam-raidh *f*.

**butterfly** *n* dealan-dè *m*.

**buttery** *adj* ìmeach.

**buttock** *n* màs *m*.

**button** *n* putan *m*. • *v* putanaich.

**buxom** *adj* tiugh.

**buy** *v* ceannaich.

**buyer** *n* ceannaiche *m*.

**buzz** *n* srann *f*. • *v* srann.

**buzzard** *n* clamhan *m*.

**by** *adv* seachad; (*aside*) an dara taobh. • *prep* fasg air; le; **by and by** *adv* a dh' aithghearr, dh' aith-gearr.

**by-election** *n* frith-thaghadh *m*.

**bypass** *n* seach-rathad *m*.

**byre** *n* bàthach *f*.

**bystander** *n* fear-amhairc *m*.

# C

**cab** *n* tagsaidh *m*.

**cabbage** *n* càl *m*.

**caber** *n* cabar *m*.

**cabin** *n* seòmar luinge, cèaban *m*.

**cadaverous** *adj* cairbheach.

**cadence** *n* dùnadh *m*.

**cadger** *n* fear-faoighe *m*.

**café** *n* cafaidh *m*.

**cage** *n* cèidse *f*.

**cairn** *n* càrn *m*.

**cajole** *v* breug.

**cake** *n* breacag *f*.

**calamitous** *adj* dosgainneach.

**calamity** *n* dosgainn *f*.

**calculate** *v* tomhais.

**calculation** *n* tomhas *m*.

**calculator** *n* àireamhair *m*.

**calculus** *n* riaghailt-àireamh *f*.

**Caledonia** *n* Albann *f*.

**calendar** *n* mìosachan *m*.

**calf** *n* laogh *m*; (*leg*) calpa *m*.

**calibre** *n* meudachd *f*.

**call** *v* glaodh.

**call-box** *n* bocsa-fòn *m*.

**calligraphy** *n* làmh-sgrìobhaidh *f*.

**calling** *n* eigheachd *f*; (*vocation*) dreuchd *f*.

**calliper** *n* cailpear *m*.

**callous** *adj* cruaidh-chridheach.

**calm** *adj* ciùin; fèathach.

**calm** *v* ciùinich.

**calumniate** *v* cùl-chàin.

**calve** *v* beir laogh.

**camel** n càmhal m.

**camera** n camara m.

**camouflage** n breug-riochd m.

**camp** n càmpa m.

**camp** v càmpaich.

**campaign** n còmhrag f.

**can**[1] n canastair m.

**can**[2] v (may) faod; (be able) is urrainn do.

**Canadian** adj Canèideanach.

**canal** n clais-uisge f.

**cancel** v dubh a-mach.

**cancellation** n dubhadh a-mach
m.

**cancer** n aillse f.

**cancerous** adj aillseach.

**candid** adj neo-chealgach.

**candidate** n fear-iarraidh m.

**candle** n coinneal f.

**candlestick** n coinnlear m.

**candour** n fosgarrachd f.

**canine** adj conail.

**cannibal** n canabail m.

**canny** adj cùramach.

**canonise** v cuir an àireamh nan
naomh.

**canter** n trotan m.

**canvas** n canabhas m.

**canvass** v beachd-rannsaich.

**canvasser** n sireadair m.

**cap** n bonaid m/f, ceap m.

**cap** v còmhdaich; (fig) thoir bàrr
air.

**capability** n cumhachd m.

**capable** adj comasach.

**capacious** adj farsaing.

**capacity** n comas m.

**cape** n rubha m; cleòc m.

**caper** v leum.

**capital** n ceanna-bhaile m.

**capital letter** n corr-litir f.

**capitalism** n calpachas m.

**capitalist** n calpaire m.

**capitulate** v strìochd.

**capitulation** n strìochdadh m.

**caprice** n neònachas m.

**capricious** adj neònach.

**capsule** n capsal m.

**captain** n caiptean m.

**caption** n tiotal m; fo-thiotal m.

**captive** n ciomach m.

**captivity** n ciomachas m.

**capture** n glacadh m.

**capture** v glac.

**car** n càr, carbad m.

**carbohydrate** n gualaisg m.

**carbon** n gualan m.

**carcass** n cairbh m.

**card** n cairt f.

**card** v càrd.

**cardboard** n cairt-bhòrd m.

**cardiac** adj cridhe.

**cardiac disease** n tinneas cridhe
m.

**cardinal** adj prìomh. • n càirdineal.

**card index** n clàr-amais cairt m.

**care** n cùram m. • v gabh cùram.

**career** n (rush) rèis f; (work)
dreachd f.

**careful** adj cùramach.

**careless** adj mì-chùramach.

**carelessness** n mì-chùram m.

**caress** v cnèadaich.

**caretaker** n fear-aire m.

**cargo** n luchd m.

**caricature** n dealbh-magaidh m.

**carnage** n àr m.

**carnal** adj feòlmhor.

**carnival** n fèill f.

**carnivorous** adj feòil-itheach.

**carousal** n fleadh m.

**carpark** n pàirc-chàraichean f.

**carpenter** n saor m

**carpet** n brat-ùrlair m.

**carriage** n carbad m; (gait) giùlan m.

**carrier** n fear-ghiùlain m.

**carrion** n ablach m.

**carrot** n curran m.

**carry** v giùlain, iomchair, thoir.

**cart** n cairt f. • v giùlain le cairt.

**cartilage** n maoth-chnàimh m.

**cartoon** n dealbh-èibhinn m/f.

**cartridge** n catraisde f.

**carve** v geàrr; snaigh.

**carving** n snaigheadh m.

**cascade** n eas m.

**case** n còmhdach m; ceus m; staid m; cùis m; tuiseal m.

**cash** n airgead ullamh m.

**cash-book** n leabhar-airgid m.

**cashier** n gleidheadair airgid m.

**cash machine** n inneal-airgid m.

**cash register** n inneal-cùnntaidh airgid m.

**cask** n buideal m.

**cassock** n casag f.

**cast** v tilg, cuir; **cast loose** v sgaoil.

**caste** n dual-fhine f.

**castigate** v cronaich.

**castle** n caisteal m.

**castrate** v spoth.

**casual** adj tuiteamach.

**casualty** n leòinteach m.

**cat** n cat m.

**catalogue** n ainm-chlàr m.

**catalyse** v cruth-atharraich.

**catapult** n tailm m.

**cataract** see cascade; (eye) n meam-ran sùla m.

**catarrh** n an galar smugaideach m.

**catastrophe** n droch thubaist f.

**catch** n glacadh m. • v glac, greimich.

**catching** adj gabhaltach.

**catechism** n leabhar-cheist m.

**categorical** adj làn-chinnteach.

**category** n gnè f.

**cater** v solair.

**caterpillar** n burras m.

**caterpillar-tracked** adj burras-ach.

**cathedral** n cathair-eaglais f.

**Catholic** adj Caitligeach.

**catholic** adj coitcheann.

**cattle** n spreidh f.

**cattle show** n fèill a' chruidh f.

**cauldron** n coire mòr m.

**cauliflower** n colag f.

**causal** adj adhbharach.

**causation** n adhbharachadh m.

**cause** n adhbhar m; cùis m. • v dèan, thoir gu buil.

**causeway** n cabhsair m.

**caustic** adj loisgeach.

**caution** n cùram m. • v cuir air fhaicill.

**cautious** adj cùramach.

**cavalry** n marc-shluagh m.

**cave** n uamh f.

**cavity** n lag m/f, sloc f.

**cease** v stad.

**cease-fire** n stad-losgaidh m.

**ceaseless** adj gun stad.

**cedar** n seudar m.

**cede** v gèill.

**ceilidh** n cèilidh m/f.

**ceiling** n mullach m.

**celebrate** v glèidh; bi subhach.

**celebrity** n neach iomraiteach m.

**celestial** adj nèamhaidh.

**celibacy** n aontamhachd f.

**celibate** adj aontamhach.

**cell** n cealla; prìosan f.

**cellar** n seilear m.

**cello** n beus-fhidheall f.

**cellular** adj ceallach.

**celluloid** n ceallaloid m.

**Celt** n Ceilteach m.

**Celtic** adj Ceilteach.

**cement** n saimeant m. • v tàth.

**cemetery** n cladh m.

**censor** n caisgire m. • v caisg.

**censorious** adj cronachail.

**censure** n coire f. • v coirich.

**census** n cùnntas-sluaigh m.

**centenary** n ceud blianna m.

**centennial** adj ceud-bhliannach.

**centimetre** n ciadameatair m.

**central** adj anns a' mheadan.

**central heating** n teasachadh meadhanach m.

**central processing unit** n prìomh ghnìomh-inneal m.

**centre** n meadhan m.

**centrifugal** adj meadhan-sheach-nach.

**centripetal** adj meadhan-aoma-chail.

**century** n ceud blianna, linn m.

**cereal** n gràn m.

**ceremony** n deas-ghnàth m.

**certain** adj cinnteach.

**certainly** adv gu cinnteach.

**certainty** n cinnt f.

**certificate** n teisteanas m.

**certify** v teistich.

**cesspool** n poll-caca m.

**chagrin** n mìghean m.

**chain** n slabhraidh f. • v cuibhrich.

**chain store** n bùth-sreatha f.

**chair** n cathair f.

**chairman** n fear-cathrach m.

**chalk** n cailc f.

**challenge** n dùbhshlan m.

**chamber** n seòmar m.

**chambered** adj seòmrach.

**champ** v cagainn.

**champion** n gaisgeach m.

**championship** n urram gaisgeachd m.

**chance** n tuiteamas m.

**change** n caochladh m; (money) iomlaid f. • v mùth.

**changeable** adj caochlaideach.

**channel** n amar, caolas m.

**chant** v sianns.

**chanter** n feadan m.

**chaos** n eucruth m.

**chapel** n caibeal m.

**chapter** n caibideil m/f.

**character** n beus, mèinn f; (story) pearsa m.

**characteristic** adj coltach.

**charcoal** n gual-fiodha m.

**charge** n earbsa f; ionnsaigh f; prìs f. • v earb; thoir ionnsaigh; cuir.

**charity** n gràdh, coibhneas m.

**charm** n mealladh m; (spell) ortha f. • v meall; cuir fo dhraoidheachd.

**chart** n cairt-iùil f.

**charter** v fasdaidh.

**chase** n sealg. • v ruith.

**chaste** adj geanmnaidh.

**chastity** n geanmnachd f.

**chat** v dèan còmhradh.

**chatter** v dèan cabaireachd.

**cheap** adj saor; air bheag prìs.

**cheapness** n saoiread m.

**cheat** n mealltair m. • v dèan foill air.

**check** n casg m. • v caisg.

**checkmate** n tul-chasg m.

**cheek** n gruaidh f.

**cheer** v brosnaich.

**cheese** n càise m, càbag f.

**chemical** adj ceimiceach.

**chemist** n ceimicear m; fear-chungaidhean.

**cheque** n seic f.

**cherry** n sirist f.

**chess** n fidhcheall m.

**chest** n ciste f; cliabh f.

**chew** v cagainn.

**chicken** n isean m.

**chief** n ceann-feadhna m.

**chilblain** n cusp f.

**child** n leanabh m.

**childhood** n leanabas m.

**childless** adj gun sliochd.

**children** n clann f.

**chill** v fuaraich.

**chilly** adj fuar.

**chimney** n similear m.

**chin** n smig m.

**China** n Sìna.

**chocolate** n teòclaid f.

**choice** n roghainn m.

**choir** n còisir-chiùil f.

**choke** v tachd.

**choose** v roghnaich.

**chop** n staoig. • v sgud.

**chord** n còrda f.

**chorus** n sèist f; co-sheirm f.

**Christ** n Crìosd m.

**christen** v baist.

**Christmas** n Nollaig f.

**chronic** adj leantalach.

**chronicle** n eachdhraidh f.

**church** n eaglais f.

**churchyard** n cladh m.

**churlish** adj mùgach.

**cigarette** n toitean m.

**cinema** n taigh-dhealbh m.

**circle** n cearcall; còmhlan m. • v cuairtich.

**circuit** n cuairt f.

**circular** adj cruinn.

**circulate** v cuir mun cuairt.

**circumnavigate** v seòl mun cuairt.

**circumstance** n cùis f.

**circus** n soircas m.

**citizen** n fear-àiteachaidh m.

**city** n cathair f.

**civil** adj sìobhalta.

**civilian** n sìobhaltair m.

**civilisation** n sìobhaltachd f.

**civilise** v sìobhail.

**claim** n tagairt f. • v tagair.

**claimant** n fear-tagraidh m.

**clan** n fine f, cinneadh m.

**clanship** n cinneadas m.

**clap** n buille f. • v buail ri chèile.

**claret** n clàireat f.

**clarify** v soilleirich.

**clash** v dèan glagadaich.

**clasp** n dubhan m.

**class** n buidheann f, clas m. • v seòrsaich.

**classical** adj clasaiceach.

**classify** v seòrsaich.

**claw** n iongna f.

**clay** n crèadh f.

**claymore** n claideamh-mòr m.

**clean** adj glan. • v glan.

**cleanness** n gloinead m.

**clear** adj soilleir. • v soilleirich.

**cleft** n sgoltadh m.

**cleg** n crèithleag f.

**clench** v dùin.

**clergy** n clèir f.

**clergyman** n pears-eaglais m.

**clever** adj tapaidh.

**click** v cnag.

**clientèle** n luchd-dèilig m.

**cliff** n creag f, sgùrr m.

**climate** n clìomaid f.

**climb** v dìrich, streap.

**climber** n streapaiche m.

**climbing** n dìreadh m.

**cling** v slaod.

**clinic** n clionaic f.

**clink** v thoir gliong.

**clip** v geàrr.

**clipper** n gearradair m.

**clock** n uaireadair, cleoc m.

**clod** n ploc m.

**clog** v tromaich.

**cloister** n clabhstair m.

**clone** n lethbhreac ginteil m. • v mac-samhlaich.

**close**[1] adj (near) faisg; (stuffy) dùmhail. • n (entry) clobhsa m.

**close**[2] v dùin. • n dùnadh m.

**clot** n meall m.

**cloth** n aodach m.

**clothe** v còmhdaich.

**clothes** npl aodach, trusgan m.

**cloud** n neul m.

**cloudy** adj neulach.

**clout,** n (cloth) clùd m.

**clover** n clòbhar m.

**clown** n amadan m.

**cloy** v sàsaich.

**club** n (stick) cuaille, caman m.

**cluck** v dèan gogail.

**clump** n tom m.

**clumsy** adj cearbach.

**cluster** n bagaid f.

**clutch** n grèim m; (car) put. • v greimich.

**coagulate** v binndich.

**coal** n gual m.

**coalesce** v aonaich.

**coarse** adj garbh.

**coast** n oirthir f.

**coastguard** n freiceadan-oirthire m.

**coastline** n iomall-fairge m.

**coat** n còta m. • v cuir brat air.

**coax** v tàlaidh.

**cobweb** n eige f.

**cockle** n coilleag f.

**cocksure** adj coccanta, spairisteach.

**cock** n coileach m.

**cod** n trosg m.

**code** n riaghailt f.

**co-education** n co-fhoglam m.

**coerce** v ceannsaich.

**coeval** adj co-aimsireach.

**co-exist** v bi beò le.

**coffee** n cofaidh m.

**coffin** n ciste-laighe f.

**cog** n fiacaill f.

**cogent** adj làidir.

**cohabitation** n co-fhuireachd f.

**cohere** v lean.

**coherent** adj so-leantainn.

**coil** n cuibhleachadh m. • v cuibhlich.

**coin** n bonn airgid m.

**coinage** n cùinneadh m.

**coincide** v co-thirit.

**coincidence** n co-thuiteamas m.

**cold** adj fuar. • n fuachd m; cnatan m.

**coldness** n fuairead m.

**collaborate** v co-oibrich.

**collapse** v tuit am broinn a chèile.

**collapsible** adj so-sheacaich.

**collar** n coilear m.

**collarbone** n ugan m.

**colleague** n co-oibriche m.

**collect** v cruinnich.

**collective** adj co-choitcheann.

**college** n colaisde f.

**collision** n co-bhualadh m.

**collusion** n co-rùn m.

**colonel** n còirneal m.

**colony** n tìr-imrich f.

**colour** n dath m. • v dath.

**column** n colbh m.

**coma** n trom-neul m.

**comb** n cìr f. • v cìr.

**combination** n co-aontachadh m.

**combine** v co-aontaich.

**come** v thig; (imper) trobhad!

**comedian** n cleasaiche m.

**comedy** n cleas-chluich f.

**comet** n reul-chearbach f.

**comfort** n cofhurtachd f.

**comfortable** adj cofhurtail.

**comic** adj àbhachdach.

**coming** n teachd m.

**comma** n cromag f.

**command** n òrdugh m.

**commemorate** v cuimhnich.

**commend** v mol.

**commendable** adj ri a mholadh.

**comment** n facal m. • v thoir tar-raing.

**commerce** n malairt f.

**commercial** adj malairteach.

**commiserate** v co-bhàidhich.

**commission** n ùghdarras m.

**commit** v earb; (crime, etc) cion-taich.

**committee** n comataidh f.

**commodious** adj luchdmhor.

**commodity** n badhar m.

**common** adj coitcheann.

**Commonwealth** n Co-fhlaitheas m.

**communicate** v com-pàirtich.

**communication** n com-pàir-teachadh m; **communications** npl eadar-cheangal m.

**community** n pobal m.

**commute** v malairtich; triall.

**compact** adj teann.

**compact disc** n meanbh-chlàr m.

**companion** n companach m.

**company** n cuideachd f; compa-naidh f.

**compare** v coimeas.

**compass** n combaist f; meud m.

**compassion** n truas m.

**compatible** adj co-fhulangach.

**compatriot** n co-fhear-dùthcha m.

**compel** v co-èignich.

**compensate** v diol.

**compete** v strì.

**competition** n co-fharpais f.

**competitor** n farpaiseach m.

**complacent** adj somalta.

**complain** v gearain.

**complaint** n gearan m; (illness) galar.

**computer** n coimpiutair m.

**conjugate** v co-naisg.

**conjunction** n naisgear m.

**conjure** v cuir impidh air.

**connection** n ceangal m.

**connoisseur** n fear-eòlach m.

**conquer** v ceannsaich.

**conquest** n buaidh f.

**conscience** n cogais f.

**conscientious** adj cogaisach.

**conscious** adj mothachail.

**consciously** adv le mothachadh.

**consecrate** v coisrig.

**consecutive** adj leanmhainneach.

**consent** n aonta m.

**consent** v aontaich.

**consequence** n toradh m.

**consequently** adv uime sin.

**conservancy** n glèidhteachas m.

**conservation** n gleidheadh m.

**conserve** v taisg.

**consider** v smaoinich.

**considerable** adj math, cudro-mach.

**consideration** n tuigse f.

**consignment** n lìbhrigeadh m.

**consistency** n seasmhachd f.

**consolation** n sòlas m.

**console** v furtaich.

**consonant** n co-fhoghar m.

**consort** n cèile m.

**conspicuous** adj faicsinneach.

**conspire** v dèan co-fheall.

**constancy** n neo-chaochlai-deachd f.

**constant** adj daingeann.

**constellation** n reul-bhad m.

**constipation** n teannachadh-in-nidh m.

**constituency** n roinn-taghaidh f.

**constitution** n dèanamh, nàdar m; (political) bonn-stèidh.

**constriction** n teannachadh m.

**construct** v tog.

**construction** n togail f.

**consult** v gabh comhairle.

**consume** v caith.

**consumer** n fear-caitheamh m.

**consummate** v crìochnaich.

**contact** v (physical) suath ann; (message) cuir fios gu.

**contain** v cùm; caisg.

**container** n bocsa-stòraidh m.

**contemplate** v beachd-smuai-nich.

**contemporary** adj co-aoiseach.

**contempt** n tàir f.

**contemptuous** adj tarcaiseach.

**content** adj toilichte.

**context** n co-theacs m.

**continent** n mòr-thìr f.

**contingent** adj tuiteamach.

**continual** adj sìor.

**continually** adv gun sgur.

**continue** v lean air.

**continuous** adj leanailteach.

**contour** n (map) loidhne àirde f.

**contraception** n casg-gineamh-ainn m.

**contract** n cùnnnradh. • v tean-naich; rèitich.

**contraction** n teannachadh m.

**contradict** v cuir an aghaidh.

**contradiction** n breugnachadh m.

**contrary** adj an aghaidh.

**contrast** v eadar-dhealaich.

**contravene** v bris.

**contribute** v cuir ri.

**contribution** n cuideachadh m.

**contrivance** n innleachd f.

**control** n smachd m.

**control** v ceannsaich; stiùir.

**controversial** adj connsachail.

**controversy** n connspaid f.

**convalescence** n iar-shlànach-adh m.

**convalescent** adj iar-shlànach.

**convener** n fear-gairm m.

**convenient** adj goireasach.

**convent** n clochar m.

**converge** v co-aom.

**conversation** n còmhradh m.

**converse** v dèan còmhradh.

**conversion** n iompachadh m.

**convert** v iompaich.

**convex** adj os-chearclach.

**conveyance** n còir-sgrìobhte f.

**conveyancer** n sgriobhadair-chòirichean m.

**convict** n ciomach m. • v dearbh.

**conviction** n dìteadh m.

**convivial** adj cuideachdail.

**convulsion** n criothnachadh m.

**cook** n còcaire m. • v deasaich, bruich.

**cooker** n cucair m.

**cookery** n còcaireachd f.

**cool** v fuaraich.

**cooperate** v co-oibrich.

**cope** v dèan an gnothach.

**copious** adj pailt.

**copper** n copar m.

**copulate** v cuplaich.

**copy** n lethbhreac m. • v ath-sgrìobh.

**copyright** n dlighe-sgrìobhaidh.

**coral** n corail m.

**cord** n còrd m.

**cordial** adj càirdeil.

**core** n cridhe m.

**cork** n àrc f. • v cuir àrc ann.

**corkscrew** n sgriubha àrc m.

**corn** n coirce m.

**corner** n oisean f.

**cornice** n bàrr-mhaise m.

**coronary** adj coronach.

**coronation** n crùnadh m.

**corpse** n corp m.

**corpuscle** n corpag f.

**correct** adj ceart. • v ceartaich.

**correspond** v co-fhreagair.

**correspondence** n (mail) co-sgrìobhadh m.

**corridor** n trannsa f.

**corrie** n coire m.

**corrode** v meirgnich.

**corrosion** n meirg f.

**corrugated** adj preasach.

**corrupt** adj grod.

**cosmetic** n cungaidh maise f.

**cosmopolitan** n os-nàiseanta m.

**cost** n cosgais f. • v cosg.

**costly** adj cosgail.

**costume** n culaidh f.

**cosy** adj seasgair.

**cottage** n bothan m.

**cotton** n cotan m.

**couch** n uirigh f.

**cough** n casd m. • v dèan casd.

**council** n comhairle f.

**councillor** n comhairliche m.

**count** v cùnnt.

**countenance** n gnùis f.

**counter** n cuntair m.

**counteract** v cuir bacadh air.

**counter-clockwise** adv tuathal.

**counterfeit** v feall-chùinneach.

**countersign** v cuir ainm ri.

**counting** n cùnntas m.

**countless** adj do-àireamh.

**country** n dùthaich, tìr m.

**countryman** n fear-dùthcha m.

**county** n siorrachd f.

**couple** n càraid f.

**couplet** n rann dà-shreathach f.

**coupon** n cùpon m.

**courage** n misneach f.

**courageous** adj misneachail.

**courier** n teachdaire m.

**course** n slighe m.

**court** n cùirt f. • v dèan suirghe.

**courtesy** n modh f.

**courthouse** n taigh-cùirte m.

**cousin** n co-ogha m.

**cove** n bàgh, camas m.

**cover** n còmhdach, brat m. • v còmhdaich.

**cow** n bò f.

**coward** n gealtaire m.

**cowardice** n geilt f.

**cowherd** n buachaille m.

**coy** adj nàrach.

**crab** n partan m, crùbag f.

**crack** n sgàinneadh m. • v sgàin.

**cradle** n creathail f.

**craft** n cèaird m; (cunning) seòltachd f; (vessel) bàta m.

**craftsman** n fear-ceàirde m.

**crag** n creag f.

**cram** v dìnn.

**crane** n crann m.

**crannog** n crannag f.

**cranny** n cùil f.

**crash** v co-bhuail.

**craving** n miann m/f.

**crawl** v snàig.

**crazy** adj às a chiall.

**creak** v dèan dìosgan.

**cream** n uachdar m.

**crease** n filleadh m.

**create** v cruthaich.

**creation** n cruthachadh m.

**creature** n creutair m.

**credible** adj creideasach.

**crèche** n ionad-là leanaban m.

**credit** n creideas m. • v creid.

**credit card** n cairt-iasaid f.

**creditor** n fear-fèich m.

**creed** n creud f.

**creel** n cliabh m.

**cremate** v loisg.

**crest** n cìrean m.

**crew** n sgioba m/f.

**crime** n eucoir f.

**criminal** adj eucoireach. • n eucoireach m.

**crimson** adj crò-dhearg.

**cringe** v crùb.

**cripple** n crioplach m.

**crisis** n gàbhadh m.

**crisp** adj brisg; fionnar.

**criterion** n slat-tomhais m.

**critic** n sgrùdair m.

**critical** adj breitheach.

**criticise** v dèan sgrùdadh.

**criticism** n breithneachadh m.

**croak** v dèan gràgail.

**crockery** npl soitheachan-crèa-dha.

**croft** n croit f.

**crofter** n croitear m.

**crook** n cromag f; (person) cruc m.

**crooked** adj cam, crom.

**croon** v crònaich.

**crop** n bàrr m. • v beàrr, buain.

**cross** adj crosta. • n crois f. • v rach tarsaing.

**cross-breed** n tair-bhrid m.

**cross-examine** v ath-cheasnaich.

**cross-roads** n crois a' rothaid f.

**crossword puzzle** n tòimh-seachan-tarsainn m.

**crotch** n gobhal m.

**crotchet** n (music) dubh-nota m.

**crouch** v crom.

**crow** n feannag f.

**crowd** n sluagh m. • v dòmhlaich.

**crowdie** n gruth m.

**crown** n crùn m. • v crùn.

**crucible** n soitheach-leaghaidh m.

**cruciform** adj crasgach.

**crude** adj amh.

**cruel** adj an-iochdmhor.

**cruelty** n an-iochdmhorachd m.

**cruise** n cùrsa mara m.

**crumb** n criomag f.

**crumple** v rocaich.

**crush** v pronn.

**crust** n plaosg m.

**crutch** n crasg f.

**cry** v èigh; guil.

**cub** n cuilean m.

**cube** n ciùb m.

**cuckoo** n cuach m.

**cuff** n bun-dùirn m.

**culprit** n ciontach m.

**cultivate** v àitich.

**culture** n saothrachadh m; (arts) cultur m.

**cup** n copan m.

**cupboard** n preas m.

**cupidity** n sannt f.

**curable** adj so-leigheas.

**curb** v bac.

**curdle** v binndich.

**cure** n leigheas m. • v leigheis.

**curious** adj ceasnachail.

**curl** n bachlag f. • v bachlaich.

**curlew** n guilbneach m.

**currency** n sgaoileadh m; airgead m.

**current** adj gnàthaichte. • n sruth m.

**curse** n mallachd f. • v mallaich.

**curtain** n cùrtair m.

**curvature** n caime f.

**curve** v crom.

**cushion** n pillean m.

**custody** n cùram m.

**custom** n àbhaist m.

**customary** adj àbhaisteach.

**cut** n gearradh m. • v geàrr.

**cutlery** n uidheam-ithe f.

**cynical** adj searbhasach.

**cyst** n ùthan m.

# D

**dabble** v crath uisge air.

**dad** n dadaidh m.

**daffodil** n lus-a-chrom-chinn m.

**dagger** n biodag f.

**daily** adj làitheil. • adv gach là.

**dainty** adj mìn.

**dairy** n taigh-bainne m.

**daisy** n neòinean m.

**dale** n dail f.

**dam** n dàm m.

**damage** n dochann m. • v do-chainn.

**damnable** adj damaichte.

**damnation** n dìteadh m.

**damp** adj tais.

**dampen** v taisich.

**dance** n dannsa m. • v danns.

**dandelion** n beàrnan-brìde m.

**dandle** v luaisg.

**danger** n cunnart m.

**dangerous** adj cunnartach.

**dappled** adj ball-bhreac.

**dare** v gabh air.

**daring** adj neo-sgàthach.

**dark** adj dorch.

**darken** v dorchaich.

**darkness** n dorchadas m.

**darling** n annsachd, eudail f, luaidh m.

**darn** v càirich.

**dash** v spealg.

**database** n stòr-dàta m.

**date** n ceann-latha m; (fruit) deit f.

**daub** v smeur.

**daughter** n nighean f.

**daughter-in-law** n ban-chlia-mhain f.

**dawn** n camhanach f.

**day** n là m.

**daylight** n solas an latha m.

**daze** v cuir bho mhothachadh.

**dazzle** v deàrrs.

**dead** adj marbh.

**deadlock** n glasadh m.

**deadly** adj marbhtach.

**deaf** adj bodhar.

**deafen** v bodhair.

**deafness** n buidhre f

**deal** n cùnnradh m. • v dèilig.

**dealer** n fear-malairt m.

**dealing** n dèiligeadh m.

**dear** adj gaolach; (cost) daor.

**dearness** n (cost) daoire f.

**dearth** n gainne f.

**death** n bàs m.

**debar** v bac.

**debase** v truaill.

**debate** n deasbad m. • v deasbair.

**debit** n fiach-shuim f. • v cuir fiach-shuim.

**debts** npl fiachan.

**decade** n deichead m.

**decadent** adj air claonadh.

**decant** v taom.

**decanter** n searrag ghlainne f.

**decay** n crìonadh m. • v caith.

**deceit** n cealg f.

**deceive** v meall, breug.

**December** n An Dùbhlachd.

**decency** n beusachd f.

**decent** adj beusach.

**deception** n mealladh m.

**decide** v co-dhùin.

**deciduous** adj seargach.

**decimal** adj deicheach.

**decision** n breith f.

**decisive** adj cinnteach.

**deck** n bòrd-luinge m. • v sgia-mhaich.

**declaration** n dearbhadh m.

**declare** v cuir an cèill.

**decompose** v lobh.

**decorate** v sgeadaich.

**decoration** *n* sgeadachadh *m*.

**decorous** *adj* cubhaidh.

**decrease** *n* lùghdachadh *m*. • *v* lùghdaich.

**decrepit** *adj* breòite.

**decry** *v* càin.

**dedicate** *v* coisrig.

**deduce** *v* tuig.

**deduct** *v* beagaich.

**deduction** *n* beagachadh *m*.

**deed** *n* gnìomh *m*; (*legal*) gnìomhas *m*.

**deep** *adj* domhainn.

**deepen** *v* doimhnich.

**deer** *n* fiadh *m*.

**deer-forest** *n* frìth *f*.

**deface** *v* mill.

**defamation** *n* tuaileas *m*.

**defame** *v* cùl-chàin.

**default** *n* dearmad *m*.

**defeat** *n* call *m*. • *v* gabh air, faigh buaidh.

**defect** *n* easbhaidh *f*.

**defective** *adj* easbhaidheach.

**defence** *n* dìon *m*; leisgeul *m*.

**defenceless** *adj* gun dìon.

**defend** *v* dìon.

**defensive** *adj* dìona.

**defer** *v* cuir air dàil.

**deference** *n* ùmhlachd *f*.

**deferment** *n* dàil *f*.

**defiance** *n* dùlan *m*.

**deficiency** *n* dìth *m*.

**deficit** *n* easbhaidh *f*.

**definable** *adj* sonnrachail.

**define** *v* sonnraich.

**definite** *adj* comharraichte.

**definition** *n* comharrachadh *m*.

**deflect** *v* aom.

**deform** *v* cuir à cumadh.

**deformity** *n* mì-dhealbh *m*.

**defraud** *v* feallaich.

**deft** *adj* ealamh.

**defy** *v* thoir dùlan do.

**degenerate** *v* meath. • *adj* meathaichte.

**degrade** *v* ìslich.

**degree** *n* inbhe *f*; (*academic*) ceum *m*; (*temp*) puing *f*.

**deign** *v* deònaich.

**deity** *n* diadhachd *f*.

**dejected** *adj* fo bhròn.

**delay** *n* maille *f*. • *v* cuir maille air.

**delegate** *n* fear-ionaid *m*.

**delegation** *n* luchd tagraidh *m*.

**delete** *v* dubh-às.

**deliberate** *adj* mall. • *v* meòraich.

**delicacy** *n* mìlseachd *f*.

**delicate** *adj* finealta.

**delicious** *adj* ana-bhlasta.

**delight** *v* toilich.

**delightful** *adj* aoibhneach.

**delinquency** *n* ciontachd *f*.

**delinquent** *adj* ciontach.

**delirium** *n* breisleach *f*.

**deliver** *v* saor; (*baby*) asaidich.

**delivery** *n* teàrnadh *m*; post *m*; (*baby*) asaid *m*.

**dell** *n* lagan *m*.

**deluge** *n* tuile *f*.

**demand** *n* tagradh *m*. • *v* tagair.

**demean** v ìslich.

**demented** adj air bhoile.

**dementia** n troimhe-chèile m.

**demerit** n lochd m.

**democracy** n sluagh-fhlaitheas m.

**democrat** n sluagh-fhlaithear m.

**demolish** v sgrios.

**demon** n deamhan m.

**demonstrable** adj so-dhearbhte.

**demonstration** n taisbeanadh m.

**demote** v thoir ceum a-nuas.

**demur** v cuir teagamh ann.

**demure** adj stuama.

**den** n saobhaidh m.

**denial** n àicheadh m.

**denigrate** v dèan dìmeas air.

**dense** adj tiugh; (mind) maol.

**density** n dlùths m.

**dent** v dèan lag ann.

**dentist** n fiaclaire m.

**denture** n deudach m.

**denude** v rùisg.

**deny** v àicheidh.

**depart** v imich.

**department** n roinn f.

**departure** n falbh m.

**depend** v (on) cuir earbsa ann.

**dependence** n eisimealachd f.

**dependent** adj eisimealach.

**depict** v dealbh.

**deplorable** adj truagh.

**deplore** v caoidh.

**deportment** n giùlan m.

**depose** v cuir às oifig.

**deposit** n tasgadh m. • v tasgaich.

**depravity** n truailleachd f.

**depreciate** v cuir an dìmeas.

**depress** v brùth sìos.

**depressant** n ìocshlaint-ìsleach-aidh f.

**depression** n ìsleachadh m.

**deprive** v toirt air falbh.

**depth** n doimhneachd f.

**depute** adj leas-. • v sonnraich.

**derelict** adj trèigte.

**deride** v dèan fanaid air.

**derision** n fanaid f.

**derivation** n sìolachadh m.

**derive** v sìolaich.

**descend** v teirinn.

**descent** n teàrnadh m.

**describe** v thoir tuairisgeul air.

**description** n tuairisgeul m.

**desert**[1] n fàsach m/f.

**desert**[2] v trèig.

**deserve** v toill.

**design** n rùn m; (art) dealbh m.

**design** v rùnaich; deilbh.

**designer** n dealbhadair m.

**desire** n miann m. • v miannaich.

**desist** v stad.

**desk** n deasg m.

**despair** n eu-dòchas m. • v leig thairis dòchas.

**desperate** adj eu-dòchasach; dam-ainnte.

**despicable** adj suarach.

**despise** v dèan tàir air.

**despite** prep a dh'aindeoin.

**dessert** n mìlsean m.

**destiny** n dàn m.

**destitute** *adj* falamh.

**destroy** *v* sgrios.

**destruction** *n* milleadh *m*.

**detach** *v* dealaich.

**detail** *n* mion-chùnntas *m*; mion-phuing *f*.

**detain** *v* cùm air ais.

**detect** *v* lorg.

**detective** *n* lorg-phoileas *m*.

**determination** *n* diongbhaltas *m*.

**determine** *v* cuir roimh.

**determinism** *n* cinnteachas *m*.

**detest** *v* fuathaich.

**detestation** *n* fuath *m*.

**detonate** *v* toirm-spreadh.

**detour** *n* bealach *m*.

**detract** *v* thoir air falbh.

**detriment** *n* dolaidh *f*

**devalue** *v* di-luachaich.

**devastate** *v* lèir-sgrios.

**devastation** *n* lèir-sgrios *m*.

**develop** *v* leasaich; fàs.

**development** *n* leasachadh *m*.

**deviate** *v* claon.

**device** *n* innleachd *f*.

**devil** *n* diabhal *m*.

**devious** *adj* seachranach.

**devise** *v* innlich.

**devolve** *v* thig fo chùram; (*political*) sgaoil cumhachd.

**devolution** *n* sgaoileadh-cumhachd *m*.

**devotion** *n* cràbhadh *m*; teas-ghràdh *m*.

**devour** *v* sluig.

**dew** *n* dealt *m*.

**dexterity** *n* deisealachd *f*.

**diagnose** *v* breithnich.

**diagnosis** *n* breithneachadh *m*.

**diagonal** *adj* trasdanach.

**dial** *n* aodann *m*. • *v* comharraich àireamh.

**diameter** *n* meadhan-thrasdan *m*.

**diarrhoea** *n* a' bhuinneach *f*.

**dice** *npl* dìsnean.

**dictate** *v* deachd.

**dictionary** *n* faclair *m*.

**die** *v* bàsaich.

**diesel** *n* dìosail *m*.

**diet** *n* riaghailt bidhe *f*.

**differ** *v* eadar-dhealaich.

**difference** *n* eadar-dhealachadh *m*.

**different** *adj* air leth.

**differentiate** *v* diofaraich.

**difficult** *adj* duilich.

**difficulty** *n* duilgheadas *m*.

**dig** *v* cladhaich.

**digest** *v* cnàmh.

**digestible** *adj* so-chnàmh.

**digit** *n* meur *f*; (*number*) meur-àireamh *f*.

**digital** *adj* meurach.

**dignified** *adj* urramaichte.

**dilate** *v* leudaich.

**dilemma** *n* imcheist *f*.

**diligent** *adj* dìcheallach.

**dilute** *v* tanaich.

**dim** *adj* doilleir; (*person*) mall 'na intinn.

**dimension** *n* tomhas *m*.

**diminish** *v* lùghdaich.

**dimple** n tibhre m.

**din** n toirm f.

**dine** v gabh dìnnear.

**dining-room** n seòmar-bidhe m.

**dinner** n dìnnear f.

**dinner-time** n tràth-dìnneireach m.

**dip** n tumadh m. • v tum, bog.

**diplomacy** n seòltachd f.

**dipsomania** n miann-daoraich m/f.

**direct** adj dìreach. • v seòl.

**direction** n seòladh m; àird f.

**direction-finder** n àird-lorgair m.

**directly** adv air ball; dìreach.

**director** n fear-stiùiridh m.

**dirk** n biodag f.

**dirt** n salchar m.

**dirty** adj salach.

**disability** n neo-chomas m.

**disadvantage** n mì-leas m.

**disagree** v rach an aghaidh.

**disagreement** n eas-aonta f.

**disappear** v rach à sealladh.

**disappoint** v meall.

**disapprove** v coirich.

**disaster** n mòr-thubaist f.

**disbelieve** v na-creid.

**disc** n clàr m.

**discard** v cuir dhe.

**discerning** adj tuigseach.

**discharge** n di-luchdachadh m. • v di-luchdaich; cuir à dreuchd.

**disclaim** v àicheidh.

**disclose** v foillsich.

**discomfort** n anshocair f.

**disconnect** v sgaoil.

**disconsolate** adj brònach.

**discontented** adj mì-thoilichte.

**discord** n mì-chòrdadh m; (mus) dì-chòrda m.

**discount** n lasachadh m. • v lasaich.

**discourage** v mì-mhisnich.

**discover** v nochd; leig ris.

**discovery** n nochdadh m.

**discrepancy** n diofar m.

**discretion** n cùram m.

**discriminate** v (in favour of) gabh taobh; (against) rach an aghaidh.

**discuss** v deasbair.

**discussion** n deasbaireachd f.

**disease** n euslaint f.

**disembark** v cuir air tìr.

**disengage** v dealaich.

**disentangle** v fuasgail.

**disfavour** n mì-fhàbhar m.

**disgrace** n masladh m. • v maslaich.

**disgraceful** adj maslach.

**disguise** n breug-riochd m. • v cuir breug-riochd air.

**disgust** n gràin f.

**disgusting** adj gràineil.

**dish** n soitheach m.

**dish-cloth** n tubhailt-shoithichean f.

**dishearten** v mì-mhisnich.

**dishonest** adj mì-onorach.

**dishonesty** n mì-onair f.

**dishwasher** n nigheadair-shoithichean m.

**disillusion** n bristeadh-dùil m.

**disinclined** adj neo-thoileach.

**disinherit** v buin còir bhreith o.

**disinterested** adj neo-fhèin-chuiseach.

**disjointed** adj an-altaichte.

**disk** n clàr m.

**disk drive** n clàr-inneal m.

**dislike** v mì-thaitneamh.

**dislodge** v cuir à àite.

**disloyal** adj neo-dhìleas.

**dismal** adj dubhach.

**dismay** n uabhas m.

**dismember** v spion o chèile.

**dismiss** v cuir air falbh.

**disobedience** n eas-ùmhlachd f.

**disobey** v bi eas-umhail do.

**disorder** n mì-riaghailt f.

**disown** v na gabh ri.

**disparity** n neo-ionnanachd f.

**dispel** v fògair.

**dispensation** n riarachadh m.

**dispense** v riaraich.

**dispersal** n sgàpadh m.

**displace** v cuir à àite.

**display** n foillseachadh m. • v foillsich.

**displease** v mì-thoilich.

**dispose** v suidhich.

**disprove** v breugnaich.

**disputatious** adj connsachail.

**dispute** v connsaich.

**disqualification** n neo-iomchaidheachd f.

**disqualify** v dèan neo-iomchuidh.

**disregard** v dèan dìmeas air.

**disrepair** n droch-chàradh m.

**disrespect** n eas-urram m.

**disrupt** v bris, reub.

**disruption** n briseadh m.

**dissatisfaction** n mì-thoileachadh m.

**dissatisfied** adj mì-riaraichte.

**dissect** v sgrùd; gèarr suas.

**dissertation** n tràchd f.

**disservice** n droch-chomain f.

**dissimilar** adj eu-coltach.

**dissipate** v sgap.

**dissociate** v eadar-sgar.

**dissolute** adj drùiseil.

**dissolve** v leagh; fuasgail.

**dissuade** v comhairlich an aghaidh.

**distance** n astar m, fad m.

**distant** adj cèin.

**distaste** n droch bhlas m.

**distasteful** adj neo-bhlasta.

**distil** v tarraing.

**distiller** n grùdaire m.

**distillery** n taigh-staile m.

**distinct** adj soilleir.

**distinction** n eadar-dhealachadh m; (merit) cliù m.

**distinctive** adj so-aithnichte.

**distinguish** v eadar-dhealaich.

**distort** v fiaraich.

**distract** v buair.

**distress** n àmghar m. • v sàraich.

**distribute** v roinn, compàirtich.

**district** n ceàrn m.

**district nurse** n banaltram sgìreachd f.

**distrust** v an-earbsa.

**disturb** v cuir dragh air.

**disturbance** n aimhreit f.

**disunite** v eadar-sgar.

**disunity** n eadar-sgaradh m.

**disuse** n mì-cleachdeach m.

**ditch** n clais f.

**ditto** adv an nì ceudna.

**ditty** n luinneag f.

**dive** v daoibhig.

**diver** n daoibhear m.

**diverge** v iomsgair.

**diverse** adj eugsamhail.

**diversify** v sgaoil.

**diversion** n claonadh m; (pas-time) fearas-chuideachd f.

**diversity** n eugsamhlachd m.

**divert** v claon.

**divide** v roinn, pàirtich.

**dividend** n earrann f.

**divination** n fàistneachd f.

**divine** adj diadhaidh. • v dèan a-mach.

**divisible** adj so-roinn.

**division** n roinn f.

**divorce** n dealachadh pòsaidh m. • v dealaich ri.

**dizzy** adj tuainealach.

**do** v dèan.

**dock**[1] n port m.

**dock**[2], **docken** n copag f.

**dockyard** n doca m.

**doctor** n lighiche, doctair m; (academic) ollamh m.

**doctrine** n teagasg m.

**document** n sgrìobainn f.

**documentary** adj aithriseach.

**dodge** v seachainn.

**doe** n maoiseach f.

**dog** n cù m.

**dogged** adj doirbh, dùr.

**dogmatic** adj dìorrasach.

**dole** n dòil m.

**dollar** n dolair m.

**domain** n tighearnas m.

**domestic** adj teaghlachail.

**domesticate** v càllaich.

**domicile** n fàrdach f.

**dominate** v ceannsaich.

**domineer** v sàraich.

**dominion** n uachdranachd f.

**donate** v thoir tabhartas.

**donor** n tabhartaiche m.

**doom** n binn m. • v dìt.

**doomsday** n latha-luain m.

**door** n doras m.

**dope** n druga, drugaichean f.

**dose** n tomhas m.

**dot** n puing f.

**dotage** n leanabachd na h-aoise f.

**double** adj dùbailte. • n dùbladh m. • v dùblaich.

**double-bass** n prò-bheus m.

**doubt** n teagamh m. • v cuir an teagamh.

**doubtful** adj teagmhach.

**doubtless** adv gun teagamh.

**dough** n taois f.

**dour** adj dùr.

**down** prep shìos, a-nuas.

**downfall** n tuiteam m.

**downhill** adv leis a' bruthach.

**downright** adv air fad.

**downstairs** adv shìos staidhre.

**downward** adj le bruthach.

**downwards** adv sìos.

**dowry** n tochradh m.

**doze** v rach an clò-chadal.

**dozen** n dusan m.

**drag** v slaod.

**drain** n drèana f. • v sìolaidh.

**drake** n dràc m.

**dram** n dràm, drama m.

**dramatist** n dràmaire m.

**draught** n (drink) tarraing f; (wind) gaoth troimh tholl. f

**draughts** n dàmais f.

**draughtsman** n fear-tarraing m.

**draw** v tarraing; (liquid) deoghail; (art) dèan dealbh.

**drawer** n drabhair m.

**drawing** n dealbh m/f.

**drawing-pin** n tacaid f.

**dread** n oillt f. • v oilltich.

**dreadful** adj eagalach.

**dream** n aisling f. • v bruadair, faic aisling.

**dreamer** n aislingiche m.

**dredge** v glan grùnnd.

**dregs** npl druaip f.

**drench** v dèan bog-fliuch.

**dress** v cuir aodach air.

**dresser** n dreasair m.

**dressing** n ìoc-chòmhdach m.

**dribble** v sil; (sport) drioblaig.

**drift** v siab.

**drill** v drilich.

**drilling platform** n clàr-tollaidh m.

**drink** n deoch f. • v òl, gabh.

**drinker** n fear-òil m.

**drip** v snigh.

**drive** v greas; (car) stiùir.

**drivel** n briathran gorach mpl, sgudal m.

**driver** n dràibhear m.

**driving licence** n cead-dràibhidh m.

**drizzle** n ciùthran m.

**droll** adj neònach; èibhinn.

**drone** n torman m; (pipes) dos m.

**droop** v searg.

**drop** n boinne f. • v leig às.

**drought** n turadh m.

**drove** n dròbh m.

**drover** n dròbhair m.

**drown** v bàth.

**drowsy** adj cadalach.

**drudgery** n dubh-chosnadh m.

**drug** n droga f.

**drug addict** n tràill-dhrogaichean m.

**druggist** n drogadair m.

**druid** n draoidh m.

**druidism** n draoidheachd f.

**drum** n druma f.

**drum-major** n màidseir-druma m.

**drummer** n drumair m.

**drumstick** n bioran-druma m.

**drunk** adj air misg.

**drunkard** n misgear m.

**drunkenness** n misg f.

**dry** adj tioram. • v tiormaich.

**dub** v dùblaich.

**duck**[1] n tunnag f.

**duck²** v tum; crùb.

**dud** n rud gun fheum m.

**due** adj dligheach.

**duel** n còmhrag-dithis f.

**duet** n òran-dithis m.

**dull** adj trom-inntinneach; tiugh.

**dullness** n truime m.

**dulse** n duileasg m.

**duly** adv gu riaghailteach.

**dumb** adj balbh.

**dummy** n fear-brèige m, breagag f.

**dump** n òcrach m. • v caith air falbh.

**dumpling** n turraisg f.

**dunce** n ùmaidh m.

**dung** n innear f.

**dunghill** n dùnan m.

**duplicate** n dùblachadh m.

**duplicity** n dùbailteachd f.

**durable** adj maireannach.

**duration** n fad m, rè f.

**during** prep rè.

**dusk** n duibhre f.

**dusky** adj ciar.

**dust** n dust, stùr m. • v glan stùr dhe.

**dustbin** n biona-stùir m.

**Dutch** adj Duitseach.

**dutiful** adj umhail.

**duty** n dleasdanas m; (customs) diùtaidh m.

**duty-free** adj saor o dhiùtaidh.

**dwarf** n troich m.

**dwell** v tuinich.

**dwelling** n fàrdach f.

**dwindle** v crìon.

**dye** n dath m. • v dath.

**dyke** n gàradh m.

**dynamic** adj fiùghantach.

**dynamite** n dinimit m.

**dynasty** n rìgh-shliochd m.

**dyspepsia** n an do-chnàmh m.

# E

**each** adj gach, gach aon. • pron gach aon; an duine.

**eager** adj dealasach.

**eagle** n iolair f.

**ear** n cluas f.

**earphone** n cluasan m.

**earring** n cluas-fhail f.

**earl** n iarla m.

**early** adj tràth.

**earn** v coisinn.

**earnest** adj dùrachdach.

**earth** n talamh f.

**earthenware** n soitheach criadha m.

**earthly** adj talmhaidh.

**earthworm** n daolag f.

**ease** n fois f.

**easel** n dealbh-thaic f.

**east** n ear, an àirde an ear f.

**Easter** n Càisg f.

**easterly** adj an ear.

**easy** adj furasda.

**eat** v ith.

**eatable** adj so-ith.

**ebb** n tràghadh m. • v tràigh.

**eccentric** adj iomrallach.

**eccentricity** n iomrallachd f.

**echo** n mac-talla m.

**eclipse** n dubhadh grèine m; (lunar) dubhadh gealaich m.

**ecology** n eag-eòlas m.

**economics** n eaconomachd m.

**ecomomist** n eaconomair m.

**economise** v caomhain.

**economy** n eaconomaidh m; banas-taighe m.

**ecstasy** n àrd-èibhneas m.

**ecstatic** adj àrd-èibhneach.

**ecumenical** adj uil-eaglaiseil.

**eddy** n saobh-shruth m.

**edge** n oir, iomall m; faobhar m. • v dèan oir.

**edgewise** adv air oir.

**edible** adj so-ithe.

**edict** n reachd m.

**edifice** n aitreabh m.

**edify** v teagaisg.

**Edinburgh** n Dun Eideann.

**edit** v deasaich.

**edition** n deasachadh m.

**editor** n fear-deasachaidh m.

**educate** v foghlaim.

**education** n foghlam m.

**educational** adj oideachail.

**effect** n buaidh f. • v thoir gu buil.

**effective** adj buadhach.

**effeminate** adj boireannta.

**effervescent** adj bruichneach.

**efficacy** n èifeachd f.

**efficient** adj èifeachdach.

**effigy** n ìomhaigh f.

**effluent** n sruthadh m.

**effort** n dìcheall m.

**egg** n ugh m.

**egghead** n eanchainn mhòr m.

**egotism** n fèin-spèis f.

**Egypt** n An Eiphit f.

**eight** n ochd m.

**eighth** adj ochdamh.

**eighteen** n ochd-deug.

**eightsome** n ochdnar m.

**eightsome reel** n ruidhle-ochdnar m.

**eighty** n ochdad.

**either** conj **either . . . or . . .** an dara cuid . . . no . . . . • adv a bharrachd, nas motha.

**ejaculate** v cuir a-mach.

**eject** v tilg a-mach.

**elaborate** adj saothraichte.

**elapse** v rach seachad.

**elastic** adj sùbailte.

**elate** v tog suas.

**elbow** n uileann f.

**elder** n (church) eildear m; (tree) droman m. • adj as/nas sine.

**elderly** adj sean.

**elect** v tagh.

**election** n taghadh.

**electioneering** n taghadaireachd f.

**elector** n taghadair m.

electorate *n* luchd-taghaidh *m*.
electric *adj* dealain.
electricity *n* dealan *m*.
electrification *n* dealanachadh *m*.
electrocute *v* dealan-marbh.
electronic *adj* eleactronach.
elegance *n* grinneas *m*.
elegant *adj* grinn.
elegiac *adj* caointeach.
elegy *n* tuireadh *m*.
element *n* dùil *f*.
elementary *adj* bun.
elephant *n* ailbhean *m*.
elevate *v* àrdaich.
eleven *n* aon.... deug.
eligible *adj* ion-tagha.
eliminate *v* geàrr às.
elixir *n* ìocshlaint *f*.
elm *n* leamhan *m*.
elongate *v* fadaich.
elope *v* teich.
eloquence *n* deas-bhriathrachd *f*.
else *adj*/*adv* eile.
elude *v* seachainn.
elusive *adj* èalaidheach.
e-mail *n* post dealain *m*.
emancipate *v* saor.
embalm *v* spìosraich.
embargo *n* bacadh *m*.
embark *v* cuir air bòrd.
embarrass *v* cuir troimhe chèile.
embarrassment *n* beag-nàrach-adh *m*.
embassy *n* tosgaireachd *f*.
ember *n* èibhleag *f*.

embezzle *v* dèan maoin-èalach-adh.
emboss *v* gràbhail.
embrace *v* iath an glacaibh.
embroider *v* cuir obair-ghrèis air.
embryo *n* suth *m*.
emerald *n* smàrag *f*.
emerge *v* thig an uachdar.
emergency *n* bàlanaich *m*.
emigrant *n* eilthireach *m*.
emigrate *v* dèan eilthireachd.
eminent *adj* àrd.
emit *v* leig a-mach.
emotion *n* tòcadh *m*.
emotional *adj* tòcail.
emphasis *n* cudrom *m*.
emphatic *adj* làidir.
empire *n* ìompaireachd *f*.
empirical *adj* deuchainneach.
employ *v* fasdaich.
employee *n* fear-obrach *m*.
employer *n* fastaidhear *m*.
empty *adj* falamh.
emulation *n* strì *f*.
enable *v* dèan comasach.
enact *v* òrdaich.
enamel *n* cruan *m*.
enchant *v* cuir fo gheasaibh.
enchantment *n* draoidheachd *f*.
enclosure *n* crò *m*.
encourage *v* misnich.
encroach *v* thig a-steach.
encumbrance *n* uallach *m*.
end *n* deireadh *m*, crìoch *f*. • *v* cuir crìoch air.
endemic *adj* dùthchasach.

**endless** *adj* neo-chrìochnach.

**endorse** *v* cùl-sgrìobh.

**endowment** *n* bronnadh *m*.

**enemy** *n* nàmhaid *m*.

**energetic** *adj* brìoghmhor.

**energy** *n* brìogh *f*.

**enforce** *v* co-èignich.

**engagement** *n* gealladh-pòsaidh *m*.

**engine** *n* inneal *m*.

**engineer** *n* innleadair *m*. • *v* inn-lich.

**England** *n* Sasainn *f*.

**English** *n* Beurla *f*.

**Englishman** *n* Sasannach *m*.

**enhance** *v* meudaich.

**enigma** *n* dubhfhacal *m*.

**enjoy** *v* meal.

**enlarge** *v* meudaich.

**enlighten** *v* soillsich.

**enlist** *v* liostaig.

**enormous** *adj* uabhasach.

**enough** *adv* gu leòr.

**enquire** *v* feòraich.

**enrage** *v* feargaich.

**ensue** *v* lean.

**ensure** *v* dèan cinnteach.

**enter** *v* rach/thig a-steach.

**enterprise** *n* iomairt *f*.

**enterprising** *adj* ionnsaigheach.

**entertainer** *n* oirfideach *m*.

**entertainment** *n* aoigheachd *f*.

**enthusiasm** *n* dìoghras *m*.

**entice** *v* tàlaidh.

**entire** *adj* iomlan.

**entirely** *adv* gu lèir.

**entitle** *v* thoir còir.

**entrance** *n* dol a-steach *m*.

**entreat** *v* guidh.

**entrepreneur** *n* fear-tionnsgain *m*.

**envelope** *n* cèis *f*.

**environment** *n* comhearsnachd *f*; (*ecology*) àrainn-eachd *f*.

**envy** *n* farmad *m*.

**ephemeral** *adj* geàrr-shaoglach.

**episode** *n* tachartas *m*.

**epitaph** *n* leac-sgrìobhadh *m*.

**epoch** *n* tùs-aimsir *f*.

**equal** *adj* seise.

**equalise** *v* dèan co-ionann; (*game*) ruig an aon àireamh.

**equation** *n* co-ionannas *m*.

**equator** *n* meadhan-chearcall na tal-mhainn *m*.

**equidistant** *adj* co-fhad air falbh.

**equinox** *n* co-fhreagradh nan tràth *m*.

**equip** *v* uidheamaich.

**equipment** *n* uidheam *f*.

**equipped** *adj* uidheamaichte.

**equity** *n* ceartas *m*; (*fin*) stoc-roinn *f*.

**equivalent** *adj* co-ionann.

**erase** *v* dubh às.

**erect** *v* tog.

**erection** *n* togail *m*.

**erode** *v* meirg.

**erotic** *adj* drùis-mhiannach.

**err** *v* rach iomrall.

**errand** *n* gnothach *m*.

**erratic** *adj* iomrallach.

**error** *n* mearrachd *f*.

**eruption** *n* brùchdach *m*.

**escalator** *n* streapadan *m*.

**escape** *n* èaladh *m*. • *v* teich.

**esoteric** *adj* às an rathad.

**essay** *n* aiste *f*.

**essence** *n* gnè *f*.

**essential** *adj* riatanach.

**establish** *v* suidhich.

**estate** *n* oighreachd *f*.

**esteem** *n* meas *m*.

**estimate** *v* meas.

**estrange** *v* dèan fuathach.

**estuary** *n* inbhir *m*.

**eternal** *adj* bith-bhuan.

**eternity** *n* sìorraidheachd *f*.

**ethical** *adj* modhannach.

**ethnic** *adj* cinnidheach.

**eunuch** *n* caillteanach *m*.

**Europe** *n* An Roinn Eòrpa *f*.

**European** *adj* Eòrpach.

**evaporate** *v* deataich.

**even** *adj* rèidh. • *adv* eadhon; fèin.

**evening** *n* feasgar *m*.

**event** *n* tuiteamas *m*.

**ever** *adv* aig àm sam bith, idir.

**evergreen** *adj* sìor-uaine.

**everlasting** *adj* sìorraidh.

**evermore** *adv* gu bràth.

**every** *adj* gach, na h-uile.

**everyday** *adj* làitheil.

**everyone** *pron* gach duine.

**everything** *pron* gach nì.

**evict** *v* fuadaich.

**eviction** *n* fuadachadh *m*.

**evidence** *n* fianais *f*.

**evident** *adj* soilleir.

**evil** *adj* olc. • *n* olc *m*.

**ewe** *n* othaisg *f*.

**exact** *adj* pongail.

**exact** *v* buin.

**exactly** *adv* dìreach.

**exaggerate** *v* cuir am meud.

**examination** *n* ceasnachadh *m*.

**examine** *v* ceasnaich.

**example** *n* eisimpleir *m*.

**excavate** *v* cladhaich.

**excavation** *n* cladhach *m*.

**exceed** *v* rach thairis air.

**exceedingly** *adv* glè.

**excel** *v* thoir bàrr.

**excellence** *n* feabhas *m*.

**excellent** *adj* barrail.

**except** *v* fàg a-mach. • *prep* ach a-mhàin; **except for** saor o.

**exceptional** *adj* sònraichte.

**exchange** *v* malairtich.

**exchange rate** *n* co-luach cùinnidh *m*.

**exchequer** *n* stàitchiste *f*.

**exciseman** *n* gàidsear *m*.

**excite** *v* gluais.

**excitement** *n* brosnachadh *m*.

**exclaim** *v* glaodh.

**exclamation** *n* glaodh *m*.

**exclamation mark** *n* clisgphuing *f*.

**exclusive** *adj* dlùth.

**excrement** *n* cac *m*.

**excrete** *v* cac.

**excuse** *n* leisgeul *m*. • *v* gabh leisgeul, math.

**executive** n fear-gnìomha m.

**executor** n fear-cùraim tiomnaidh m.

**exercise** n eacarsaich f. • v obraich, cleachd.

**exertion** n spàirn f.

**exhaust** v falmhaich.

**exhaustion** n traoghadh m.

**exile** n fògarrach m.

**exist** v bi, bi beò.

**existence** n bith f.

**exit** n dol a-mach m.

**exonerate** v fìreanaich.

**exorbitant** adj ana-cuimseach.

**exotic** adj coimheach.

**expand** v sgaoil.

**expatriate** adj às-dhùthchach.

**expect** v bi dùil aig.

**expedient** adj coltach.

**expedite** v luathaich.

**expedition** n turas m.

**expeditious** adj cabhagach.

**expend** v caith.

**expenditure** n caiteachas m.

**expensive** adj cosgail.

**experience** n cleachdadh m. • v mothaich.

**experiment** n deuchainn f.

**expert** adj ealanta. • n eòlaiche m.

**expire** v analaich; (die) bàsaich.

**explain** v mìnich.

**explanation** n mìneachadh m.

**explicit** adj fosgailte.

**explode** v spreadh.

**exploit** n euchd m. • v dèan feum de.

**explore** v rannsaich.

**export** n eas-tharraing f. • v cuir thairis.

**expose** v nochd.

**exposure** n nochdadh m.

**express**[1] v cuir an cèill.

**express**[2] adj luath.

**express train** n luath-thrèana.

**expression** n fiamh m.

**exquisite** adj òirdheirc.

**extensive** adj leathann.

**exterior** n taobh a-muigh m.

**extinct** adj bàthte.

**extinguish** v smàl.

**extinguisher** n smàladair m.

**extra** adj fìor, ro-. • adv a bharrachd.

**extraordinary** adj anabarrach.

**extravagant** adj ana-caiteach.

**extreme** adj fìor.

**extricate** v saor.

**extrovert** n duine fosgarra m.

**exuberance** n braise.

**exuberant** adj bras.

**eye** n sùil f. • v seall.

**eyesight** n fradharc m.

**eyesore** n cùis mhì-thlachd f.

**eyrie** n nead iolaire m.

# F

**fable** *n* uirsgeul *m*.

**fabric** *n* aodach *m*; togalach *m*.

**facade** *n* aghaidh *f*.

**face** *n* aghaidh, gnùis *f*.

**facet** *n* taobh *m*.

**facilitate** *v* soirbhich.

**facilities** *npl* goireasan.

**fact** *n* beart *m*.

**factor** *n* seumarlan *m*.

**factory** *n* taigh-cèairde, fac-taraidh *m*.

**faculty** *n* comas *m*; (*university*) dàmh *m*.

**fad** *n* àilleas *m*.

**fade** *v* searg.

**fail** *v* dìobair.

**failure** *n* fàilinn *f*.

**faint** *adj* fann. • *v* fannaich.

**fair** *n* fèill.

**fairly** *adv* an ìre mhath.

**fairness** *n* maisealachd *f*.

**fairway** *n* prìomh-raon *m*.

**fairy** *adj* sìdh. • *n* sìdhiche *m*.

**faith** *n* creideamh *m*.

**faithful** *adj* dìleas.

**fake** *n* rud brèige *m*.

**fall** *n* tuiteam *m*. • *v* tuit.

**fallacy** *n* saobh-chiall *f*.

**fallow** *adj* bàn.

**false** *adj* meallta.

**falsehood** *n* breug *f*.

**falter** *v* lagaich.

**fame** *n* cliù *m*.

**familiar** *adj* càirdeil.

**familiarise** *v* gnàthaich.

**family** *n* teaghlach *m*.

**famine** *n* goirt *f*.

**famous** *adj* ainmeil.

**fanatic** *n* eudmhoraiche *m*.

**fancy** *adj* guanach. • *v* smaoinich.

**fank** *n* faing *f*.

**fantastic** *adj* ro-iongantach.

**fantasy** *n* sgeul guaineis *m*.

**far** *adj* fada, fas às. • *adv* fada, fas às.

**fare** *n* faradh *m*; biadh *m*.

**farewell** *n* soraidh *m*.

**farm** *n* baile-fearainn, tuathanas *m*.

**farmer** *n* tuathanach *m*.

**fart** *n* braidhm *m*; tùd *m*.

**farther** *adv* nas fhaide.

**fascinate** *v* cuir fo gheasaibh.

**fascination** *n* geasachd *f*.

**fascism** *n* faisisteachas *m*.

**fashion** *n* fasan *m*. • *v* cum.

**fashionable** *adj* fasanta.

**fast** *adj* luath; daingeann.

**fasten** *v* ceangail.

**fast food** *n* grad-bhiadh *m*.

**fastidious** *adj* àilleasach.

**fat** *adj* reamhar. • *n* reamhrachd *m*.

**fatal** *adj* marbhtach.

**fate** *n* dàn *m*.

**father** *n* athair *m*. • *v* bi mar athair.

**father-in-law** *n* athair-cèile *m*.

**fatherly** *adj* athaireil.

**fathom** *v* ruig air.

**fatigue** *n* sgìos *f*. • *v* sgìthich.

**fatuous** *adj* baoth.

**fault** *n* coire *f*.

**faultless** *adj* neo-chiontach.

**faulty** *adj* easbhaidheach.

**favour** *v* bi fàbharach.

**favourite** *n* annsachd *m/f*.

**fawn** *n* mang *f*.

**fax** *n* facs *m*.

**fear** *n* eagal *m*. • *v* gabh eagal.

**fearful** *adj* eagalach.

**fearless** *adj* gun eagal.

**feast** *n* fèisd *f*, fleadh *m*.• *v* dèan
fèist.

**feat** *n* euchd *m*.

**feather** *n* ite *f*.

**February** *n* Feabruari *f*, An Gearran *m*.

**federal** *adj* feadarail.

**fee** *n* duais *f*.

**feeble** *adj* fann.

**feed** *v* biath.

**feel** *v* fairich.

**feeling** *n* faireachdainn *f*.

**felicitous** *adj* sona.

**feline** *adj* mar chat.

**fellowship** *n* companas *m*.

**felon** *n* slaoightear *m*.

**female** *adj* boireann, baineann.

**feminine** *adj* banail.

**fence** *n* lann. • *v* dùin.

**fender** *n* dìonadair *m*.

**ferment** *n* brachadh *m*. • *v* brach.

**fermentation** *n* brachadh *m*.

**fern** *n* raineach *f*.

**ferret** *n* feocallan *m*.

**ferry** *n* aiseag *f*. • *v* aisig.

**ferry-boat** *n* bàta-aiseig.

**fertile** *adj* torach.

**fertility** *n* torachas *m*.

**fertilise** *v* toraich.

**fervent** *adj* dian.

**fervour** *n* dèine *f*.

**fester** *v* at.

**festive** *adj* fleadhach.

**fetch** *v* faigh.

**feu** *n* gabhail *m*.

**feud** *n* falachd *f*.

**fever** *n* fiabhras *m*.

**feverish** *adj* fiabhrasach.

**few** *adj* beag, tearc. • *n* beagan *m*.

**fibre** *n* snàithleach *m*.

**fibrous** *adj* snàithlainneach.

**fickle** *adj* caochlaideach.

**fiction** *n* uirsgeul *m*.

**fiddle** *n* fidheall *f*. • *v* dèan
fìdhleireachd; foillich.

**fiddler** *n* fìdhlear *m*.

**fidelity** *n* dìlseachd *f*.

**field** *n* achadh *m*.

**field-glasses** *n* prosbaig *f*.

**field-mouse** *n* luch-fheòir *f*.

**fierce** *adj* garg.

**fierceness** *n* gairge *f*.

**fiery** *adj* teinnteach.

**fifteen** *n* còig-deug.

**fifth** *adj* còigeamh.

**fifty** *n* leth-cheud.

**fiftieth** *adj* leth-cheudamh.

**fig** *n* fiogais *f*.

**fight** n còmhrag f. • v còmhraig.

**figure** n dealbh m; figear m.

**file** n eighe f; (documents) còmhlachadh m. • v lìomh; còmhlaich.

**filial** adj macail.

**fill** v lìon.

**fillet** v colpaich.

**filly** n loth m/f.

**film-star** n reul film m, reultag film f.

**filter** n sìolachan m. • v sìolaidh.

**filth** n salchar m.

**filthy** adj salach.

**final** adj deireannach.

**finalise** v thoir gu crìch.

**finance** n maoineachas m. • v maoinich.

**financier** n maoiniche m.

**find** v faigh, lorg.

**fine**[1] adj grinn.

**fine**[2] n ùnnlagh m. • v leag ùnnlagh.

**finery** n rìomhachas m.

**finger** n meur, corrag f.

**fingernail** n ìne f.

**finish** n crìoch f. • v crìochnaich.

**fir** n giuthas m.

**fire** n teine m. • v cuir 'na theine.

**fire-arm** n airm-theine m.

**fire-escape** n staidhre èalaidh f.

**fire-proof** adj teine-dhìonach.

**fireside** n teallach m.

**firewood** n fiodh connaidh m.

**firm**[1] adj teann.

**firm**[2] n companaidh f.

**first** adj a'chiad. • adv (time) an toiseach; (sequence) air toiseach.

**first aid** n ciad-fuasgladh m.

**first-born** n ciad-ghin m.

**firth** n caol m.

**fiscal** adj fioscail.

**fish** n iasg m. • v iasgaich.

**fisher** n iasgair m.

**fishing** n iasgaireachd f.

**fishing-line** n driamlach m.

**fishing rod** n slat-iasgaich f.

**fishy** adj mar iasg; neònach.

**fist** n dòrn m.

**fit**[1] adj freagarrach.

**fit**[2] n taom m.

**five** adj/n còig.

**fix** v dèan teann; suidhich.

**fixture** n rud socraichte m.

**fizz** n copraich f.

**flabby** adj plamach.

**flag** n bratach f.

**flagrant** adj follaiseach.

**flagstone** n leac f.

**flair** n liut m.

**flake** n bleideag f.

**flame** n lasair f.

**flannel** n flannain f.

**flap** n cleitearnach m. • v crath.

**flare** n lasair-bhoillsg m.

**flash** n lasair f. • v boillsg.

**flask** n searrag f.

**flat**[1] adj còmhnard; (mus) maol, flat.

**flat**[2] n còmhnard m; flat m.

**flatten** v laigh ri; (mus) maolaich.

**flatter** v dèan sodal.

**flattery** *n* sodal *m*.

**flautist** *n* cuisleannach *m*.

**flavour** *n* blas *m*. • *v* blasaich.

**flea** *n* deargann *f*.

**fleece** *n* rùsg *m*. • *v* rùisg.

**fleecy** *adj* rùsgach.

**fleet** *n* cabhlach *m*.

**fleeting** *adj* siùbhlach.

**flesh** *n* feòil *f*.

**fleshy** *adj* sultmhor.

**flex** *n* fleisg *f*.

**flexible** *adj* so-lùbadh.

**flicker** *v* priob.

**flight** *n* itealadh *m*.

**flimsy** *adj* tana.

**flinch** *v* clisich.

**flint** *n* ailbhinn *f*.

**flippant** *adj* beadaidh.

**flit** *v* èalaidh; (*house*) dèan imrich.

**float** *v* snàmh.

**flock** *n* treud *m*.

**flood** *n* tuil *f*. • *v* còmhdaich le uisge.

**floodlight** *n* tuil-sholas *m*.

**floor** *n* ùrlar *m*. • *v* cuir ùrlar ann.

**floppy disk** *n* clàr sùbailte *m*.

**floral** *adj* flùranach.

**flounder** *n* leòbag *f*.

**flour** *n* flùr *m*.

**flourish** *v* fàs gu math; beartaich.

**flow** *v* ruith.

**flower** *n* blàth, flùr *m*.

**fluctuate** *v* atharraich.

**fluency** *n* fileantachd *f*.

**fluent** *adj* fileanta.

**fluid** *adj* silteach. • *n* lionn *m*.

**flush** *v* fàs dearg; (*toilet*) sruthlaich.

**fluster** *v* cuir gu cabhaig.

**flute** *n* cuisle chiùil *f*.

**fly**[1] *n* cuileag *f*; (*fishing*) maghar *m*.

**fly**[2] *v* theirig air iteig.

**fly**[3] *adj* carach.

**foal** *n* searrach *m*.

**foam** *n* cop *m*. • *v* cuir cop dhe.

**focus** *n* cruinn-ionad *m*; fòcas *m*. • *v* faigh cruinn-shealladh.

**fodder** *n* fodar *m*.

**foetus** *n* toircheas *m*.

**fog** *n* ceò *m/f*.

**foggy** *adj* ceòthach.

**foil** *v* cuir casg air.

**fold** *n* buaile *f*. • *v* cuir an crò.

**folded** *adj* fillte.

**foliage** *n* duilleach *m*.

**folk** *n* muinntir *f*.

**folk-song** *n* mith-òran *m*.

**folk-tale** *n* mith-sgeul *m*.

**folklore** *n* beul-aithris *f*.

**follow** *v* lean.

**folly** *n* amaideachd *f*.

**fond** *adj* dèidheil.

**fondle** *v* cniadaich.

**food** *n* biadh *m*.

**fool** *n* amadan *m*. • *v* thoir an car à.

**foolproof** *adj* do-mhillte.

**foolish** *adj* gòrach.

**foot** *n* cas, troigh *f*.

**footpath** *n* frith-rathad *m*.

**footwear** *n* caisbheart *f*.

**for** *prep* air; a chionn; an àite; do bhrìgh; ri; gu; fad; do.

**forage** *v* solair.

**forbid** *v* toirmisg.

**forbidding** *adj* gruamach.

**force** *n* neart *m.* • *v* co-èignich.

**forceps** *n* teanchair *m.*

**ford** *n* àth *m.*

**fore** *adj* toisich.

**forearm** *n* ruighe *f.*

**forecast** *n* roimh-aithris *f.* • *v* roimh-aithris.

**forefather** *n* sinnsear *m.*

**forefinger** *n* sgealbag *f.*

**forego** *v* fàg.

**foreground** *n* roimh-ionad *m.*

**forehead** *n* bathais *m.*

**foreign** *adj* gallda, coimheach.

**foreigner** *n* Gall, coigreach *m.*

**foreknow** *v* roimh-aithnich.

**foreknowledge** *n* roimh-aithne *f.*

**foremost** *adj* prìomh.

**forerunner** *n* roimh-ruithear *m.*

**foresail** *n* seòl-toisich *m.*

**foresee** *v* faic roimh làimh.

**foresight** *n* roimh-shealladh *m.*

**forest** *n* coille *f.*

**forester** *n* forsair *m.*

**forestry** *n* forsaireachd *f.*

**foretaste** *n* roimh-bhlasad *m.*

**foretell** *v* roimh-innis.

**forever** *adv* a chaoidh.

**forewarn** *v* cuir air earalas.

**foreword** *n* roimh-ràdh *m.*

**forge** *v* dèan goibhneachd.

**forger** *n* fallsaidhear *m.*

**forget** *v* dìochuimhnich.

**forgetful** *adj* dìochuimhneach.

**forgetfulness** *n* dìochuimhne *f.*

**forgive** *v* thoir mathanas.

**forgotten** *adj* air dìochuimhne.

**fork** *n* greimire, forc *m.* • *v* fàs gòbhlach.

**forlorn** *adj* aonaranach.

**form** *n* cumadh *m.* • *v* dealbh, cum.

**formal** *adj* dòigheil, foirmeil.

**formality** *n* deas-ghnàth *m.*

**format** *n* cruth *m.*

**formidable** *adj* cumhachdach.

**formula** *n* foirmle *f.*

**formulate** *v* riaghailich.

**fornicate** *v* dèan strìopachas.

**fornication** *n* strìopachas *f.*

**forsake** *v* cuir cùl ri.

**forsaken** *adj* trèigte.

**fort** *n* daingneach *f*, dùn *m.*

**forth** *adv* a-mach.

**forthwith** *adv* gun dàil.

**fortitude** *n* cruadal *m.*

**fortnight** *n* cola-deug *f.*

**fortuitous** *adj* tuiteamach.

**fortunate** *adj* fortanach.

**fortune** *n* sealbh *m.*

**fortuneteller** *n* fiosaiche *m.*

**forty** *adj/n* ceathrad.

**forward** *adj* iarrtach. • *adv* air adhart.

**forwards** *adv* air adhart.

**fossil** *n* fosail *f.*

**foster** *v* altrum.

**foster-sibling** *n* co-alta *m.*

**foster-father** n oide m.

**foster-mother** n muime f.

**foul**[1] adj breun.

**foul**[2] n fealladh m.

**found** v stèidhich.

**foundation** n stèidh f.

**founder**[1] n fear-stèidheachaidh f.

**founder**[2] v theirig fodha.

**foundling** n faodalach m.

**fountain** n fuaran m.

**four** adj/n ceithir; (persons) ceathrar.

**foursome** n ceathrach f.

**fourteen** adj/n ceithir-deug.

**fourteenth** adj ceathramh deug.

**fourthly** adv sa' cheathramh àite.

**fowl** n eun m.

**fox** n sionnach m.

**fraction** n bloigh f.

**fracture** n bristeadh m.

**fragile** adj brisg.

**fragment** n fuigheall m.

**fragrant** adj cùbhraidh.

**frail** adj lag.

**frailty** n laige f.

**frame** n cèis f.

**France** n An Fhraing f.

**frank** adj faoilidh.

**frank** v (stamp) saor.

**frantic** adj air bhoile.

**fraternal** adj bràithreil.

**fraud** n foill f.

**freak** n tuiteamas m.

**freckles** npl breacadh-seunain m.

**freckled** adj breac-bhallach.

**free** adj saor; an asgaidh.

**freedom** n saorsa f.

**freelance** adj neo-cheangailte.

**freemason** n saor-chlachair m.

**free-range** adj saor-thogta.

**free trade** n saor-mhalairt f.

**free will** n saor-thoil f.

**freeze** v reòdh.

**freezer** n reodhadair m.

**freight** n luchd m.

**French** adj Frangach. • n Fraingis f.

**frenzy** n boile f.

**frequency** n tricead m.

**frequent** adj tric. • v tadhail.

**fresh** adj (air) fionnar; (food) ùr.

**fret** v luaisg.

**fretful** adj frionasach.

**friar** n bràthair-bochd m.

**friction** n suathadh m.

**Friday** n Dihaoine m.

**friend** n caraid m, bana-charaid f.

**friendliness** n càirdeas m.

**friendly** adj càirdeil.

**fright** n eagal m.

**frighten** v cuir eagal air.

**frightful** adj oillteil.

**frigid** adj fuar.

**frill** n grinneas m.

**frisky** adj mireagach.

**frivolity** n faoineas m.

**frivolous** adj faoin.

**fro** adv air ais.

**frock** n froca m.

**frog** n losgann m.

**from** prep o, bho, à.

**front** n aghaidh f.

**front-door** n doras-mòr m.
**frontier** n crìoch f.
**frost** n reothadh m.
**frostbitten** adj reo-sheargte.
**frosty** adj (frozen) reòta.
**frown** n gruaim f.
**frugal** adj glèidhteach.
**frugality** n glèidhteachd f.
**fruit** n meas m.
**fruity** adj measach.
**frustrate** v mill dùil.
**fry** v ròsd.
**frying pan** n aghann f.
**fuck** v rach air muin.
**fuel** n connadh m.
**fugitive** n fògarrach m.
**fulfil** v coilion.
**fulfilment** n coilionadh m.
**full** adj làn.
**full-grown** adj aig làn fhàs.
**full stop** n stad phuing f.
**full-time** adj làn-aimsireach.

**fumble** v làimhsich gu cearbach.
**fun** n spòrs f.
**function** n dreuchd f.
**function key** n (comput) inchair-gnìomha f.
**fundamental** adj bunaiteach.
**funeral** n adhlacadh m.
**funny** adj sùgach, èibhinn.
**fur** n bian m.
**furnish** v uidheamaich.
**furniture** n àirneis f.
**furrow** n clais f.
**furry** adj molach.
**further, furthermore** adv rud eile, a bhàrr air sinn.
**fury** n cuthach m.
**fuse** n leagadh m.
**fusty** adj malcaidh.
**futile** adj dìomhain.
**futility** n dìomhanas m.
**future** adj ri teachd. • n àm ri teachd m.

# G

**gable** n stuadh f.
**gadget** n uidheam f.
**Gael** n Gaidheal m.
**Gaelic** adj/n Gàidhlig.
**gaiety** n cridhealas m.
**gaily** adv gu cridheil.
**gain** v buannaich.
**gale** n gaoth mhòr f.
**gallant** adj basdalach.

**gallery** n lobhta m.
**galley** n birlinn f.
**gallon** n galan m.
**gallop** v luath-mharcaidh.
**Galloway** n A'Ghall-Ghaidheal-tachd f.
**gallows** n croich f.
**galore** adv gu lèor.
**gamble** v iomair air gheall.

**gambler** n cèarraiche m.
**gambling** n cèarrachas m.
**game** n cluiche f; (*meat*) sitheann f.
**gamekeeper** n geamair m.
**gander** n gànradh m.
**gang** n buidheann f.
**gannet** n sùlaire m.
**gaol** n prìosan m.
**gap** n beàrn m.
**gape** v spleuchd.
**garage** n garaids f.
**garbage** n fuighleach m.
**garble** v cuir às a riochd.
**garden** n lios m.
**gardener** n gàirnealair m.
**garland** n blàth-fhleasg f.
**garlic** n creamh m.
**garment** n bad aodaich m.
**garron** n gearran m.
**garrulity** n goileam m.
**garrulous** adj cabach.
**garter** n gartan m.
**gas-cooker** n cucair-gas m.
**gas fire** n teine gas m.
**gash** n gearradh m.
**gasp** v plosg.
**gastronomic** adj sòghail.
**gastronomy** n sòghalachd f.
**gate** n geata m.
**gather** v cruinnich.
**gathering** n cruinneachadh m.
**gaudy** adj basdalach.
**gauge** n tomhas m.
**gaunt** adj lom.
**gawky** adj sgleòideach.

**gay** adj sùnndach; (*sexuality*) co-sheòrsach.
**gaze** v dùr-amharc.
**gear** n (*car*) gèar m.
**gem** n seud m.
**gender** n gnè f.
**genealogical** adj sloinnnteach-ail.
**genealogist** n sloinntear m.
**genealogy** n sloinntearachd f.
**general** adj coitcheann.
**generalise** v ginearalaich.
**generally** adv am bitheantas.
**generation** n àl m; linn m.
**generator** n gineadair m.
**generic** adj gnèitheach.
**generosity** n fialaidheachd m.
**generous** adj fial.
**genetic** adj ginteil.
**genial** adj coibhneil.
**genitals** npl buill gineamhainn.
**genius** n sàr-ghin m.
**genteel** adj suairce.
**gentle** adj ciùin.
**gentleman** n duine uasal m.
**gentlewoman** n bean uasal f.
**gentry** npl uaislean.
**genuine** adj fìor.
**geography** n cruinn'-eòlas m.
**geological** adj geòlâch.
**geologist** n geòlaiche m.
**geology** n geòlas m.
**geometry** n geoimeatras m.
**germ** n bitheag f.
**German** n Gearmailt f. • adj Gear-mailteach.

**Germany** n A' Ghearmailt f.
**germinate** v ginidich.
**gestation** n torrachas m.
**gesture** n gluasad m.
**get** v faigh, coisinn.
**ghastly** adj oillteil.
**ghost** n taibhse m/f, bòcan m.
**ghostly** adj taibhseil.
**giant** adj ana-mhòr. • n famhair m.
**gibber** v dèan goileam.
**gibe** n sgeig f.
**giddy** adj guanach.
**gift** n tiodhlac m.
**gifted** adj tàlantach.
**gigantic** adj fuamhaireil.
**gild** v òraich.
**gill** n giùran m.
**gin** n sine f; (trap) ribe f.
**gingerbread** n aran-crì m.
**gipsy** n giofag f.
**giraffe** n sioraf m.
**girdle** n greideal f.
**girl** n caileag, nighean f.
**girth** n giort f.
**give** v thoir.
**glaciation** n eighreachadh m.
**glacier** n eighre-shruth m.
**glad** adj toilichte.
**glance** n grad-shealladh m. • v grad-amhairc.
**gland** n fàireag f.
**glare** n deàrrsadh m.
**Glasgow** n Glaschu f.
**glass** n glainne f.
**glassy** adj glainneach.

**gleam** v soillsich.
**glean** v dìoghlam.
**glee** n mire f.
**glen** n gleann m.
**glib** adj cabanta.
**glide** v gluais.
**glimmer** n fann-sholas m.
**glister** v deàrrs.
**glitter** n lainnir f.
**gloaming** n fionnaraigh f.
**global** adj domhanta.
**global warming** n blàthachadh na cruinne m.
**globe** n cruinne f.
**gloom** n duibhre f.
**gloomy** adj doilleir.
**glory** n glòir f.
**glossy** adj lìomharra.
**glove** n miotag f.
**glow** n luisne f. • v luisnich.
**glower** v seall fo na mùgan.
**glue** n glaodh m.
**glum** adj gruamach.
**glutton** n craosaire m.
**gluttony** n craos m.
**gnash** v gìosg.
**gnaw** v creim.
**go** v falbh, imich, theirich, rach, gabh.
**goal** n crìoch f; gòil m.
**goalie** n fear-bàire m.
**goalpost** n post-bàire m.
**goat** n gobhar m.
**goblin** n bòcan m.
**god** n dia m.
**goddess** n ban-dia f.

**going** n falbh m.

**gold** n òr m.

**golden** adj òir, òrach.

**golf** n goilf m.

**good** adj math, deagh.

**goodbye** interj slàn leat; beannachd leat.

**goodness** n mathas m.

**goodwill** n gean math m.

**goods** npl bathar m; (possessions) cuid f.

**goose** n gèadh f.

**gooseberry** n gròiseid f.

**gore** v sàth.

**gorge**$^1$ n clais-mhòr f.

**gorge**$^2$ v lion craos.

**gorgeous** adj greadhnach.

**gorse** n conasg m.

**gory** adj gaorrach.

**gospel** n soisgeul m.

**gossip** n goistidh m. • v bi a' gobaireachd.

**govern** v riaghail.

**government** n riaghaltas m.

**gown** n gùn m.

**grab** v gabh grèim air.

**grace** n gràs m; (prayer) altachadh m; (manner) loinn m. • v sgeadaich.

**grace-note** n nota-altaidh m.

**graceful** adj maiseach.

**gracious** adj gràsmhor.

**grade** n ceum m.

**gradient** n àrdachadh m.

**gradual** adj beag is beag.

**gradually** adv beag is beag.

**graduate** n fear-ceuma m.

**graduation** n ceumnachadh m.

**graft** n nòdachadh m. • v nòdaich; (toil) saothraich.

**grain** n gràinne f.

**graip** n gràpa m.

**granary** n sìol-lann f.

**grand** adj mòr, uasal.

**grandchild** n ogha m.

**grandeur** n mòrachd m.

**grandfather** n seanair m.

**grandmother** n seanmhair f.

**granite** n clach-ghràin f.

**grant** n tabhartas m.

**granular** adj cnapach.

**grape** n fìon-dearc f.

**grapefruit** n seadag f.

**grapple** v greimich.

**grasp** n grèim m. • v dèan grèim air, glac.

**grass** n feur m.

**grassy** adj feurach.

**grate** n cliath-theine f.

**grate** v sgrìob.

**grateful** adj taingeil.

**grater** n sgrìoban m.

**gratitude** n taingealachd f.

**gratuity** n tiodhlac m.

**grave**$^1$ adj stòlda.

**grave**$^2$ n uaigh f.

**gravel** n grinneal m.

**gravestone** n leac-uaghach f.

**graveyard** n cladh m.

**gravity** n iom-tharraing f.

**graze**$^1$ v (browse) feuraich.

**graze**$^2$ v (scrape) suath.

**grease** *n* saill *f.* • *v* crèisich.

**greasy** *adj* crèiseach.

**great** *adj* mòr; àrd.

**greatness** *n* mòrachd *f.*

**Greece** *n* A' Ghreig *f.*

**Greek** *adj* Greugach. • *n* Greugais *f.*

**greed** *n* sannt *m.*

**greedy** *adj* sanntach.

**green** *adj* uaine.

**greenness** *n* uainead *m.*

**greet** *v* fàiltich.

**greeting** *n* fàilte *f.*

**gregarious** *adj* greigheach.

**grey** *adj* glas, liath.

**grey-haired** *adj* liath.

**grid** *n* cliath *f.*

**griddle** *n* greideal *f.*

**grief** *n* mulad *m.*

**grieve** *v* cràidh.

**grill** *v* grìosaich.

**grilse** *n* bànag *f.*

**grim** *adj* gnù.

**grimace** *n* mùig *m.*

**grin** *n* braoisg *f.* • *v* cuir braosg air.

**grind** *v* meil.

**gristle** *n* maothan *m.*

**grit** *n* grian *m.*

**grizzled** *adj* grìsfhionn.

**groan** *n* cnead *m.* • *v* dèan cnead.

**groceries** *n* bathair grosaireach *m.*

**groin** *n* loch-bhlèin *f.*

**groove** *n* clais *f.*

**grope** *v* rùraich.

**gross**[1] *adj* dòmhail.

**gross**[2] *n* dà dhusan deug *m.*

**grotesque** *adj* mì-nàdurrach.

**ground** *n* grùnnd *m.* • *v* socraich.

**group** *n* còmhlan *m.*

**grouse**[1] *n* (*bird*) eun-fhraoich *m.*

**grouse**[2] *n* (*grumble*) gearan *m.*

**grove** *n* doire *m.*

**grovel** *v* snàig.

**grow** *v* fàs, meudaich.

**growl** *n* dranndan *m.* • *v* dèan dranndan.

**growth** *n* fàs *m.*

**grudge** *n* diomb *m.* • *v* talaich.

**grumble** *v* gearain.

**grunt** *n* gnòsail *f.* • *v* dèan gnòsail.

**guarantee** *n* barrantas *m.*

**guard** *n* faire *f*; (*individual*) freiceadan *m.* • *v* dìon.

**guardian** *n* (*tutor*) taoitear *m.*

**guess** *n* tomhas *m.* • *v* tomhais.

**guest** *n* aoigh *m.*

**guide** *n* fear-treòrachaidh *m.* • *v* treòraich.

**guided missile** *n* urchair thrèoraichte *f.*

**guillemot** *n* eun dubh an sgadain *m.*

**guilt** *n* ciont *m.*

**guilty** *adj* ciontach.

**gulf** *n* camas *m.*

**gully** *n* gil *f.*

**gulp** *n* slugadh *m.* • *v* sluig.

**gum** *n* càireas *m.*

**gumption** *n* ciall *f.*

**gun** *n* gunna *m.*

**gunwale** *n* beul-mòr *m.*

**gurgle** n glugan m.

**gust** n oiteag f.

**gusto** n cridhealas m.

**gusty** adj stoirmeil.

**gut** n caolan m.

# H

**habit** n cleachdadh m; (monk) earradh m.

**habitual** adj gnàthach.

**hack** v geàrr.

**haddock** n adag f.

**haft** n cas m.

**hag** n cailleach f.

**haggis** n taigeis f.

**haggle** v dèan còmhstri mu phrìs.

**hailstones** npl clachan-meallain.

**hair** n falt m.

**hairy** adj molach.

**half** n leth m.

**half-bottle** n leth-bhotal m.

**half-way** adj letheach-slighe.

**hall** n talla m/f.

**Hallowe'en** n Oidhche Shamhna f.

**hallucination** n mearachadh m.

**halo** n fainne f.

**halt** v stad.

**halter** n aghastar m.

**halve** v roinn 'na dhà leth.

**ham** n hama m.

**hamlet** n clachan m.

**hammer** n òrd m. • v buail le òrd.

**hamper**[1] n bascaid bidhe f.

**hamper**[2] v bac.

**hand** n làmh, cròg f. • v sìn.

**handbag** n poca làimhe m.

**handful** n dòrlach m.

**handicap** n bacadh m.

**handkerchief** n neapaigear f.

**handle** n làmh, cas f. • v làimhsich.

**handshake** n crathadh làimhe m.

**handsome** adj eireachdail.

**handwoven** adj làmh-fhighte.

**handy** adj deas.

**hang** v croch.

**hangover** n ceann daoraich m.

**happen** v tachair.

**happening** n tachartas m.

**happiness** n sonas m.

**happy** adj sona.

**harass** v sàraich.

**harbour** n cala, acarsaid m. • v gabh ri.

**hard** adj cruaidh.

**hard disk** n clàr cruaidh m.

**harden** v cruadhaich.

**hardihood** n cruadal m.

**hardly** adv gann.

**hardship** n cruaidh-chàs m.

**hardware** n cruaidh-bhathar m; (comput) bathar cruaidh m.

**hare** n maigheach f.

**hare-brained** adj gaoitheanach.

**harm** n cron m. • v dèan cron air.

**harmful** adj cronail.

**harmless** adj neo-chronail.

**harmonic** adj co-cheòlach.

**harmonious** adj co-chòrdach.

**harmonise** v ceòl-rèim.

**harmony** n co-sheirm m.

**harp** n clàrsach f.

**harper** n clàrsair m.

**Harris** n Na Hearadh.

**Harris tweed** n clò na Hearadh m.

**harrow** v cliath.

**harsh** adj garg.

**harshness** n gairge f.

**hart** n damh-fèidh m.

**harvest** n buain f.

**haste** n cabhag f.

**hasten** v greas.

**hasty** adj cabhagach.

**hat** n ad f.

**hatch** n gur m; (ship) saidse f.

**hatchet** n làmh-thuagh f.

**hate** n fuath m. • v fuathaich.

**hateful** adj fuathach.

**hauteur** n àrdan m.

**haughty** adj àrdanach.

**haul** v tarraing.

**haunch** n leis f.

**haunt** v tathaich.

**have** v bi aig; seilbhich; (eat, etc) gabh; (have to) feum.

**hawk** n seabhag m/f.

**hawser** n taod m.

**hawthorn** n sgitheach m.

**hay** n feur, feur caoin m.

**haystack** n goc, tudan m.

**haze** n ceò m.

**hazy** adj ceòthach.

**he** pron e.

**head** n ceann m.

**headmaster** n maighstir-sgoile m.

**headmistress** n bana-mhaighstir-sgoile f.

**headache** n cràdh-cinn m.

**header** n buille-cinn f.

**headland** n rubha m.

**headlight** n solas-mòr m.

**headquarters** n prìomh-àros m.

**headstrong** adj ceann-làidir.

**headway** n adhartas m.

**heady** adj bras.

**heal** v leighis.

**healer** n slànaighear m.

**health** n slàinte f.

**healthy** adj slàn.

**heap** n tòrr m. • v cruach.

**hear** v cluinn, èisd.

**hearer** n fear-èisdeachd m.

**hearing** n claisneachd f.

**hearing-aid** n inneal-claistinn m.

**hearsay** n iomradh m.

**hearse** n carbad-mharbh m.

**heart** n cridhe m.

**hearten** v misnich.

**hearth** n teinntean m.

**hearty** adj sùnndach.

**heat** n teas m. • v teasaich.

**heater** n uidheam teasachaidh f.

**heathen** n pàganach m. • adj pàganta.

**heather** n fraoch m.

**heathery** adj fraochach.

**heave** n togail f. • v tarraing.

**heaven** n nèamh m.

**heavenly** adj nèamhaidh.

**heaviness** n truime f.

**heavy** adj trom.

**Hebrides** n Innse Gall.

**heckle** v tras-cheusnaich.

**hedge** n callaid f.

**hedgehog** n gràineag f.

**heed** n aire m. • v thoir aire.

**heedful** adj faicilleach.

**heedless** adj neo-aireach.

**heel** n sàil f.

**heifer** n agh f.

**height** n àirde f.

**heighten** v àrdaich.

**heir** n oighre m.

**heiress** n ban-oighre f.

**helicopter** n helicoiptear m.

**hell** n ifrinn, iutharn f.

**help** n cuideachadh m. • v cuidich.

**helpful** adj cobhaireach.

**hem** n faitheam m.

**hemisphere** n leth-chruinne m.

**hen** n cearc f.

**hence** adv às a seo.

**henceforth** adv o seo a-mach.

**her** pron i, ise. • poss adj a, aice.

**herald** n teachdaire m.

**herb** n lus m.

**herbal** adj lusragach.

**herd** n treud, buar m. • v buachaillich.

**herdsman** n buachaille m.

**here** adv seo. an seo.

**hereafter** n an ath shaogal m.

**hereby** adv le seo.

**hereditary** adj dùthchasach.

**heredity** n dùchas m.

**heresy** n saobh-chreideamh m.

**heritage** n oighreachd f.

**hermit** n aonaran m.

**hero** n curaidh, laoch m.

**heroic** adj gaisgeach.

**heroine** n bana-ghaisgeach f.

**heron** n corra-ghrìtheach f.

**herring** n sgadan m.

**herring-gull** n faoileag f.

**herself** pron ise, i fhèin.

**hesitate** v bi an imcheist.

**hesitation** n imcheist f.

**hiccup** n aileag f.

**hide** v ceil.

**hideous** adj gràineil.

**hiding-place** n àite-falaich m.

**high** adj àrd; mòr; urramach.

**high-frequency** adj àrd-tricead.

**Highland** adj Gaidhealach.

**Highlander** n Gaidheal m.

**Highlands** n A'Ghaidhealtachd f.

**highlight** v leig cudthrom air.

**high-minded** adj ard-intinneach.

**high-powered** adj mòr-chumhachdach.

**high tide** n muir-làn m/f.

**highway** n rathad-mòr m.

**hike** v bi a'heidhceadh.

**hill** n cnoc m.

**hillock** n cnocan, sìthean m.

**hillside** n leathan m.

**hilly** adj cnocach.

**hilt** *n* dòrn *m*.

**himself** *pron* e fhèin.

**hind** *n* eilid *f*.

**hinder** *v* bac.

**hinge** *n* bann *m*.

**hint** *n* sanas *m*.

**hip** *n* cruachann *f*.

**hire** *v* fasdaidh.

**hire purchase** *n* cìs-cheannach *m*.

**his** *pron* a. • *poss adj* a, aige.

**hiss** *v* siosarnaich.

**historian** *n* eachdraiche *m*.

**historical** *adj* eachdraidheil.

**history** *n* eachdraidh *f*.

**hit** *n* buille *f*. • *v* buail.

**hither** *adv* an seo.

**hive** *n* sgeap *f*.

**hoard** *n* ulaidh *f*. • *v* taisg.

**hoar-frost** *n* liath-reodhadh *m*.

**hoarse** *adj* tùchanach.

**hoarseness** *n* tùchadh *m*.

**hobby** *n* cur-seachad *m*.

**hobnail** *n* tacaid *f*.

**hoe** *n* todha *m*. • *v* todhaig.

**Hogmanay** *n* Callain, Oidhche Challain *f*.

**hold** *v* cùm.

**hole** *n* toll *m*.

**holiday** *n* saor-là *m*.

**hollow** *n* còs *m*.

**hollowness** *n* falamhachd *m*.

**holly** *n* cuileann *m*.

**holy** *adj* naomh.

**homage** *n* ùmhlachd *f*.

**home** *n* dachaigh *f*. • *adv* dhach-aigh.

**home rule** *n* fèin-riaghladh *m*.

**homesick** *adj* cianalach.

**homesickness** *n* cianalas *m*.

**homespun** *adj* dachaigheil.

**homosexual** *adj* co-sheòrsach.

**honest** *adj* onorach.

**honesty** *n* onair *f*.

**honey** *n* mil *f*.

**honeymoon** *n* mìos nam pòg *f*.

**honeysuckle** *n* iadh-shlat *f*.

**honour** *n* onair *f*; urram *m*. • *v* onaraich.

**hood** *n* cochall *m*.

**hoof** *n* iongna *f*.

**hook** *n* dubhan *m*.

**hooked** *adj* crom.

**hooligan** *n* ùpraidiche *m*.

**hoot** *v* goir.

**hop** *n* sìnteag *f*. • *v* dèan sìnteag.

**hope** *n* dòchas *m*. • *v* tha dùil aig.

**hopeful** *adj* dòchasach.

**hopeless** *adj* eu-dòchasach.

**horizon** *n* fàire *f*.

**horizontal** *adj* còmhnard.

**horn** *n* adharc *f*; (*musical instrument, drink*) còrn *m*.

**hornet** *n* connspeach *f*.

**horoscope** *n* reul-shealladh *m*.

**horrible** *adj* oillteil.

**horrid** *adj* dèisinnneach.

**horror** *n* uamhann *m*.

**horse** *n* each *m*.

**horseman** *n* marcaiche *m*.

**horseshoe** *n* crudha *m*.

**hose** *n* (*sock*) osan *m*; (*pipe*) pìob *f*.

**hospitable** *adj* fial.

**hospital** *n* taigh-eiridinn *m*.

**hospitality** *n* aoigheachd *f*.

**host** *n* fear-taighe *m*; sluagh *m*.

**hostage** *n* bràigh *m*.

**hostess** *n* bean-taighe *f*.

**hostile** *adj* nàimhdeil.

**hostility** *n* nàimhdeas *m*.

**hot** *adj* teth.

**hotel** *n* taigh-òsda *m*.

**hour** *n* uair *f*.

**hourly** *adv* gach uair.

**house** *n* taigh *m*. • *v* thoir taigh do.

**household** *n* teaghlach *m*.

**hover** *v* fo-luaimnich.

**how** *adv* ciamar?; dè cho?

**however** *adv* co-dhiù.

**howl** *n* donnal *m*. • *v* dèan donnal.

**huddle** *v* còmhlaich.

**hug** *v* glac teann.

**hull** *n* cochall *m*.

**hum** *n* srann *f*. • *v* dèan torman.

**human** *adj* daonna.

**humane** *adj* caomh.

**humanity** *n* daonnachd *f*.

**humankind** *n* an cinne daonna *m*.

**humble** *adj* umhal. • *v* ùmhlaich.

**humid** *adj* tais.

**humorist** *n* fear àbhachdach *m*.

**humorous** *adj* àbhachdach.

**humour**[1] *n* àbhachd *f*.

**humour**[2] *v* toilich.

**hump** *n* croit *f*.

**hundred** *adj/n* ceud.

**hundredth** *adj* ceudamh.

**hunger** *n* acras *m*.

**hungry** *adj* acrach.

**hunt** *n* sealg *m*. • *v* sealg.

**hunter** *n* sealgair *m*.

**hurricane** *n* doinnean *f*.

**hurry** *n* cabhag *f*. • *v* luathaich.

**hurt** *n* dochann *m*. • *v* goirtich.

**hurtful** *adj* cronail.

**husband** *n* fear-pòsda, cèile *m*.

**hush** *v* sàmhaich.

**hut** *n* bothan *m*.

**hybrid** *n* cros-chineal *m*.

**hydro-electric** *adj* dealan-uis-geach.

**hydro-electricity** *n* dealan-uisge *m*.

**hygiene** *n* slàinteachas *m*.

**hymn** *n* laoidh *m*.

**hypocrisy** *n* breug-chràbhadh *m*.

**hypocrite** *n* breug-chràbaiche *m*.

**hysterical** *adj* reachdail.

**hysterics** *npl* reachd *f*.

# I

**I** *pron* mi; mise.

**ice** *n* deigh *f*.

**iceberg** *n* cnoc-eighre *m*.

**ice-cream** *n* reòiteag *f*.

**icicle** *n* caisean-reòta *m*.

**icing** *n* còmhdach-siùcair *m*.

**icy** *adj* reòta.

**idea** *n* beachd-smuain *f.*

**ideal** *adj* sàr. • *n* sàr-beachd *m.*

**identical** *adj* ionann.

**identification** *n* aithneachadh *m.*

**identify** *v* dearbh-aithnich.

**identity** *n* dearbh-aithne *f.*

**idiom** *n* gnathas-cainnt *m.*

**idiot** *n* amadan *m.*

**idle** *adj* dìomhain.

**idleness** *n* dìomhanas *m.*

**idler** *n* leisgean *m.*

**idol** *n* iodhal *m.*

**if** *conj* ma, nan, nam.

**if not** *conj* mur.

**ignite** *v* cuir teine ri.

**ignition** *n* adhnadh *m.*

**ignominious** *adj* nàr.

**ignorance** *n* aineolas *m.*

**ignorant** *adj* aineolach.

**ignore** *v* leig le.

**ill** *adj* tinn.

**ill-health** *n* euslainte *f.*

**illegal** *adj* neo-laghail.

**illegality** *n* mì-laghalachd *f.*

**illegible** *adj* do-leughadh.

**illegitimate** *adj* dìolain.

**illiterate** *adj* neo-litireach.

**illness** *n* tinneas *m.*

**illogical** *adj* mì-reusanta.

**illuminate** *v* soilleirich.

**illumination** *n* soillseachadh *m.*

**illusion** *n* mealladh *m.*

**illusory** *adj* meallach.

**illustrate** *v* dealbhaich.

**illustrator** *n* dealbhadair *m.*

**ilustrious** *adj* ainmeil.

**image** *n* ìomhaigh *f.*

**imaginable** *adj* so-smuainich.

**imaginary** *adj* mac-meanmnach.

**imagination** *n* mac-meanmainn *m.*

**imagine** *v* smaoinich.

**imbecile** *n* lethchiallach *m.*

**imbibe** *v* òl.

**imbue** *v* lìon.

**imitate** *v* dèan atharrais air.

**imitation** *n* atharrais *f.*

**immaculate** *adj* fìorghlan.

**immaterial** *adj* neo-chorporra; coma.

**immature** *adj* an-abaich.

**immaturity** *n* an-abaichead *m.*

**immediate** *adj* ciad.

**immediately** *adv* gun dàil.

**immense** *adj* an-mhòr.

**immerse** *v* cuir fodha.

**immigrant** *n* inn-imriche *m.*

**immigration** *n* inn-imrich *f.*

**imminent** *adj* gus teachd.

**immodest** *adj* mì-nàrach.

**immoral** *adj* mì-bheusach.

**immorality** *n* mì-bheus *f.*

**immortal** *adj* neo-bhàsmhor.

**immortality** *n* neo-bhàsmhorachd *f.*

**immunise** *v* dìon bho ghalar.

**immunity** *n* saorsa *f*; dìon *m.*

**imp** *n* spruis.

**impair** *v* mill.

**impalpable** *adj* do-fhaireach-dainn.

**impart** v compàirtich.

**impartial** adj ceart-bhreitheach.

**impassable** adj do-shiubhal.

**impassive** adj socair.

**impatience** n mì-fhoighidinn f.

**impatient** adj mì-fhoighidneach.

**impede** v bac.

**impediment** n bacadh m.

**impel** v greas.

**impenetrable** adj do-inntrig.

**imperative** adj òrduigheach.

**imperceptible** adj do-mhoth-aichte.

**impersonal** adj neo-phearsanta.

**impersonate** v pearsonaich.

**impertinence** n mì-mhodh f.

**impertinent** adj mì-mhodhail.

**impervious** adj do-ruighinn.

**impetuous** adj cas, bras.

**impetus** n dèine f.

**impinge** v buail.

**implacable** adj gamhlasach.

**implement** n inneal m.

**implement** v thoir gu buil.

**implicate** v cuir an sàs.

**implication** n ribeadh m.

**implicit** adj fillte.

**implore** v aslaich.

**imply** v ciallaich.

**impolitic** adj neo-sheòlta.

**import** n brìgh f; (goods) badhar o chèin m. • v thoir a-steach ba-dhar.

**importance** n cudrom m.

**important** adj cudromach.

**impose** v cuir air.

**impossibility** n nì do-dhèanta m.

**impossible** adj do-dhèanta.

**impostor** n mealltair m.

**impotence** n eu-comas m.

**impotent** adj eu-comasach.

**impoverish** v dèan bochd.

**impracticable** adj do-dhèanta.

**impregnable** adj do-ionnsaighe.

**impressive** adj drùidhteach.

**imprison** v cuir am prìosan.

**improbability** n mì-choltas m.

**improbable** adj mì-choltach.

**improper** adj neo-iomchuidh.

**improve** v leasaich.

**improvement** n leasachadh m.

**improvident** adj neo-fhreas-dalach.

**imprudent** adj neo-chùramach.

**impudence** n dànachd f.

**impulsive** adj spreigearra.

**impure** adj neòghlan.

**impute** v cuir às leth.

**in** prep an, ann an. • adv ann; a-steach, a-staigh.

**in-shore** adj cladaich.

**inability** n neo-chomas.

**inaccurate** adj neo-chruinn.

**inadequate** adj uireasach.

**inadvertent** adj neo-aireach.

**inane** adj faoin.

**inarticulate** adj gagach.

**inasmuch as** conj aig a'mheud 's a.

**incarnate** adj san fheòil.

**incense**¹ n tùis f.

**incense**² v feargaich.

**incest** n col m.

**incestuous** adj colach.

**inch** n òirleach f.

**inclement** adj an-iochdmhor.

**inclination** n aomadh m.

**incline** v aom.

**include** v cuir san àireamh.

**incognito** adv gu dìomhair.

**income** n teachd-a-steach m.

**income tax** n càin-teachd-a-steach f.

**incomparable** adj gun choimeas.

**incompatible** adj neo-fhreagarrach.

**incomplete** adj neo-choileanta.

**incomprehensible** adj do-thuigsinn.

**inconvenience** n neo-ghoireasachd f.

**inconvenient** adj mì-ghoireasach.

**incorrect** adj mearachdach.

**increase** n meudachadh m. • v meudaich; rach am meud.

**incredible** adj do-chreidsinn.

**incredulous** adj às-creideach.

**incriminate** v ciontaich.

**incubate** v guir.

**incur** v bi buailteach do.

**incurable** adj do-leigheas.

**indebted** adj an comain.

**indecent** adj mì-chuibheasach.

**indeed** adv gu dearbh.

**indelible** adj do-sgriosta.

**indemnify** v theirig an urras air.

**indent** v eagaich.

**independence** n neo-eisimeileachd f.

**independent** adj neo-eisimeileach.

**index** n clàr-amais m. • v clàraich.

**indicate** v comharraich.

**indifferent** adj coma.

**indigestion** n cion-meirbhidh m.

**indignant** adj diombach.

**indignation** n diomb m.

**indiscreet** adj neo-chrìonna.

**indiscretion** n neo-chrìonnachd f.

**individual** adj air leth.

**individual** n urra f.

**indoor** adj a-staigh.

**indulge** v leig le.

**indulgent** adj bàigheil.

**industrial** adj tionnsgalach.

**industrious** adj gnìomhach.

**industry** n (abstract) saothair f; gnìomhachas f.

**inedible** adj do-ithe.

**inept** adj baoth.

**inequality** n neo-ionnanachd f.

**inert** adj marbhanta.

**inexcusable** adj neo-leisgeulach.

**inexpensive** adj saor.

**inexperienced** adj neo-eòlach.

**inexplicable** adj do-mhìneachadh.

**inextricable** adj do-fhuasgladh.

**infallible** adj do-mhearachdach.

**infant** n naoidhean m.

**infantile** adj leanabail.

**infantry** n cois-shluagh m.

**infect** *v* cuir galar air.
**infection** *n* galar-gabhail *m*.
**inferior** *adj* ìochdarach.
**infertile** *adj* mì-thorrach.
**infest** *v* claoidh.
**infinitesimal** *adj* beag-bìodach.
**infirm** *adj* anfhann.
**inflammable** *adj* so-lasadh.
**inflate** *v* sèid.
**inflation** *n* (*money*) at cùinnidh *m*.
**inflict** *v* leag peanas air.
**influence** *n* buaidh *f*. • *v* treòraich.
**influenza** *n* fliù *f*.
**inform** *v* innis.
**informal** *adj* neo-fhoirmeil.
**information** *n* fiosrachadh *m*.
**information technology** *n* teicneolas fiosrachaidh *m*.
**infrequent** *adj* ainmig.
**infringe** *v* bris.
**ingenious** *adj* innleachdach.
**ingenuous** *adj* fosgarra.
**ingot** *n* uinge *f*.
**ingredient** *n* tàthchuid *f*.
**inhabit** *v* àitich.
**inhabitable** *adj* so-àiteachadh.
**inhabitant** *n* fear-àiteachaidh *m*.
**inhale** *v* tarraing anail.
**inherit** *v* faigh mar oighreachd.
**inhibit** *v* cùm air ais.
**inhibition** *n* urchall *m*.
**inhospitable** *adj* neo-fhialaidh.
**inhuman** *adj* mì-dhaonna.
**initial** *adj* ciad. • *n* ciad litir *f*.
**inject** *v* ann-steallaich.

**injection** *n* ann-stealladh *m*.
**injure** *v* ciurr.
**injurious** *adj* cronail.
**injury** *n* ciurradh *m*.
**ink** *n* dubh *m*.
**inland** *adj* a-staigh san tìr.
**inlet** *n* caolas *m*.
**inn** *n* taigh-òsda *m*.
**innate** *adj* dualach.
**inner** *adj* as fhaide a-staigh.
**innkeeper** *n* òsdair *m*.
**innocent** *adj* neo-chiontach.
**innovate** *v* ùr-ghnàthaich.
**innovation** *n* ùr-ghnàthachadh *m*.
**innovator** *n* ùr-ghnàthadair *m*.
**innuendo** *n* fiar-shanas *m*.
**inoculate** *v* cuir a' bhreac air.
**inquire** *v* feòraich.
**inquiry** *n* ceasnachadh *m*.
**inquisitive** *adj* faighneachail.
**insane** *adj* air chuthach.
**insanitary** *adj* mì-shlàinteil.
**insanity** *n* cuthach *m*.
**insect** *n* meanbh-fhrìde *f*.
**insecure** *adj* neo-thèarainte.
**inseparable** *adj* do-sgaradh.
**insert** *v* cuir a-steach.
**inside** *prep* am broinn. • *adv* air an taobh a-staigh.
**insincere** *adj* neo-onorach.
**insipid** *adj* neo-bhlasda.
**insist** *v* cùm air.
**insolvency** *n* bristeadh *m*.
**insolvent** *adj* briste.
**insomnia** *n* bacadh cadail *m*.
**inspect** *v* sgrùd.

**inspection** n sgrùdadh m.
**instal** v cuir an dreuchd.
**instalment** n earrann f.
**instance** n eisimpleir m.
**instant** adj grad. • n tiota m.
**instead** prep an àite. • adv an àite sin.
**instil** v teagaisg.
**instinct** n dùchas m.
**instinctive** adj dùchasach.
**institute** n stèidheachadh m.
**institution** n stèidheachadh m.
**instrument** n inneal m, beart f.
**insular** adj eileanach.
**insulate** v dealaich.
**insult** n tàmailt f. • v tàmailtich.
**insurance** n urras m.
**insurance policy** n poileasaidh urrais m.
**insure** v faigh urras air.
**intact** adj slàn.
**integrity** n ionracas m.
**intellect** n inntinn f.
**intellectual** adj inntleachdail.
**intelligence** n tuigse f.
**intelligible** adj so-thuigsinn.
**intend** v cuir roimh.
**intense** adj teann.
**intensify** v teinnich.
**intensity** n dèine f.
**intention** n rùn m.
**intentional** adj a dh'aon rùn.
**intercede** v dèan eadar-ghuidhe.
**intercept** v ceap.
**intercourse** n co-chomann m; (sexual) co-ghineadh m.

**interest** n ùidh f.
**interesting** adj ùidheil.
**interfere** v buin ri.
**internal** adj san leth a-staigh.
**international** adj eadar-nàiseanta.
**driver** n dràibhear m.
**internet** n eadarlìon m.
**interpret** v mìnich.
**interpreter** n fear-mìneachaidh m.
**interrupt** v cuir casg air.
**interruption** n casgadh m.
**intertwine** v eadar-thoinn.
**intervene** v thig eadar.
**intervention** n eadar-ghabhail m.
**interview** n agallamh m. • v agallaich.
**intestine** n greallach f.
**intimacy** n dlù-chaidreamh m.
**intimate** adj dlù-chaidreach.
**into** adv a-steach do; ann an.
**intonation** n guth-cheòl m.
**intricate** adj eadar-fhighte.
**intrigue** n cluaineireachd f. • v dèan cluaineireachd.
**intrinsic** adj gnèitheach.
**introduce** v cuir an aithne.
**introduction** n cur an aithne.
**intrude** v brùth a-steach.
**intruder** n bruthaiche-steach m.
**intuition** n imfhios m.
**invalid**[1] adj neo-bhrìgheach.
**invalid**[2] adj (ill) tinn. • n eu-slainteach m.
**invariable** adj neo-chaochlaideach.

**invent** *v* innlich.
**invention** *n* innleachd *f*.
**inventor** *n* tionnsgalair *m*.
**inventory** *n* cùnntas *m*.
**Inverness** *n* Inbhir Nis.
**invert** *v* cuir bun-os-cionn.
**invest** *v* èid; (*money*) cuir an seilbh.
**invisible** *adj* do-fhaicsinneach.
**invitation** *n* cuireadh *m*.
**invite** *v* iarr.
**invoice** *n* maoin-chlàr *m*.
**involuntary** *adj* neo-shaor-thoileach.
**involve** *v* gabh a-steach.
**inward** *adv* a-staigh.
**inwards** *adv* a-steach.
**Ireland** *n* Eirinn *f*.
**Irish** *adj* Eireannach.
**irksome** *adj* buaireasach.
**iron** *n* iarann *m*. • *adj* iarrain. • *v* iarnaich.
**ironic** *adj* ìoronta.
**irony** *n* ìoronas *m*.

**irrational** *adj* eu-cèillidh.
**irregular** *adj* mì-riaghailteach.
**irrelevant** *adj* nach buin ri.
**irreverent** *adj* eas-urramach.
**irrigate** *v* uisgich.
**irrigation** *n* uisgeachadh *m*.
**irritable** *adj* crosda.
**irritation** *n* frionas *m*.
**island** *n* eilean *m*.
**islander** *n* eileanach *m*.
**Islay** *n* Ile *f*.
**isolated** *adj* air leth.
**issue** *n* ceist *f*; (*descendants*) sliochd *m*.
**isthmus** *n* aoidh *f*.
**it** *pron* e, i.
**Italian** *adj* Eadailteach.
**Italy** *n* An Eadailt *f*.
**itch** *n* tachas *m*.
**itchy** *adj* tachasach.
**itinerary** *n* cùrsa *m*.
**its** *pron* aige, aice.
**itself** *pron* e fhèin, i fhèin.
**ivory** *n* ìbhri *f*.

# J

**jab** *n* briogadh *m*. • *v* briog.
**jacket** *n* seacaid *f*.
**jacobite** *adj* seumasach.
**jagged** *adj* eagaich.
**jail** *n* carcair *m*.
**jam** *n* silidh *m*; (*traffic*) dòmhlachd *m*.

**jamb** *n* ursainn *f*.
**jangle** *v* dèan gleadhraich.
**janitor** *n* dorsair *m*.
**jar** *n* sileagan *m*.
**jargon** *n* goileam *m*.
**jaundice** *n* a' bhuidheach *f*.
**jaunt** *n* cuairt *f*.

**jaunty** *adj* sgeilmeil.

**jaw** *n* giall *f*.

**jawbone** *n* peirceall *m*.

**jealous** *adj* eudmhor.

**jealousy** *n* eud *m*.

**jeans** *npl* dìnichean.

**jeer** *v* mag.

**jelly** *n* slaman-milis *m*.

**jellyfish** *n* muir-tiachd *m*.

**jerkin** *n* còta-geàrr *m*.

**jersey** *n* geansaidh *m*.

**jest** *n* abhcaid *f*.

**jester** *n* cleasaiche *m*.

**jet plane** *n* diet-itealan *m*.

**jettison** *v* tilg a-mach.

**jetty** *n* cidhe *m*.

**jewel** *n* seud *m*.

**jib**¹ *n* dioba *f*.

**jib**² *v* cuir stailc ann.

**jig** *n* port-cruinn *m*.

**jilt** *v* trèig.

**job** *n* car-òibre, gnothach *m*.

**jockey** *n* marcach *m*.

**jog** *v* put; (*run*) dèan dabhdail.

**join** *v* ceangail.

**joiner** *n* saor *m*.

**joinery** *n* saorsinneachd *m*.

**joint** *adj* coitcheann. • *n* alt *m*; spòld *m*.

**jointed** *adj* altach.

**jointly** *adv* le chèile.

**joke** *n* fealla-dhà *f*.

**jollity** *n* cridhealas *m*.

**jolly** *adj* cridheil.

**jolt** *n* crathadh *m*. • *v* crath.

**jostle** *v* brùth.

**jot** *n* pong *m*.

**journal** *n* leabhar-latha; pàipear làith–eil *m*.

**journalism** *n* naidheachdas *m*.

**journalist** *n* naidheachdair *m*.

**journey** *n* turas *m*, cuairt *f*.

**jovial** *adj* fonnmhor.

**jowl** *n* giall *f*.

**joy** *n* aoibhneas *m*.

**joyful** *adj* aoibhneach.

**joyfully** *adv* gu h-aoibhinn.

**jubilant** *adj* lùthghaireach.

**jubilee** *n* àrd-fhèill *f*.

**judge** *n* britheam *m*. • *v* thoir breith.

**judgment** *n* breitheanas *m*.

**judicial** *adj* dligheil.

**judicious** *adj* geur-chuiseach.

**jug** *n* siuga *f*.

**juggle** *v* dèan cleasachd.

**jugular** *adj* sgòrnanach.

**juice** *n* sùgh *m*.

**juicy** *adj* sùghmhor.

**July** *n* Iuchar *m*.

**jump** *n* leum *m*. • *v* leum.

**jumper** *n* leumadair *m*; siumpar *m*.

**junction** *n* ceangal *m*.

**June** *n* An t-Og-mhìos *m*.

**jungle** *n* dlùth-fhàsach *m*.

**junior** *adj* às òige; (*rank*) iar-.

**juniper** *n* aiteann *m*.

**junk** *n* truilleis *m*.

**junket, junketing** *n* cuirm *f*.

**juror** *n* fear/bean diùraidh *m/f*.

**just** *adj* còir. • *adv* dìreach; air èiginn.

**justice** n còir f.
**justifiable** adj reusanta.
**justification** n fìreanachadh m.
**justify** v fìreanaich.

**jut** v seas a-mach.
**juvenile** adj òganta.
**juxtapose** v cuir ri chèile.

# K

**kail** n càl m.
**keel** n druim m.
**keen**[1] adj geur.
**keen**[2] v caoin.
**keenness** n gèire f.
**keep** n daingneach f. • v cùm, glèidh.
**keeping** n glèidheadh m.
**keepsake** n cuimhneachan m.
**kelp** n ceilp f.
**kennel** n taigh-chon m.
**kerb** n cabhsair m.
**kernel** n eitean m.
**kettle** n coire m.
**key** n iuchair f; (mus) gleus f.
**keyboard** n meur-chlàr f.
**keystone** n clach-ghlasaidh f.
**kick** n breab m. • v breab.
**kid** n meann m.
**kidnap** v goid air falbh.
**kidney** n dubhag f.
**kill** v marbh.
**killer** n marbhaiche m.
**kilogram** n cile-gram m.
**kilometre** n cilemeatair m.
**kilowatt** n cileavat m.
**kilt** n fèileadh, fèileadh beag m.

**kin** n cinneadh m.
**kind**[1] adj coibhneil.
**kind**[2] n gnè f.
**kindle** v las, fad.
**kindly** adj bàigheil.
**kindred** adj dàimheil.
**kindred** n muinntir f.
**king** n rìgh m.
**kingdom** n rìoghachd m.
**kinsfolk** npl luchd-dàimh.
**kinsman** n caraid m.
**kinswoman** n bana-charaid f.
**kiosk** n ciodhosg f.
**kipper** n ciopair m.
**kiss** n pòg f. • v pòg.
**kit** n trusgan m.
**kitbag** n màileid f.
**kitchen** n cidsin m.
**kite** n clamhan m; (model) iteileag f.
**kitten** n piseag m.
**knack** n liut f.
**knapsack** n aparsaig f.
**knave** n slaightear m.
**knead** v fuin.
**knee** n glùn f.
**kneecap** n failmean m.

**kneel** *v* sleuchd.

**knickers** *npl* drathars.

**knife** *n* sgian *f*.

**knight** *n* ridire *m*.

**knighthood** *n* ridireachd *m*.

**knit** *v* figh.

**kniter** *n* figheadair *m*.

**knitting needle** *n* bior-fighe *m*.

**knob** *n* cnap *m*.

**knock** *n* buille *f*. • *v* buail.

**knoll** *n* tolm *m*.

**knot** *n* snaidhm *m*. • *v* snaidh-mich.

**knotted, knotty** *adj* snaidh-meach.

**know** *v* aithnich; tuig; bi eòlach air.

**knowing** *adj* eòlach.

**knowingly** *adv* gu h-eòlach.

**knowledgeable** *adj* fiosrach.

**knuckle** *n* rùdan *m*.

**kyle** *n* caol *m*.

# L

**label** *n* bileag *f*.

**labial** *adj* liopach.

**laboratory** *n* deuchainn-lann *f*.

**laborious** *adj* deacair.

**labour** *v* saothraich.

**labourer** *n* oibriche *m*.

**labyrinth** *n* ioma-shlighe *f*.

**lace**¹ *n* lios *f*.

**lace**² *n* barrall *f*. • *v* (*shoe, etc*) dùin.

**lacerate** *v* reub.

**laceration** *n* reubadh *m*.

**lack** *n* easbhaidh *f*. • *v* bi a dh'eas-bhaidh.

**lad, laddie** *n* gille *m*.

**ladder** *n* fàradh *m*.

**ladle** *n* liagh *f*.

**lady** *n* bean-uasal *f*.

**ladybird** *n* an daolag dhearg-bhreac *f*.

**ladylike** *adj* bainndidh.

**lair** *n* saobhaidh *f*.

**laird** *n* tighearna *m*.

**lake** *n* linn *f*, loch *m*.

**lamb** *n* uan *m*; (*roast*) uainfheòil *m*.

**lame** *adj* bacach.

**lameness** *n* crùbaiche *f*.

**lament** *n* cumha *m*.

**lament** *v* caoidh.

**lamentable** *adj* tùrsach.

**lamp** *n* làmpa *m*.

**lance** *v* leig fuil.

**lancet** *n* lannsa *f*.

**land** *n* tìr, dùthaich *f*. • *v* rach air tìr.

**landholder** *n* fear-fearainn *m*.

**landing** *n* ceann staidhre *m*; (*of aeroplane*) laighe *m*.

**landing strip** *n* raon-laighe *m*.

**landlady** *n* bean-an-taighe *f*.

**landlocked** *adj* tìr-dhruidte.

**landmark** *n* comharradh *m*.

**landscape** *n* dealbh tìre *m/f*.

**landslide** *n* beum-slèibhe *m*.

**landward** *adv* gu-tìr.

**lane** *n* lònaid *f*.

**language** *n* cànan *m*; (*speech*) cainnt *f*.

**languish** *v* fannaich.

**lanky** *adj* fada caol.

**lantern** *n* lanntair *m*.

**lap**¹ *n* uchd *m*.

**lap**² *v* sùgh.

**lapel** *n* liopaid *f*.

**lapse** *n* mearachd *f*. • *v* sleamhnaich.

**lapwing** *n* currcag *f*.

**larceny** *n* braide *f*.

**larch** *n* learag *f*.

**lard** *n* blonag *f*.

**larder** *n* preas-bidhe *m*.

**large** *adj* mòr.

**lark** *n* uiseag *f*.

**lass, lassie** *n* nighean *f*.

**last**¹ *adj* deireannach, mu dheireadh. • *adv* mu dheireadh.

**last**² *v* mair.

**lasting** *adj* maireannach.

**late** *adj* anmoch.

**lately** *adv* o chionn ghoirid.

**lateness** *n* fadalachd *f*.

**latent** *adj* dìomhair.

**lather** *n* cop *m*. • *v* dèan cop.

**Latin** *n* Laideann *f*.

**latitude** *n* leud *m*; (*line*) domhan-leud *m*.

**latter** *adj* deireannach.

**laugh** *n* gàire *m*. • *v* dèan gàire.

**laughter** *n* gàireachdaich *f*.

**launch** *v* cuir air bhog.

**laurel** *n* labhras *m*.

**lavatory** *n* taigh-failcidh, taigh beag *m*.

**lavish** *adj* sgapach. • *v* sgap.

**law** *n* lagh, reachd *m*.

**law-suit** *n* cùis lagha *f*.

**lawful** *adj* laghail.

**lawn** *n* rèidhlean *m*.

**lawyer** *n* fear-lagha *m*.

**laxative** *n* purgaid *f*.

**lay** *v* càirich, cuir, leag sìos.

**lay-by** *n* far-rathad *m*.

**layer** *n* filleadh *m*.

**layman** *n* neo-chlèireach *m*.

**laziness** *n* leisge *f*.

**lazy** *adj* leisg.

**lead**¹ *n* luaidhe *m/f*.

**lead**² *n* (*dog*) iall *f*. • *v* treòraich.

**leaden** *adj* luaidhe.

**leader** *n* ceannard *m*.

**leaf** *n* duilleag *f*.

**leafy** *adj* duilleagach.

**league** *n* co-cheangal *m*; (*sport*) lìg *m*.

**leak** *v* leig a-steach.

**leaky** *adj* ao-dìonach.

**lean**¹ *adj* caol.

**lean**² *v* leig do thaic air.

**leap** *v* leum.

**leap-year** *n* bliadhna-leum *f*.

**learn** *v* ionnsaich.

**learner** *n* neach-ionnsachaidh *m*.

**lease** n gabhail m/f.

**least** adj as lugha.

**leather** n leathar m.

**leave** n fòrladh m. • v fàg, trèig.

**lecher** n drùisire m.

**lecherous** adj drùiseil.

**lecture** n òraid f. • v teasgaig.

**ledge** n oir m.

**ledger** n leabhar-cùnntais m.

**lee, lee-side** n taobh an fhas-gaidh m.

**leech** n deala f.

**leek** n cainneann m.

**leet** n (list) ciad-thaghadh m.

**left** n an taobh ceàrr m.

**left hand** n làmh chlì f.

**left-handed** adj ciotach.

**leg** n cas f.

**legacy** n dìleab f.

**legalise** v dèan laghail.

**legend** n fionnsgeul f.

**legendary** adj fionnsgeulach.

**legibility** n so-leughtachd f.

**legible** adj so-leughadh.

**legislate** v dèan lagh.

**legitimate** adj dligheach.

**leisure** n suaimhneas m.

**leisurely** adj athaiseach.

**lemon** n liomaid f.

**lend** v thoir an iasad.

**lender** n iasadaiche m.

**length** n fad m.

**lengthen** v cuir am fad.

**lengthwise** adv air fhad.

**lenient** adj tròcaireach.

**lenition** n sèimheachadh m.

**lens** n lionsa f.

**Lent** n Carghas m.

**leper** n lobhar m.

**leprechaun** n luchraban m.

**less** adj nas lugha.

**lessen** v lùghdaich.

**lesson** n leasan m.

**lest** conj air eagal gu.

**let¹** n bacadh m; (house) n gabhail m/f.

**let²** v leig; thoir air ghabhail.

**lethal** adj bàsmhor.

**letter** n litir f.

**letter-box** n bocsa-litrichean m.

**lettuce** n leiteis f.

**level** adj còmhnard.

**level** n còmhnard m. • v dèan còmhnard.

**lever** n luamhan m.

**lewd** adj draosda.

**lewdness** n draosdachd f.

**Lewis** n Leòdhas m.

**liability** n buailteachd f.

**liable** adj buailteach.

**liar** n breugaire m.

**libel** v dèan cliù-mhilleadh.

**liberal** adj pailt-làmhach.

**Liberal** n Liberaileach m.

**librarian** n leabhar-lannaiche m.

**library** n leabhar-lann f.

**licence** n cead m.

**license** v ceadaich.

**lichen** n crotal m.

**lick** v imlich.

**lid** n ceann m.

**lie¹** v laigh.

**lie¹** n breug f. • v innis breug.

**life** n beatha f.

**lifeboat** n bàta-teasairginn m.

**lifestyle** n seòl-beatha m.

**lifeguard** n freiceadan m.

**lift** n (*elevator*) àrdaichear m. • v tog.

**light¹** adj aotrom; suarach; guanach; soilleir.

**light²** n solas m. • v las.

**light-headed** adj gog-cheannach.

**lighten** v deàlraich.

**lighthouse** n taigh-solais m.

**lightness** n aotromachd m.

**lightning** n dealanach m.

**like¹** adj coltach. • n samhail f.

**like²** v is toigh le.

**liken** v samhlaich.

**likeness** n coltas m.

**likewise** adv mar an ceudna.

**limb** n ball m.

**lime** n aol m; (*fruit*) n teile f.

**limestone** n aol-chlach f.

**lime tree** n teile f.

**limit** n crìoch m. • v cuir crìoch ri.

**limited** adj (*Ltd*) earranta.

**limp¹** adj bog.

**limp²** n ceum m. • v bi crùbach.

**limpet** n bàirneach f.

**linden tree** n teile f.

**line¹** n loidhne f; streath f.

**line²** v lìnig.

**lineage** n linn, sliochd m.

**lineal** adj dìreach.

**linear** adj streathach.

**linen** n anart m.

**linger** v gabh ùine.

**linguist** n cànanaich m.

**link** n tinne f. • v co-cheangail.

**links** npl machair goilf f.

**linnet** n breacan-beithe m.

**lion** n leòghann m.

**lioness** n ban-leòghann f.

**lip** n bile f.

**liquefy** v leagh.

**liquid** adj lionnach. • n lionn m.

**liquidate** v glan air falbh.

**lisp** n liotachas m. • v bi liotach.

**list** n liosta f; (*items*) clàr-ainm f. • v liostaig; cuir sìos.

**listen** v èisd.

**listener** n fear-èisdeachd m.

**listless** adj coma; gun smior.

**literacy** n litireachd f.

**literal** adj litireil.

**literate** adj litir-foghlaimte.

**literature** n litreachas m.

**litre** n liotair m.

**litter** n treamsgal m; (*young*) cuain m. • v dèan treamsgal; beir.

**little** adj beag.

**littoral** n cladach m.

**liturgy** n ùrnaigh choitcheann f.

**live¹** adj beò.

**live²** v bi beò.

**livelihood** n teachd-an-tìr m.

**lively** adj beothail.

**liver** n adha m.

**livid** adj dùghorm.

**lizard** n laghairt m.

**load** n luchd m. • v luchdaich.

**loaf** n buileann f, lof m/f.

**loan** *n* iasad *m*.

**loath** *adj* aindeonach.

**loathe** *v* fuathaich.

**loathing** *n* gràin *f*.

**loathsome** *adj* gràineil.

**lobster** *n* giomach *m*.

**lobster-pot** *n* cliabh-ghiomach *f*.

**local** *adj* ionadail.

**locality** *n* àite *m*.

**locate** *v* cuir 'na àite.

**loch** *n* loch *m*.

**lock**[1] *n* glas *f*. • *v* glais.

**lock**[2] *n* (*hair*) dual *m*

**locket** *n* glasag-mhuineil *f*.

**locksmith** *n* gobha-ghlasan *m*.

**lodge** *n* taigh-gheata *m*. • *v* suidhich; gabh còmhnaidh.

**lodger** *n* lòisdear *m*.

**loft** *n* lobhta *m*.

**log** *n* sgonn *m*.

**logic** *n* ealain reusanachaidh, loidig *f*.

**logical** *adj* loidigeach.

**loiter** *v* dèan màirneal.

**loll** *v* seas ri taic.

**London** *n* Lunnainn.

**lone** *adj* aonarach.

**loneliness** *n* aonaranachd *f*.

**long**[1] *adj* fada; buan.

**long**[2] *v* miannaich.

**long ago** *adv* o chionn fhada.

**long-term** *adj* fad-ùineach.

**longevity** *n* fad-shaoghalachd *f*.

**longing** *n* miann *m*.

**longitude** *n* domhan-fhad *m*.

**long-suffering** *adj* fad-fhulangach.

**long-wave** *adj* fad-thonnach.

**long-winded** *adj* fad-anaileach.

**look** *n* fiamh *m*; sùil *f*. • *v* seall, amhairc; **look for** sir.

**looking-glass** *n* sgàthan *m*.

**loop** *n* lùb *f*.

**loophole** *n* fosgladh *m*.

**loose** *adj* sgaoilte. • *v* fuasgail.

**lop** *v* sgath.

**lop-sided** *adj* leathoireach.

**lord** *n* tighearna, morair *m*.

**lore** *n* oilean *m*.

**lorry** *n* làraidh *f*.

**lose** *v* caill.

**loser** *n* fear a chaill *m*.

**loss** *n* call *m*.

**lost** *adj* air chall.

**lotion** *n* cungaidh *f*.

**lottery** *n* crannchur *m*.

**loud** *adj* labhar.

**loudness** *n* faram *m*.

**loudspeaker** *n* glaodhaire *m*.

**lounge** *n* seòmar-searraidh *m*. • *v* seàrr.

**lour, lower** *v* (*face*) bi an gruaim.

**louse** *n* mial *f*.

**lousy** *adj* mialach.

**lout** *n* burraidh *m*.

**love** *n* gaol, gràdh *m*.

**lovely** *adj* àlainn.

**lover** *n* leannan *m*.

**lovesick** *adj* tinn le gaol.

**loving** *adj* gràdhach.

**low** *adj* ìosal.

**lower¹** v ìslich.

**lower²** see **lour**.

**lowest** adj as ìsle.

**Lowland** adj Gallda.

**Lowlands** n A' Ghalltachd f.

**lowly** adj iriosal.

**loyal** adj dìleas.

**loyalty** n dìlse f.

**lubricate** v lìomh.

**lucid** adj soilleir.

**luck** n fortan m.

**lucky** adj fortanach.

**lucrative** adj buannachail.

**ludicrous** adj amaideach.

**luggage** n treallaich f.

**lukewarm** adj meadh-bhlàth.

**lull** v cuir a chadal.

**lullaby** n òran tàlaidh m.

**luminous** adj deàlrach.

**lump** n meall m.

**lumpy** adj meallanach.

**lunacy** n cuthach m.

**lunar** adj gealachail.

**lunch** n ruisean m.

**lung** n sgamhan m.

**lurch¹** n sitheadh m.

**lurch²** v dèan sitheadh.

**lure** n mealladh m. • v meall, buair.

**lurid** adj cròn.

**lurk** v falaich.

**luscious** adj sòghmhor.

**lust** n ana-miann m.

**lustre** n deàlradh m.

**lusty** adj sultmhor.

**luxuriant** adj fàsmhor.

**luxurious** adj sòghail.

**luxury** n sògh m, n sòghalachd f.

**lyre** n cruit f.

**lyric** n liric f.

# M

**mace** n cuaille suaicheantais m.

**machine** n inneal m.

**machinery** n innealradh. m.

**mackerel** n rionnach m.

**magazine** n iris f.

**magic** adj draoidheil. • n draoi-dheachd f.

**magician** n draoidh m.

**magistrate** n bàillidh m.

**magnet** n clach-iùil f.

**magnification** n meudachadh m.

**magnificence** n greadhnachas m.

**magnificent** adj òirdheirc.

**magnify** v meudaich.

**magnitude** n meudachd m.

**magpie** n pioghaid f.

**maid** n maighdeann f.

**mail** n litrichean pl; post m. • v cuir sa' phost.

**mail order** n òrdugh tron phost m.

**main** adj prìomh.

**mainland** n tìr-mòr m.

**mainly** *adv* anns a' mhòr-chuid.

**maintain** *v* glèidh.

**maintenance** *n* glèidheadh *m.*

**majestic** *adj* flathail.

**majesty** *n* mòrachd *f.*

**major** *adj* as motha. • *n* màidsear *m.*

**make** *v* dèan, dealbh; **make to do** thoir air; **make towards** dèan air. • *n* dèanamh *m.*

**maker** *n* dealbhadair *m.*

**make-up** *n* rìomhadh *m.*

**making** *n* dèanamh *m.*

**male** *adj* fireannach. • *n* fireannach *m.*

**malevolence** *n* gamhlas *m.*

**malice** *n* mì-rùn *m.*

**malicious** *adj* mì-runach.

**malign** *v* càin.

**malignant** *adj* millteach; (*med*) aillseach.

**mallet** *n* fairche *m.*

**malt** *n* braich *f.*

**maltster** *n* brachadair *m.*

**maltreat** *v* droch ghrèidh.

**mam, mammy** *n* mam, mamaidh *f.*

**mammal** *n* sineach *m.*

**man** *n* duine, fear *m.*

**manage** *v* stiùir.

**manageable** *adj* so-riaghladh.

**management** *n* riaghladh *m.*

**manager** *n* manaidsear *m.*

**manageress** *n* bana-mhanaidsear *f.*

**mane** *n* muing *f.*

**manful** *adj* duineil.

**manger** *n* prasach *f.*

**mangle** *v* reub.

**manhood** *n* fearalas *m.*

**maniac** *n* dearg amadan *m.*

**manifest** *v* taisbein.

**manifestation** *n* foillseachadh *m.*

**manifesto** *n* gairm-fhollaiseach *f.*

**manipulate** *v* oibrich.

**mankind** *n* cinne-daonna *m.*

**manner** *n* modh *m/f.*

**mannerism** *n* magaid *f.*

**mannerly** *adj* modhail.

**manners** *npl* modh *m/f.*

**manse** *n* mansa *m.*

**mansion** *n* taigh-mòr *m.*

**mantelpiece** *n* breus *m.*

**manual** *adj* làmhach. • *n* leabhar-tuairisgeil *m.*

**manufacture** *v* saothraich.

**manure** *n* mathachadh *m.* • *v* mathaich.

**manuscript** *n* làmh-sgrìobhainn *m.*

**many** *adj* mòran; iomadh. • *n* mòran, tòrr *m.*

**map,** *n* map *m.*

**mar** *v* mill.

**marble** *n* màrmor *m.*

**March** *n* Am Màrt *m.*

**march** *n* màrsail *f.* • *v* dèan màrsail.

**mare** *n* làir *f.*

**marijuana** *n* a' bhang *f.*

**marine** *adj* mara.

**mariner** *n* maraiche *m.*

**maritime** *adj* fairgeach.

**mark** *n* comharradh *m*.

**market** *n* fèill *f*, margadh *m*/*f*.

**marketable** *adj* a ghabhas reic.

**maroon** *v* cuir air eilean uaigneach.

**marquee** *n* puball *m*.

**marriage** *n* pòsadh *m*.

**marriageable** *adj* aig aois pò-saidh.

**married** *adj* pòsda.

**marry** *v* pòs.

**marshy** *adj* bog, fèitheach.

**marten** *n* taghan *m*.

**martial** *adj* gaisgeanta.

**martyr** *n* martarach *m*.

**marvel** *n* iongnadh *m*. • *v* gabh iongnadh.

**marvellous** *adj* iongantach.

**mascot** *n* suaichnean *m*.

**masculine** *adj* fireannta.

**mash** *v* pronn.

**mask** *n* aghaidh choimheach *f*.

**mason** *n* clachair *m*.

**masonry** *n* clachaireachd *m*.

**mass** *n* tomad *m*; meall *m*; (*church*) aif reann *m*.

**massacre** *n* casgradh *m*. • *v* casgair.

**massage** *n* suathadh *m*.

**massive** *adj* tomadach.

**mast** *n* crann *m*.

**master** *n* maighstir *m*.

**masterly** *n* ealanta *m*.

**masterpiece** *n* euchd *m*.

**masturbate** *v* brod.

**mat** *n* brat *m*.

**match** *n* lasadair *m*; seise *m*. • *v* freagair.

**matchless** *adj* gun choimeas.

**mate** *n* cèile *m*; (*ship*) meite *m*; (*chess*) clos *m*. • *v* cuir clos air.

**material** *n* stuth *m*.

**maternal** *adj* màithreil.

**maternity** *n* màthaireachd *f*.

**mathematics** *n* eòlas matamata-ic.

**matins** *npl* maidnean.

**matrimony** *n* dàimh-pòsaidh *m*/*f*.

**matter** *n* stuth *m*; brìgh *f*; gnoth-ach *m*.

**mattress** *n* leabaidh-ìochdrach *f*.

**mature** *adj* abaich.

**maul** *v* pronn.

**mavis** *n* smeòrach *m*.

**maw** *n* goile *f*.

**maximum** *n* os-mheud *m*.

**May** *n* A' Mhàigh *f*; An Cèitean *m*.

**may** *v* faod.

**May Day** *n* Là-Bealltainn.

**maze** *n* ioma-shlighe *f*.

**me** *pron* mi, mise.

**meadow** *n* lòn *m*.

**meagre** *adv* gann.

**meagreness** *n* gainne *f*.

**meal** *n* min *f*; (*repast*) biadh *f*.

**mealy** *adj* mar mhin.

**mean**[1] *adj* suarach.

**mean**[2] *n* cuibheasachd *f*.

**mean**[3] *v* ciallaich.

**meaning** *n* ciall *f*.

**means** *npl* comas *m*; seilbhean *fpl*.

**meantime** *adv* an dràsda.

**measles** *n* a' ghriùthlach *f*.

**measurable** *adj* a ghabhas tomhas.

**measure** *v* tomhais. • *n* tomhas *m*.

**measurement** *n* tomhas *m*.

**meat** *n* feòil *f*.

**mechanic** *n* meicnic *m*.

**mechanism** *n* meadhan *m*.

**medal** *n* bonn *m*.

**meddle** *v* buin ri.

**mediate** *v* rèitich.

**mediation** *n* eadraiginn *f*.

**mediator** *n* eadar-mheadhanair *m*.

**medical** *adj* lèigh.

**medicinal** *adj* ìocshlainteach.

**medicine** *n* eòlas-leighis; ìocshlaint *m*.

**medieval** *adj* meadhan-aoiseil.

**mediocre** *adj* meadhanach.

**meditate** *v* beachd-smuainich.

**meditation** *n* beachd-smuaineachadh *m*.

**medium** *n* meadhan *m*.

**medium-wave** *adj* meadhanthonnach.

**meek** *adj* macanta.

**meekness** *n* macantas *m*.

**meet** *v* coinnich.

**meeting** *n* coinneachadh *m*; (*official*) coinneamh *f*.

**megalith** *n* tursa *m*.

**melancholy** *adj* dubhach.

**melancholy** *n* leann-dubh *m*.

**mellifluous** *adj* mealach.

**mellow** *adj* tlàth.

**melodious** *adj* fonnmhor.

**melody** *n* binneas *m*; fonn *m*.

**melon** *n* meal-bhucan *m*.

**melt** *v* leagh.

**member** *n* ball *m*.

**member of parliament** *n* ballpàrla-maid *m*.

**membership** *n* ballrachd *f*.

**memento** *n* cuimhneachan *m*.

**memoir** *n* tràchdas *m*; beatha-aisneis *m*.

**memorable** *adj* ainmeil.

**memorise** *v* cùm air mheomhair.

**memory** *n* cuimhne *f*.

**mend** *v* càraich.

**menstrual** *adj* mìosach.

**menstruation** *n* fuil-mìos *f*.

**mental** *adj* inntinneil.

**mention** *v* ainmich.

**menu** *n* cairt-bidhe *f*.

**merchant** *n* ceannaiche *m*.

**mercy** *n* tròcair *m*.

**mere** *adj* a-mhain.

**merely** *adv* a-mhain.

**merge** *v* rach an aon.

**merit** *n* luach *m*.

**mermaid** *n* maighdeann-mhara *f*.

**merriment** *n* aighear *m*.

**mess** *n* truidhleis *f*.

**message** *n* teachdaireachd *f*.

**messenger** *n* teachdaire *m*.

**metal** *n* meatailt *f*.

**metallic** *adj* meatailteach.

**meteor** *n* dreag *f*.

**meter** *n* inneal-tomhais *m*.

**method** n dòigh f.

**metre** n meatair m; (verse) rann-aigh-eachd m.

**mettle** n smioralachd f.

**microbe** n bitheag f.

**microwave oven** n àmhainn mheanbh-thonn f.

**mid** adj eadar-mheadannach.

**middle** n meadhan m.

**middle-aged** adj leth-shean.

**midge** n meanbh-chuileag f.

**midnight** n meadhan-oidhche m.

**midwife** n bean-ghlùine f.

**might** n cumhachd m.

**migrate** v dèan imrich.

**mild** adj ciuin.

**mile** n mìle f.

**military** adj cogail.

**milk** n bainne m. • v bleoghain.

**milky** adj bainneach.

**mill** n muileann m/f.

**millennium** n am mìle-bliadhna m.

**miller** n muillear m.

**million** n millean m.

**mime** n mìm f.

**mimicry** n atharrais f.

**mince** n mions m.

**Minch** n An Cuan Sgìth.

**mind** n inntinn f.

**mind** v thoir an aire; cuimhnich.

**mine**[1] n mèinne f.

**mine**[2] poss pron agam; leam.

**mineral** adj mèinneach. • n mèin-nearach m.

**mingle** v measgaich.

**miniature** n meanbh-dhealbh m/f.

**minister** n ministear m. • v fri-theil.

**minor** n neach fo làn-aois m. • adj beag, as lugha.

**minstrel** n oirfideach m.

**minus** prep as aonais; mìonas.

**minute**[1] adj meanbh.

**minute**[2] n mionaid f.

**minx** n aigeannach f.

**miracle** n mìorbhail f.

**mirage** n mearachadh-sùla m.

**mirror** n sgàthan m.

**misapprehension** n mì-thuig-sinn f.

**misbehaviour** n droch-ghiùlan m.

**miscarriage** n asaid anabaich f.

**mischief** n aimhleas m.

**mischievous** adj aimhleasach.

**misdeed** n dò-bheart f.

**miser** n spìocaire m.

**miserable** adj truagh.

**misinterpret** v mì-bhreithnich.

**misogyny** n fuath-bhan m.

**Miss** n A' Maighdeann, A' Mh f.

**miss** v rach iomrall; ionndrainn.

**missing** adj a dhìth.

**missionary** n misionairidh m.

**mist** n ceò m.

**mistake** v mì-aithnich.

**Mister** n Maighstir, Mgr m.

**mistletoe** n an t-uil-ìoc m.

**mistress** n bana-mhaighstir f; coileapach f.

**misty** adj ceòthach.

**misunderstand** v mì-thuig.

**mite** n fineag f.

**mix** v measgaich.

**mixture** n measgachadh m.

**moan** n gearan m. • v gearain.

**mob** n gràisg f.

**mobile phone** n fòn shiubhail f.

**mock** v mag.

**model** n cumadh m. • v deilbh.

**moderate** adj stuama.

**moderation** n stuaim m.

**modern** adj ùr, nodha.

**modernise** v ùraich.

**modest** adj nàrach.

**modesty** n beusachd f.

**moist** adj tais, bog.

**moisten** v taisich.

**mole**[1] n famh f.

**mole**[2] (spot) ball-dòrain m.

**molest** v cuir dragh air.

**mollify** v maothaich.

**mollusc** n maorach m.

**moment** n tiota m.

**momentary** adj grad-ùineach.

**momentous** adj cudromach.

**monarch** n monarc m.

**monastery** n mannachain f.

**Monday** n Diluain m.

**money** n airgead m.

**monitor** n foillsear m.

**monk** n manach m.

**monkey** n muncaidh m.

**monopoly** n lèir-shealbhachd f.

**monotony** n aon-ghuthachd f.

**monster** n uilebheist m.

**month** n mìos m/f.

**monthly** adj mìosach.

**monument** n carragh f.

**mood** n gleus m.

**moody** adj gruamach.

**moon** n gealach f.

**moor**[1] n mòinteach f.

**moor**[2] v tilg acair.

**moral** n beus f.

**morale** n misneach f.

**morality** n deagh bheusachd f.

**more** adv tuilleadh. • n tuilleadh m.

**moreover** adv a thuilleadh.

**morning** n madainn f.

**mortal** adj bàsmhor.

**mosquito** n còrr-mhial m.

**moss** n còinneach f.

**most** adj as mò. • n a' mhòr chuid m.

**mostly** adv mar as trice.

**moth** n leòman m.

**mother** n màthair f.

**mother-in-law** n màthair-cèile f.

**motherly** adj màithreil.

**motion** n gluasad m.

**motive** n adhbhar m.

**motor** n motair m.

**motorist** n motairiche m.

**motto** n facal-suaicheantais m.

**mould** n molldair m.

**mouldy** adv cloimh-liathach.

**moult** v tilg fionnadh.

**mound** n tom m.

**mountain** n beinn f, meall m.

**mountaineer** n streapaiche m.

**mourn** v caoidh.

**mourning** *n* bròn *m*.
**mouse** *n* luch *f*.
**moustache** *n* stais *f*.
**mouth** *n* beul *m*.
**mouth-music** *n* port-a-beul *m*.
**mouthful** *n* balgam *m*.
**move** *v* gluais; luaisg; imich.
**mow** *v* geàrr.
**Mrs** *n* A' Bhean, A' Bh *f*.
**much** *adv* mòran.
**muck** *n* salchar *m*.
**mud** *n* poll *m*.
**muddle** *n* troimhe-chèile *f*.
**muddy** *adj* eabarach.
**mug** *n* muga *f*.
**Mull** *n* Muile *f*.
**multiple** *adj* ioma-sheòrsach.
**multiply** *v* meudaich.
**mumble** *v* dèan brunndail.
**mumps** *n* an tinneas-plocach *m*.
**murder** *n* mort *m*.
**murderer** *n* mortair *m*.
**murmur** *n* monmhor *m*.
**muscle** *n* fèith *f*.

**museum** *n* taigh-tasgaidh *m*.
**mushroom** *n* balgan-buachrach *m*.
**music** *n* ceòl *m*.
**musical** *adj* ceòlmhor.
**musical instrument** *n* inneal ciùil *m*.
**mussel** *n* feusgan *m*.
**must** *v* feum, 's èiginn, 's fheudar.
**muster** *n* cruinneachadh *m*.
**mutation** *n* mùthadh *m*.
**mute** *adj* balbh.
**mutilate** *v* ciorramaich.
**mutiny** *n* ceannairc *f*.
**mutton** *n* feòil caorach *f*.
**mutual** *adj* aontachail.
**my** *pron* mo, m', agam.
**myself** *pron* mi fhìn.
**mysterious** *adj* dìomhair.
**mystery** *n* dìomhaireachd *f*.
**mystical** *adj* fàidheanta.
**myth** *n* miotas *m*.
**mythical** *adj* miotasach.
**mythology** *n* miotas-eòlas *m*.

# N

**nag** *v* dèan dranndan.
**nail** *n* tarrag *f*.
**naive** *adj* soineannta.
**naked** *adj* lomnochd.
**name** *n* ainm *m*. • *v* ainmich.
**nap** *n* dùsal *m*.
**narrate** *v* aithris.

**narrative** *n* aithris *m*.
**narrow** *adj* cumhang.
**nasal** *adj* srònach.
**nasty** *adj* truaillidh.
**nation** *n* nàisean *m*.
**national** *adj* nàiseanta.
**nationalism** *n* nàiseantachd *f*.

**nationalist** *n* nàiseantach *m*.

**nationality** *n* dùthchas *m*.

**native** *adj* gnèitheach. • *n* gnàth-fhear *m*.

**natural** *adj* nàdurrach.

**nature** *n* nàdur *m*.

**naughty** *adj* dona.

**nausea** *n* dèistinn *f*.

**nauseous** *adj* sgreamhail.

**nautical** *adj* seòlaidh.

**navel** *n* imleag *f*.

**neap-tide** *n* conntraigh *f*.

**near** *adj* faisg.

**near-sighted** *adj* geàrr-fhradharcach.

**nearly** *adv* faisg air. • *adv* (*conj*) cha mhòr (nach).

**neat** *adj* grinn.

**necessary** *adj* riatanach.

**necessity** *n* èiginn; aimbeart *f*.

**neck** *n* amhach *f*.

**need** *n* feum *m*. • *v* feum.

**needle** *n* snàthad *f*.

**needy** *adj* feumach.

**negative** *adj* àicheanach.

**neglect** *v* dèan dearmad.

**negligent** *adj* dearmadach.

**negotiate** *v* dèan gnothach ri.

**neighbour** *n* nàbaidh *m*.

**neither** *adv/conj/pron* cha mhò.

**nephew** *n* mac peathar *m*.

**nerve** *n* fèith-mhothachaidh *f*; (*cheek*) aghaìdh *f*.

**nest** *n* nead *m*.

**Netherlands** *n* An Isealtìr *f*.

**net** *n* lìon *m*.

**nettle** *n* feanntag *f*.

**neutral** *adj* neo-phàirteil.

**never** *adv* a chaoidh, gu brath.

**nevertheless** *adv* gidheadh.

**new** *adj* ùr, nuadh.

**New Year** *n* A' Bhliadhna Ur *f*.

**news** *n* naidheachd *f*.

**next** *adj* an ath.

**nice** *adj* gasta.

**niche** *n* oisinn *f*.

**nickname** *n* farainm *m*.

**niece** *n* nighean peathar *f*.

**night** *n* oidhche *f*.

**nightingale** *n* spideag *f*.

**nil** *n* neo-ni *m*.

**nine** *adj/n* naodh, naoi.

**nineteen** *adj* naodh-deug.

**ninety** *adj* naochad.

**ninth** *adj* naodhamh.

**nip** *n* teumadh *m*; (*whisky*) tè bheag *m*.

**nipple** *n* sine *f*.

**noble** *adj* uasal, flathail.

**nod** *n* cromadh *m*.

**noise** *n* fuaim *m*.

**noisy** *adj* fuaimneach.

**nominate** *v* ainmich.

**non-stop** *adj* gun stad.

**nonconformity** *n* neo-aontachd *f*.

**nonsense** *n* amaideas *m*.

**noon** *n* meadhan-latha *m*.

**nor** *conj* no, nas mò.

**normal** *adj* gnàthach.

**normally** *adv* an cumantas.

**north** *adj* tuath. • *n* tuath *m*, an àirde tuath *f*.

**northeast** n ear-thuath m.

**northern** adj tuathach.

**northwest** n iar-thuath m.

**nose** n sròn f.

**note** n nota f. • v thoir fa-near.

**notebook** n leabhar-notaichean m.

**nothing** n neo-ni m.

**notice** n sanas, fios m. • v thoir fa-near.

**notify** v thoir fios do.

**nuclear** adj niuclasach.

**nuclear waste** n sgudal niuclasach m.

**numb** adj meilichte; (cold) air lathadh.

**number** n àireamh f; mòran f. • v cùnnt, àir.

**numeral** n cùnntair m.

**numerous** adj lìonmhor.

**nurse** n banaltram f. • v altraim.

**nursery** n plannd-lann f; sgoil-àraich f.

**nursing home** n taigh-altraim m.

**nut** n cnò f.

**nutshell** n plaosg-cnotha m.

# O

**oak** n darach m.

**oar** n ràmh m.

**oatcake** n bonnach coirce m.

**oath** n bòid f.

**oatmeal** n min-choirce f.

**obdurate** adj rag-mhuinealach.

**obedience** n ùmhlachd f.

**obey** v gèill do.

**object**[1] n adhbhar m.

**object**[2] v cuir an aghaidh.

**objection** n gearan m.

**oblige** v cuir mar fhiachaibh air; (help) cuir fo chomain.

**oblique** adj siar.

**oblivion** n dìochuimhne f.

**oboe** n òboidh f.

**obscene** adj drabasda.

**obscenity** n drabasdachd f.

**observant** adj aireil.

**observe** v amhairc.

**obsession** n beò-ghlacadh m.

**obsolete** adj bho fheum.

**obstinate** adj rag-mhuinealach.

**obstinacy** n rag-mhuinealas m.

**obvious** adj follaiseach.

**occasion** n fàth; cothrom m.

**occasional** adj corra.

**occult** adj dìomhair.

**occupancy** n seilbh f.

**occupy** v gabh sealbh.

**ocean** n cuan m, fairge f.

**octagon** n ochd-shliosach f.

**octave** n ochdad m.

**October** n Octòber, An Dàmhair m.

**octopus** n ochd-chasach m.

**ocular** *adj* sùl, shùilean.
**odd** *adj* còrr.
**ode** *n* duanag *f*.
**odour** *n* boladh *m*.
**of** *prep* de, dhe, a.
**off** *adv* dheth, às, air falbh. • *prep* de, dhe, o, bhàrr, a-mach bho.
**offence** *n* oilbheum *m*.
**offend** *v* dèan oilbheum do.
**offer** *n* tairgse *f*.
**office** *n* oifis *f*; gnothach *f*; dreuchd *f*.
**officer** *n* oifigeach *m*.
**officious** *adj* bleideil.
**often** *adv* tric; *adv* gu tric.
**ogle** *v* caog.
**oil** *n* ola *f*. • *v* olaich.
**oil-field** *n* ola-raon *m*.
**oil-rig** *n* crann-ola *m*.
**oily** *adj* uilleach.
**ointment** *n* ol-ungaidh *f*.
**old** *adj* aosda, sean.
**old-fashioned** *adj* sean-fhasanta.
**omen** *n* manadh *m*.
**ominous** *adj* droch-fhàistinneach.
**omit** *v* fàg às.
**on** *adv* air. • *prep* air.
**once** *adv* uair.
**one** *adj* aon. • *n* a h-aon *m*.
**onion** *n* uinnean *m*.
**only** *adj* aon. • *adv* a-mhàin. • *conj* ach.
**onward** *adv* air adhart.
**ooze** *v* sil.
**open** *adj* fosgailte. • *v* fosgail.

**opening** *n* fosgladh *m*.
**operation** *n* gnìomhachd *m*; (*surgical*) opairèisean *m*.
**opinion** *n* barail *f*.
**opponent** *n* nàmhaid *m*.
**opportune** *adj* tràthail.
**opportunity** *n* cothrom *m*.
**oppose** *v* cuir an aghaidh.
**opposite** *prep* fa chomhair.
**oppress** *v* claoidh.
**oppressive** *adj* fòirneartach.
**optic** *adj* fradharcach.
**optimism** *n* soirbh-dhùil *f*.
**optimistic** *adj* soirbh-dhùileach.
**or** *conj* no, air neo.
**oral** *adj* troimhn bheul.
**orange** *adj* orainds.
**orator** *n* cainntear *m*.
**orbit** *n* reul-chuairt *f*.
**orchard** *n* ubhalghort *m*.
**ordain** *v* socraich.
**order** *n* òrdugh *m*. • *v* òrdaich.
**ordinary** *adj* gnàthaichte.
**ore** *n* mèinn *f*.
**organ** *n* ball *m*; orghan *m*.
**organic** *adj* innealach.
**organise** *v* eagraich.
**organiser** *n* fear-eagraidh *m*.
**orgasm** *n* reachd *f*.
**orgy** *n* ruitearachd *f*.
**oriental** *adj* earach.
**origin** *n* tùs, bun *m*.
**originality** *n* bun-mhèinn *f*.
**originate** *v* tàrmaich.
**Orkney** *n* Arcaibh.
**ornithology** *n* eun-eòlas *m*.

**orphan** n dìlleachdan m.
**osprey** n iolair-uisge f.
**ostensible** adj a-rèir-coltais.
**ostrich** n oistric f.
**other** pron eile.
**otherwise** adv air modh eile.
**otter** n dòbhran m.
**ought** v bu chòir (dhomh, etc).
**ounce** n ùnnsa m.
**our** pron ar, ar n-.
**ours** pron ar ..... -ne, againne, leinne.
**ourselves** pron sinn fhèin.
**out** adv a-muigh.
**out-of-date** adj às an fhasan.
**outdo** v buadhaich air.
**outlaw** n fear-cùirn m.
**outrage** n sàrachadh m.
**outright** adv gu buileach. • adj dearg.
**outside** adv a-muigh.
**outskirts** n iomall m.
**outspoken** adj fosgarra.
**outward** adj faicsinneach.

**outwit** v thoir an car às.
**oven** n àmhainn f.
**over** prep os cionn; thairis air. • adv (here) a-null; (there) a-nall.
**overall** adv thar a chèile.
**overboard** adv thar bòrd.
**overcharge** v cuir tuilleadh 's a' chòir.
**overflow** n cur thairis m. • v tar-shruth.
**overnight** adj ri linn oidhche.
**overrrule** v cuir fo smachd.
**overseas** adv thall thairis.
**overtake** v beir air.
**overtime** n seach-thìm f.
**overturn** v cuir bun-os-cionn.
**overweight** adj ro-throm.
**owe** v bi fo fhiachaibh.
**owl** n comhachag f.
**own** pron fèin, fhèin.
**owner** n fear-seilbhe m.
**oxter** n achlais f.
**oyster** n eisir m.

# P

**pace** n ceum m. • v ceumnaich.
**pacifism** n sìochantas m.
**pacifist** n sìochantair m.
**pack** v paisg.
**packet** n pacaid f.
**pact** n cùmhnant f.
**pad** n pada f.
**paddle** v pleadhagaich.
**paddling** n plubraich f.

**padlock** n glas-chrochaidh f.
**page** n duilleag f; (boy) pèidse m.
**pageant** n taisbeanadh m.
**pain** n pian f.
**painful** adj piantach.
**painless** adj neo-phiantach.
**paint** n peant m. • v peant.
**painting** n dealbh m.
**pair** n càraid f.

**palace** n lùchairt f.
**palate** n bràighe-beòil m.
**pale** adj bàn. • v bànaich.
**pallid** adj bàn.
**palm** n bas f.
**pamper** v dèan peata dhe.
**pan** n pana f.
**pancake** n foileag f.
**pane** n gloinne f.
**panic** n clisgeadh m.
**pant** v plosg.
**pantry** n seòmar-bìdh m.
**pants** npl pantaichean.
**papal** adj pàpanach.
**paper** n pàipear m.
**parable** n cosamhlachd f.
**paradise** n pàrras m.
**paradox** n frith-chosamhlachd f.
**paragraph** n earran sgrìobhaidh f.
**parallel** adj co-shìnteach.
**paralysis** n pairilis m.
**parapet** n uchd-bhalla m.
**parcel** n parsail m.
**pardon** n mathanas m. • v math.
**parent** n pàrant m.
**parish** n sgìre f.
**park** n pàirce f.
**Parliament** n Parlamaid f.
**parody** n sgig-athrais f.
**parrot** n pearraid f.
**parsimonious** adj spìocach.
**parsley** n peirsill f.
**part**¹ n cuid f.
**part**² v dealaich.
**partake** v com-pàirtich.
**participate** v com-pàirtich.

**particle** n gràinean m.
**particular** adj àraidh.
**parting** n dealachadh m.
**partition** n roinneadh m; (wall) cailbhe m.
**partly** adv ann an cuid; gu ìre bhig.
**partner** n companach m.
**partridge** n cearc-thomain m.
**party** n cuideachd f; pàrtaidh f.
**pass**¹ n bealach m.
**pass**² v gabh seachad; (sport) pasaig.
**passable** adj cuibheasach.
**passage** n turas m; (in building) trannsa f.
**passion** n boile f.
**passionate** adj dìoghrasach.
**passive resistance** n aghaidh-eachd fhulangach f.
**passivity** n fulangachd m.
**passport** n cead dol thairis m.
**past** adj seachad. • n an t-àm a dh'fhalbh m.
**pastry** n pastra f.
**pasture** n feurach m. • v feuraich.
**pat** v slìob.
**patch** n tùthag f.
**paternal** adj athaireil.
**path** n ceum m, slighe f.
**pathetic** adj tiamhaidh.
**patience** n foighidinn f.
**patient** n euslainteach m. • adj foighidneach.
**patrimony** n dualchas m.
**patronymic** n ainm sinnsireil m.

**pattern** *n* pàtran *m*.

**paunch** *n* maodal *f*.

**pause** *n* stad *m*. • *v* fuirich.

**paw** *n* spòg *f*.

**pawn**[1] *n* pàn *m*.

**pawn**[2] *v* thoir an geall.

**pay** *n* pàigheadh *m*. • *v* pàigh.

**pea** *n* peasair *f*.

**peace** *n* sìth, fois *f*.

**peaceful** *adj* sìothchail.

**peach** *n* pèitseag *f*.

**peak** *n* stùc *f*, binnean *m*.

**pear** *n* peur *f*.

**pearl** *n* neamhnaid *f*.

**peat** *n* mòine *f*; (*single*) fad *m*.

**peat-stack** *n* cruach-mhònach *f*.

**pebble** *n* dèideag *f*.

**peck** *v* pioc.

**pectoral** *adj* uchdail.

**peculiar** *adj* àraid.

**pedal** *n* troighean *m*.

**pedantry** *n* rag-fhoglam *m*.

**peddle** *v* reic.

**pedestrian** *n* coisiche *m*.

**pee** *v* dèan mùn.

**peel** *n* rùsg *m*. • *v* ruisg.

**peep** *n* caogadh *m*. • *v* caog.

**peevish** *adj* dranndanach.

**peewit** *n* curracag *f*.

**pelt** *v* caith air.

**pen** *n* peann *m*.

**penalty** *n* peanas *m*.

**penance** *n* aithridh *f*.

**pending** *adj* ri thighinn.

**penetrate** *v* drùidh.

**peninsula** *n* leth-eilean *m*.

**penis** *n* bod *m*.

**penny** *n* peighinn *f*.

**pension** *n* peinnsean *m*.

**pensioner** *n* fear-peinnsein *m*, bean peinnsein *f*.

**people** *n* sluagh, poball *m*.

**pepper** *n* piobair *m*.

**perceive** *v* tuig, mothaich.

**per cent** *adv* sa' ceud.

**perch** *n* spiris *f*. • *v* rach air spiris.

**percolator** *n* sìolachan *m*.

**percussion** *n* faram *m*.

**perennial** *adj* maireannach.

**perfect** *adj* foirfe. • *v* dèan foirfe.

**perform** *v* coimhlion.

**perfume** *n* cùbhrachd *f*.

**perhaps** *adv* is dòcha, ma dh' fhaoite.

**period** *n* cuairt *f*.

**perish** *v* faigh bàs.

**perishable** *adj* neo-sheasmhach.

**permanence** *n* maireannachd *f*.

**permanent** *adj* buan.

**permissive** *adj* ceadachail.

**permit** *n* bileag-cead *f*. • *v* ceadaich.

**perpendicular** *adj* dìreach.

**perquisite** *n* frith-bhuannachd *f*.

**persecute** *v* geur-lean.

**persevere** *v* lean air.

**persistent** *adj* leanailteach.

**person** *n* neach *m*.

**personal** *adj* pearsanta.

**persuade** *v* cuir ìmpidh air.

**persuasion** *n* ìmpidheachd *f*.

**pertinent** *adj* iomchuidh.

**peruse** v leugh.

**perverse** adj claon.

**pervert** n claonair m.

**pessimist** n fear gun dòchas m.

**pest** n plàigh f.

**pestle** n plocan m.

**pet** n peata m.

**petition** n iarrtas m. • v aslaich.

**petrol** n peatroil m.

**petticoat** n còta-bàn m.

**pew** n suidheachan m.

**phantom** n faileas m.

**pheasant** n easag f.

**phenomenon** n iongantas m.

**philosopher** n feallsanach m.

**philosophy** n feallsanachd f.

**phlegmatic** adj ronnach.

**phone** n fòn m. • v fòn.

**phosphorescence** n teine-ghea-lan m.

**photograph** n dealbh m.

**phrase** n abairt m.

**physical** adj fisiceach; corporra.

**piano** n piàno m.

**pianist** n cluicheadair piàno m.

**pibroch** n pìobaireachd, ceòl-mòr f.

**pick** v tagh.

**pickle** v saill.

**Pict** n Cruithneach m.

**picture** n dealbh m.

**picturesque** adj àillidh.

**pie** n pai m.

**piece** n pìos m.

**pier** n ceadha m.

**pierce** v toll.

**pig** n muc f.

**pigeon** n calman m.

**pigsty** n fail muice f.

**pile** v cruach.

**pilfer** v dèan braide.

**pilgrim** n eilthireach m.

**pill** n pile f.

**pillar** n carragh f.

**pillow** n cluasag f.

**pilot** n pìleat m. • v treòraich.

**pimple** n plucan m.

**pin** n dealg f.

**pinch** v fàisg.

**pine** n giuthas m.

**pink** adj pinc.

**pipe** n pìob f.

**piper** n pìobaire m.

**pirate** n spùinneadair mara m.

**piss** n mùn m. • v mùin.

**pistol** n daga m.

**pitch** n bìth f; (mus) àirde f; (field) raon-cluiche m.

**pitiful** adj truacanta.

**pittance** n suarachas m.

**pity** n truas m. • v gabh truas de.

**place** n àite m. • v suidhich.

**placidity** n ciùineachd f.

**plague** v plàighich.

**plaice** n lèabag-mhòr f.

**plaid** n breacan m.

**plain** adj còmhnard; soilleir.

**plait** n figheachan m.

**plan** n innleachd, plana f. • v innlich.

**planet** n planaid f.

**plank** n clàr m.

**plant** n luibh m. • v cuir.

**plantation** n planntachadh m.

**plaster** n sglàib f; plàsd m.

**plastic** adj plastaic; coineallach.
• n plastaic f.

**plate** n truinnsear m.

**plateau** n àrd-chlàr m.

**plausible** adj beulach.

**play** v cluich.

**player** n fear-cluiche m; cleasaiche m.

**plead** v tagair.

**pleasant** adj taitneach.

**please** v toilich, riaraich, taitinn,
còrd.

**pleasure** n tlachd f.

**pleat** n pleat f.

**plenty** adv gu leòr.

**plenty** n pailteas m.

**plight** n cor m.

**plod** v saothraich.

**plot** n goirtean m; (scheme) cuilbheart f.

**plough** n crann m. • v treabh.

**plug** n plucan m.

**plum** n plumas m.

**plumb** v feuch doimhneachd.

**plump** adj sultmhor.

**plunder** n cobhartach m. • v
spùinn.

**plunge** v tum.

**plural** adj iolra.

**plus** prep agus.

**poach** v poidsig.

**poacher** n poidsear m.

**pocket** n pòcaid f.

**poem** n dàn m.

**poet** n bàrd m.

**poetry** n bàrdachd f.

**point** v comharraich.

**poison** n puinnsean m.

**police** n poileas m.

**polish** n lìomh f.

**polite** adj modhail.

**pollute** v truaill.

**pompous** adj mòrchuiseach.

**pond** n linne f.

**pony** n pònaidh m.

**pool** n linne f.

**poor** adj bochd.

**Pope** n am Pàpa m.

**popular** adj coiteanta.

**population** n sluagh m.

**porch** n sgàil-thaigh m.

**porridge** n lite f.

**port** n port m.

**portable** adj so-ghiùlan.

**portion** n earrann f.

**Portugal** n A' Phortagail f.

**positive** adj cinnteach.

**possess** v sealbhaich.

**possible** adj comasach.

**possibly** adv is dòcha.

**post** v cuir air falbh.

**postal order** n òrdugh-puist m.

**postcard** n cairt-phostachd f.

**postcode** n còd-puist m.

**postman** n posta m.

**post office** n oifis a' phuist f.

**pot** n poit f.

**potato** n buntàta m.

**pottery** n crèadhadaireachd f.

**pound** n pùnnd m.

**pour** v dòirt; (*rain*) sil.

**powder** n fùdar m.

**power** n cumhachd f.

**power station** n stèisean dealain m.

**practicable** adj so-dhèanamh.

**practice** n cleachdadh m.

**practise** v cleachd.

**praise** n moladh m. • v mol.

**prank** n cleas m.

**prawn** n muasgan-caol m.

**pray** v guidh.

**prayer** n guidhe f.

**preach** v searmonaich.

**precarious** adj cugallach.

**precaution** n roi-chùram m.

**precentor** n fear togail fuinn m.

**precious** adj prìseil.

**precipitous** adj cas.

**precise** adj pongail.

**precocious** adj roi-abaich.

**predatory** adj creachach.

**predict** v roi-innis.

**predominant** adj buadhach.

**preface** n roi-ràdh m.

**prefer** v is fheàrr (leam, etc).

**pregnant** adj trom.

**prehistoric** adj roi-eachdraidheil.

**prejudice** n claon-bhàigh f.

**preliminary** adj tòiseachail.

**premises** n aitreabh m.

**premonition** n roi-fhiosrachadh f.

**prepare** v ullaich.

**preposterous** adj mì-reusanta.

**prescription** n riaghailt-lèigh f.

**presence** n làthaireachd f.

**present**[1] n an t-àm tha làthair m

**present**[2] n (*gift*) tiodhlac m. • v thoir do.

**presently** adv an ceart uair.

**president** n ceann-suidhe m.

**press release** n aithris-naidheachd f.

**pretence** n leigeil air m.

**pretend** v leig air.

**pretty** adj brèagha.

**prevailing** adj buadhach.

**previously** adv roimh làimh.

**prey** n creach f. • v creach.

**price** n prìs f.

**prick** v stuig.

**prickly** adj biorach.

**pride** n àrdan m.

**priest** n sagart m.

**prim** adj frionasach.

**primary school** n bun-sgoil f.

**primitive** adj tùsach.

**primrose** n sòbhrach f.

**prince** n prionnsa m.

**print** v clò-bhuail.

**printer** n (*comput*) clò-bhualadair m.

**print-out** n lethbhreac clo-bhuailte m.

**private** adj uaigneach.

**privilege** n sochair f.

**prize** n duais f.

**probable** adj coltach.

**probably** adv is dòcha.

**probity** n treibhdhireas m.

**problem** n ceist f.

**problematic** adj ceisteach.

**process** n cùrsa m.
**proclaim** v èigh.
**procurator fiscal** n fioscail m.
**prod** v stob.
**produce** n toradh m. • v thoir gu cinneas.
**producer** n riochdaire m.
**profession** n dreuchd f.
**professor** n proifeasair m.
**profit** n buannachd f. • v tairbhich.
**profound** adj domhainn.
**profuse** adj pailt.
**program(me)** n prògram m.
**programming language** n cànan-prògramaidh m.
**progress** n imeachd f; piseach f.
**prohibit** v toirmisg.
**prolific** adj torrach.
**prominent** adj faicsinneach.
**promise** n gealladh m. • v geall.
**promontory** n rubha m.
**prompt** adj deas.
**pronoun** n riochdair m.
**pronounce** v fuaimnich.
**proof** n dearbadh m.
**prop** v cùm suas.
**proper** adj iomchuidh.
**property** n seilbh f.
**prophesy** v fàisnich.
**proportion** n co-rèir m.
**proprietor** n sealbhadair m.
**propulsion** n sparradh m.
**prose** n rosg m.
**prosecute** v dlù-lean.
**prosper** v soirbhich.
**prostitute** n strìopach f.

**prostrate** adj sleuchdte.
**protect** v dìon.
**protection** n dìon m.
**protest** v tog casaid.
**Protestant** adj Pròsdanach.
**proud** adj uaibhreach.
**prove** v dearbh.
**proverb** n seanfhacal m.
**provide** v solair.
**province** n roinn f.
**provocation** n buaireadh m.
**provoke** v buair.
**provost** n pròbhaist m.
**prow** n toiseach m.
**prowl** v èalaidh.
**prude** n leòmag f.
**prudent** adj glic.
**prune** v sgath.
**pry** v lorgaich.
**psalm** n salm m.
**psalter** n salmadair m.
**psychic** adj anamanta.
**ptarmigan** n tàrmachan m.
**pub** n taigh-seinnse m.
**public** adj follaiseach.
**publicity** n follaiseadh m.
**public relations** n dàimh phoblach f.
**publish** v foillsich.
**pudding** n marag; mìlsean f.
**puddle** n lòn m.
**puffin** n buthaid m.
**pull** v tarraing.
**pulpit** n cùbaid f.
**pulse** n cuisle f.
**pump** n pumpa m; bròg-dannsa f.

**punctual** *adj* pongail.
**puncture** *n* tolladh *m*.
**punish** *v* peanasaich.
**punishment** *n* peanasachadh *m*.
**pupil** *n* sgoilear *m*; (*eye*) clach na sùla *m*.
**puppy** *n* cuilean *m*.
**pure** *adj* fiorghlan.
**purge** *v* glan.
**purity** *n* glaine *f*.
**purple** *adj* còrcair.
**purse** *n* sporan *m*.

**pursue** *v* lean.
**pursuer** *n* fear-tòire *m*.
**pursuit** *n* tòir *f*.
**push** *n* bruthadh *m*. • *v* brùth.
**pussy cat** *n* piseag *f*.
**put** *v* cuir, suidhich.
**putrid** *adj* grod.
**putt** *v* amas.
**puzzle** *n* imcheist. • *v* cuir an imcheist, bi an imcheist.
**pylon** *n* paidhleon *m*.
**pyramid** *n* biorramaid *f*.

# Q

**quack** *v* dèan gàgail.
**quaint** *adj* neònach.
**qualification** *n* feart *m*.
**qualify** *v* ullaich.
**quality** *n* gnè *f*.
**quantify** *v* àirmhich.
**quarrel** *n* còmhstri *m*. • *v* connsaich.
**quarrelsome** *adj* connspaideach.
**quarry** *n* cuaraidh *m*; creach *m*. • *v* cladhaich.
**quarter** *n* ceathramh *m*; (*season*) *n* ràith *f*.
**quartz** *n* èiteag *f*.
**quaver** *n* crith *f*; (*mus*) *n* caman *m*.
**queasy** *adj* sleogach.
**queen** *n* ban-rìgh *f*.
**quell** *v* smachdaich.
**quench** *v* bàth.
**quern** *n* brà *f*.

**question** *n* ceist *f*. • *v* ceasnaich.
**question-mark** *n* comharradh ceiste *m*.
**queue** *n* ciudha *f*.
**quibble** *v* car-fhaclaich.
**quick** *adj* bras, luath.
**quicksand** *n* beò-ghainmheach *f*.
**quiet** *adj* sàmhach.
**quiet** *n* sàmhchair *m*.
**quieten** *v* sàmhaich.
**quilt** *n* cuibhrig *m*.
**quirk** *n* car *m*.
**quit** *v* fàg.
**quite** *adv* gu tur, gu lèir; gu math.
**quiver**[1] *n* balg-shaighead *m*.
**quiver**[2] *v* dèan ball-chrith.
**quiz** *n* ceasnachadh *m*.
**quotation** *n* luaidh *m*; (*price*) luach *m*.
**quote** *v* luaidh; thoir mar ùghdarras.

# R

**rabbit** n coineanach m.

**rabid** adj cuthachail.

**race** n rèis f; (human) cinneadh f.

**racism** n cinneadachd f.

**racket** n gleadhraich f.

**radiant** adj lainnireach.

**radiate** v deàlraich.

**radiator** n rèididheator m.

**radical** adj bunasach.

**radio** n rèidio m.

**raffle** n crannchur-gill m.

**raft** n ràth m.

**rafter** n taobhan m.

**rag** n luideag f.

**rage** n boile f.

**raid** n ruaig f.

**railway** n rathad-iarainn m.

**rain** n uisge m; frasachd f. • v sil, dòirt.

**rainbow** n bogha-frois m.

**rainy** adj frasach.

**raise** v àrdaich, tog.

**rake** v ràc.

**ram** n reithe m.

**ram** v spàrr.

**rambler** n fear-fàrsain m.

**rampant** adj sùrdagach.

**rancid** adj breun.

**random** adj tuaireamach.

**range** n sreath m. • v siubhail.

**rank** n inbhe f; sreath m/f.

**rankle** v feargaich.

**ransom** n èirig f. • v fuasgail.

**rapacious** adj gionach.

**rape** n toirt air èiginn f. • v èiginich.

**rapidity** n braise f.

**rare** adj tearc.

**rarity** n annas m.

**rash**[1] n broth m.

**rash**[2] adj dàna.

**raspberry** n subh-craoibh m.

**rat** n ratan m.

**rate** n luach m; ràta f.

**rather** adv rudeigin.

**ravage** v sgrios.

**rave** v bi air bhoile.

**raven** n fitheach m.

**ravenous** adj cìocrach.

**raw** adj amh.

**razor** n ealtainn f.

**reach** n ruigheachd f. • v ruig.

**read** v leugh.

**reader** n leughadair m.

**readily** adv gu rèidh.

**readiness** n ullamhachd f.

**ready** adj ullamh.

**real** adj fìor.

**realise** v tuig.

**reality** n fìrinn f.

**really** adv gu dearbh.

**reap** v buain.

**rear** n deireadh m.

**reason** n reusan m.

**rebate** n lùghdachadh m.

**rebel** n reubalach m. • v dèan ar-a-mach.

**rebuff** n diùltadh m.

**rebuild** v ath-thog.

**recall** v cuimhnich air.

**recede** v rach air ais.

**receive** v gabh.

**recent** adj ùr.

**recently** adv o chionn ghoirid.

**reception** n fàilteachadh m.

**receptive** adj so-ghabhail.

**recession** n ìsleachadh m.

**recipe** n modh m.

**reciprocal** adj malairteach.

**recital** n aithris; (mus) ceadal f.

**reckless** adj neo-chùramach.

**reckon** v cùnnt.

**reclaim** v ath-leasaich.

**recline** v sìn.

**recognise** v aithnich.

**recommend** v cliùthaich.

**reconcile** v rèitich.

**reconnoitre** v feuch.

**record** n cùnntas m; clàr m. • v sgrìobh; clàraich.

**recover** v faigh air ais; fàs nas fheàrr.

**recovery** n faotainn air ais f; fàs nas fheàrr m.

**recreation** n cur-seachad m.

**rectify** v ceartaich.

**rector** n ceannard m, reactor m.

**recur** v tachair a-rithist.

**red** adj dearg; ruadh.

**redeem** v ath-cheannaich.

**redirect** v ath-sheòl.

**redouble** v dùblaich.

**reduce** v ìslich.

**redundant** adj anbharra.

**reed** n cuilc f; (mus) ribheid f.

**reef** n sgeir f.

**reel** n ruidhle m; (thread) piorna f.

**refer** v cuir gu.

**referee** n breitheamh, reaf m.

**reference** n iomradh m; teistean-as m.

**refill** v ath-lìon.

**refit** v ath-chàirich.

**reflect** v tilg air ais; (think) smaoinich.

**reform** n leasachadh m. • v ath-leasaich.

**refrain** n luinneag f.

**refresh** v ùraich.

**refreshment** n ùrachadh m; deoch f.

**refuge** n tèarmann m.

**refund** v ath-dhìol.

**refusal** n diùltadh m.

**refuse** v diùlt.

**refute** v breugnaich.

**regard** n suim f. • v gabh suim ann.

**register** n clàr m.

**regret** n duilchinn f. • v bi duilich.

**regulate** v riaghlaich.

**rehearsal** n ath-aithris f.

**rehearse** v ath-aithris.

**reign** v rìoghaich.

**reimburse** v ath-phàigh.

**rein** n srian f.

**reinforce** *v* ath-neartaich.

**rejoice** *v* dèan aoibhneas.

**relate** *v* innis.

**related** *adj* (*akin*) càirdeach.

**relation** *n* caraid *m*, ban-charaid *f*.

**relative** *adj* dàimheach.

**relax** *v* lasaich.

**release** *v* cuir ma sgaoil.

**relent** *v* taisich.

**relentless** *adj* neo-thruacanta.

**relevant** *adj* a' buntainn ri.

**reliable** *adj* earbsach.

**relic** *n* fuidheall *m*.

**relief** *n* furtachd *f*.

**relieve** *v* furtaich.

**religion** *n* diadhachd *f*.

**relish** *n* tlachd *f*. • *v* gabh tlachd de.

**reluctant** *adj* aindeonach.

**rely** *v* earb.

**remain** *v* fuirich.

**remains** *npl* fuidhleach *m*; (*human*) duslach *m*.

**remark** *n* facal *m*. • *v* thoir fa-near.

**remarkable** *adj* suaicheanta.

**remedy** *n* leigheas *m*.

**remember** *v* cuimhnich.

**remind** *v* cuimhnich do.

**reminiscence** *n* cuimhneachadh *m*.

**remorse** *n* agartas-cogais *m*.

**remorseful** *adj* cogaiseach.

**remote** *adj* iomallach.

**renaissance** *n* ath-bheothachadh *m*.

**rend** *v* srac.

**renew** *v* nuadhaich.

**rent** *n* sracadh *m*; (*fee*) màl *m*. • *v* gabh air mhàl.

**repair** *n* càireadh *m*. • *v* càirich.

**repay** *v* ath-dhìol.

**repeat** *v* aithris.

**repel** *v* tilg air ais.

**replace** *v* cuir an àite.

**replay** *v* ath-chluich.

**replete** *adj* làn.

**reply** *n* freagairt *f*. • *v* freagair.

**report** *v* thoir iomradh.

**representative** *n* riochdaire *m*.

**reprieve** *n* stad-bhreith *f*.

**reprimand** *n* casaid *f*.

**reprisal** *n* èirig *f*.

**reproach** *v* cronaich.

**reproduce** *v* gin.

**reproduction** *n* gintinn *m*; mac-samhlachadh *m*.

**reptile** *n* pèist *f*.

**republic** *n* poblachd *f*.

**reputation** *n* cliù *m*.

**request** *n* iarrtas *m*. • *v* iarr.

**rescue** *n* fuasgladh *m*. • *v* fuasgail.

**research** *v* rannsaich.

**researcher** *n* neach-rannsachaidh *m*.

**resent** *v* gabh tàmailt dhe.

**resentment** *n* doicheall *m*.

**reserve** *n* tasgadh *m*. • *v* caomhain.

**reservoir** *n* tasgadh-uisge *m*.

**residence** *n* ionad-còmhnaidh *m*.

**resign** *v* thoir suas, gèill.

**resistance** *n* strì *f.*

**resolute** *adj* gramail.

**resonant** *adj* glòrach.

**resource** *n* goireas *m.*

**respect** *n* urram *m.* • *v* thoir urram do.

**respectable** *adj* measail.

**respectful** *adj* modhail.

**respective** *adj* àraidh.

**respite** *n* anail *f.*

**responsibility** *n* cùram *m.*

**responsive** *adj* freagairteach.

**rest** *n* fois *f*; (*mus*) clos *m.* • *v* gabh fois.

**restaurant** *n* taigh-bidhe *m.*

**restful** *adj* sàmhach.

**restless** *adj* mì-fhoisneach.

**restore** *v* thoir air ais.

**restrict** *v* grab.

**result** *n* buil *f.*

**retain** *v* cùm.

**reticent** *adj* tosdach.

**retire** *v* rach air chluainidh, leig dreuchd dhe.

**retirement** *n* cluaineas *m.*

**retreat** *v* teich.

**retribution** *n* ath-dhìoladh *m.*

**return** *n* tilleadh *m.* • *v* till.

**reveal** *v* nochd.

**revelation** *n* taisbeanadh *m.*

**revenge** *n* dìoghaltas *m.*

**reverend** *adj* urramach.

**reverent** *adj* iriosal.

**review** *v* ath-bheachdaich.

**revise** *v* ath-sgrùd.

**revival** *n* dùsgadh *m.*

**revive** *v* dùisg.

**revolve** *v* iom-chuartaich.

**reward** *n* duais *f.* • *v* dìol.

**rheumatic** *adj* lòinidheach.

**rheumatism** *n* lòinidh *m/f.*

**rhubarb** *n* rùbarb *m.*

**rhyme** *n* comhardadh *m.* • *v* dèan rann.

**rib** *n* aisean *f.*

**ribbon** *n* rioban *m.*

**rice** *n* rus *m.*

**rich** *adj* beairteach.

**riddle** *n* tòimhseachan *m*; ruideal *f.*

**ride** *v* marcaich.

**rider** *n* marcaiche *m.*

**ridge** *n* druim *m.*

**ridiculous** *adj* amaideach.

**right** *adj* ceart; (*hand*) deas. • *n* ceartas *m*; dlighe *f.* • *v* cuir ceart.

**rigid** *adj* rag.

**rigour** *n* cruas *m.*

**rim** *n* oir *m.*

**rind** *n* rùsg *m.*

**ring** *n* fàinne *m/f*; cearcall *m.* • *v* seirm.

**rinse** *v* sgol.

**ripe** *adj* abaich.

**ripen** *v* abaich.

**ripple** *n* luasgan *m.*

**rise** *v* èirich.

**risk** *n* cunnart *m.* • *v* feuch.

**rival** *n* co-dheuchainniche *m.* • *adj* còistritheach.

**rivalry** *n* còmhstri *f.*

**river** *n* abhainn *f.*
**rivulet** *n* sruthan *m.*
**road** *n* rathad *m*, slighe *f.*
**roam** *v* rach air fàrsan.
**roar** *n* beuc *m.* • *v* beuc.
**roast** *v* ròist.
**rob** *v* spùinn, spùill.
**robber** *n* spùilleadair *m.*
**robbery** *n* goid *f.*
**robe** *n* fallaing *f.*
**robin** *n* brù-dhearg *m.*
**rock**[1] *n* carraig *f.*
**rock**[2] *v* luaisg.
**rod** *n* slat *f.*
**roe** *n* earba, ruadhag *f*; (*fish*) glasag *f.*
**rogue** *n* slaoightear *m.*
**roll** *n* rolla *f.* • *v* fill.
**romance** *n* romansachd *f*; (*tale*) ròlaist *m.*
**romantic** *adj* romansach.
**roof** *n* mullach *m.*
**rook** *n* ròcas *m.*
**room** *n* seòmar, rùm *m.*
**roomy** *adj* farsaing.
**root** *n* freumh *m.*
**rope** *n* ròpa, ball *m.*
**rosary** *n* paidirean *m.*
**rose** *n* ròs *m.*
**rosy** *adj* ruiteach.
**rot** *n* grodadh *m.*
**rotten** *adj* grod.

**rough** *adj* garbh, molach.
**round** *adj* cruinn. • *adv* mun cuairt.
**rouse** *v* dùisg.
**rout** *n* ruaig *f.*
**routine** *n* gnàth-chùrsa *m.*
**row** *n* (*rank*) sreath *m/f*; (*fight*) sabaid *f.*
**rowan** *n* caorann *f.*
**rower** *n* ràmhaiche *m.*
**rub** *v* suath.
**rubbish** *n* salchar, brusgar *m.*
**rudder** *n* stiùir *f.*
**rude** *adj* borb.
**rue** *v* crean.
**rueful** *adj* dubhach.
**ruffian** *n* brùid *f.*
**rug** *n* bràt-urlair *m.*
**ruin** *n* sgrios *m*; (*house*) làrach *m.*
**rule** *n* riaghailt *f.* • *v* riaghail.
**rumble** *v* dèan rùcail.
**rummage** *v* rannsaich.
**rumour** *n* fathann *m.*
**run** *v* ruith.
**runnel** *n* srùlag *f.*
**rural** *adj* dùthchail.
**rush** *v* brùchd.
**rushes** *npl* luachair *f.*
**rust** *n* meirg *f.*
**rut** *n* clais *f*; (*animal*) dàmhair *f.*
**ruthless** *adj* neo-thruacanta.

# S

sabbath *n* sàbaid *f.*

sack[1] *n* poca *m.*

sack[2] *v* sgrios; cuir à obair.

sacred *adj* naomh.

sacrifice *n* ìobairt *f.* • *v* ìobair.

sad *adj* brònach.

sadden *v* dèan brònach.

saddle *n* dìollaid *f.*

sadness *n* bròn, mulad *m.*

safe *adj* sàbhailte.

safety *n* tèarainteachd *f.*

saffron *n* cròch *m.*

sag *v* tuit.

sagacious *adj* geurchuiseach.

sail *n* seòl *m.* • *v* seòl.

sailor *n* seòladair *m.*

saint *n* naomh *m.*

sake *n* sgàth *m.*

salad *n* sailead *m.*

sale *n* reic *m.*

saleable *adj* so-reic.

saliva *n* seile *m.*

sallow *adj* lachdann.

salmon *n* bradan *m.*

salmon trout *n* bànag *f.*

salt *n* salann *m.*

salt-cellar *n* saillear *m.*

salutary *adj* slàinteil.

salute *v* fàiltich.

salvage *n* tàrrsainn *m.*

same *adj* ionann, ceudna.

sameness *n* co-ionannachd.

sample *n* samhla *m.*

sanctify *v* naomhaich.

sanctuary *n* comraich *f.*

sand *n* gainmheach *f.*

sandstone *n* clach-ghainmhich *f.*

sandy *adj* gainmheil.

sane *adj* ciallach.

sapling *n* faillean *m.*

sapphire *n* gorm-leug *f.*

sarcasm *n* searbhas *m.*

sacrcastic *adj* searbh.

satanic *adj* diabhlaidh.

satchel *n* màileid *f.*

satellite *n* saideal *m.*

satiate *v* sàsaich.

satin *n* sròl *m.*

satire *n* aoir *f.*

satirical *adj* aoireil.

satirist *n* èisg *f.*

satisfaction *n* sàsachadh *m.*

satisfied *adj* sàsaichte.

satisfy *v* sàsaich.

Saturday *n* Disathairne *m*, Sath-airne *f.*

sauce *n* sabhs *m.*

saucepan *n* sgeileid *f.*

saucer *n* sàsar *m.*

sausage *n* ìsbean *m.*

save *v* sàbhail.

saved *adj* saorte.

savour *v* feuch blas.

savoury *adj* blasda.

saw *n* sàbh *m.* • *v* sàbh.

say *v* abair.

**saying** n ràdh, facal m.
**scald** v sgàld.
**scale** n cothrom m; (fish) lann m; (mus) sgàla m.
**scaly** adj lannach.
**scalp** n craiceann a' chinn m.
**scan** v sgrùd.
**scandal** n sgainneal m.
**scandalise** v sgainnealaich.
**scandalous** adj maslach.
**scanty** adj gann.
**scar** n leòn m.
**scarce** adj tearc.
**scare** v cuir eagal air.
**scarecrow** n bodach-ròcais m.
**scarf** n stoc m.
**scatter** v sgap.
**scattering** n sgapadh m.
**scene** n sealladh m.
**scent** n fàileadh m.
**scented** adj cùbhraidh.
**sceptical** adj às-creideach.
**scheme** n innleachd f.
**school** n sgoil f.
**schoolmaster** n maighstir-sgoile m.
**schoolmistress** n bana-maigh-stir-sgoile f.
**science** n saidheans m.
**scientific** adj saidheansail.
**scissors** n siosar f.
**scold** v troid.
**scone** n bonnach m, sgona f.
**scorch** v dadh.
**score** v cuir; sgrìob.
**scorn** n tàir f.

**scornful** adj tàireil.
**Scotland** n Alba f.
**Scottish** adj Albannach.
**scour** v nigh.
**scourge** v sgiùrs.
**scout** n beachdair m.
**scowl** v bi fo ghruaim.
**scrape** n sgrìob f.
**scratch** n sgròbadh m. • v sgròb.
**scream** n sgreuch m. • v sgreuch.
**scree** n sgàirneach f.
**script** n sgrìobhadh m.
**scroll** n rolla f.
**scrotum** n clach-bhalg m.
**scrub** v nigh.
**scruple** n teagamh m.
**scrupulous** adj teagmhach.
**scuffle** n tuasaid f.
**sculptor** n deilbhear m.
**sculpture** n deilbheadh m.
**scythe** n speal f. • v speal.
**sea** n muir m/f, cuan m, fairge f.
**seagull** n faoileag f.
**seal** n ròn m; (official) seula m. • v seulaich.
**sea level** n àirde-mara f.
**seaport** n longphort m.
**sear** v crannaich.
**search** n lorg m. • v lorg, rann-saich.
**seashore** n cladach m.
**season** n ràith f.
**seasonable** adj tràthail.
**seaweed** n feamainn f.
**second** adj dara.
**secondary** adj dàrnach.

**secondary school** n àrd-sgoil f.

**second-hand** adj ath-dhìolta.

**secondly** adv anns an dara h-àite.

**secrecy** n cleith f.

**secret** adj dìomhair. • n rùn.

**secretary** n rùnaire m, ban-rùnaire f.

**secretive** adj ceilteach.

**secretly** adv gun fhiosda.

**sect** n dream m.

**secular** adj saoghalta.

**secure** adj seasgair. • v glais, glac.

**security** n dìon m.

**seduce** v truaill.

**seduction** n truailleadh m.

**see** v faic, seall, amhairc.

**seed** n sìol m. • v sìolaich.

**seeing** n lèirsinn f.

**seek** v iarr.

**seer** n fiosaiche m.

**seize** v glac, cuir làmh ann.

**seldom** adv gu tearc.

**select** v tagh.

**self** pron fèin, fhèin, fhìn.

**self-interest** n fèin-bhuannachd f.

**selfish** adj fèineil.

**sell** v reic.

**semiquaver** n leth-chaman m.

**semitone** n leth-phong m.

**senate** n seanadh m.

**send** v cuir.

**senile** adj seantaidh.

**senior** adj as sine.

**sensation** n mothachadh m.

**sense** n ciall f.

**senseless** adj gun chiall.

**sensible** adj ciallach.

**sensitive** adj mothachail.

**sensual** adj feòlmhor.

**sensuous** adj ceudfaidheach.

**sentence** n rosg-rann m; (law) binn f.

**sentimental** adj maoth-inntinneach.

**separate** v dealaich.

**separation** n dealachadh.

**September** n September m; An t-Sultuine f.

**septic** adj seaptaic.

**sepulchral** adj tuamach.

**sequence** n leanmhainn m.

**serene** adj soinneanta.

**sergeant** n seàirdeant m.

**series** n sreath m.

**serious** adj suidhichte.

**serpent** n nathair f.

**serrated** adj eagach.

**servant** n seirbheiseach m.

**serve** v riaraich, fritheil.

**service** n seirbheis f; dleasnas m.

**serviceable** adj feumail.

**session** n seisean m.

**set** v suidhich, cuir.

**setter** n cù-luirg m.

**settle** v socraich.

**settlement** n suidheachadh; tuineachadh m.

**seven** adj seachd. • n (people) seachdnar.

**seventeen** n seachd-deug.

**seventh** *adj* seachdamh.

**seventy** *n* seachdad, trì fichead 's a deich.

**sever** *v* sgar.

**severe** *adj* cruaidh.

**severity** *n* cruas *m*.

**sew** *v* fuaigh.

**sewage** *n* giodar *m*.

**sewing** *n* fuaigheal *m*.

**sex** *n* gnè *f*, sex *m*.

**sextet** *n* ceòl-sianar *m*.

**sexual intercourse** *n* co-ghineadh *m*.

**shade** *n* sgàil *f*. • *v* sgàil.

**shadow** *n* faileas *m*.

**shady** *adj* dubharach.

**shaggy** *adj* molach.

**shallow** *adj* tana; faoin.

**sham** *adj* mealltach.

**shame** *n* nàire *f*. • *v* nàraich.

**shameful** *adj* nàr.

**shape** *n* cumadh *m*. • *v* cum, dealbh.

**shapely** *adj* cuimir.

**share** *n* roinn *f*. • *v* roinn, pàirtich.

**shark** *n* siorc *m*.

**sharp** *adj* geur.

**sharpen** *v* geuraich.

**sharpness** *n* gèire *f*.

**shave** *v* beàrr.

**shawl** *n* seàla *f*.

**she** *pron* i, ise.

**shear** *v* rùsg.

**shearing** *n* rùsgadh *m*.

**sheath** *n* truaill *f*.

**shed**[1] *n* bothan *m*.

**shed**[2] *v* dòirt.

**sheep** *n* caora *f*.

**sheep-dog** *n* cù-chaorach.

**sheet** *n* duilleag *f*.

**sheiling** *n* àirigh *f*.

**shelf** *n* sgeilp *f*; (*rock*) sgeir *f*.

**shellfish** *n* maorach *m*.

**shelter** *n* dìon *m*.

**shepherd** *n* cìobair *m*.

**sheriff** *n* siorraidh *m*.

**Shetland** *n* Sealtainn *m*.

**shield** *n* sgiath *f*. • *v* dìon.

**shine** *v* deàlraich.

**shinty** *n* iomain *f*.

**shinty stick** *n* caman *m*.

**ship** *n* long *f*.

**shipwreck** *n* long-bhriseadh *m*.

**shire** *n* siorrachd *f*.

**shirt** *n* lèine *f*.

**shiver** *v* crith.

**shoal** *n* bogha; sgaoth *m*.

**shock** *n* sgannradh *m*. • *v* criothnaich.

**shoe** *n* bròg *f*.

**shoelace** *n* barrall *f*.

**shoemaker** *n* greusaiche *m*.

**shoot** *v* tilg, loisg; (*grow*) fàs.

**shop** *n* bùth *f*.

**shore** *n* tràigh *f*.

**short** *adj* goirid.

**shortage** *n* dìth *m*.

**shorten** *v* giorraich.

**shortly** *adv* a dh' aithghearr.

**short-sighted** *adj* geàrr-sheallach.

**shorts** *npl* briogais ghoirid *f*.

**short-wave** *n* geàrr-thonnach *m*.

**shot** *n* urchair *f*.

**shoulder** *n* gualainn *f*.

**shout** *n* glaodh *m*.

**shove** *n* putadh *m*. • *v* put.

**show** *v* seall.

**shower** *n* fras *f*.

**shred** *n* mìr *m*.

**shriek** *n* sgread *m*.

**shrimp** *n* carran *m*.

**shrink** *v* seac.

**shrub** *n* preas *m*.

**shudder** *v* criothnaich.

**shuffle** *v* tarraing; (*cards*) measgaich.

**shut** *v* druid, dùin. • *adj* dùinte.

**shy** *adj* sochaireach.

**sick** *adj* tinn.

**sickness** *n* tinneas *m*.

**side** *n* taobh *m*.

**sidelong** *adv* air fhiaradh.

**sideways** *adv* an comhair a thaoibh.

**siege** *n* sèisd *f*.

**sieve** *n* criathar *m*.

**sigh** *v* leig osna.

**sight** *n* sealladh *m*; lèirsinn *f*.

**sign** *n* comharradh *m*.

**signature** *n* ainm *m*.

**significant** *adj* brìgheil.

**signpost** *n* post-seòlaidh *m*.

**silence** *n* sàmhchair *f*, tosd *m*.

**silent** *adj* tosdach.

**silk** *n* sìoda *m*.

**sill** *n* sòlla *f*.

**silly** *adj* gòrach.

**silver** *n* airgead *m*.

**similar** *adj* coltach.

**simple** *adj* sìmplidh.

**simplify** *v* sìmplich.

**simultaneous** *adj* còmhla.

**sin** *n* peacadh *m*. • *v* peacaich.

**since** *conj* a chionn is gu. • *prep* o, bho, o chionn.

**sincere** *adj* onorach.

**sing** *v* seinn, gabh òran.

**singer** *n* seinneadair *m*.

**single** *adj* singilte; gun phòsadh.

**singular** *adj* sònraichte.

**sinister** *adj* droch thuarach.

**sink** *n* since *f*. • *v* cuir fodha; rach fodha.

**sip** *v* gabh balgam.

**sister** *n* piuthar *f*.

**sister-in-law** *n* piuthar-chèile *f*.

**sit** *v* suidh.

**sitting room** *n* seòmar-suidhe *m*.

**six** *adj* sia. • *n* (*people*) sianar.

**sixteen** *adj/n* sia-deug *m*.

**sixty** *adj/n* trì-fichead, seasgad.

**size** *n* meud *m*.

**skate**[1] *n* bròg-spèilidh *f*. • *v* spèil.

**skate**[2] *n* (*fish*) sgait *f*.

**skeleton** *n* cnàimhneach *m*.

**skerry** *n* sgeir *f*.

**sketch** *n* tarraing *f*.

**ski** *v* sgithich.

**skid** *v* sleamhnaich.

**ski-lift** *n* àrdaichear-ski *m*.

**skill** *n* sgil *m*.

**skim** *v* thoir uachdar dhe.

**skin** *n* craiceann *m*. • *v* feann.

**skinny** *adj* caol.

**skip** *v* leum.

**skirmish** *n* arrabhaig *f.*

**skirt** *n* sgiort *f.*

**skull** *n* claigeann *m.*

**sky** *n* adhar *m.*

**Skye** *n* An t-Eilean Sgitheanach *m.*

**skylark** *n* uiseag *f.*

**slam** *v* toir slàr do.

**slander** *n* sgainneal *m.*

**slant** *n* claonadh *m.* • *v* claon.

**slap** *n* sgailc *f.*

**slash** *v* geàrr.

**slate** *n* sglèat *m.*

**slaughter** *n* marbhadh *m.*

**slave** *n* tràill *f.*

**sledge** *n* càrn-slaoid *m.*

**sleek** *adj* slìom.

**sleep** *n* cadal *m.*

**sleepy** *adj* cadalach.

**sleet** *n* flin *m.*

**sleeve** *n* muinchill *m.*

**slice** *n* sliseag *f.*

**slide** *v* sleamhnaich.

**slip** *n* tuisleadh *m.* • *v* tuislich.

**slipper** *n* slapag *f.*

**slippery** *adj* sleamhainn.

**slit** *n* sgoltadh *m.*

**slogan** *n* sluagh-ghairm *f.*

**slope** *n* leathad *m.*

**sloven** *n* luid *f.*

**slovenly** *adj* luideach.

**slow** *adj* slaodach.

**slowness** *n* slaodachd *f.*

**slur** *n* tàir *f*; (*speech*) slugadh *m.*

**sly** *adj* carach.

**smack** *n* sglais *f.*

**small** *adj* beag.

**smart** *adj* tapaidh.

**smattering** *n* bloigh eòlais *m.*

**smear** *v* smiùr.

**smell** *n* fàileadh *m.* • *v* feuch fàile-adh.

**smile** *n* snodha-gàire *m.* • *v* dèan snodha-gàire.

**smith** *n* gobha *m.*

**smoke** *n* ceò *m.* • *v* smocaig.

**smoky** *adj* ceòthach.

**smooth** *adj* mìn.

**smoothe** *v* mìnich.

**smother** *v* mùch.

**smoulder** *v* cnàmh-loisg.

**smuggle** *v* dèan cùl-mhùtair-eachd.

**smuggler** *n* cùl-mhùtaire *m.*

**snack** *n* blasad bìdh *m.*

**snake** *n* nathair *f.*

**snatch** *v* glac.

**sneak** *v* snàig.

**sneer** *v* dèan fanaid.

**sneeze** *v* dèan sreothart.

**sniff** *n* boladh *m.* • *v* gabh boladh.

**snipe** *n* naosg *m.*

**snivel** *v* smùch.

**snob** *n* sodalan *m.*

**snooze** *n* norrag *f.*

**snore** *v* dèan srann.

**snout** *n* soc *m.*

**snow** *n* sneachd *m.* • *v* cuir sneachd.

**snowdrift** *n* cith *m.*

**snug** *adj* còsach.

**snuggle** *v* laigh dlùth ri.

**so** *adv* cho; mar seo; mar sin.

**soak** *v* drùidh.

**soap** *n* siabann *m*.

**soapy** *adj* làn siabainn.

**sober** *adj* stuama; sòbair.

**sociable** *adj* cuideachdail.

**socialism** *n* sòisealachd *f*.

**society** *n* comann *m*.

**sock** *n* socais *f*.

**sod** *n* fòid *f*.

**soft** *adj* bog.

**soften** *v* bogaich.

**softness** *n* buige *f*.

**software** *n* bathar bog *m*.

**soil** *n* ùir *f*. • *v* salaich.

**solar** *adj* na grèine.

**soldier** *n* saighdear *m*.

**sole** *n* bonn na coise *m*; (*fish*) lèa-bag *m*.

**solemn** *adj* sòlaimte.

**solicit** *v* aslaich.

**solicitor** *n* fear-lagha *m*.

**solid** *adj* teann.

**solidarity** *n* dlùthachd *f*.

**solitude** *n* uaigneas *m*.

**solo** *n* òran aon-neach *m*.

**soloist** *n* òranaiche *m*.

**soluble** *adj* so-sgaoilte.

**solve** *v* fuasgail.

**solvent** *adj* comasach air pàigh-eadh.

**some** *pron* cuid, feadhainn; pàirt.

**somebody** *n* cuideigin *m*.

**somehow** *adv* air dòigh air choreigin.

**something** *n* rudeigin *m*.

**sometime** *adv* uaireigin.

**sometimes** *adv* air uairibh.

**somewhere** *adv* an àiteigin.

**son** *n* mac *m*.

**son-in-law** *n* cliamhainn *m*.

**soon** *adv* a dh' aithghearr.

**sophisticated** *adj* ionnsaichte.

**sordid** *adj* suarach.

**sore** *n* creuchd *m*. • *adj* goirt.

**sorrow** *n* bròn *m*.

**sorry** *adj* duilich.

**sort** *n* seòrsa *m*. • *v* seòrsaich.

**soul** *n* anam *m*.

**sound** *n* fuaim *m*. • *v* seirm, seinn.

**soup** *n* eanraich *f*, *n* brot *m*.

**sour** *adj* geur.

**south** *adj/n* deas *f*.

**southerly** *adj/adv* deas, à deas.

**sow** *n* cràin *f*.

**space** *n* rùm *m*.

**space probe** *n* taisgealadh fànais *m*.

**spacious** *adj* farsaing.

**Spain** *n* An Spàinn *f*.

**spaniel** *n* cù-eunaich *m*.

**Spanish** *n* Spàinnis *f*.

**spare** *v* caomhainn.

**spark** *n* sradag *f*.

**sparkle** *v* lainnrich.

**spawn** *v* sìolaich.

**speak** *v* bruidhinn.

**spear** *n* sleagh *f*.

**special** *adj* àraidh.

**species** *n* seòrsa *m*.

**spectacles** *npl* speuclairean.

**spectre** n tannasg m.

**speech** n cainnt f; òraid f.

**speed** n luas m.

**speed** v luathaich.

**spell** v litrich.

**spend** v caith.

**spider** n damhan-allaidh m.

**spill** v dòirt.

**spin** v snìomh.

**spine** n cnàimh-droma f.

**spinning wheel** n cuibhle-shnìomh f.

**spirit** n spiorad m.

**spirited** adj misneachail.

**spit** v tilg smugaid.

**spite** n gamhlas m.

**splendid** adj greadhnach.

**split** v sgoilt.

**spoil** v mill.

**spoon** n spàin f.

**sporran** n sporan m.

**sport** n spòrs f.

**spot** n ball m.

**spouse** n cèile m.

**spreadsheet** n duilleag-cleithe f.

**spree** n daorach f.

**Spring** n earrach m.

**spring** n fuaran m; leum m.

**spume** n cathadh-mara m.

**spur** v spor.

**spy** n beachdair m.

**squalid** adj sgreamhail.

**squall** n sgal m.

**square** adj ceithir-cheàrnach. • n ceàrnag f.

**squash** v brùth.

**squat** adj cutach.

**squeak** n bìog m.

**squirrel** n feòrag f.

**squirt** v steall.

**stable**[1] adj bunailteach.

**stable**[2] n stàball m.

**stag** n damh m.

**stair** n staidhre f.

**stale** adj cruaidh; goirt.

**stalk** n gas f.

**stallion** n àigeach m.

**stammer** v bruidhinn gagach.

**stamp** n stampa f; (embossing) stàmpa f.

**stand** v seas, stad.

**standstill** n stad m.

**star** n rionnag, reul f; prìomh act-air f.

**starboard** n deasbhòrd m.

**stare** v spleuchd.

**starfish** n crosgan m.

**starry** adj rionnagach.

**start** v clisg; (motor) cuir a dhol.

**starvation** n goirt f.

**state**[1] n staid f; (country) stàit f.

**state**[2] v cuir an cèill.

**station** n stèisean m.

**statue** n ìomhaigh f.

**stature** n àirde f.

**stave** n earran f; cliath f.

**stay** n stad m. • v fuirich.

**steak** n staoig f.

**steal** v goid.

**steam** n toit f.

**steel** n stàilinn f.

**steep** adj cas.

**steer** v stiùir.

**step** n ceum m.

**sterile** adj seasg.

**stern**[1] adj cruaidh.

**stern**[2] n deireadh m.

**stick**[1] n maide m.

**stick**[2] v sàth; (adhere) lean.

**stiffen** v ragaich.

**still**[1] adv fhathast; an dèidh sin.

**still**[2] n poit-dhubh f.

**sting** n gath m. • v guin.

**stink** n tòchd m.

**stir** v gluais.

**stitch** n grèim m.

**stocking** n stocainn f.

**stomach** n stamag f.

**stone** n clach f.

**stool** n stòl m.

**stop** v stad.

**store** v stòir.

**storehouse** n taigh-stòir m.

**stork** n corra bhàn f.

**storm** n doineann, stoirm f.

**stormy** adj stoirmeil.

**story** n sgeul m.

**stove** n stòbha f.

**straight** adj dìreach.

**strain**[1] n teannachadh m; (mental) uallach.

**strain**[2] v teannaich; (filter) sìolaidh.

**strange** adj iongantach.

**stranger** n coigreach m.

**strath** n srath m.

**straw** n connnlach f.

**strawberry** n subh-làir m.

**streaky** adj stiallach.

**stream** n sruth m.

**street** n sràid f.

**strength** n neart m.

**stretch** v sìn.

**strict** adj teann.

**stride** n sìnteag f.

**strike** v buail; (work) rach air stailc.

**string** n sreang f; teud f.

**stringed** adj teudaichte.

**stroke** v slìog.

**stroll** v siubhail.

**strong** adj làidir.

**struggle** n gleac m. • v gleac.

**stubble** n asbhuain f.

**stubborn** adj rag.

**stuff** n stuth m.

**stupid** adj baoghalta.

**sturdy** adj bunanta.

**sty** n fail mhuc f.

**stye** n leamhnagan m.

**style** n modh m.

**stylish** adj baganta.

**subject** adj umhal, fo smachd. • v ceannsaich.

**sublime** adj òirdheirc.

**submit** v gèill.

**subside** v traogh.

**subsidy** n còmhnadh m.

**substance** n stuth m; brìgh f.

**substitute** v cuir an ionad.

**subtle** adj seòlta.

**subtract** v thoir o.

**succeed** v soirbhich; lean.

**successful** adj soirbheachail.

**such** *adj/pron* a leithid de, den t-seòrsa.

**suck** *v* deoghail.

**suckle** *v* thoir cìoch.

**sudden** *adj* grad.

**suddenly** *adv* gu h-obann.

**sue** *v* tagair.

**suffer** *v* fuiling.

**sufferer** *n* fulangaiche *m*.

**sufficient** *adj* lèor.

**sugar** *n* siùcar *m*.

**suggest** *v* mol, comhairlich.

**suicide** *n* fèin-mhort *m*.

**suit** *n* deise *f*. • *v* freagair.

**suitable** *adj* freagarrach.

**sum** *n* àireamh, suim *f*.

**summer** *n* samhradh *m*.

**summit** *n* mullach *m*.

**summon** *v* gairm.

**sun** *n* grian *f*.

**sunbathe** *v* blian.

**Sunday** *n* Di-Dòmhnaich *m*, Là na Sàbaid *m*.

**sunny** *adj* grianach.

**sunrise** *n* èirigh na grèine *f*.

**sunset** *n* laighe na grèine *m*.

**supernatural** *adj* os-nàdurrach.

**superstition** *n* saobh-chràbadh *m*.

**supper** *n* suipear *f*.

**supple** *adj* sùbailte.

**supply** *v* sòlaire ù.

**support** *v* cùm taic ri.

**suppose** *v* saoil.

**suppress** *v* cùm fodha.

**supreme** *adj* sàr.

**sure** *adj* cinnteach.

**surely** *adv* gun teagamh.

**surface** *n* uachdar *m*.

**surge** *v* brùchd.

**surgeon** *n* làmh-leigh *m*.

**surgery** *n* (*doctor's*) ionad doctair *m*.

**surly** *adj* iargalta.

**surname** *n* sloinneadh *m*.

**surplus** *n* còrr *m*.

**surprise** *n* iongnadh *m*. • *v* cuir iongnadh air.

**surprising** *adj* neònach.

**surrender** *n* gèilleadh *m*.

**surround** *v* cuartaich.

**survive** *v* mair beò.

**suspect** *v* cuir an amharas.

**suspend** *v* croch.

**suspense** *n* teagamh *m*.

**suspension bridge** *n* drochaid croch-aidh *f*.

**suspicious** *adj* amharasach.

**swallow**[1] *v* sluig.

**swallow**[2] *n* gòbhlan-gaoithe *m*.

**swamp** *n* fèith *f*.

**swan** *n* eala *f*.

**swarm** *v* sgaothaich.

**swear** *v* mionnaich.

**sweat** *n* fallas *m*. • *v* cuir fallas dhe.

**swede** *n* (*neep*) snèip *f*.

**Sweden** *n* An t-Suain *f*.

**sweep** *v* sguab.

**sweet** *adj* milis.

**sweeties** *npl* siùcairean.

**sweetheart** *n* eudail *f*; leannan *f*.

**swim** v snàmh.
**swimming pool** n amar-snàimh m.
**swing** n dreallag f.
**switch** n suidse f.
**sword** n claidheamh m.
**symbol** n samhla m.

**symbolic** adj samhlachail.
**sympathetic** adj co-mhothachail.
**sympathise** v co-mhothaich.
**syringe** n steallaire m.
**syrup** n siorap f.
**system** n riaghailt f.

# T

**table** n bòrd; clàr m.
**tablet** n pile f; clàr m.
**tacit** adj gun bhruidhinn.
**taciturn** adj dùinte.
**tack** n tacaid f.
**tacket** n tacaid f.
**tacksman** n fear-baile m.
**tadpole** n ceann-pholan m.
**tail** n earball m.
**taint** v truaill.
**take** v gabh, thoir.
**tale** n sgeulachd f.
**talent** n tàlann m.
**talk** v bruidhinn.
**tall** adj àrd.
**tame** adj calla. • v callaich.
**tangle** n sàs m; (seaweed) stamh m.
**tanker** n tancair m.
**tantalise** v tog dòchas.
**tap** n goc m.
**taper** v dèan caol.
**tapestry** n grèis-bhrat m.
**target** n targaid f.
**tart**[1] adj searbh.
**tart**[2] n pithean m.

**task** n obair f.
**taste** v blais.
**tasty** adj blasta.
**tawny** adj lachdann.
**tawse** n stràic m.
**tax** v leag cìs.
**tea** n teatha, tì f.
**teach** v teasgaig.
**teacher** n fear-teagaisg, tìdsear m.
**teach-in** n seisean connsachaidh m.
**teacup** n cupan teatha m.
**team** n sgioba m/f.
**tear** n deur m; (rip) sracadh m.
**tease** v farranaich.
**tedious** adj liosda.
**teenager** n deugaire m.
**telephone** n fòn, teilefon m.
**television** n teilebhisean m.
**tell** v innis.
**temper** n nàdur m.
**temperament** n càil f.
**temperature** n teodhachd f.
**tempest** n doineann f.
**temple** n teampall m.

**temporary** *adj* sealach.

**tempt** *v* buair.

**ten** *adj/n* deich; (*persons*) deich-near.

**tenacious** *adj* leanailteach.

**tenant** *n* fear-aonta *m*.

**tender** *adj* maoth.

**tennis** *n* cluich-cneutaig *f*.

**tent** *n* teanta *f*.

**tenth** *n* an deicheamh earrann *f*.

**term** *n* teirm *f*; briathar *m*.

**tern** *n* steàrnan *m*.

**terrier** *n* abhag *f*.

**terrorism** *n* oillteachas *m*.

**test** *n* deuchainn *f*.

**testament** *n* tiomnadh *m*.

**testicle** *n* magairle *m*, clach *f*.

**than** *conj* na.

**thank** *v* thoir taing.

**thanks** *npl* tapadh leat, tapadh leibh; taing *f*.

**thankful** *adj* taingeil.

**that** *adj/pron* sin, ud, siud. • *conj* gu, chum. • *adv* a chionn, do brìgh.

**thatch** *n* tughadh *m*.

**thaw** *v* dèan aiteamh.

**the** *art* an, am, a', na, na h-, nan.

**theft** *n* meirle *m*.

**their** *pron* an, am, aca.

**them** *pron* iad, iadsan.

**themselves** *pron* iad fhèin.

**then** *adv* an sin; an dèidh sin; a-rèist.

**thence** *adv* às a sin.

**theory** *n* beachd *m*.

**therapy** *n* leigheas *m*.

**there** *adv* an sin, an siud.

**thereby** *adv* le sin.

**therefore** *adv* uime sin.

**these** *pron* iad seo.

**they** *pron* iad, iadsan.

**thick** *adj* tiugh.

**thief** *n* meirleach *m*.

**thigh** *n* sliasaid *f*.

**thin** *adj* tana.

**thing** *n* nì, rud *m*.

**think** *adj* smaoinich.

**third** *adj* treas.

**thirst** *n* pathadh *m*. • *v* bi pàiteach.

**thirteen** *adj/n* trì-deug.

**thirty** *adj/n* trìthead.

**this** *pron* seo.

**thistle** *n* cluaran *m*.

**thorny** *adj* driseach.

**those** *pron* iad sin.

**though** *conj* ge, ged.

**thought** *n* smaoin *f*.

**thousand** *adj/n* mìle.

**thrash** *v* slaic; (*corn*) buail.

**threat** *n* bagairt *f*.

**threaten** *v* bagair.

**three** *adj/n* trì; (*persons*) triùir.

**thrilling** *adj* gaoireil.

**throat** *n* amhach *f*.

**through** *prep* tre, troimh, trìd.

**throw** *v* tilg.

**thrush** *n* smeòrach *m*.

**thumb** *n* òrdag *f*.

**thunder** *n* tàirneanach *m*.

**thunderous** *adj* torranach.

**Thursday** *n* Diardaoin *m*.

**thus** *adv* mar seo.

**ticket** *n* bileag *f*.

**ticking** *n* diogadaich *f*.

**tide** *n* seòl-mara *m*.

**tidy** *v* sgioblaich.

**tiger** *n* tìgeir *m*.

**till** *prep* gu, gus, gu ruig.

**tiller** *n* ailm *f*.

**time** *n* ùine, aimsir *f*.

**timely** *adj* an deagh àm.

**timeous** *adj* an deagh àm.

**tinker** *n* ceàrd *m*.

**tiny** *adj* crìon.

**tipsy** *adj* froganach.

**tired** *adj* sgìth.

**tiresome** *adj* sgìtheachail.

**title** *n* tiotal *m*.

**to** *prep* do, gu, chun, ri, aig, an aghaidh.

**toad** *n* muile-mhàg *f*.

**toast** *v* òl deoch-slàinte; tostaig.

**tobacco** *n* tombaca *m*.

**today** *adv* an-diugh.

**together** *adv* le chèile, còmhla.

**toilet** *n* taigh-beag *m*; sgeadachadh *m*.

**tomb** *n* tuam *m*.

**tomorrow** *adv* a-màireach.

**tone** *n* fonn *m*; tòna *f*.

**tongue** *n* teanga *m*.

**tonight** *adv* a-nochd.

**too** *adv* cuideachd.

**tool** *n* inneal *m*.

**tooth** *n* fiacail *f*.

**top** *n* mullach, uachdar *m*.

**torch** *n* leus *m*.

**torrent** *n* bras-shruth *m*.

**tortoise** *n* sligeanach *m*.

**Tory** *n* Tòraidh *m*.

**toss** *v* luaisg.

**total** *adj* iomlan.

**touch** *v* bean do, suath ann.

**tough** *adj* righinn.

**tour** *n* turas *m*.

**tourists** *npl* luchd-turais.

**towards** *prep* a chum.

**tower** *n* tùr *m*.

**town** *n* baile *m*.

**toy** *n* dèideag *f*.

**trace** *v* lorg.

**track** *v* lorg.

**trade** *n* malairt *f*.

**tradition** *n* beul-aithris *m*; tradisean *m*.

**train** *n* trèana *f*; (*retinue*) muinntir *f*. • *v* àraich.

**traitor** *n* fear-brathaidh *m*.

**trance** *n* neul *m*.

**transfer** *v* thoir thairis.

**transient** *adj* diombuan.

**translate** *v* eadar-theangaich.

**transmitter** *n* crann-sgaoilidh *m*.

**transparent** *adj* trìd-shoilleir.

**trap** *n* ribe *f*. • *v* rib.

**travel** *n* siubhal *m*. • *v* siubhail.

**tray** *n* sgàl *m*.

**treasure** *n* ionmhas *m*. • *v* taisg.

**treat** *n* cuirm *f*. • *v* riaraich.

**tree** *n* craobh *f*.

**tremor** *n* crith *f*.

**trespass** *n* cionta *m*; peacadh *m*. • *v* rach thar chrìochan.

**trews** *npl* triubhas *m*.

**trial** *n* deuchainn *f*.

**tribe** *n* treubh *f*, sliochd *m*.

**tributary** *n* leas-abhainn *f*.

**trick** *n* car *m*.

**trim** *adj* cuimir.

**trip** *v* tuislich.

**triumph** *n* gàirdeachas *m*.

**triumph** *v* thoir buaidh.

**trivial** *adj* suarach.

**trot** *v* dèan trotan.

**trouble** *n* dragh *f*. • *v* cuir dragh air.

**trousers** *n* briogais *f*.

**trout** *n* breac *m*.

**true** *adj* fìor.

**trump card** *n* buadh-chairt *f*.

**trust** *n* earbsa *f*. • *v* earb à.

**truth** *n* fìrinn *f*.

**try** *v* feuch; cuir gu deuchainn.

**tub** *n* balan *m*.

**Tuesday** *n* Dimàirt *m*.

**tumble** *v* tuit, leag.

**tumult** *n* iorghail *f*.

**tune** *n* fonn, port *m*. • *v* gleus.

**tuneful** *adj* fonnmhor.

**tup** *n* reithe *m*.

**turf** *n* sgrath, fòd *f*.

**turn** *v* tionndaidh; cuir air falbh.

**turtle** *n* turtur *f*.

**tutor** *n* (*guardian*) taoitear *m*.

**tweak** *v* teannaich.

**tweed** *n* clò *m*.

**twelfth** *adj* dara-deug.

**twelve** *adj/n* dà-deug.

**twentieth** *adj* ficheadamh.

**twenty** *adj/m* fichead.

**twice** *adv* dà uair.

**twilight** *n* eadar-sholas *m*.

**twin** *n* leth-aon *m*.

**twist** *v* toinn.

**two** *adj/n* dà; (*persons*) dithis.

**two-faced** *adj* beulach.

**typical** *adj* dualach.

**typography** *n* clò-bhualadh *m*.

**tyrant** *n* aintighearna *m*.

**tyro** *n* foghlamaiche *m*.

# U

**udder** *n* ùth *m*.

**ugliness** *n* grànndachd *f*.

**ugly** *adj* grànnda.

**ulcer** *n* neasgaid *f*.

**ultimate** *adj* deiridh.

**umbrella** *n* sgàilean *m*.

**unable** *adj* neo-chomasach.

**unaccustomed** *adj* neo-chle-achdte.

**unanimous** *adj* aon-inntinneach.

**unarmed** *adj* neo-armaichte.

**unavoidable** *adj* do-sheachanta.

**unaware** *adj* gun fhios.

**unbolt** *v* thoir an crann de.

**uncle** *n* bràthair-athar, bràthair-màthar *m*.

**uncomfortable** *adj* anshocrach.

**uncommon** *adj* neo-gnàthach.

**unconditional** *adj* gun chùmh-nantan.

**uncork** *v* às-àrcaich.

**unction** *n* ungadh *m.*

**undecided** *adj* neo-chinnteach.

**under** *prep* fo.

**undergo** *v* fuiling.

**underground** *adj* fo thalamh.

**underneath** *adv* fodha. • *prep* fo.

**understand** *v* tuig.

**underwear** *n* fo-aodach *m.*

**undeserved** *adj* neo-thoillteanach.

**undistinguished** *adj* neo-chomharraichte.

**undisturbed** *adj* neo-bhuairte.

**undo** *v* fuasgail.

**unemployed** *adj* dìomhain, gun obair.

**unequal** *adj* neo-ionnan.

**uneven** *adj* corrach.

**unexpected** *adj* gun dùil.

**unfair** *adj* mì-cheart.

**unfinished** *adj* neo-chrìochnaichte.

**unfold** *v* fosgail.

**unfriendly** *adj* neo-chàirdeil.

**unfurl** *v* sgaoil.

**ungrateful** *adj* mì-thaingeil.

**uniform** *n* culaidh *f.*

**unimportant** *adj* neo-chudromach.

**uninhabited** *adj* neo-àitichte.

**union** *n* aonadh *m.*

**unique** *adj* air leth.

**unit** *n* aonad *m.*

**unity** *n* aonachd *f.*

**universal** *adj* coitcheann.

**universe** *n* domhan *m.*

**university** *n* oilthigh *m.*

**unless** *conj* mur, mura.

**unlike** *adj* neo-choltach.

**unload** *v* thoir an luchd dhe.

**unmask** *v* leig ris.

**unmusical** *adj* neo-cheòlmhor.

**unnecessary** *adj* neo-fheumail.

**unoccupied** *adj* bàn.

**unpack** *v* fosgail.

**unpardonable** *adj* gun leisgeul.

**unpleasant** *adj* mì-thaitneach.

**unpopular** *adj* neo-ionmhainn.

**unpremeditated** *adj* gun roi-smuain.

**unproductive** *adj* neo-thorrach.

**unreal** *adj* neo-fhìor.

**unreasonable** *adj* mì-reusanta.

**unrest** *n* aimhreit *f.*

**unripe** *adj* an-abaich.

**unsafe** *adj* mì-shàbhailte.

**unsatisfactory** *adj* mì-shàsail.

**unsightly** *adj* duaichnidh.

**unsuccessful** *adj* mì-shealbhar.

**unsuitable** *adj* neo-iomchuidh.

**untidy** *adj* luideach.

**untie** *v* fuasgail.

**until** *adv* gu, gus, gu ruig.

**unto** *prep* do, gu.

**unused** *adj* neo-chleachdte.

**unusual** *adj* neo-àbhaisteach.

**unwanted** *adj* gun iarraidh.

**unwieldy** *adj* trom.

**unwise** *adj* neo-ghlic.

**unworthy** *adj* neo-airidh.

**unwrap** *v* fuasgail.

**up** *prep* suas. • *adv* suas; a-nìos; shuas.

**upbringing** *n* togail *f.*

**uphill** *adv* ri bruthach.

**uphold** *v* cùm suas.

**upland** *n* aonach *f.*

**upon** *prep* air, air muin.

**upper** *adj* uachdrach.

**upright** *adj* dìreach; onorach.

**uproar** *n* gleadhar *m.*

**upset** *n* cur troimhe-chèile *m.*

**upshot** *n* co-dhùnadh *m.*

**upside-down** *adj/adv* bun os cionn.

**upstairs** *adv* shuas staidhre; suas staidhre.

**upward** *adv* suas.

**urban** *adj* cathaireil.

**urge** *v* spàrr.

**urgency** *n* dèine *f.*

**urgent** *adj* dian.

**urinal** *n* ionad-mùin *m.*

**us** *pron* sinn, sinne.

**usage** *n* àbhaist *f.*

**use** *n* feum *m.* • *v* gnàthaich, dèan feum de.

**useful** *adj* feumail.

**usefulness** *n* feumalachd *f.*

**useless** *adj* gun fheum.

**usual** *adj* gnàthach.

**usurp** *v* glèidh gun chòir.

**uterus** *n* machlag *f.*

**utmost** *adj* as motha

**utter**[1] *v* abair, labhair.

**utter**[2] *adj* coilionta; dearg.

**utterly** *adv* gu tur.

# V

**vacancy** *n* beàrn *m.*

**vacant** *adj* falamh.

**vaccinate** *v* cuir breac-a-chruidh air.

**vagabond** *n* fear-fuadain *m.*

**vagina** *n* faighean *f.*

**vague** *adj* neo-dheimhinn.

**vain** *adj* dìomhain.

**vale** *n* srath *m.*

**valid** *adj* tàbhachdach.

**valley** *n* gleann, srath *m.*

**valour** *n* gaisge *f.*

**valuable** *adj* prìseil.

**value** *n* luach *m.*

**value-added tax** *n* cìs luach-leasaichte *f.*

**valve** *n* pìob-chòmhla *f.*

**van** *n* vana *f.*

**vandal** *n* creachadair, milltear *m.*

**vanish** *v* rach às an t-sealladh.

**vapour** *n* deatach *f.*

**varied** *adj* iomadh.

**variegated** *adj* breac.

**variety** *n* atharrachadh *m.*

**various** *adj* iomadh.

**vary** *v* caochail.

**vase** n vàsa f.

**veal** n laoigh-fheòil f.

**vegetable** n glasraich f.

**vegetarian** n feòil-sheachnair m.

**vegetation** n fàs m.

**vehement** adj dealasach.

**vehicle** n carbad m.

**veil** n sgàile f. • v còmhdaich.

**vein** n cuisle f.

**velvet** n meileabhaid f.

**vengeance** n dìoghaltas m.

**venison** n sitheann m.

**venom** n nimh m.

**venture** n tuaiream m.

**venue** n làthair m.

**verdict** n breith f.

**verge** n oir f.

**verify** v dearbh.

**vermin** npl mìolan.

**vernacular** n cainnt na dùthcha f.

**verse** n dànachd f; (stanza) rann m.

**version** n innse f.

**vertical** adj dìreach.

**vertigo** n tuaineal m.

**very** adv fìor, ceart.

**vest** n peitean m.

**vestige** n lorg f.

**vet** n veat m.

**vex** v buair.

**viable** adj so-obrachadh.

**vibrate** v crith, cuir air chrith.

**vicarious** adj ionadach.

**vice** n dubhailc f; (tool) teanchair m.

**victim** n ìobairteach m.

**victor** n buadhair m.

**victory** n buaidh f.

**video recorder** n chàradair bhidio m.

**view** n sealladh m; beachd m. • v gabh sealladh; beachdaich.

**viewpoint** n àite-seallaidh m; ionad-beachd m.

**vigil** n faire f.

**vigour** n spionnadh m.

**vile** adj gràineil.

**village** n baile-beag m.

**villain** n slaoightear m.

**vindicate** v fìreanaich.

**vine** n fìonan, crann-fìona m.

**vintage** n fìon-fhoghar m.

**violence** n fòirneart m.

**violent** adj fòirneartach.

**violin** n fidheall f.

**violinist** n fìdhleir m.

**viper** n nathair-nimhe f.

**virgin** n maighdeann, òigh f.

**virginity** n maighdeannas m.

**virile** adj fearail.

**virility** n fearachas m.

**virtual** adj dha-rìribh.

**virtue** n subhailc f.

**virtuous** adj beusach.

**virus** n vìoras m.

**visibility** n lèireas m.

**visible** adj faicsinneach.

**vision** n fradharc m; (mental) bruadar m, taibhs f.

**visit** v tadhail.

**visitor** n aoigh m.

**visual** adj fradharcach.

**vital** *adj* riatanach; beò.
**vitality** *n* beathalachd *f*.
**vivacious** *adj* aigeannach.
**vocal** *adj* guthach.
**vocalist** *n* òranaiche, seinneadair *m*.
**vocation** *n* gairm *f*.
**voice** *n* guth *m*.
**void** *adj* fàs. • *n* fàsalachd *f*.
**voluble** *adj* deas-chainnteach.

**voluntary** *adj* toileach.
**vomit** *n* sgeith *m*. • *v* sgeith.
**vote** *n* vòta *f*. • *v* thoir vòta.
**voucher** *n* fianais *f*.
**vow** *n* bòid *f*. • *v* bòidich.
**voyage** *n* turas-mara *m*.
**voyager** *n* taisdealaich *m*.
**vulgar** *adj* gràisgeil.
**vulnerable** *adj* so-leònte.

# W

**wade** *v* siubhail troimh.
**wafer** *n* abhlan *m*.
**wag** *v* crath.
**wager** *n* geall *m*.
**wagon** *n* cairt *f*.
**wagtail** *n* breacan-buidhe *m*.
**wail** *v* dèan caoineadh.
**waist** *n* meadhan *m*.
**wait** *v* feith; fritheil.
**waitress** *n* caileag-fhrithealaidh *f*.
**wake** *n* taigh-fhaire *m*. • *v* dùisg.
**waken** *v* dùisg.
**Wales** *n* A' Chuimrigh *f*.
**walk** *n* cuairt *f*. • *v* coisich.
**walking stick** *n* bata *m*.
**wall** *n* balla *m*.
**walrus** *n* each-mara *m*.
**wan** *adj* glas-neulach.
**wander** *v* rach air seachran.
**wanderer** *n* seachranaiche *m*.

**want** *n* dìth *m*; bochdainn *f*. • *v* iarr; thig geàrr.
**war** *n* cogadh *m*.
**warble** *v* ceileirich.
**wardrobe** *n* preas-aodaich *m*.
**warehouse** *n* taigh-tasgaidh *m*.
**warlike** *adj* coganta.
**warm** *adj* blàth.
**warmth** *n* blàths *m*.
**warn** *v* thoir rabhadh.
**warren** *n* broclach *f*.
**warship** *n* long-chogaidh *f*.
**wart** *n* foinne *f*.
**wary** *adj* faicilleach.
**wash** *v* nigh.
**washing** *n* nigheadaireachd *f*.
**wasp** *n* speach *f*.
**waste** *n* ana-caitheamh *m*. • *v* cosg, caith.
**watch** *n* uaireadair; faire *m*. • *v* dèan faire.

**watchdog** n cù-faire m.

**water** n uisge m. • v uisgich.

**water-power** n neart-uisge m.

**waterfall** n eas m.

**waterproof** adj uisge-dhìonach.

**watershed** n uisge-dhruim m.

**watertight** adj dìonach.

**waulk** v luaidh.

**waulking** n luadhadh m.

**wave** n tonn m. • v smèid; crath.

**wax** n cèir f.

**way** n slighe f.

**waylay** v dèan feall-fhalach.

**we** pron sinn, sinne.

**weak** adj lag.

**weaken** v lagaich.

**weave** v figh.

**weaver** n breabadair m.

**web** n eige, lìon f.

**webbed** adj eigeil.

**wed** v pòs.

**wedding** n banais f.

**Wednesday** n Diciadain m.

**weed** n luibh m. • v priog.

**week** n seachdain f.

**weep** v guil.

**weigh** v cothromaich.

**weight** n cudthrom m.

**weir** n cairidh f.

**welcome** n fàilte f. • v fàiltich.

**well**[1] adj math; faillain. • adv gu math.

**well**[2] n tobar m.

**west** adj siar. • n an iar f. • adv an iar.

**westerly** adj on iar.

**westward** adv chun na h'àirde an iar.

**wet** adj fliuch.

**whale** n muc-mhara f.

**what** interr pron de? • rel pron na.

**wheat** n cruineachd m.

**wheel** n cuibhle f.

**wheeze** v dèan pìochan.

**whelk** n faochag f.

**when** conj nuair. • interr pron cuin?

**whence** adv co às.

**whenever** adv gach uair.

**where** conj far. • interr pron càite?

**whereas** adv do bhrìgh gu.

**whereby** adv leis, leis am bheil.

**wherever** adv ge be ar bith càite.

**whereupon** adv leis sin.

**whether** adv co-dhiù. • pron co aca.

**which** rel pron a, (neg) nach. • interr pron dè?, cò?

**while** conj fhad is a. • n tacan m, greis f.

**whin** n conasg m.

**whip** n cuip f. • v sgiùrs.

**whirlpool** n cuairt-shlugan m.

**whiskers** npl feusag f.

**whisky** n uisge-beatha m.

**whisper** n cagar m. • v cagair.

**whistle** n feadag f. • v dèan fead.

**white** adj geal, bàn, fionn.

**who** rel pron a, (neg) nach. • interr pron cò?

**whoever** pron cò air bith.

**whole** *adj* slàn, iomlan.

**wholefood** *adj* slàn-bhiadh.

**wholesale** *n* mòr-reic *m*.

**whoop** *n* glaodh *m*.

**whose** *interr pron* co leis?

**why** *adv* carson?

**wick** *n* siobhag *f*.

**wicked** *adj* olc.

**wide** *adj* leathann.

**widow** *n* banntrach *f*.

**widower** *n* banntrach *m*.

**width** *n* leud *m*.

**wife** *n* bean *f*.

**wild** *adj* fiadhaich.

**wildcat** *n* cat fiadhaich *m*.

**wilderness** *n* fàsach *m*.

**will** *n* toil *f*; (*last*) tiomnadh *m*.

**willing** *adj* toileach.

**willow** *n* seileach *m*.

**willpower** *n* neart toile *m*.

**wily** *adj* seòlta.

**win** *v* coisinn.

**wind** *n* gaoth *f*.

**window** *n* uinneag *f*.

**windward** *n* fuaradh *m*.

**windy** *adj* gaothach.

**wine** *n* fìon *m*.

**wing** *n* sgiath *f*.

**wink** *v* caog.

**winter** *n* geamhradh *m*. • *v* geamhraich.

**wintry** *adj* geamhrachail.

**wipe** *v* suath.

**wire** *n* uèir *m*.

**wiry** *adj* seang.

**wisdom** *n* gliocas *m*.

**wise** *adj* glic.

**wish** *n* miann *m*. • *v* miannaich.

**wit** *n* toinisg *f*; eirmse *f*.

**witch** *n* bana-bhuidseach *f*.

**with** *prep* le, còmhla ri.

**wither** *v* searg.

**withered** *adj* crìon.

**within** *adv* a-staigh.

**without** *adv* a-muigh. • *prep* gun.

**witness** *n* fianais *f*; fear-fianais *m*.

**witty** *adj* eirmseach.

**wizard** *n* draoidh *m*.

**wolf** *n* madadh-allaidh *m*.

**woman** *n* boireannach *f*.

**womanly** *adj* banail.

**womb** *n* machlag *f*.

**wonder** *n* iongnadh *m*; iongantas *m*. • *v* gabh iongantas.

**woo** *v* dèan suirghe.

**wood** *n* coille *f*; (*timber*) fiodh *f*.

**woodland** *n* fearann coillteach *m*.

**woodlouse** *n* reudan *m*.

**woodwork** *n* saoirsneachd *f*.

**wool** *n* clòimh *f*.

**woollen** *adj* de chlòimh.

**word** *n* facal *m*; (*bond*) gealladh *m*.

**word processor** *n* facladair *m*.

**wordy** *adj* briathrach.

**work** *n* obair *f*. • *v* oibrich.

**worker** *n* oibriche *m*.

**workmanship** *n* ealain *f*.

**world** *n* saoghal *m*.

**worldly** *adj* saoghalta.

**world-wide web** *n* lìonra domhanta *m*.

**worm** n cnuimh, durrag f.
**worn** adj caithte.
**worry** n dragh m. • v buair, dèan dragh do.
**worse** adj nas miosa.
**worsen** v fàs nas miosa.
**worship** n adhradh m.
**worst** adj as miosa.
**worth** n luach m. • adj fiù.
**worthless** adj gun fhiù.
**worthy** adj airidh.
**wound** n leòn m. • v leòn, lot.
**wrangle** n connsachadh m. • v connsaich.
**wrap** v paisg, fill.
**wrapper** n filleag f.
**wrath** n corraich f.
**wrathful** adj feargach.
**wreath** n blàth-fhleasg f.

**wreck** n long-bhriseadh m. • v sgrios.
**wren** n dreadhan-donn m.
**wrench** v spìon.
**wrest** v spìon.
**wrestle** v gleac.
**wrestling** n gleac m.
**wring** v fàisg.
**wrinkle** n preas m. • v preas.
**wrist** n caol an dùirn m.
**wristwatch** n uaireadair làimhe m.
**write** v sgrìobh.
**writer** n sgrìobhadair m.
**writhe** v snìomh.
**writing** n sgrìobhadh m.
**wrong** adj ceàrr; coireach. • n eu-coir f; euceart m.
**wry** adj cam.

# XYZ

**xenophobe** n gall-gamhlasaiche m.
**xenophobia** n gall-gamhlas m.
**X-ray** n x-ghath m.
**yacht** n sgoth-long f.
**yard** n gàrradh m; (length) slat f.
**yarn** n sgeulachd f; (thread) snàth f.
**yarrow** n eàrr-thalmhainn f.
**yawl** n geòla f.
**yawn** n mèanan m. • v dèan mèananaich.
**year** n bliadhna f.

**yearly** adj gach bliadhna.
**yearn** v iarr gu làidir.
**yearning** n iarraidh m/f.
**yeast** n beirm f.
**yellow** adj/n buidhe m.
**yelp** v dèan tathann.
**yes** adv (non-affirmative) seadh (affirmative replies repeat verb used in question).
**yesterday** adv an-dè.
**yet** adv fhathast. • conj gidheadh, an dèidh sin, ach.
**yew** n iubhar m.

**yield** *v* gèill.

**yoke** *n* cuing *f*. • *v* beartaich.

**yolk** *n* buidheagan *m*.

**yon** *adv* thall, ud, an siud.

**you** *pron* (*sing*) thu, thusa; (*pl*) sibh, sibhse.

**young** *adj* òg.

**youngster** *n* òganach *m*.

**your** *pron* (*sing*) do, d', t', agad; (*pl*) bhur, ur, agaibh.

**yourself** *pron* thu fhèin.

**yourselves** *pron* sibh fhèin.

**youth** *n* òigear *m*; (*state*) òige *m*.

**youthful** *adj* ògail.

**zeal** *n* eud *m*.

**zealous** *adj* eudmhor.

**zebra** *n* asal-stiallach *f*.

**zenith** *n* bàrr *m*.

**zero** *n* neoni *f*.

**zest** *n* smior *m*.

**zigzag** *adj* lùbach.

**zip** *n* sip *f*.

**zodiac** *n* grian-chrios *m*.

**zoo** *n* sutha *f*.

**zoology** *n* ainmh-eòlas *m*.